A LIFE ON THE LEFT

By the same author:

A History of the Association of Engineering and Shipbuilding Draughtsmen, McGibbon & Kee

Industrial Relations, Heinemann

British Trade Unions Today, Pergamon (jointly with Clive Jenkins)

The Kind of Laws the Unions Ought to Want, Pergamon (jointly with Clive Jenkins)

Trade Unions and Technological Change, Oxford University Press

History of the Boilermakers' Society, Volumes 1 and 2, George Allen and Unwin

History of the Boilermakers' Society, Volume 3, Verso

A Professional Union: The Evolution of the Institution of Professional Civil Servants, George Allen & Unwin (jointly with Valerie Ellis)

A LIFE ON THE LEFT

J.E. (Jim) Mortimer

The Book Guild Ltd
Sussex, England

The Book Guild Ltd
25 High Street,
Lewes, Sussex

First published 1998
© J.E. Mortimer, 1998

Set in Times

Typesetting by
Acorn Bookwork, Salisbury, Wiltshire

Printed in Great Britain by
Antony Rowe Ltd, Chippenham, Wiltshire

A catalogue record for this book is
available from the British Library

ISBN 1 85776 337 8

CONTENTS

PREFACE

During recent years the Labour Party, under the influence of its leadership, has moved sharply to the right. Labour has become New Labour. I oppose this trend and believe that the aspirations of most of the supporters of Labour, whether as Party members, trade unionists or voters, remain much as they always have been. They want an end to periodic mass unemployment, gross inequality and the threat of poverty in old age. They attach great importance to the National Health Service, to education and to employment rights.

I have written this book because I wanted to try to explain, through the ideas and experiences of a participant in the labour movement for more than 60 years, why I think Labour should adhere to a socialist commitment and should develop its policies accordingly. It offers a political account and there is, I hope, nothing in it that will feed an appetite for personal scandal.

In 1947 the Labour Party published an educational booklet entitled *A Guide to the Elements of Socialism*, written by the late Professor G.D.H. Cole. He was the Professor of Political and Social Theory at Oxford whilst I was a full-time adult student on a TUC award at Ruskin College. I owe much to his lectures and books. His views on socialism and the importance of democracy in every walk of life as the guarantee against the abuse of power and bureaucracy are as relevant as ever.

In the Labour Party's educational booklet Cole wrote:

'Socialism, in the broadest and most general sense, is the doctrine that the resources of production ought to be used, not for the profit of a class of capitalists, but for the common service of all people. In order to bring this about, socialists have urged that the principal and basic industries shall be publicly owned and administered under some form of public control ... They have held, further, that there can be no guarantee, except democracy, that the resources of production will, in fact, be used for the benefit of all; and, both for this reason and because they believe in democracy on principle, they have sought to bring about the widest possible diffusion both of political and economic and social power and of the knowledge needed for putting such power to effective use.'

I am sometimes asked whether I am a Marxist. My reply is that I have been strongly influenced by the writings and example of Marx and Engels and of others of different countries who share the Marxist tradition. I have also been strongly influenced, however, by the writings and activities of men and women who, through the centuries, have inspired and led the struggle against autocracy in all its forms, exploitation and inherited privilege. They include British radicals and the thinkers who inspired the French Revolution and the independence of the United States.

Through my own activities I have also learnt much from colleagues in the unions and in the wider labour movement. This book will give some idea of this debt.

Finally, I owe a great deal to my parents. My mother started work at 12 years of age as a half-timer in a textile mill, and my father started work at 13 years of age after an interrupted education caused by prolonged periods of absence from school following a childhood accident. He was left physically crippled for life. Nevertheless my parents, despite their very limited formal education, were the first to arouse within me a consciousness of social injustice. They were the first to give me a vision of a different kind of society, and they taught me from an early age to value and to subscribe to the culture of Nonconformity.

Both my parents were brought up as Methodists in the city of Bradford in West Yorkshire. To my mother, who was a committed Methodist all her life, religion and politics were inseparable. To my father, who abandoned his formal religion as a young man, his Nonconformity expressed itself in a readiness to look critically at everything and to challenge whatever he thought was wrong. Both my parents were political radicals.

The struggle continues.

J.E. MORTIMER

1

Bradford

The Manningham Mills of Bradford are a monument to the prosperity, power and confidence of the owners of the textile industry in Britain in the late nineteenth century. They are built of stone as though to last for ever. They have a grandeur about them which can be likened to some of the buildings in Whitehall. At the same time, when blackened with smoke, as I remember them as a schoolboy, they generated a forbidding and ominous atmosphere, as though to remind everyone that they existed for the purpose of work and not for architectural contemplation.

Some time after the Second World War the Manningham Mills were externally cleaned. Some of the surrounding old streets were also cleared. What emerged was a magnificent collection of industrial buildings, more impressive than anything I have seen elsewhere as an industrial landscape. The one other mill to stand comparison is only a few miles away, Salt's of Saltaire.

The Manningham Mills are served by a giant chimney stack. It was built in a style which suggests that no money was spared in its design and construction. Stories used to circulate that horses and a carriage could be driven around its summit. I have no idea whether this was true or just a wild exaggeration. The Manningham Mills chimney can be seen for miles around, and when I was a boy dense smoke emerged from it to remind everyone that the woollen textile industry had its home in Bradford. Coal provided the motive power, and steam emerged from a thousand windows in the manufacturing sheds.

To the people of our neighbourhood the Manningham Mills were more frequently known as Lister's, after the name of the original proprietor and wealthy textile magnate, who was later to become Lord Masham. People who worked in the mills usually said that they worked at Lister's, but the works football and cricket teams were always known as Manningham Mills. Their sports ground, at the top of the road where my parents lived, offered good facilities. I went there frequently to watch both football and cricket. My recollection is that there was paid admission when the first teams were playing at home.

Cricket was a serious business in those days in Yorkshire, and it was customary in local cricket leagues to take a collection for any player who scored a half-century or who, as a bowler, took six wickets for less than six runs each. Gossip had it that if the county side were in difficulty on the last day of a county championship game at the Bradford ground of Park Avenue the word would go round the mills, including Lister's, to stoke up and throw a heavy curtain of smoke over the city. The newspapers next day would report: 'Fog stops play – Yorkshire saved by bad light'. Perhaps the story is untrue, but it has been told many times and illustrates the attitude of some among the male population to the then cricketing prowess of the Yorkshire county club. They were partisan to the point where they could joke about cheating, providing it was in Yorkshire's favour.

Much seemed to revolve around Lister's during my childhood in Bradford. Even the air we breathed was influenced by the mills. If Lister's was busy the smoke poured from the chimney. The grime descended on the surrounding streets, in which many of the houses were occupied by the families of the operatives. On Monday mornings the housewives did the family washing, and the clothes were hung across the streets immediately adjoining Lister's. They were 'no go' areas for traffic, particularly for horses and carts delivering coal. People would watch the Lister's chimney and expect the stokers to limit the smoke output when the washing was being dried in the streets.

Family Influence

My father was a street newspaper seller. His pitch was at one of the busy corners near to the main entrance of Manningham Mills. He collected the newspapers in a tram shed from the first tram out of the centre of Bradford, sorted them and then walked, with his newspapers in a large bag slung across his shoulders, to the mill corner in time for the earliest shift. He tied placards to a lamppost and sat on a camp stool to sell his papers. He was there six mornings every week in all weathers. He worked 52 weeks in the year, and his only days off, apart from Sunday each week, were at Christmas and Easter, when newspapers were not published. He never went away for a holiday, though sometimes on Sundays my parents would take an outing to the many attractive areas in the Pennines and dales surrounding Bradford.

There was a crisis in our family life when a new manager was appointed to the terminus tram shed where my father collected his newspapers. The new manager, in a display of officiousness, ordered my father off the premises. It was the only place, under cover, where he could sort the newspapers for his morning pitch. My father, who always disliked the abuse of authority, felt deeply aggrieved. He was, however, not a person to accept without protest such a challenge to his means of livelihood.

My father was a cripple as a result of an accident as a small child. He walked with two sticks and was not therefore able to compete on equal terms in the normal labour market. He felt that if he were denied the opportunity to sort his newspapers under the cover of the tram shed where they were delivered from the wholesaler, his livelihood would be taken away.

The tram shed was owned by the Bradford Corporation. One of my father's friends was a Labour councillor by the name of George Carter. He was, I think, at the time the Bradford district secretary of the Amalgamated Engineering Union. My father asked for help, and George Carter successfully intervened.

Both my parents were born in Bradford. My paternal grand-

3

father was a textile worker, but in his early life had been a miner. According to my father, my grandfather started work underground when he was nine years of age, in about 1861. He was then living near Leeds, but later came to Bradford when he found work in textiles. He eventually became a cloth presser, a job in which it was often necessary to carry heavy pieces of cloth. In his later years he suffered from a bad back, sustained through his employment. At that time it was much more difficult to obtain industrial compensation, and he spent his final years in poverty, dependent on the support of his children.

All my relatives spoke well of my paternal grandfather. He was said to have been a kindly and thoughtful man with a keen and intelligent interest in social affairs and in nature. He was a strong trade unionist and a radical in politics. He loved the open air, and one of his favourite walks was to the wild solitude of the moors near to west Bradford where he lived. He was influenced by the poetry of Shelley and Byron. I inherited from him, through my father, two volumes of their poetry, but unfortunately they were lost in the bombing in the Second World War.

A number of my grandfather's brothers were interested in politics. One of them I knew reasonably well. He too had been a textile worker, but was already retired when I was a boy. I remember him for his flashing blue eyes and his fluency. He had strong socialist convictions and had spent many years as an active member of the Independent Labour Party. When I was about 14 years of age, after my family had left Bradford, I remember him explaining to me his vision of the socialist society of the future. One of his sons was a full-time trade union official and later encouraged my interest in the labour movement.

My mother was the daughter of a railwayman. I remember him as an engine driver, though in earlier years he had been an engine-cleaner and then a fireman. He worked all his life on the railway, from 13 to 65 years of age. He claimed that during these 52 years he had never been late for work and had been absent ill for only two days. He slipped from a locomotive and injured his leg. In his retirement this injury still continued to give him pain.

My maternal grandfather had no pretensions of intellectual interests. My grandmother said, half-jokingly, that he never read anything except the football results. He was, for me, a lovable character. He seemed always to be in a good temper and ready, immediately we arrived at his house, to send out for ice cream or fish and chips. In the cellar head – so called because it was at the head of the stairs leading to the underground cellar – there was always a crate of mineral waters, lemonade, dandelion and burdock and American cream soda.

My maternal grandfather took great interest in his grandchildren, of whom I was the eldest. He would talk to us, hold and comfort us with affection when we were hurt and join in any game we were playing. He rarely engaged in serious conversation, though his pride in being an engine-driver and his loyalty to the railway were apparent even to his grandchildren. When, from his living room, he heard the whistles of the trains he would check by his watch whether they were running to time. He would tell us stories of the railway, of his pranks when he started work as a fire-lighter in the engine shed, of the delays in fog or snow when he was a fireman and later a driver, of the hard work stoking a coal-fired boiler on a long-distance express, of the effect of different qualities of coal on locomotive power and of what was meant by 'learning the road' to become a top link driver.

My maternal grandfather had no great interest in politics. He was a 'Lib-Lab' and the politician he admired most was David Lloyd George. He spoke of the Liberal Government elected in 1906 in much the same way as some Labour supporters of a later generation speak of the Labour Government of 1945. He identified the 1906 Liberal Government with social reform, and he regarded Lloyd George as the principal reformer. He also spoke favourably of Lloyd George's toughness in pursuing his ideas.

If the Liberals had maintained their political strength I do not think my maternal grandfather would have voted anything but Liberal. With the decline of the Liberal Party, however, he became a wavering Labour voter. He never spoke of 'changing the social order', unlike a number of relatives of my father's side. He was opposed to the Tories, and when Labour represented the stronger challenge he would be tempted to vote Labour. He did not do it with any particular enthusiasm.

On the other hand, my maternal grandfather was a loyal member of the footplatemen's union, the Associated Society of Locomotive Engineers and Firemen. He did not speak of his membership in the vocabulary of the class struggle. Such expressions as 'organised labour' or 'workers' solidarity' were not part of his language. He was proud of the railways and of his knowledge as a footplateman. His membership of the Society was an expression of this pride and of his sense of community with others who shared his skill or who aspired to it.

During the General Strike of 1926 my grandfather served on the local strike committee and supported the strike action. When questioned about it in later years he would express his sympathy with the miners, who were facing wage cuts and an extension of the working day. His readiness to take strike action in support of the miners was, as he saw it, an expression of human fellowship. Certainly, it had nothing to do with challenging the government or social revolution.

My grandfather was not a supporter of amalgamation between ASLEF and the National Union of Railwaymen. He was not an opponent of the NUR, but he felt that footplatemen had separate and identifiable interests.

My grandfather's support for the General Strike was solid. He refused for years afterwards to speak to another driver who lived nearby, who had gone to work during the strike. He regarded him as someone who had acted in a totally immoral manner towards the men who shared his daily working life.

My maternal grandmother also had very little political interest, though like my grandfather she was not a Tory. She was able to read fluently in the Yorkshire dialect, and her grandchildren, myself included, loved to hear her read dialect stories.

My grandfather retired from the London North Eastern

Railway well before the outbreak of the Second World War. During my schooldays in Bradford he was already a top link driver, confined largely and, perhaps, exclusively to long-distance express trains. By working-class standards he and my grandmother had a high standard of living. My grandfather's basic pay was £4 and 10 shillings per week (£4.50p in modern currency), and he earned one hour's mileage for every 15 miles over 140 miles per shift. As a long-distance driver he thus had an average and regular weekly income of at least twice that of a normal male industrial worker. He occasionally earned even more by taking special Sunday excursion trains from Bradford to Bridlington or Scarborough. Every year he and my grandmother had summer holidays, with privilege tickets, at resorts in various parts of England.

My maternal grandparents owned their own house. This was another indication of their relative affluence. True, the house would not be described as a 'desirable residence' by modern standards. It had an outside lavatory, and there was no bathroom. There were two rooms downstairs and two upstairs. The main living room served as a kitchen, washing area, dining and sitting room. It was heated by a coal fire in an open range which also accommodated an oven. Even in the hottest weather the oven could be used only if there was a blazing fire. The coal was stored in the cellar. The second room downstairs, known always as the 'front room', was used only on Sundays or on festive occasions when visitors were received.

The house of my maternal grandparents was very similar to the house in which I lived with my parents. There was one interesting difference. The lavatory of my grandparents' house had a flush mechanism. This was the hallmark of modernity. The lavatory in my parents' house was a 'tippler'. It was at the bottom of the backyard and was built well below ground level. It was reached by descending steps. The lavatory was part of a larger structure, always referred to as 'the midden'. The rest of the structure accommodated ashes and other rubbish.

The principle of 'the tippler' was that a bowl or large pot, hinged off-centre, would tipple as it filled. Thus there was no flushing mechanism, but equally the sewage found its way automatically into the main drainage. The outlet pipe from the kitchen sink and the main rainwater drainpipes also fed into 'the tippler'. When there was heavy rain the frequent sound of tippling tipplers could be heard up and down the street.

The elementary school I attended in Bradford was immediately opposite one of the main buildings of the Manningham Mills. Many of the pupils were the children of textile operatives. The poorest came from the streets immediately adjoining Lister's. Behind these streets were others, dignified by the title 'Road', where the standard of living was rather higher. It was in one of these roads that my parents lived. The houses were occupied mainly by workers with regular employment, either in industry or in the public services.

Many of the children in the poorest streets were from Irish families and went to the local Catholic school. In the road where my parents lived many of the families were of Nonconformist background and the children went to the local state school. A number of my boyhood friends were Catholics from the streets 'at back o't mill'. On Saturday mornings, when we played cricket or football in the back streets or on the local recreation ground, we had to wait for them to return from confession.

Among the Nonconformist families there was sometimes an unfortunate attitude of moral superiority towards the neighbouring Catholic Irish. The Catholic Irish families often had more children and were thus said to worsen their own poverty. They were more inclined to frequent public houses and to spend their money on drink. Nonconformists, in contrast, were usually conscious of the virtue of thrift, and a higher proportion of them were attracted to temperance. Indeed, among the children with a Nonconformist background, many, including myself, were attenders of the Band of Hope, where we were shown magic lantern slides and given talks about the evils of alcoholic drink. We were given a card to record our attendance and received a blue star every time we went to a session. We were encouraged to save money even from a very early age. We contributed a penny per week to a savings account of the Yorkshire Penny Bank.

My parents and grandparents all had a Nonconformist upbringing. On my mother's side the family were Wesleyan Methodists, and on my father's side some were Primitive Methodists and some Wesleyan Methodists. Later these churches – or chapels as they were always called in the Bradford of my childhood – all amalgamated into modern Methodism.

My mother retained her Methodist convictions throughout her life. She went to chapel until the deterioration in her health made it impossible for her to walk unaided out of doors. Her earliest ambition for me was that I should become a Methodist minister.

Her religion and her politics were inseparable. She believed that Jesus Christ was a good man in his everyday conduct and that he sided with and spoke fearlessly for the interests of the poor. He was persecuted, she said, by the ruling class of his time and finally crucified. His humble and unostentatious manner was, she thought, the example to be followed by contemporary organised religion. Hence, she disliked the rituals, the ornaments, the special robes and the wealth of both the Church of England and the Roman Catholic Church. To my mother, religion was a personal affair to be reflected in human conduct. Each individual was answerable to God and to his/her own conscience for behaviour. The idea of a confession made through a priest was not merely objectionable; it was repulsive. She disliked set prayers and believed that worshippers should pray in their own words. She rejected any notion that worshippers should kneel in church. On the contrary, they should stand proudly and proclaim their beliefs. To be a Christian was to be an evangelist. The hymns of the church were the battle songs of a confident and proselytising faith.

My father retained much of the Nonconformist culture which he had absorbed as a child and as a youth, but in his manhood he was without religion. In all the years I knew him I do not remember him going to a church service, other than to hear my mother sing in an oratorio. He probably had more sympathy with Methodism than with any of the other

9

organised churches, but he did not believe in the divinity of Christ and he rejected the notion of a virgin birth. His general attitude was that organised religion had too frequently given its support to whoever constituted the ruling group in society. He commented often that the church in Britain had supported the British government in the First World War and that the church in Germany had supported the German government. Both claimed that God was on their side. They could not both have been right. In my father's view, the First World War was caused by imperialist rivalry and neither the British nor the German government were pursuing a just cause.

Despite their differences of belief, my parents never argued about religion. My mother went regularly to chapel and to choir practice, but my father never regarded himself as a Christian. Their respective points of view led them to much the same practical conclusions, though my mother was much more aware of the need for good personal conduct. I think she sometimes regarded my father – with justification – as too selfish, too concerned with thrift and occasionally bad-tempered.

My mother thought of herself as very much inferior to my father in mental ability, so much so that it was not until I was older that I began to question her poor view of her own capacity. Before that I was inclined to accept almost without thought, and certainly without argument, her self-estimation. How many millions of working-class women have suffered from the same unjustifiable sense of inferiority?

It is a criticism of my father that he did little to encourage my mother to have more self-esteem for her own talent. She accepted her role in the home and, though she read many books, she did not challenge her subordinate status. She carried out nearly all the household chores, except that of making the fire and clearing the ashes from the grate. My father, for example, never helped with washing-up.

It was not until after my father's death that my mother began to pursue her own interest in politics. She became an active member of the Cooperative Women's Guild, and I remember her, when she was already well into her sixties, spending hours writing a report of a weekend school she attended. She went to political meetings and even to meetings of the National Secular Society. She was a member of the Labour Party up to the day of her death, when she was 91 years of age.

Before her marriage my mother was a textile worker. She started as a half-timer at 12 years of age in Tankard's mill in the Bowling district of Bradford. Her first job was that of 'doffer' in a spinning shed. It was her task to take the full bobbins from the spinning machinery and to replace them with empty bobbins. The starting time for the mill was 6 a.m. and, with a break for breakfast, the half-timers were required to work until midday. In the afternoons the half-timers went to school.

When she was 13 years of age my mother went into full-time employment. She became a spinner in a textile mill and was employed for about 54 or 55 hours a week. She would later describe how she would run home for her dinner and then hurry back before the mill hooter sounded for the afternoon session. The dinner break was 40 minutes only. From the spinning shed my mother graduated into weaving. This was considered a rather better job. From being a weaver she became a burler and mender, responsible for repairing small weaving defects in pieces of cloth. This was regarded as a skilled job and was often performed in small firms operating on commission from larger manufacturing firms.

My mother had a lifelong interest in music. She could play the piano, but her main interest was in singing, which probably developed in the first place from her participation in a chapel choir as a teenage girl. She was actively associated with the Prospect Street Wesleyan chapel in Bradford. When my mother was a girl it had about 1,000 pupils in the Sunday school. Many years later it became an Islamic mosque. I do not know whether it still exists or whether it has been demolished, as it was in a part of Bradford which has been extensively redeveloped.

From the chapel choir my mother began to take singing lessons. She had a contralto voice. Her ambition was to be accepted into the Bradford Festival Choral Society. It was not easy to gain entry, and she would sometimes recall how nervous she was when she took a test for acceptance. She was successful, and from then onwards until my parents left Bradford the Choral Society occupied an important place in my mother's life. Every week she went to the choir practice and looked forward keenly to the big subscription concerts held in the magnificent St George's Hall in the centre of the city.

I do not know why the concerts were known as 'subscription concerts', but my parents always used this description. The concerts attracted Britain's leading conductors and solo singers. My mother described how when she was a young woman the carriages would arrive on the concert evenings at St George's Hall, conveying local well-off people in their evening dress.

Always around our house were the musical scores of oratorios and other well known choral pieces. At Christmas my mother would sing in a chapel choir in *The Messiah* and at Easter in *Elijah*. It was a special occasion when the Carl Rosa Opera Company came to the city. My parents would try to attend a couple of times during the week of performances. In later years, when we had moved to Portsmouth, I was introduced to the operas of the Carl Rosa Company.

On Sundays during the summer my parents frequently went to Manningham Park – also known as Lister Park – for a walk and to listen to the playing of a band. The band performances were very well attended, particularly if the weather was good. Listeners had to pay to sit in the enclosure around the bandstand, but the music could be heard clearly in the main promenading area outside the enclosure.

Many of the brass bands to play in Manningham Park were associated with factories or collieries in Yorkshire. Most of the big pits in the county had bands of high quality, but for Bradford the pride of place was occupied by the Black Dyke Mills Band from the mills of the same name located high in the Pennines at Queensbury on the outskirts of the city. My parents awaited eagerly each year the result of the brass band national contests at the Crystal Palace or Belle Vue. I learnt to share their pleasure whenever the Black Dyke Band did well in these contests.

My mother had a lifelong friendship with a lady whose maiden name was Gladys Corney. Gladys married John Cryer and their son, Bob Cryer, became the Labour Member of Parliament for Bradford South. He was earlier the MP for Keighley and later a Member of the European Parliament for a constituency in south Yorkshire. Unfortunately he was killed in a motor accident. He was a very good MP, and his death was a great loss to the labour movement. Both his wife, Ann, and his son, John, were elected to parliament in the 1997 general election. I do not know how my mother met Gladys, but it was through her and John Cryer that my parents met. My father was a friend of John Cryer. They probably met in the labour movement before the First World War. My father's brother also married John Cryer's sister, so the relationship between them all was close.

All her life my mother had a great admiration for Gladys Cryer (née Corney). She described her as an extremely talented person. She was a self-taught pianist with a very good ear for music and a sensitive touch. My mother also described her as the best costume-maker she had ever encountered. After leaving Bradford my mother kept in touch with Gladys Cryer, and they were still exchanging occasional messages right up to the time of my mother's death. Gladys Cryer outlived my mother and died in 1990. My mother took pleasure in the political commitment and progress of Gladys's son, Bob, and was glad that he was consistently on the left.

Roots

Before the First World War my father was attracted by syndic-alist and socialist ideas. He was influenced by the political radicalism and trade union convictions of his father and probably by the support for the Independent Labour Party expressed by other members of my grandfather's family. The

13

ILP was founded in Bradford, largely as the result of a strike against proposed wage reductions at Manningham Mills. The strike began in 1890 and lasted for 19 weeks. The strike was defeated, but it aroused widespread support among the working class of the West Riding of Yorkshire. There were street demonstrations with tens of thousands of participants. There was very little violence, but troops were brought into the city and the Riot Act was read. Attempts were made to forbid demonstrations and meetings. The Poor Law Guardians were unsympathetic to claims for relief for the families of striking workers. The strikers were dependent on voluntary collections and donations from other trade unionists.

Careful accounts were kept of the collections and donations to assist the Manningham Mills' strikers. Some of them were reproduced in 1975 in a University of Hull publication, entitled *The Manningham Mills Strike, Bradford, December 1890 – April 1891*, by Cyril Pearce. There is a short list of individual subscriptions. One of the contributors was a person by the name of Mortimer. He contributed £2, the equivalent of between one-and-a-half and two weeks' wages. It may well have been my paternal grandfather. My father always described him as a strong trade unionist who was generous in donations when other workers were engaged in industrial disputes.

West Bradford, where my father was born in 1888, became a centre of socialist activity. In 1892, before the formation of the ILP, the Manningham ward elected its first two socialist councillors. One of them was Fred Jowett, a textile worker, who, many years later as an MP for one of the Bradford constituencies, became a Labour Cabinet Minister.

The ILP was formed at a national conference held in Bradford in January 1893. Its purpose was to establish a political party, primarily to represent working-class interests, but independent of the other two principal political parties, the Liberals and the Tories. There was, of course, little or no likelihood that those who sought working-class political representation would do so through the Tory Party. There was, however, a tradition of seeking representation through the Liberal Party.

14

In Bradford the experience of the Manningham Mills strike had underlined the need for real political independence for the labour movement. Some individual Liberals had sympathised with the strikers, but the Bradford Council, under Liberal control, sided much more with the Tory employer, Samuel Lister, than with the Manningham Mills' workers. Lister was unusual as a wool textile employer in being a Tory. Most of them at that time were Liberals.

The formation of the ILP represented a coming together of trade unionism and socialist ideas. Previously in Bradford there had been a branch of the Socialist League, whose most prominent supporter nationally was probably William Morris. The distinctive feature of the Bradford branch of the Socialist League was that it included a number of Germans who had come to Bradford to work in the textile industry. Even at that time Germany was said to be ahead of Britain in the development and use of dyes for textiles. In the last century and before the First World War there was a substantial colony of German immigrants in Bradford. Indeed, one part of central Bradford was known as 'little Germany'. Some of these German immigrants brought with them the socialist ideas of the German labour movement.

It was not, however, until the Manningham strike of 1890 that the early socialists established a close and leading relationship with a substantial group of workers engaged in an industrial dispute. One of the strike leaders was a man called Willie Drew. He was also a pioneer of the ILP. Very dimly in my memory I seem to recall, when I was a small boy, going to his house. My memory may be wrong because my father often spoke of Willie Drew. Drew emigrated to Canada but returned shortly afterwards to Bradford. He lived to a good age.

In the 1892 General Election the socialists of Bradford West selected the famous dockers' leader, Ben Tillett, to stand as an Independent Labour candidate. He was opposed by both Tory and Liberal candidates. Tillett came within 557 votes of victory. This was the General Election where Keir Hardie was a successful Independent Labour candidate for West Ham South. The Bradford West result was, however, arguably the

15

more impressive because Hardie, unlike Tillett, did not have a Liberal opponent.

I do not know when or exactly how my father became interested in the labour movement, but it was certainly well before the First World War, as he always spoke approvingly of Lloyd George's opposition to the Boer War. He would have been no more than 12 or 13 years of age at the time, so he probably was influenced by the attitude of his father.

My father spoke also of an event, known as the 'Girlington Klondike', which occurred in 1906 in an area of west Bradford where he was born and where he was then living. Girlington is a district of Bradford, not too far from Manningham, which at that time consisted largely of streets of back-to-back houses inhabited by textile workers.

In 1906 a group of unemployed workers, led by a Councillor Charles Glyde – a pioneer socialist in Bradford – occupied some unused land, owned by a railway company, with a view to establishing a camp. They announced that they intended to cultivate the land and establish a residence to be named Klondike Villa. The first residence was to be a large tent supplied by miners at Hemsworth. This land-grabbing exercise was intended as a protest against unemployment and against the capitalist system, which was held to be responsible for mass unemployment. The name Klondike was taken from the district of the Yukon in Alaska where in a 'gold rush' at the end of the nineteenth century thousands of fortune-seekers had dug for the newly found precious metal.

The 'Girlington Klondike' was established on a site very near to where my father was born and went to school. The 'Girlington diggers', as the land-grabbers were known, took their inspiration not only from their experience of unemployment and poverty in the capitalist society of their day but from the Diggers of the English Civil War in the seventeenth century. The Diggers were a small group associated with the Levellers, the democratic wing of the Cromwellian forces. They set up a small community in Surrey in 1649 based upon the principle of the common ownership and cultivation of land. It was short-lived. So too was the 'Girlington Klondike'. It lasted

16

for about three months, but during that period the occupants had brought much of the land under cultivation.

My father was, however, above all influenced by the unrest of the years before the First World War. These years saw a significant rise in militancy in the labour movement, not only in Britain but in a number of other countries. These were years of trade union struggles on a scale unprecedented in British history. There was also some disillusionment with the ineffectiveness of the first substantial group of Labour Members of Parliament elected in 1906. Most of them, with a few significant exceptions, were little different from the Liberals with whose support they had been elected. My father's low estimation of the Labour Party, based on his experience of the years before the First World War, remained with him for the rest of his life.

In the period before the First World War the need for social reform was being widely discussed. The demand for change was supported by working class opinion, whether Liberal or Labour, in the textile and mining areas of the West Riding of Yorkshire. Another issue at the centre of public attention was that of Irish home rule. The movement for Irish independence reached a new height, with accompanying threats of civil war from top Unionists in Northern Ireland who feared a parliamentary majority for Irish home rule. Yet another issue with radical implications was the challenge to democracy represented by the power of the House of Lords to frustrate the will of the elected House of Commons. The Lords rejected Budget proposals of the Liberal Government. Eventually the power of the House of Lords was curtailed.

The other major influence on my father's point of view when he was a young man was the preparation for war on the part of all the great powers, particularly Germany, Britain, Russia and France. He remained persuaded throughout his life that the First World War was motivated by the imperialist rivalry of the great powers.

In this period my father came close to the views, not of the Labour Party or even of the ILP, but of the then Socialist Labour Party. With the benefit of hindsight it is not difficult to

17

recognise both the strengths and weaknesses of the orientation of the SLP. It claimed to be Marxist, but in many ways it advocated a crude application of militancy in all its forms. Its contribution was its vigorous support for socialist ideas and its recognition of the importance of working-class struggle. Its weakness was that it underestimated the need for stable trade union organisation and for parliamentary representation.

My father often spoke of a strike of textile workers in Lawrence, New England, USA, some three or four years before the outbreak of the First World War. This strike was influenced by the Industrial Workers of the World, an American organisation closely associated with the Socialist Labour Party. It emphasised the necessity for union militancy but underestimated the need for continuing trade union organisation with negotiating procedure agreements and day-to-day collective bargaining. It was hostile to anything which it suspected might degenerate into a bureaucracy. It was also less than enthusiastic about any kind of socialist political movement which was not firmly rooted in workplace militancy.

In Bradford there was a solidarity movement with the New England textile strikers, and my father was sympathetic to it and associated with it. It is possible that it was there that he first met and established a friendship with John Cryer, the father of Bob Cryer MP.

The syndicalist and militant views of my father remained with him, certainly throughout the 1920s and early 1930s. Some members of the SLP joined the Communist Party when it was formed after the First World War. My father did not, but equally he never joined the Labour Party. He abhorred right-wing social democracy and held it responsible for the betrayal of the anti-war movement in both Britain and Germany in the First World War, for the defeat of social revolution in post-war Germany and for the failures of both the first and second Labour Governments in 1924 and 1931. He was condemnatory of the role of right-wing trade union leaders in what he regarded as the 'sell-out' of the 1926 General Strike. He was strongly opposed to imperialism and, during my childhood, I have a clear impression that my parents were in favour of Irish and Indian independence and had no sympathy with the celebration of Empire Day.

On all these issues the views of my father were close to those of the Communist Party in the 1920s and early 1930s. Indeed, he was sympathetic to the 'class against class' policy, later recognised by the Communist Party as mistaken, in which social democracy was regarded with hostility. One of the expressions used by my father to describe right-wing Labour leaders was that they were 'labour fakirs'.

My father's objection to the Communist Party was not on grounds of militancy or of any difference about right-wing social democracy, but was based entirely upon his strong objection to any kind of bureaucracy or uniformity imposed from above. One of his favourite sayings was that workers should be wary of anyone in a peaked cap. My father would under no circumstances have accepted the Leninist theory of 'democratic centralism'.

During my childhood my parents were not inhibited from speaking to me about their ideas. My mother would frequently put her views within a religious or moral context, but my father was explicitly political. Their conclusions, though expressed in different ways, were very similar. It is sometimes said that children react against their parents' views. I experienced no such reaction, though in later years in my teens I had political arguments with my father.

My parents did not batter me with their views but explained their standpoint when issues arose in the course of everyday life. I occasionally went to open-air meetings with my father, and I remember on one occasion in a textile strike in 1930 or 1931 being chased by police following a demonstration of striking workers. During the period 1929–31 stoppages of work in textiles, both cotton and wool, accounted for approximately two-thirds of all working days lost in Britain through industrial disputes. Bradford was a centre of industrial struggle.

In the Bradford of my schooldays there were three professional football teams, two following the Association code, Bradford and Bradford City, and one, Bradford Northern, following the Rugby League code. As a young man my father

19

supported Bradford City, whose ground, Valley Parade, was situated off one of the main roads through Manningham. In our house we had a large framed photograph of the Bradford City team that won the Football Association cup in 1911.

By the time I became interested in football in the late 1920s, the loyalty of our household had switched from Bradford City to Bradford. I was always a Bradford supporter. It was only later that I learnt of the reason for this change in my father's loyalty. In 1916 he had been deeply upset by the execution by the British of the militant Irish socialist, James Connolly, who was the Commandant-General of the Dublin Division of the Army of the Irish Republic in the abortive Easter Rising of 1916. Connolly was taken from hospital and executed by a firing squad on 12 May, 1916.

My father had a great admiration for Connolly, whose social-ist activities were firmly rooted in the working-class movement and who had a vision of socialism based on extensive reading and study. Connolly was both an activist and a theorist. My father, in a symbolic gesture, changed his loyalty after the First World War from Bradford City to Bradford because, he said, most of the Irish in the city supported Bradford. At one time they played in green and white colours. Later they changed to red, amber and black. Bradford (also known as Bradford Park Avenue) eventually lost their place in the Football League.

My parents sometimes went to the Mechanics' Institute in Bradford for Sunday evening lectures and lantern shows. My only recollection is of lantern shows connected with foreign travel. More usually, Sunday was the day on which visits were exchanged with relatives. With my mother's family the discus-sion was mainly about family matters, issues of local interest and sport. With my father's family it was more often about politics and the state of industry.

When I was about eleven years of age my father fell ill. He collapsed at his street-corner newspaper stand. My mother had to take over, collecting the newspapers early in the morning, selling them outside the Manningham Mills and then delivering a newspaper round both in the mornings and in the evenings. I helped a little in the evenings.

This arrangement could not last. Both of my parents felt that it was not right that my mother should carry this burden. They decided to seek their livelihood elsewhere. Two of my father's brothers were by this time living in the south of England, and they offered to accommodate my parents whilst my father looked for a leasehold shop. My parents had always lived frugally and they had small savings. My mother went to live with her parents for a short while, I went to relatives in Bradford, and my father went to his brother in Poole.

Before my father left Bradford my parents were informed that I had been granted a place at Bradford Grammar School as a result of what was then universally known in Bradford as the 'scholarship' examination. My 'scholarship' carried with it a financial award, known as the Nutter award. Unfortunately, because of my parents' intended departure from the city I was not able to take advantage of the grammar school place. My mother, however, bought me, as a consolation, a Bradford Grammar School cap. It was the nearest I came to a place in the school.

2

The South Coast

When my parents decided to leave Bradford, the intention was to find and rent a leasehold tobacconist shop somewhere near to the south coast of England. My father's two elder brothers were already living in the Bournemouth–Poole area. The elder of the two, who was originally a textile worker, had been successful in developing a thriving fish and chip business in Dorchester. He then sold it at a considerable profit and developed another, similarly prosperous, fish and chip business in Poole.

The other brother had gone into semi-retirement whilst still in his thirties. He had emigrated to British Columbia in Canada and had done very well for himself; so well, in fact, that some years earlier my parents were also persuaded to emigrate. However, they got no further than to have passport photographs taken. A slump led them to change their minds. In the meanwhile my father's brother and his wife returned to England, where their first child was born. They bought themselves an antique shop in Bournemouth, and this too did very well. They then bought a very large bungalow, with something like twelve rooms and two acres of ground, in a then largely underdeveloped area between Bournemouth and Poole.

The bungalow, so it was said, served at one time as a convalescent home for wounded officers in the First World War. It had an attractive setting with a wooded area and pine trees, a dell, small open meadows, a large barn and a house separate from the bungalow. It was located in the country, and my uncle was said to have bought it because it reminded him of

Canada. He was an even-tempered and kind man and loved the open air. He was very good at any sport to which he turned his hand. He ran the estate as a homestead, growing vegetables, keeping chickens and working in the woods.

After leaving Bradford my father first went to live with his elder brother and wife in Poole. My mother returned to live with her parents in the expectation that my father would find a leasehold shop fairly quickly. I went to live with my mother's sister and husband in another part of Bradford. They had two young children. My aunt and uncle treated me with great kindness and consideration.

After a few weeks it became clear that my father was unlikely very quickly to find a suitable shop. He was extremely cautious and reluctant to commit the small savings he had accumulated. He did not have the speculative flair of his two brothers, and his physical infirmity added to his fear of business failure. Both his brothers were generous, and it was agreed that my mother should join my father in Poole and live with his brother and his wife who owned the fish and chip business. I was to live with my father's other brother and his wife on their estate.

Altogether it was 15 months before I was reunited with my parents. During this period my parents had no income at all. As an unemployed former street newspaper seller, my father was not eligible for unemployment benefit. We were fortunate to have such generous close relatives.

When the time came for my mother and me to leave Bradford for the South Coast, it seemed as though we were to travel to some distant land. I had little idea what to expect except that I imagined the climate to be much warmer. My maternal grandfather, the engine-driver, as always affectionate and considerate, came to see us off on a train destined for Bournemouth. It was called 'The Pine Express'. It was typical of my grandfather that as we prepared to get on the train he gave my mother money so that we could have a meal in the restaurant car. This was an experience of luxury which was not only new to me but also to my mother.

I remember the meal because after the sweet course the

attendant asked my mother whether we wanted coffee. My mother was always a tea drinker, but when told that tea was not available she said that we would both have coffee. The attendant then asked whether we wanted black or white coffee. My mother was flustered. The only coffee with which she had any familiarity came as an essence out of a bottle and was called Camp coffee. The essence was very dark, and so my mother assumed that this was what was meant by black coffee. She had no idea what white coffee might be. She asked for black coffee and that was what we received. I think she was then too embarrassed to ask for milk.

I have pleasant memories of my stay of near 15 months on my uncle's estate near Bournemouth. Naturally I looked forward to seeing my parents when they visited us from Poole, but my days were fully and enjoyably occupied. The school I went to was a long way away, and my cousin and I had to walk across fields for the journey. When we were not at school there were always jobs to do on the estate, and my uncle had the knack of making us feel that we were pioneers. In the mornings he worked on the estate, but in the early afternoons he rested. Afterwards we would sometimes play outdoor games. My parents later spent short periods on the estate, and in the evenings would join my aunt and uncle to listen to music, to read or to play cards.

My father eventually found a suitable leasehold shop on the outskirts of Portsmouth. He went there because his brother with the fish and chip business in Poole sold his shop profitably and found another new shop in Portsmouth. This once again proved to be a very good business. My uncle had a talent for spotting business opportunities. He was not physically a hard worker, but my father always admired his intelligence and business sense. He was eccentric in his ways. In his house he had a large room for his personal use where he would shut himself away and read for hours on end. He never sat down at a table with others for a meal, but took his food either in a chair or in his own room. Sometimes when my parents visited him at his house in Portsmouth he would not emerge from his room until it was almost time for my parents to depart. His wife would keep calling him, but he would be immersed in a book on philosophy or religion.

There was no ill-feeling in his eccentricity, and my parents accepted it with rather more amusement than complaint. He was also generous to my parents and always good-tempered. He lived, as my mother would say, in another world of philosophy, religion, politics, stocks and shares and business opportunities.

On Saturdays, after playing football or cricket in the morning, I often went to my uncle's house and fish and chip shop for lunch. I was always assured of a massive meal. I would sit at the table by myself and eat my fill of fish and chips. My uncle would give me money to buy custard pies or anything else I fancied for a sweet. It would all be washed down with lemonade. Sometimes he would come into the room to talk to me and outline his views on society and life. Occasionally he would lie full-length on the floor to engage in conversation. He cared nothing for convention.

This same uncle of mine helped two other relatives from Bradford to find businesses in Portsmouth. Both had been workers before becoming shopkeepers. One of them was sometimes visited by one of my grandfather's brothers. My grandfather's brother was then in his seventies and was retired. He had been a textile worker all his working life, and he was a strong socialist. He had been a member of the ILP from the early days of its formation in Bradford. He spoke to me of his vision of a new socialist society. It was an inspiring message, and he delivered it in persuasive tones. He was fluent and his eloquence was all the more impressive because he believed strongly in the views he expressed. One of his sons, who was a full-time trade union official in Leeds, later encouraged my interest in the labour movement. I continued to correspond with him until his death when he was in his middle nineties.

Before my parents left Bournemouth for Portsmouth I was able to sit the secondary school examination. I was awarded a place at Bournemouth High School but was unable to take it. Nevertheless the local authority indicated that it would probably be possible to transfer the award to a similar school in Portsmouth. This, indeed, proved to be the case. Soon after our arrival in Portsmouth my parents were informed that a place would be available for me at one of the city's secondary schools (later called grammar schools).

Unfortunately my father turned down the offer. He took me out for a walk one evening and explained his reasons. He doubted whether we could afford my staying at school until I was at least 16 years of age, and he was aware that other continuous expenses would be incurred by attendance at such a school. He was also of the view that it would probably be better for me to learn a trade when I left school. His own experience of life had led him to attach importance to becoming a skilled worker.

My father's low estimation of the value of formal education was one of his principal weaknesses. He never looked at a school report of mine and never once attended any school function or parents' day interview. He would talk to me patiently about politics but showed no interest in the subjects I was being taught at school. His attitude was that it was sufficient to be able to read, to write and to make elementary arithmetical calculations. He might have shown some interest in history, except that he regarded as very biased the kind of history taught in schools. He was opposed to imperialism, hostile to the existence of the Empire and felt that we should be ashamed of Britain's history of conquest in other lands. I grew up to support the movements for Indian independence and for a united independent Ireland.

For about a year after arriving in Portsmouth I attended an elementary school adjacent to a large council estate. When I was twelve years of age there came an opportunity to sit for entrance to the Portsmouth Junior Technical School. The syllabus of this school had a strong technical bias. It was a three-year course and many of the pupils became apprentices in Portsmouth Dockyard or artificer apprentices in the Royal Navy. I was awarded a place in the junior technical school, and this time my father agreed I should take it. This determined the course of much of my subsequent life.

I was not a suitable pupil for a technical school, although I maintained a place in the A stream throughout my three years. The emphasis of the tuition was on technical training. We spent many hours on engineering drawing and either one or two afternoons a week in the workshops. Academic studies were directed towards physics, mechanics, dynamics, hydraulics, chemistry and mathematics. The amount of time we spent on history, geography and English was limited, yet these were my favourite subjects and also the subjects at which I was best. Conversely, I was never any good at drawing and, although I enjoyed the workshops, I had no aptitude for craftsmanship.

Despite my unsuitability for a technical education, I was fortunate to find in my three years at Portsmouth Junior Technical School a group of teachers who were interested in history, geography and English and who taught it well. I won a number of school prizes in these subjects. In my third year I selected a number of books on socialism and Marxism as my prizes, including a book by a German refugee, Dr Edward Conze, entitled, *An Introduction to Dialectical Materialism*. The headmaster thought it an odd choice, but he acceded to my request.

My life in the technical school could not be described as particularly successful, and for a period I was made unhappy by the sarcasm of a drawing instructor who could not bring himself to accept that anyone could be so hopeless at freehand drawing as I was. My ability in engineering drawing was, fortunately, rather better. We spent about six hours a week in drawing lessons, and this was considered an important part of the curriculum. Nevertheless, despite these failings I was made a prefect in my final year and elected as house captain. All pupils at the school were divided into four houses.

In each of the three years at the junior technical school each of the pupils in the A stream was required, as part of the English course, to deliver a short lecture on a subject of his own choosing. (There were no girls in the school.) In the first year I chose 'disarmament', in the second 'trade unionism' and in the third 'socialism'. I very much enjoyed preparing the material for these lectures. I have no doubt that they were very crude in substance, but they were important for my own development. They led me to use the public library for the preparation of my own notes.

Initiation

My interest in the labour movement was quickening. One of my relatives, the full-time union official, arranged to send me his union journal every month. I also went to my first meeting of the Labour Party League of Youth. It was the Portsmouth North branch. I was very disappointed because, although the meeting was very well attended, no-one spoke to me. The emphasis of the meeting appeared to be on social arrangements and, as a schoolboy, I was probably thought to be too young to participate in hiking, cycling or dancing.

Nevertheless, I acquired one or two pamphlets which made my initiation into the League of Youth worthwhile. They had been published many years earlier. I remember three particular pamphlets: one by George Hicks MP, another by Tom Kennedy MP and the third by Harry Quelch, entitled *The Economics of Labour*. They were all, I think, originally published by the old Social Democratic Federation. I have no idea how they came to be available at a meeting of the Portsmouth North Labour League of Youth; I have a vague recollection that I found them discarded in a cupboard and that the secretary of the branch, the daughter of a Portsmouth Labour councillor, said that I could have them.

I read these three pamphlets with great interest, though I found the one by Harry Quelch rather difficult. They seemed to confirm so many of the ideas which I had heard expressed by my parents. These ideas were not only interesting but inspiring. They were fired by a deep sense of injustice against poverty and unemployment and a determination to build a new society through the struggles of the labour movement.

At about this time my relative who was a union official suggested in a letter that I should get in touch with the National Council of Labour Colleges. He gave me an address in Southampton of the full-time organiser for the Hampshire area. I knew virtually nothing of the NCLC, though I had heard from my father of the existence of Ruskin College, Oxford, which, he said, provided places for working-class students from the labour movement. He also mentioned that many years earlier there had been a strike of students at Ruskin and that this had led to the establishment of the short-lived Central Labour College in London. This reference to Ruskin College by my father led me to inquire from the headmaster of the Junior Technical School whether he knew anything about it. He indicated that he did not, and I felt from his attitude that he would not have encouraged me even if he had.

I wrote to the full-time organiser for the NCLC, and he put me in touch with what I found to be a thriving branch in Portsmouth. The branch was led by a former Mancunian called Will Greaves. Other keen supporters included a Dockyard electrician called Tom Farnes, a Cooperative worker called Russell who later became the Labour candidate for the ward in which my family lived, a Labour councillor, Robert Mack, who stood as a candidate in the 1935 General Election, and a Cooperative Party secretary whose name I have forgotten. I started to attend NCLC classes and there I met another young person, David Priscott, who was about two years older than I and who by this time was an apprentice in the Dockyard.

Dave Priscott suggested that I should attend the meetings of the Portsmouth Central branch of the Labour League of Youth which, he said, were more political than the meetings of the Portsmouth North branch. I accepted his suggestion and found the Portsmouth Central branch more to my liking. I there met another Dockyard apprentice, Gordon Jeffery, later to become an author and an executive committee member of a civil service trade union. I am still in touch to this day with Gordon and his wife, Joan, another former member of Portsmouth Central League of Youth branch. Dave Priscott eventually joined the Communist Party and was employed full-time by the Party for many years. He was a District Secretary, a member of their Executive Committee and of their Political Committee.

My introduction to the classes of the NCLC was an exciting

29

experience. I had already picked up fragments about socialism, trade unionism and the struggle against social injustice from my parents and some of my relatives, but the classes of the NCLC, with their emphasis on Marxism, put these fragments into a theoretical framework. In particular, the labour theory of value and the concept of surplus value – a surplus derived from the employment of wage labour and appropriated by private employers because of their ownership of the means of production – gave new substance to ideas which were developing in my mind.

Similarly, I was being introduced to a whole new area of thought, the world outlook of dialectical materialism. In a very crude manner I became acquainted with the 'laws' of dialectics: that everything is in movement, that to understand change it is necessary to look for internal contradictions, that the struggle of opposites, the unity of opposites and the interpenetration of opposites are all aspects of matter in motion, that in all phenomena quantitative change leads to qualitative change, which in turn leads to further quantitative change, that development through the struggle of contradictory forces can be perceived as the success of what appears to be a negation, and that this in turn is followed by the negation of the negation, but on a higher scale.

I was also increasingly influenced by the view that human thought reflects the material conditions of life and that as conditions change, so too do the ideas of mankind. It was this concept which finally led me to question the religious beliefs which I still held in my mid-teens.

The leading NCLC supporter in Portsmouth, Will Greaves, had a strong interest in philosophy and was a follower of another Manchester NCLC tutor, Fred Casey. Casey was strongly influenced by the German philosopher, Josef Dietzgen, who claimed to have developed a method of thinking based upon the application of dialectics. Some of the attenders at the Portsmouth classes were less enthusiastic than Will Greaves about the emphasis to be given to the ideas of Dietzgen. They preferred to concentrate their studies on the texts of Marx and Engels.

This was my first introduction to philosophical controversy and its implications for the practical work of the labour movement. I found it all fascinating. I remember spending hours in a room above my father's shop, writing page after page of notes on the evolution of society.

I could not at this stage afford to buy books. I had, therefore, to rely on the public library and on occasional pamphlets to be bought at NCLC classes, at the League of Youth branch or at a left-wing bookshop, then run by the Communist Party in Portsmouth. In the public library I found a number of books on socialism. I do not think I read any from cover to cover except, perhaps, *A History of British Socialism* by Max Beer. Nevertheless I gained something from odd chapters and pages in whatever I could find. There was one book, *Marxism and Modern Thought*, edited by Bukharin (later to be executed in the Stalin purges of the late 1930s), which intrigued me, but I understood little of its contents. It consisted of a number of contributions on the application of Marxism to various areas of learning. It seemed to confirm that Marxism was truly an all-embracing world outlook.

My father suggested that I should read John Stuart Mill. Mill, he said, was a great liberal philosopher who had come to accept the necessity for socialism. It is possible that my father's suspicion of all bureaucratic authority had been influenced by Mill's writings on liberty and representative government. The only work of Mill's that I could find in the public library was on political economy. I tried to read it but did not get very far. It was not until some years later when I was a student at Ruskin College and at the London School of Economics that I came to appreciate the value and contemporary relevance of Mill's political philosophy.

My other main interest of this period was centred on the Methodist church. No doubt due to the influence of my mother, I was a regular attender at Sunday school and a keen member of a Methodist boys' club. They were happy experiences. All my friends were drawn from the boys' club and we had a strong sense of identity as young Methodists. We had a football team and occasionally played a team from the local church of the Church of England. It was hardly an ecumenical affair, though I cannot think why there should have been such rivalry. We drew a fair number of our boys from a local council housing estate, whereas the Church of England team seemed to be drawn from more prosperous avenues in the locality.

The teenage youths in the Methodist boys' club were also invited to attend a weekly Bible class, often taken by the Minister. I frequently went and found it a stimulating experience. The class would read a short passage from the Bible – always from the New Testament, as far as I recall – and then we would discuss it. Everyone was encouraged to express an opinion, and there was no 'official' doctrine handed to us by the Minister. He saw it as his task to guide our discussion by pointing out inconsistencies and illogicalities in our contributions. We were encouraged to become thinking and articulate Nonconformists with a strong social conscience.

Sometimes on Sunday afternoons I would go to the Brotherhood meeting in the Portsmouth Wesley Central Hall. The father of one of my friends in the Methodist boys' club was a regular attender at the Brotherhood and he suggested that we might go. The meetings were very well attended, particularly when there was an interesting speaker.

The Methodist boys' club also introduced me to camping. Our club used a site some three or four miles from Chichester. I developed a liking for camping and for outdoor life which always remained with me. As an adult I spent many happy weekends and holidays on camp sites both in Britain and abroad.

Work

When I was 15 years of age I became an apprentice ship fitter in Portsmouth Dockyard. When I had been accepted for entry as an apprentice I went with my father to choose my trade. All the available trades, and there were many of them, were listed on a wall chart. I have now little idea why I chose ship fitting.

It had the word 'ship' in the title, and this probably appealed to me. I had also been told that the various fitting trades, including engine fitter, electrical fitter, ordnance fitter and ship fitter, were all based on similar engineering skills. The basic skills were fitting and machining, including turning, milling, drilling, grinding, shaping and slotting.

I started work in a large machine shop. My instructor was a heavy turner. He was highly skilled and could use a lathe to produce work within very 'fine tolerances'. He knew how to make adjustments to a thousandth of an inch, even on machine tools which had seen better days. With a gentle tap here or there, the occasional use of very thin cigarette papers as packing and an ability to eliminate 'backlash' from worn-out lead screws, he could produce work of the highest quality in circumstances where skill was being used as a substitute for modern precision machinery.

Though I had no particular aptitude for the work in which I was now engaged, I liked the atmosphere of the machine shop and all the activity of shipbuilding and ship repair. There were so many different trades and workshops to see. There was also the activity on the building stocks, in the dry docks and in the basins. Sometimes too it was necessary to go 'afloat' for work on ships at anchor.

There was also an unattractive side to work in the Dockyard. The starting time was 7 a.m. To reach the Dockyard I had to cycle about five or six miles in all kinds of weather. I left home shortly after 6 a.m. because time had to be allowed not only for the cycle ride but for parking the cycle, walking to one of the Dockyard gates and then walking to a clocking-on stand in the machine shop where I worked. I attended night school three nights a week, and there was insufficient time to go home before the night school sessions.

There was one particular feature of life in the Dockyard which I found specially objectionable. The lavatories in the machine shop where I worked had no doors. I assume that this degrading practice was introduced by top management who, in the comfort of their private offices, assumed that doors on lavatories would encourage workers to malinger.

There was also at that time no provision for the delivery of tea to workers during the long morning session from 7 a.m. to 12 noon or during the afternoons. The consequence was that many workers rigged up for themselves various devices for boiling water and making tea. They tapped into the electricity supply in the Dockyard. This led in turn to the surreptitious washing of cups and utensils in unhygienic containers of water. It was also the practice before finishing time to wash hands in containers hidden behind machines or benches so that workers would not be caught assembled in washing troughs during official working hours.

At the time I found all these practices unattractive but it was only in later years, long after my experience in the Dockyard, that I realised how foolish they were from the standpoint of industrial efficiency. These primitive and degrading practices were the consequence of a managerial attitude that had little regard for the dignity, safety and health of manual workers.

My entry into the Dockyard introduced me to a new world of trade union activity. I joined the union as soon as I could and was 'read in' at an initiation ceremony at the branch where my application for membership had been accepted. It was a moving occasion. I remember little of the wording of the ceremony, but the main message left a lasting impression. It was that as a union member I should have regard to the common interests of the members of the union and that it was through workers' cooperation and solidarity that our occupational welfare would be advanced.

My first official position as a trade union member was that of branch teller. This required that I should sit at the ballot box in the branch room whenever there was an election. Elections were frequent. Voters had to be marked on a register and checked against the membership records. I attended the branch meetings regularly. Members used to file through the meeting room to pay their subscriptions but would remain to hear the business if there was an item of particular interest or if there was a good speaker.

The branch president and branch secretary were indulgent

towards me because of my youth. I received their permission to sell *The Socialist*, a publication of the Socialist League. As a branch teller I was strategically placed to display copies for sale. I was also listened to respectfully whenever I wanted to join in the discussion. I am sure that this was not because my views had any particular merit but because it was considered right to encourage a young and interested member.

My experience as a trade union branch teller gave me an insight into how members vote in union elections. The big problem is that the electorate often know very little of the candidates. They may have read the officially circulated election addresses, but often these addresses do not convey much beyond the trade union experience of the candidates and assertions of their intention to work for the good of the union and the strengthening of trade union democracy.

Members who regularly attend branch meetings are nearly always better informed. They will have listened to or participated in discussions about union policy and will have become familiar with the points of view of different individuals or groups. Even so, candidates from large establishments have an advantage over candidates from small establishments where they are known to fewer active members.

When members came to vote in the branch room some knew already their preferred candidate. Others, however, had very little idea and would ask who the branch was supporting. This, in my view, is a legitimate enquiry and branch officials are entitled to indicate their views.

Postal voting has the big disadvantage that it does not encourage members to attend their branch meetings and to participate in discussion. In the absence of discussion or of other information, members may be unduly influenced in national union elections by newspaper campaigns which reflect the preferences and prejudices of their wealthy proprietors.

There is no perfect way of choosing union officials. In my youth I was a strong supporter of the system which requires all full-time officials to stand for periodic election, with elections conducted either at branch meetings or in the workplace. Later, through experience, I became aware that this system had its defects. On the other hand, all other systems also have their defects. A system under which most full-time officials are appointed may perpetuate an existing hierarchy. Care has to be taken in any system to prevent abuse, but this is not always as easy as some critics suggest. Unions depend upon voluntary officials at branch level. Perhaps the one valid conclusion is that no one system suits all circumstances, but that in every union the emphasis should be on informed membership participation. How this is achieved depends upon the organisation and structure of the union.

Trade union membership entitled me, free of charge, to the full facilities of the National Council of Labour Colleges. I took advantage of them. Over a six or seven year period I completed a number of NCLC correspondence courses, including three on economics, at various levels, and separate courses on finance, the 'scientific way of thinking', socialism, employment law and English. I also went to NCLC classes, to day schools and weekend schools. My first weekend school was at Cowes in the Isle of Wight. I owed much to the NCLC.

In the days when the NCLC was in existence it was often argued that the facilities for the education of trade unionists offered by the NCLC, the Workers' Educational Association, the Workers' Educational Trade Union Committee, the TUC itself and the correspondence courses offered by Ruskin College should be brought together under the auspices of the TUC. There were undoubtedly weaknesses resulting from this divided pattern of organisation. The TUC was instrumental in bringing about a rationalisation of facilities, and from the late 1950s onwards substantially extended its own educational services.

Nevertheless, one of the consequences of these changes was that the NCLC lost its identity and merged its organisation within a wider structure. This brought some advantages, but the emphasis of trade union education was henceforth more on training for effective trade unionism than on wider social education. The increased training facilities were welcome, but the distinctive role of much of the NCLC's contribution has never been satisfactorily replaced.

I had not long been active at branch level in the Amalgamated Engineering Union when a vacancy arose for Trades Council delegate. I was elected to fill the vacancy. The Portsmouth Trades Council held well attended meetings, with 60 or 70 delegates present. The meetings were interesting, with discussions ranging from local to national issues of concern to trade unionists.

It was at the Trades Council that I had my first experience of debate between left and right in the trade union movement. I generally sided with the left, though I remember that when the Franco rebellion started in Spain, with the support of Hitler and Mussolini, I was inclined to sympathise with the view that the best way to help the legitimately elected Spanish Government was to campaign for effective international non-intervention, which would have prevented German and Italian military assistance to Franco.

It was a naive view, and I changed my mind fairly quickly. The British Government sympathised with the fascists, and so-called non-intervention was no more than a device to prevent the Spanish Government exercising its right to buy arms for its defence. Hitler and Mussolini continued to give armed assistance to Franco, and the British Government had no intention to stop this one-sided arrangement. The appeasement of fascism by the British Conservative leadership, which reached its height in the Munich agreement of 1938, when parts of Czechoslovakia were handed to Hitler, was already apparent in the Spanish war.

My desire to be associated with the left of the movement led me to join the Socialist League, which was affiliated to the Labour Party, and which included many prominent left-wingers. The leading personality was Stafford Cripps, but among others, as far as I recall, were William Mellor, George Strauss, G.R. Mitchison, Aneurin Bevan and Barbara Castle (then Barbara Betts).

I attended a national conference of the Socialist League in 1937 to discuss a proposed unity campaign with the ILP and the Communist Party. It was held in London, and this was my first visit to the capital. I had to ask for time off from work to attend the conference. The charge-hand ship fitter gave me permission and so, fortunately, no problems were raised about my employment. I was accommodated free of charge in London by a Hampstead doctor.

It was at the Socialist League conference that I first encountered Trotskyists. One of their leading spokesmen was Reg Groves. I was more attracted by the arguments put forward by Cripps and Mellor, and supported the unity campaign.

I bought the first issue of *Tribune* and became a regular reader. The editor was William Mellor. It was strongly left-wing and backed the unity campaign. The Labour Party then disaffiliated the Socialist League, but *Tribune* remained as a focal point for the left.

In the Labour Party League of Youth in Portsmouth opinion was overwhelmingly in favour of the unity campaign as a means of rousing public opinion against fascism, against the appeasement policy of the British Government and in favour of 'arms for Spain'. I began to speak at open-air meetings on a big council estate on the outskirts of Portsmouth, outside the Dockyard gates and once or twice on the sea front at Southsea. I also cycled to Petersfield to speak at open-air meetings. The League of Youth was very active and attracted numerous young people to the anti-fascist movement. I joined with others in helping to form another branch of the League in Cosham, on the outskirts of Portsmouth, where I lived.

In the Dockyard in the spring of 1937 a number of apprentices sought to develop a solidarity movement with engineering and shipbuilding apprentices on the Clyde and in Manchester who had struck work for trade union recognition and higher pay. The AEU called a meeting of apprentices, but it was not well attended. I argued for solidarity action among ship fitter apprentices but was unsuccessful. I had the disadvantage of being a young apprentice. Moreover, Dockyard apprentices were conscious that they were provided with the opportunity of further education in the Dockyard School and that this education opened doors to promotion. The pay for apprentices was poor, starting at 12 shillings a week (60p) in the first year, but it was better than having to pay a premium for an apprenticeship in a private firm.

It was about this time that I had an indirect encounter with security in the Dockyard. I was advised in a friendly manner by the shop superintendent in the workshop where I was employed that a security officer had made enquiries about my activities. Apparently he was interested in my speaking in favour of the unity campaign at open-air meetings outside the Dockyard gates and in the attempt to promote solidarity action with the Clydeside and Manchester apprentices. There were also in the neighbourhood of the Dockyard numerous whitewashed slogans calling for arms for Spain. Members of the League of Youth had formed part of the whitewashing squad. I found particularly disturbing the information given to me by the shop superintendent that another employee in the workshop had made complaints to someone in authority about my 'subversive' activities.

It was rumoured that security officers were enquiring about the activities of a number of Dockyard workers. At Rosyth Dockyard a group were dismissed from their employment. The Labour Party raised the matter in the House of Commons but, as with all security matters, there is no public accountability for the actions of the official agencies. No doubt there are genuine issues of security, but it is all too easy under the guise of security to exercise discrimination against people on the left whose activities are designed to arouse opinion and promote legitimate political or industrial action. In the meanwhile the real culprits – those in high places who were appeasing fascism – were left untouched. Indeed, it was they who were ultimately in charge of the so-called security operations.

My relations with my father had by now become more difficult. He was sympathetic to my union activities and was more pleased by my election as a Trades Council delegate than by anything that I had ever done at school. On the other hand, he was much less sympathetic towards my speaking at open-air meetings on behalf of the Labour League of Youth. He had retained his scepticism about the Labour Party, and this had been reinforced by what he regarded as the betrayal of the principal Labour leaders in the Labour Government of 1931. He held them partially responsible for his own misfortunes in the early 1930s. He had voted Labour in the 1935 General Election, but only because he disliked the Tories even more than he distrusted the right-wing Labour leadership.

His distrust of Labour did not make him a Communist Party sympathiser. He was closer to the Communist Party on a number of issues of policy, but he strongly objected to any kind of authoritarian political conduct whether by a party or by a state.

These political attitudes were reinforced by other considerations. His business was becoming more prosperous, and this to some extent blunted his radicalism. He took the view that the majority of people in Britain, particularly in the south, did not want to change the social system because they were relatively comfortable under the existing order. They were satisfied with minor reforms. There was very little in the record of Labour governments to offer them a convincing vision of an alternative future. Any change towards socialism was, therefore, unlikely. All that might happen, even on the most optimistic assumptions, was the election of yet another right-wing dominated Labour Government and eventually more disillusionment.

This attitude of my father was hardly compatible with my youthful enthusiasm and my conviction that the anti-fascist struggle was of pressing urgency. I think my father perhaps feared for the effect on his business of my activities. He may also have resented the emphatic manner in which I sometimes argued with him, particularly because the differences were not so much about ultimate social objectives but about the extent of my activities. When I suggested to my parents that I might be sacked if and when I completed my apprenticeship and that it might be better to break my apprenticeship and go to London, my father did not object. My mother was upset but accepted that I might be right. Both had a fear of unemployment.

I found myself a job in London with the London County Council and applied to break my apprenticeship in the Dockyard. My request was granted.

3

London

When I moved to London I found lodgings in Gresham Road, Brixton, near to the busy centre of the borough of Lambeth. The landlady and her daughter ran a large house with about 12 lodgers, nearly all of them young men. It was a lively place in which to stay.

My room was very small and almost attic-like on the top floor. It did not have running water and it was barely furnished. There was no central heating. I had a gas fire in the room, but I very rarely used it. There was a communal sitting room which was often empty except late at night. When I wanted to read I could do so in my own room, providing the weather was not too cold, or I could use the sitting room where there was a coal fire. Those were the days before television. The rent for the room and for two meals a day, with three meals each on Saturday and Sunday, was 22 shillings a week (£1.10 per week in present currency). It was very good value.

When I arrived at my lodgings I was delighted to find that the headquarters of the Brixton Labour Party were immediately opposite in Gresham Road. It was a Saturday, and I enquired from someone who was present in the Labour Party rooms whether there was a Labour League of Youth branch. I was told that there was, that it held regular branch meetings on Friday evenings but that on most other weekday evenings a few members of the branch were present for other activities. I became a member of what must have been one of the best attended and most active branches of the League of Youth in Britain.

The Friday night meetings of the Brixton branch of the League of Youth were often packed to the door. Members assembled not only in the main meeting room, but in other rooms, in the corridors and around the refreshment bar. Outside the premises and in the approach to the front door cycles were parked in large numbers.

Some of the members of the branch remained active in the labour movement for many years afterwards, and some achieved prominence in different walks of life. The secretary of the branch when I joined was Bert Baker. He was then with the main steelworkers' union, the Iron and Steel Trades Confederation. He later worked on the *Daily Mirror*, became features editor of the *Morning Star* and was a first-class TV critic under the name of Stewart Lane. The branch chairman was Stan Moore, who became a solicitor and established a reputation as a civil rights lawyer. I seem to remember that he acted for Gerhardt Eisler when, many years later, Eisler was hounded out of the United States. Another prominent member of the branch was Bert Turner, then a student at the London School of Economics. He later had a distinguished academic career and became a foremost authority on industrial relations. He was appointed professor at Cambridge University. He and I many years later were to become members of the National Board for Prices and Incomes under the chairmanship of Aubrey Jones. Yet another active member was Eddie Appleton who, I believe, became a BBC producer.

Immediately before the Second World War the most prominent member of the Brixton branch of the Labour League of Youth was Ted Willis. He rarely, if ever, attended because of his national commitments as the unofficial leader of the League of Youth and as secretary of the Spanish Youth Foodship Committee. He lived at the time in a block of flats on Brixton Hill.

Ted Willis was brought up in a working-class family in north London. He was a number of years older than I was, and I was strongly influenced by him. I was elected to the London Advisory Committee of the League of which Ted was the chairman and the undoubted leader. He had many attractive personal qualities in addition to his very considerable intellectual ability. I occasionally visited his flat on Brixton Hill, and it was there that I first became aware of his interest in literature. This interest later flourished when he began to write 'living newspapers' for the youth movement and plays for Unity Theatre. Later still he became one of Britain's most successful writers and his name will always be associated with *The Blue Lamp* and the *Dixon of Dock Green* television series.

The Brixton branch of the League of Youth nominated Ted Willis as prospective parliamentary candidate for Brixton. We did not succeed, though if we had it is very doubtful whether the National Executive Committee would have endorsed his candidature. Ted was well known for his support for a popular front of the left. The General Management Committee of the Brixton Labour Party chose Marcus Lipton as the prospective candidate. He later won the seat for Labour.

Ted Willis later became a member of the House of Lords. Many years after leaving the youth movement I sat with him again on a committee seeking to launch a new daily Labour newspaper. We did not succeed. Others who were involved in the committee included Tom Driberg, Norman Buchan and George Elvin, the trade union leader. Ted Willis retained his socialist commitment.

The Brixton branch of the Labour League of Youth had a wide range of activities. At the Friday night branch meetings we had speakers and discussions. There was strong political interest. The branch members were overwhelmingly in favour of a popular front with communists, liberals and others, as an essential step for the urgent defeat of the Chamberlain Government. The focal point of inspiration was the resistance to fascism, symbolised above all by the struggle of the Spanish people in support of their elected Popular Front government, then threatened by the Franco rebellion, which was being assisted by the military intervention of Hitler and Mussolini. The Chamberlain Government in Britain was appeasing fascism, and many prominent Conservatives were sympathetic to Franco.

On other weekday evenings members of the League of

43

Youth branch helped in various directions. Regular open-air meetings were held at Rushcroft Road, opposite Lambeth Town Hall. Copies of the League of Youth paper, *Advance*, were sold on cinema queues and on housing estates. Money was collected for the Spanish Youth Foodship Committee. I remember how easy it was to collect money for food for Spain on the housing estates in Brixton. Most people were sympathetic.

At weekends in the summer a number of members of the branch attended a socialist youth camp near Hoddesdon. They were often joined by members of the Clapham branch of the League of Youth and by members of the Lambeth Young Communist League. The relationship between the Brixton and Clapham branches of the League of Youth was particularly close. The Clapham branch too was well attended. The Lambeth YCL regularly sent one or more of their number to the branch meetings of the Brixton branch. They did not participate in the branch business but kept the Brixton members informed of any social or political events where joint activities might be arranged. The Lambeth YCL representatives at the Brixton League of Youth branch also sold copies of their then weekly newspaper, *Challenge*. I have remained friendly with one of the pre-war members of the Lambeth YCL, Gladys Easton, to this day. She worked for many years for the Communist Party and stood as a parliamentary candidate. She is well known among the left in the labour movement, particularly in London, and she has an attractive personality. Unfortunately her husband, Sid, died some years ago. He was a taxi-driver and was for a period a member of the General Executive Council of the TGWU.

Before 1939 nearly everyone worked on Saturday mornings. In the winter months, when camping was discontinued, many members of the Brixton branch of the League of Youth regularly attended Saturday night dances organised by the Labour Party in Brixton or by other branches of the League of Youth in south London. Dances were held fairly regularly by one or other of the ward organisations of the Labour Party in Brixton. The venue was usually a local school hall and the admission price was sixpence (old money). This was before the days of the disco, and so the dancing was always to a live band of perhaps four or five musicians. Dances were also organised by trades councils and by organisations raising funds for food for Spain. Not surprisingly, a number of marriages took place between members of the Brixton League of Youth. My marriage was one of them. I separated from my wife in 1968 and have lived with my present partner, Pat, since 1969.

For Collective Security

Members of the League of Youth also participated in frequent demonstrations, usually preceded by marches, to Trafalgar Square, Hyde Park or occasionally to Mornington Crescent in Camden. These demonstrations were in support of collective security and in condemnation of the pro-fascist appeasement policy of the British Government. They expressed support for the Spanish Republic in its resistance to the Franco rebellion and condemned the so-called policy of non-intervention under which the Spanish Government was denied the right to purchase arms for its defence, even though Franco was being given military assistance by Germany and Italy. Fortunately the Spanish Government was able to obtain arms from the Soviet Union and Mexico, but in the end the fascist military intervention succeeded.

A number of young men from south-west London volunteered to fight in the International Brigade in Spain. At that time there existed a south-west London federation of League of Youth branches. The knowledge that members of youth organisations of the labour movement from Lambeth, Battersea and Wandsworth were in Spain gave the movement for solidarity a special meaning and urgency. When two of them died in the fighting, there was a huge turnout of young people for a memorial meeting in Battersea Town Hall. Both, I believe, were members of the YCL.

It was not only Spain that attracted the support and sympathy of the progressive youth movement. There was also

45

the resistance of the Chinese people to the invasion of Japan, and there was the continuing struggle for independence in the colonial empire, above all in India. The first two occasions on which I spoke (very much as a supporting speaker) in Trafalgar Square as a representative of the London Advisory Committee of the Labour League of Youth were at demonstrations called by the China Campaign Committee and the India League. I remember very little about them except that at one of the demonstrations a principal speaker was Ben Tillett, leader of the London dockers in the 1889 dock strike. The most prominent Indian in the India League was Krishna Menon, who later became a prominent statesman of independent India. Before the 1939 war he lived in London and was prospective parliamentary candidate for the Labour Party in Dundee. He was later removed by the Labour Party nationally because he did not support the war.

In London the Labour League of Youth held quarterly delegate conferences of all branches. They were well attended and took place in Transport Hall at the headquarters of the TGWU in Transport House. The main debates were between a large majority, who favoured a popular front of the left, and a relatively small minority, who to a greater or lesser extent claimed to be under Trotskyist influence, and who opposed a popular front but supported a united front of all working-class organisations. The difference, however, went much deeper. The majority saw the main task as the defeat of fascism. They believed that collective security between Britain, France, Czechoslovakia, Poland and the Soviet Union could bring the advance of fascism to an end without war. The main task in Britain was to unite all forces in Britain in favour of collective security and to bring about the replacement of the Chamberlain Government, which was seen as sympathetic to fascism. It was appeasing Hitler in the expectation that Germany would turn eastwards.

The Trotskyists in the League of Youth opposed the idea of a popular front with political parties and individuals who were not socialists. As they saw it, the struggle against fascism was inseparable from the struggle for socialism. An alliance with

46

non-socialists would, they argued, result in the labour movement, under the guise of a popular front, opposing working-class demands for social change.

These were not merely academic arguments. They had practical application in relation to Spain. Those of us who were in the majority in the League of Youth were totally supportive of the Spanish Government. We believed that the priority was to defeat Franco. We welcomed the support of all who shared this objective, whether they were socialists or not. We argued that unless Franco were defeated there would be no prospect of advance towards socialism in Spain.

Another important difference of view concerned the Soviet Union. The majority were sympathetic to the Soviet Union. We believed that economic progress was being made by the development of basic industries and by cooperative farming in agriculture. Living standards for workers and collective farmers were rising, and the foundations of a welfare state were being established. In foreign policy the Soviet Union supported collective security and opposed fascism. Alone among the major powers in the world, it was giving assistance to the democratically elected Spanish Government. The Soviet Union supported the resistance of the Chinese people to Japanese aggression and expressed solidarity with the struggle of the peoples of the colonial world for their independence.

In our attitude to the Soviet Union we were influenced also by books, particularly those circulated by the Left Book Club, including the Dean of Canterbury's *The Socialist Sixth of the World*. There was also the detailed work of the Webbs in *Soviet Communism: A New Civilisation*. The Webbs were among the foremost of British social investigators.

The Trotskyists supported the Russian Revolution but claimed that under Stalin the workers' state had degenerated into a tyrannical bureaucracy. They alleged that under the influence of communist parties throughout the world the labour movement was being influenced to serve the state interests of the Soviet bureaucracy instead of the struggle for socialism.

The great purge which took place in the Soviet Union in

47

1937–38, culminating in the Moscow trials and the execution of many leading personalities of the Bolshevik revolution, brought the controversy about the role of the Soviet Union to a high point of bitterness. It was no longer an issue of opinion, but now concerned the alleged role of Trotskyism as an agency of fascism. It was a cruel, dangerous and misleading lie, though I acknowledge I was less certain of it at the time.

My view in retrospect is that those of us who supported the idea of collective security against fascism, who believed that a popular front would provide the best and probably the only means to defeat the Chamberlain Government and thus help to maintain peace, who exposed the hypocrisy of so-called non-intervention in the Spanish war and who denounced the men of Munich for their policy of appeasing fascism, were right. We were wrong in our failure to speak out about the contradictory aspects of Soviet society. Even though there was economic and social progress in many directions, there were also injustices on an enormous scale. Whatever our misgivings about the human cost of farm collectivisation and our revulsion at the purge and the Moscow trials, we did not for the most part register our protest as vigorously or as vociferously as the injustices demanded. We saw ourselves as foot-soldiers in the front line against fascism and war, and the Soviet Union was our ally.

Among my old correspondence I still have a reply from the Moscow radio station to a letter which I sent expressing disquiet in the early days of the great purge in the Soviet Union in the second half of the 1930s. Like many others I soft-pedalled my disquiet and excused it at the time on the grounds that Russian traditions were not those of Britain and that there was no limit to the excesses and duplicity of fascism. History has demonstrated that this reluctance to speak out against injustice was wrong and had tragic consequences, not least for the Soviet Union itself.

It may be asked why this controversy, as seen through the eyes of a young socialist in the late 1930s, is portrayed as one between, on the one hand, supporters of a popular front and collective security and, on the other, those who were influenced by the writings of Trotsky. The fact was that that was where the main lines of controversy were drawn in the socialist youth movement. No doubt there were some who were more sympathetic to the official policy of the Labour Party, which was opposed to a popular front, and, at the time, took the view that the Munich surrender to Hitler had preserved peace. The Labour leadership began fairly quickly to have second thoughts about the Munich agreement, but by then the damage had been done. The Labour Party also condemned in forthright terms the purge and the executions in the Soviet Union. Nevertheless, within the socialist youth movement, support for the official policy of the Party was muted.

Trade Unionism

The London Advisory Committee of the Labour League of Youth gave me the responsibility of stimulating interest in the branches in trade unionism. I spoke on the subject at a quarterly conference of London branches, and when branches requested a speaker on trade unionism amongst youth I was usually asked to go along. The result was that I had the opportunity to visit a number of different branches.

During my relatively short period in London before the war I remember two particular industrial disputes. One was at Smithfield meat market. It was led, I think, by a trade unionist called Spencer Tribe. At one of the demonstrations in Hyde Park there was a large contingent of strikers from Smithfield. Years later, when I was a member of the National Board for Prices and Incomes and the Board conducted an investigation into Smithfield, I became more familiar with trade union organisation at Smithfield and its special characteristics.

The second dispute I remember concerned cinema projectionists, members of the then Electrical Trades Union. The strike was in the early part of 1938 and was, I seem to recall, in support of the principle of a 48-hour week. This principle was under threat, even though the union had established the 48-

hour week in a number of local agreements concluded after the First World War. The cinema projectionists went on strike in three cities, London, Manchester and Hull.

Cinemas in Brixton were affected by the strike, and our branch of the League of Youth volunteered to assist in picketing outside local cinemas. The purpose of the picketing was to persuade the public not to patronise cinemas where ETU members were on strike. One Saturday evening – always a favourite time for cinemagoers – I had a particularly disappointing experience. I was picketing a small cinema close to Lambeth Town Hall. I carried a notice urging a boycott of the cinema. About an hour after I began the picket, a commissionaire of the cinema placed a notice on the pavement to say that the house was full.

The strike in London and Hull did not achieve its purpose, but in Manchester a settlement was reached which maintained the principle of a 48-hour week. One of the weaknesses of the strike was that the ETU was not the only union representing projectionists. There were differences between the unions. It was an early lesson to me on the need for trade union cooperation.

Trade unionism was not, however, the main issue of interest to members of the League of Youth. The strongest feelings were aroused by the struggle against fascism and the threat of war. Support for Spain was central to nearly all activities. Within the League of Youth many active members identified themselves with the Spanish Youth Foodship Committee. Funds were raised and food was collected to aid the Spanish people. A member of the Norwood branch of the League was employed full-time as a lorry driver collecting material for Spain. Ted Willis acted as secretary of the committee.

I went to various parts of Britain to speak at meetings for aid to Spain. One weekend I was in Glasgow as a supporting speaker at a big rally in St Andrew's Hall. The principal speaker was Sir Peter Chalmers-Mitchell. During another weekend I spoke at a series of meetings in towns on Teesside. I remember speaking at meetings in Southampton and Margate. I also attended a socialist youth camp on the estate of Lord

Farringdon, at which solidarity with the Spanish people was the focal point of attention.

Anti-fascism

The League of Youth in London also participated in the struggle against Mosley's blackshirts. This was against the advice of the official Labour Party. Their view was that the activities of Mosley should be disregarded and that counter-demonstrations served only to give additional publicity to the fascists.

The advice of the Labour Party was, in my view, mistaken. Mosley chose to concentrate his provocative military type marches in areas where there was a substantial Jewish community or in working-class areas with a strong socialist tradition. Most of the active members of the League of Youth supported the view that Mosley's provocative anti-Semitism and red-baiting should be met with counter-demonstrations. This was the general view on the left of the labour movement.

Mosley received two decisive rebuffs in the late 1930s. First, he was stopped by a mass counter-demonstration when he and his followers attempted to stage a march through the Jewish area of Stepney in the East End. The following year he attempted a similar march through Bermondsey, the dockside area on the south bank of the river. The opposition was so strong from thousands of demonstrators that Mosley, at the request of the police, had to abandon his plans.

The defeat of Mosley in Stepney took place before I moved to London, but I participated in the counter-demonstration that led him to abandon his planned march into Bermondsey. Together with other members of the Brixton League of Youth, I joined thousands of anti-fascists in the streets near to the Borough underground station. There was a mood of determination that Mosley had to be stopped. We were supported by the inhabitants of the local blocks of flats and housing estates. The borough of Bermondsey was at that time a trade union and Labour stronghold with an almost solidly working-class population. Its pioneer welfare services were an example to all local authorities.

There was a large contingent of mounted police in the vicinity of the Borough underground station, but the size and determination of the anti-fascist demonstration was such that there was no possibility of a route being cleared for the fascist marchers. Mosley was defeated. The announcement that the march had been abandoned caused jubilation in the streets of Bermondsey. It was a day to be remembered.

Readers of a later generation may question whether the determination of so many anti-fascists to stop Mosley's marches was compatible with a belief in democracy. The fact was that the Blackshirts did more than participate in meetings and marches. Wherever they went they sought to provoke anti-Semitism. This was inseparable from attacks on Jewish people. They marched in military-style formation, and they wore the black-shirted uniform of their intolerant creed. Their style of political organisation and agitation followed closely that of Mussolini in Italy and Hitler in Germany. The labour movement in those countries had already paid a terrible price for their failure to deal with the thuggery of fascism. In Spain the fascists were demonstrating once again that they had no respect for democracy. I believe we were right, by the size of counter-demonstrations, to stop the marches of the fascists.

The defeat of the Spanish Government by fascism was a heavy blow. When the British members of the International Brigade returned to Britain they were given a tremendous reception. I was one of thousands who assembled at Victoria station in London to greet them. The British contingent of the International Brigade had demonstrated to the world that there were many British people who were not to be identified with the policies of the Chamberlain Government. These policies had contributed in no small measure to the victory of Franco and his German and Italian backers.

There could be no adequate compensation for the losses suffered by the members of the International Brigade. Hundreds of them gave their lives, some with families still in Britain. Others returned injured. A Dependants' Aid Fund,

52

whose principal organiser was Charlotte Haldane, the wife of the world-famous biochemist, Professor J.B.S. Haldane, raised thousands of pounds to help brigaders and their families.

Contrary to the impression sometimes later conveyed by commentators on the Spanish war, the great majority of British members of the International Brigade were not middle-class intellectuals, though this in no way detracts from the magnificent contribution made by the writers, lecturers, scientists, artists and doctors who volunteered their services. The majority who joined the British section of the International Brigade were workers, of whom miners formed a significant minority. Many of them came back to play an outstanding role in the trade union movement. Perhaps the best known were Jack Jones, who became the General Secretary of the TGWU, and Will Paynter, who became the General Secretary of the National Union of Mineworkers. One volunteer, who I knew very well, was Ken White. He became the convenor of shop stewards in the engineering factory where I worked for a number of years in Staines, Middlesex. Ken lost half his leg in the fighting in Spain, and when he returned he had to find a job where for most of his working time he could remain seated. He became a marker-out on the marking-off table and used his skill to great effect. He remained active in the movement until his death in the 1980s.

The defeat of the Spanish Government was not an isolated victory of fascism and fascist aggression. Throughout the 1930s fascism had been advancing. Even before Hitler, Japan had seized Manchuria from China. Appeals to the League of Nations did not result in collective security. On the contrary, international intervention by Britain and France was regarded more as a process of conciliation with aggressors than as a means of deterring aggression. In Germany Hitler introduced conscription, and in 1935 a new naval agreement was concluded with Britain which, though presented as a means of limiting German arms, in reality confirmed and sanctioned German rearmament. In 1935 Italy attacked Abyssinia. An appeal to the League of Nations was followed by a plan worked out by Britain and France – the Hoare-Laval plan –

partially to satisfy Mussolini's demands. There was no intention to build collective security. Within a few months Italy had conquered Abyssinia. In 1936 Hitler's troops marched into the demilitarised zone of the Rhineland, and in 1938 Germany annexed Austria. In the meanwhile Japan had renewed its attacks on China. Hitler then turned his attention to Czechoslovakia. The British Government in the Munich agreement accepted that concessions should be made to Germany. The Sudeten territories came under German occupation. Not long afterwards Czechoslovakia was dismembered, with much of the country under German control.

During the second half of the 1930s the Soviet Union argued strongly for collective security. The British Government were unreceptive. *The Times* spoke for the dominant circles in the Conservative Party, and their view was that Britain and Germany should be reconciled. The British Government at no stage entered into serious negotiations with the Soviet Union about a military alliance for collective security.

By the spring of 1939, when it had become clear that Poland was likely to be the next victim of German aggression, there were still further difficulties preventing an effective alliance for collective security. The Polish Government did not want to enter into an alliance with the Soviet Union and they opposed any suggestion that the stationing of Soviet troops on Polish soil might be an effective deterrent against Nazi invasion.

In March 1939 Stalin gave a clear warning to the non-aggressive Western powers that their policy of appeasement was likely to end in disaster. He pointed out in a report to the Eighteenth Congress of the Communist Party of the Soviet Union that the three aggressive states, Germany, Italy and Japan, had launched a new imperialist war for a redivision of the world. This war infringed upon the interests of the non-aggressive states, but instead of resisting the aggressors the non-aggressive capitalist states were conniving with them. The reason, said Stalin, was that the non-aggressive capitalist states did not want to hinder the aggressors from embroiling themselves in war with the Soviet Union. This big and dangerous game, he continued, might end in a serious fiasco for those who were playing it.

In August 1939 the Soviet Union concluded a non-aggression pact with Nazi Germany. In effect, Stalin had decided that because of the attitude of Britain, France and Poland there was no possibility of an effective alliance for collective security. He and his government were determined that the USSR would not be embroiled in war with Germany whilst Britain and France stood aside. The Soviet Union knew that Hitler was about to invade Poland and that any guarantees from the West would not prevent Poland's defeat. The Soviet Union entered into an understanding with Hitler for the partition of Poland. This was not disclosed at the time. They regarded such an understanding as limiting the gains which Hitler was due to make because of the absence of collective security.

The Soviet-German non-aggression treaty came as a surprise and shock to the great majority of people in Britain, including those on the left. I shared that feeling, but within days I began to appreciate that the Soviet Union was protecting its own interests in the light of the refusal of Britain, France and Poland to undertake effective collective security. I did not agree, however, with the new attitude taken by Soviet leaders towards the Nazis. Some of their statements at the time in support of the new treaty were unprincipled.

Since my arrival in London I had maintained a very frequent correspondence with my parents. I wrote to them at least four times a week and they wrote to me with barely less frequency. Much of the correspondence was concerned with family affairs, and from my father I received regular commentaries on football. He was a keen supporter of the Portsmouth football club and a regular attender at their home games. He also followed the results and reports of the then two Bradford clubs and of the Rugby League club, Bradford Northern.

My parents' correspondence also included fairly frequent references to political events. Both my mother and my father were opposed to the policy of appeasement, though momentarily my father thought that the Munich agreement might have averted the threat of war. Like many other British people, including most of the leaders of the Labour Party, he quickly revised his opinion when it became clear that Hitler would not be satisfied with the Sudeten territories.

My mother was explicit in her support, first for a united front between the Labour Party, the Communist Party and the ILP, and then for a broad Popular Front to defeat Chamberlain. She expressed disquiet about the Moscow trials but was sympathetic to the Soviet Union. She much enjoyed the Dean of Canterbury's book, *The Socialist Sixth of the World*, and she lent it to one or two acquaintances in the Methodist church.

My father was, at first, very hostile to the Soviet-German non-aggression treaty. In one of his letters he indicated that in his view the treaty had given the 'green light' to Hitler to invade Poland. He expressed his support for the criticisms made of the Soviet leaders by Trotsky. My father later modified his views, particularly in the light of the so-called 'phoney war' conducted by Britain and France against Hitler, and their enthusiasm for an anti-Soviet crusade in support of Finland. He also remained radical on many aspects of British domestic politics. He was strongly opposed, for example, to the whole system of hereditary privilege in Britain, symbolised by the monarchy and the House of Lords. He was always class-conscious and had no sympathy with imperialism. He expressed these views in his letters to me. I am glad I retained them.

The struggle in the second half of the 1930s for a broad people's front against fascism and war and for collective security did not lead to any diminution of interest in socialism or loss of support for the labour movement. On the contrary, interest in socialism and the contribution of the labour movement were stimulated by activity on the main issues of the day. Both the right wing of the Labour Party and the Trotsky-ists were mistaken in arguing that activity in support of a people's front represented some kind of political dilution and diversion from the real tasks of organised labour.

One important expression of the new interest in the theory and practice of the problems facing the left was the Left Book

Club. The books were published by the firm of Gollancz and were selected by Victor Gollancz, John Strachey and Harold Laski. For half-a-crown (12½p) a month members were sent a new book on some aspect of current politics. The Club had nearly 60,000 members. I was one of them. The Club also published a monthly journal and organised hundreds of local discussion groups. There were also supplementary books and booklets available by separate subscription.

The success of the Left Book Club was probably beyond anyone's expectations. The Labour Party, for example, has never been able to organise a book club or publishing programme to come anywhere near it. The political orientation of the Left Book Club was firmly to the left of official Labour policy, though the choice of books was not limited to any one set of political beliefs. Authors included politicians and academics from the Labour, Communist and Liberal parties, and from writers of no political affiliation.

I owed much to the books published by the Left Book Club. I still have some of them on my shelves. I particularly remember *Man's Worldly Goods* by Leo Huberman, *The Town that was Murdered* by Ellen Wilkinson, *The Labour Party in Perspective* by Clement Attlee, *The Theory and Practice of Socialism* by John Strachey, *A Philosophy for a Modern Man* by Professor Hyman Levy, *Fallen Bastions* by G.E.R. Gedye and *A People's History of England* by A.L. Morton. There was also a series of Left Book Club booklets explaining the social significance of scientific developments. They included booklets on biology, economic botany, chemistry, atomic science and heredity. No doubt they are all now very much out of date, but when they were published they helped to widen the horizon of many of us who knew virtually nothing about these subjects.

Another significant publication of the late 1930s was *The Modern Quarterly*. It was published at half-a-crown an issue but was available to Left Book Club members for one shilling and sixpence (7½p). I started buying it from the second issue in March 1938. It had an editorial council which must have been, academically, the most distinguished ever to be associated with a journal of the left. It included Bernal,

Blackett, Le Gros Clark, V. Gordon Childe, Clemens Dutt, Farrington, Haldane, Laski, Levy, Chalmers Mitchell, Needham, Pascal, Erich Roll, Susan Stebbing, George Thomson and B. Woolf. Other prominent scholars contributed to its columns, including G.D.H. Cole, Lancelot Hogben, Maurice Dobb, Christopher Hill and John Saville. *The Modern Quarterly* not only introduced lay readers like myself to new areas of knowledge but it also succeeded in giving us the feeling that study and social progress were inseparable.

I continued also with correspondence courses with the National Council of Labour Colleges and with occasional attendance at NCLC schools and classes. A new organiser for the NCLC came to live in Brixton. He was William Warbey, who later became a Member of Parliament and fought valiantly to bring to public attention the struggle of the people of Vietnam against French and American intervention. I remember Bill Warbey as a modest, studious and committed socialist.

The struggle against fascism and war in the 1930s not only generated a great amount of activity but it also stimulated labour movement studies on a scale which embraced tens of thousands of British citizens. The benefit of this activity and study was to be seen for many years afterwards. I count myself fortunate, despite many setbacks for the movement, to have participated in those stirring times.

4

The War

Britain declared war on Germany on 3 September, 1939. Up to the very last minute the British Government sought to reach an accommodation with Hitler about Poland, the latest country to be the subject of German territorial demands. The policy of appeasement was still very much alive. Many Conservative MPs, sympathetic to fascism, felt that by signing the non-aggression pact with the Soviet Union Hitler had let them down. If, however, he could be persuaded not to press his claims to the point of a full-scale occupation of Poland, conciliation might still be possible. War with Britain and France could be averted, and German ambitions might be directed ultimately even further eastwards.

Among Labour politicians the opinion was strongly held that the time had come to stand up to Hitler and that the mistake of Munich should not be repeated. This was also the view of some, though at the time not the most influential, Conservative politicians. When the British Government declared war on Germany all the old ideology of appeasement was still dominant in Government circles. The British Government had no idea how it might effectively defend Polish independence. The only possibility of effective opposition to Hitler had been through collective security, involving an alliance with the USSR. This the British Government had not wanted. Nor had the Polish Government.

Poland was defeated by the Germans within weeks. The greater part of the country fell under direct German occupation. After the collapse of the Polish state the Soviet Union occupied the eastern part of Poland where they said that the majority of the population were either Ukrainian or Byelorussian. The Soviet intervention at least had the effect of limiting the area of German occupation.

Almost immediately after the declaration of war my work with the London County Council was evacuated to Englefield Green in Surrey. Many of us who were evacuated were accommodated in what had been a teachers' training college. I left most of my books and pamphlets in Brixton. The house there in which I had been in lodgings was later destroyed by bombing and I lost my possessions, including books which had been given to me by my father.

In the early period of the war very little of military significance took place. Many women and children were evacuated from London, but within weeks thousands had returned. There was a false alarm, when the sirens sounded, about an air raid on London, but otherwise all seemed to be quiet. The blackout was introduced as a defence against air attack, and food rationing was not introduced until early in 1940. There were still many registered as unemployed. People reminded each other that there was a war with the saying: 'Don't you know there's a war on?' It was almost as if they might otherwise forget that war had been declared.

The public were told of the invincibility of the front line in France. The Maginot Line, as it was called, was supposed to be impregnable against German attack. Nothing happened until much later to challenge this belief. All was quiet on the Western Front. The British military commander, Lord Gort, was referred to in the popular press as 'Tiger' Gort.

After the collapse of Poland from German aggression the war first came to life, as far as the British Government was concerned, not with military action against Germany but with support for Finland against the Soviet Union. The Soviet Union, concerned about its security in the Baltic, entered into negotiations with Estonia, Latvia and Lithuania and concluded treaties of mutual assistance with them. Under these treaties the Soviet Union was permitted to maintain military bases in the three Baltic states. The Soviet Union agreed to transfer the city of Vilna, previously taken from Lithuania by Poland, back to Lithuania. The Soviet Union proposed a treaty of mutual assistance to Finland, but Finland declined on the grounds that such a treaty would infringe its neutrality. The Soviet Union then asked for territorial exchanges with Finland which would have had the effect of moving the frontier further from Leningrad. The existing frontier, it was said, was only 20 miles from Leningrad. The Soviet Union offered other land in exchange. They also asked for the lease of a piece of land to establish a naval base near the entrance to the Gulf of Finland. Finland refused.

The Soviet Union invaded Finland at the end of November 1939. The League of Nations, which because of the policy of the Western powers had proved so ineffective against German, Japanese and Italian aggression, found a new vitality. The USSR was expelled from the League of Nations, and in Britain a campaign was mounted to assist Finland. Preparations were made for sending troops from Britain and France. The war, however, lasted for less than four months.

I was opposed to any British involvement in war against the Soviet Union. I thought the Finnish attitude towards the Soviet request for an exchange of territory and a naval base at the entrance to the Gulf of Finland was unjustified. On the other hand, I was disturbed that the Soviet Union had taken matters into their own hands by going to war against Finland, and I did not believe their contention that the Finns had taken provocative military action.

My main concern, however, was to stop the expansion of Germany. If fascism were to be defeated a line had to be drawn against the continuous successful aggression of Hitler. It seemed to me to be unrealistic to expect that either the Baltic states or Finland would ever be able to resist German pressure except with the military help of the Soviet Union. This was the strategic consideration.

Among the young men with whom I was working at the time in the closing weeks of 1939 this recognition of what was required for effective anti-fascist action was fairly widespread. Most of them expected to be called up for the armed forces, but there was no enthusiasm for war with the Soviet Union.

We had a strong Left Book Club discussion group in our accommodation hostel and it consisted almost entirely of people under 35 years of age. Nearly all of us in the discussion group were suspicious of the British Government. We were well aware from our reading and from the experience of the Munich agreement and the Spanish war that within the Government and among prominent Conservatives there were many who were sympathetic to Germany and even to fascism. The members of our group not only discussed the danger of a switch in the war but campaigned against it.

Amongst the young people with whom I was politically active at this time there were two books, both written by D.N. Pritt, which were influential. They were *Light on Moscow* and *Must the War Spread.* They were both published as Penguin Specials. Pritt was a prominent lawyer, a KC and a Member of Parliament. Both books dealt largely with the relations between Britain and the USSR. The books argued that powerful influences among the ruling group in Britain had developed and brought near to fruition a plan for forming a common front of capitalist nations against the USSR. Within our Left Book Club group, where we were nearly all of military age, we wanted no part in this possible war against the Soviet Union. We were anti-fascist.

I have sometimes read, and I had certainly heard it from my father, that in the First World War people who opposed the war often had a very rough time from others who supported it. I had no such experience in opposing any British involvement in the war in Finland in 1939 and in the opening weeks of 1940. On the contrary, among younger people with whom I was working there was support for the view that we should keep out, and among older people there was sympathy for the view that Germany, and not Russia, was Britain's enemy. These experiences were at variance with the impression created by the press and by political leaders. Most of the newspapers were hostile to the Soviet Union, and from their reports it appeared that the Red Army was being regularly mauled in the fighting. The British Government and some of the Labour leaders were also stridently hostile to the Soviet Union.

Correspondence with my parents reinforced my opposition to any British involvement in the Finnish war. My father had by this time somewhat modified his condemnatory attitude of the Soviet Union following the Soviet-German non-aggression pact. He was now inclined, if anything, to welcome any steps taken by Stalin to limit German expansion. My mother, who throughout had remained more sympathetic to Soviet policies, was very worried at the prospect that the war might be switched and that the USSR and not Germany would become the enemy.

The ending of the Finnish war early in March 1940 brought to an end the immediate possibility of armed conflict between the Soviet Union and a British expeditionary force. I, and many other young people with whom I was working, were pleased. I remember thinking at the time that the peace terms imposed on Finland were not particularly onerous. They appeared to demonstrate that the USSR was genuinely concerned about the security of Leningrad and was not using the dispute merely as an excuse for the total domination of its neighbour.

Very quickly after the ending of the Finnish war Hitler confirmed his ambitions to move northwards. German forces occupied Denmark and moved into Norway. Britain sent a force to help Norway, but it had to withdraw. This defeat led to the downfall of the Chamberlain Government and its replacement in May 1940 by a coalition, with Labour and Liberal participation, under Winston Churchill.

Germany invaded Belgium and Holland in May 1940. These two countries quickly fell and the Germans continued into France. No effective resistance was summoned, though the total number of allied divisions on the Western Front was not less than that of the invading forces. The total tank strength was also about equal. The Maginot Line of defence fortifications seemed to have no significance. Towards the end of May Britain began the biggest military evacuation in its history. Hundreds of thousands of men were brought out from Dunkirk in an armada of ships and boats of every kind, which had been assembled at very short notice from ports and seaside resorts in Britain. The evacuation from Dunkirk, though preceded by military defeat, was an heroic achievement.

In June a new French Government asked the Germans for an armistice. Under the terms of the 'peace' agreement, stipulated by Germany, much of France, including the north and the whole of the coastline, was placed under German occupation. Most of us on the left regarded the collapse of France as yet further proof that the old ruling circles were riddled with fascist sympathisers. The French Government never sought to rally the French people to resist the Nazi invaders by life-and-death struggle. Throughout the preceding months they had been more concerned with suppressing the Communist Party than with ensuring that the Nazis would be properly resisted.

The charge to be made against the French Government and the former Chamberlain Government in Britain, that they were dominated by appeasers of fascism, could not be levelled against the new government in Britain under Winston Churchill. For years he had warned against the danger of German expansion and, though he was no friend of the Soviet Union, he did not permit his hostility to anything to do with communism or socialism to distort his view that the appeasement of Hitler would be ultimately dangerous to the interests of Britain and the then British Empire. In a series of broadcasts to the British people Churchill made it clear beyond the slightest shadow of doubt that the new British Government was resolutely opposed to Hitler and would continue the fight no matter what the setbacks.

In the late summer of 1940 I volunteered for flying duties in the Fleet Air Arm. I was rejected, but not before my parents had expressed their deep misgivings at my action. Their attitude had, I think, much more to do with parental concern for my safety – I was also an only child – than with any political considerations. I was then 19 years of age.

My parents' attitude was, nevertheless, reinforced by political hesitancies about the conduct of the war. Both my parents were anti-fascist and had opposed the policy of appeasement. Both regarded themselves as sympathisers with, rather than opponents of, the objectives of the Russian Revolution. My father had been extremely hostile to the Soviet-German non-aggression pact, but had modified his view to the extent that the Soviet Union had shown by its actions in the east that it was more effective than the Western powers in preventing the expansion of Nazi Germany.

The real conflict of considerations was centred on the new British Prime Minister, Winston Churchill. Ever since the General Strike of 1926 my father had disliked him as the most reactionary of all leading Tories. He believed that Churchill's purpose was not to defeat Hitler because he was a fascist aggressor but because he represented the resurrected strength of German big business and militarism against British imperialism.

I have reason to think that the rejection of my application to volunteer for flying duties in the Fleet Air Arm in the late summer of 1940 was on political grounds. I was in good health and of the right age. The person in charge of the establishment where I was working was asked to give a reference as to my character. I do not know whether this was the normal procedure, but it certainly applied in my case. He interviewed me and indicated that he had doubts about my political reliability. As he put it, would I 'subvert the constitution'? He was not personally hostile to me, but he had been an officer in the First World War and he wanted, as he saw it, to uphold British interests and to provide an honest estimation of my reliability according to the standards he regarded as relevant.

The problem, it seemed, centred on my attitude and my conduct during the Finnish war. I confirmed that it had been my view, and continued to be my view, that Britain should not get involved in war with the Soviet Union. I affirmed that I would not support such a war and that this was consistent with my anti-fascist convictions. I have no doubt that I expressed myself with the emphasis of youth and, perhaps, even in a provocative manner. Nevertheless, I was expressing my firmly held opinions. The interview probably ended any possibility of my being accepted into the Fleet Air Arm.

A New Job

Shortly afterwards I changed my job. I cannot now remember whether I was directed into new employment or whether I responded to an appeal for people with engineering experience to register for employment directly connected with the manufacture of armaments, particularly aircraft production. After making enquiries at a couple of firms in south-east London, where I was told that there were no immediate vacancies for lathe operators, I ended up at Lagonda's in Staines, Middlesex. I was given a job as a capstan lathe setter-operator.

The Battle of Britain, which Hitler intended as a prelude to the invasion of Britain, started in the late summer of 1940. The Germans sought to establish air superiority so that an invading force by sea would be successful. Hitler did not succeed, thanks to the heroism and sacrifice of aircrew in the Royal Air Force, the mobilisation of resources for the production and servicing of British military aircraft, and the role of Churchill in rallying support for resistance to the Nazis.

When I first went to Lagonda's to enquire about a job I had an unfortunate experience. Instead of stopping at the main gate to the factory to enquire about the whereabouts of the labour office, I walked past the gate into the factory site and down the main central road with workshops on either side. I asked a man dressed in a suit and with a collar and tie where I might enquire about a job. Instead of responding courteously to my enquiry, he ordered me off the premises and did it in terms which left me humiliated, depressed and angry. I later learnt that he was a particularly officious and unpopular shop superintendent. By walking through the main gate without enquiry I had, of course, breached security. That, however, had not been my intention. I remember the incident because it underlined to me that it is important to respond sympathetically and courteously to young workers when they enquire about a job.

I returned to the factory the next day, went through the proper procedure, was given a job and told to start work immediately. Lagonda Motors, to give the factory its full title, was a large engineering firm whose original speciality was the manufacture of luxury cars. They then broadened their activities to undertake contract work for other firms, including the aircraft manufacturer, Bristol Aeroplane Company.

The workforce did not understand the financial structure of the firm. Most of us were nominally employed by a firm called Hewitt. Presumably they had some kind of relationship with Lagonda Motors. Others were employed by Bryce Fuel Injection. This firm manufactured high-precision fuel injection equipment. Their components were, however, machined in batches together with other components going through the factory. It was said that the ultimate control was in the hands of Brush Electric of Loughborough. Later the firm seemed to be closely connected with Petter's Engines. In everyday conversation, nevertheless, the workforce described themselves as employees of Lagonda's.

The capstan lathe section was the largest section in the main machine shop. Most of the men on the section were under 30 years of age, and a significant proportion were youths or in their very early twenties. Only at a later stage of the war were women introduced onto the capstan section. In 1941 women in the machine shop were confined almost entirely to simple drilling operations. In other workshops in the factory they were employed on power presses or on repetitive bench or assembly operations.

Many of the men and youths on the capstan section had migrated from the depressed areas. They came from South Wales, the north of England and Scotland. They had been drawn to Middlesex or Slough because these were expanding industrial areas. Some of them had fascinating stories of their journey and their search for a job. Many had either hitch-hiked or travelled by other irregular means. One young Welshman, who worked on a machine next to me for a period, had secured his first job by picking up a shovel when the Great West Road was being built. Other Welshmen in the gang had suggested this method to him. When the ganger came round, he said that he had been told to start work by a 'boss' further down the road.

The men and youths on the capstan section had a very

strong sense of solidarity. Arguments about piecework times and prices were frequent. We were all on batch production, and everyone was alert to any changes in times or prices or to any special problems which might affect earnings. Thus, for example, any variation in the specification of the materials which might affect the speeds and feeds of the machine tools, any change in the tolerances on sizes or any modification of the machine setting often led to arguments. The time study department and ratefixers might seek to amend times and prices downwards because of changes which they considered made the operation quicker. Conversely operators would argue for upward adjustments when they considered that operational changes had lengthened the floor-to-floor time.

The operators on the capstan section invariably supported each other in these arguments. The disputes very rarely led to a stoppage of work, but if an operator was asked to accept a time or price which another operator, after discussions involving the rate-fixing department and the shop steward, had rejected as unfair, he also invariably refused. The requirement that times and prices should be agreed was known as the principle of mutuality. The employer did not have the unilateral right to impose piecework times and prices. Their determination was a matter for joint regulation.

The hours of work were long. We were employed on rotating day and night work. For a fortnight the normal hours of employment were from 8 a.m. to 7.30 p.m., Monday to Thursday. On Friday and Saturday work finished at 5.30 p.m. and on Sunday at noon. When the shift changed, there was no work on Sunday morning. On the night shift the hours were from 8 p.m. to 7.30 a.m. for six nights.

These very long hours were counter-productive. They could not be sustained for long periods. The rotating day and night work was particularly disturbing to health. It was very difficult to establish a regular pattern for eating and sleeping. The night shifts were also often interrupted by air raids. After a time some workers were reluctant to go the shelters unless they heard guns and aircraft. Every period spent in the shelters meant a loss of piecework earnings.

The shift system was eventually changed, partly because of representations made by the shop stewards. Most of the top management of the company worked only on day shifts. Moreover, their normal starting time was 9 a.m. They were persuaded of the necessity to change the existing shift system by the absentee figures, illnesses, lateness and disruption caused by night-time air raids. A new system was then introduced, which consisted of a double-day shift that operated for seven days a week. The early shift was from 5.30 a.m. to 1.30 p.m. and the late shift from 2 p.m. to 10 p.m. On Saturday the late shift finished at 8 p.m.

Seven-day working was also counter-productive, even with the shorter shifts. After a further period a six-day period of work was introduced. By this time, however, many of the workers had been enrolled in the factory Home Guard and were expected to attend for Sunday morning training. Some workers were also put on firewatching duty when, on one night each week, the factory was not working.

Some months after I started work at Lagonda's there was a vacancy for a shop steward for the capstan lathe section on my shift. I was elected, even though I was not yet 21 years of age. My main memory of this period as a steward was of the solidarity of the men on the section. I was involved in daily discussions about piecework times and prices, and nearly always it was possible to reach a negotiated settlement. The support given by the workers on the section was the important ingredient in the negotiations. If an immediate settlement could not be reached the shop steward had the right to seek the assistance of the convenor of stewards. On my shift the convenor at that time was the steward in the toolroom. He was always helpful. He was leftish in his views about trade unionism and politics and believed strongly in collective bargaining.

The shop stewards' committee for the factory met weekly during working hours. It was an enlightening experience. The two bastions of trade union strength in the factory were the toolroom and the sheet metal shop. Both were 100 per cent in trade union membership and both consisted entirely of craftsmen. The sheet metal shop at Lagonda's was large and, dating from the time of luxury car manufacture, had a reputation for high-quality work. The sheet metal shop was organised by the then National Union of Sheet Metal Workers. The toolroom, the machine shops, the press shop and the assembly shops were organised by the AEU. The TGWU also had a presence in the factory, and their role became more important with the recruitment of an increasing number of women workers. Some of the smaller craft unions also had members in the factory, particularly the Electrical Trades Union.

In the spring of 1941 there was a short strike of young workers in the factory. A wage claim for youths had been under negotiation for some weeks. It was related to negotiations conducted nationally. It was understood that a settlement had been secured, but for reasons which I have now forgotten the increase had not been put in our pay packets. When we arrived for work on the night shift one Friday evening we found that once again we had not been given the increase due to us. There was an immediate meeting of young workers in the main machine shop and we elected a delegation, including myself, to interview the superintendent in charge of the factory on the night shift. By chance that week it was the individual who had ordered me off the premises when I first went for a job at Lagonda's. He normally had no supervisory responsibility for the main machine shop.

At the interview he was not conciliatory despite the strength of our case. He more or less ordered us back to work without consideration of our grievance. The delegation reported back to the young workers and it was decided, unanimously as far as I recall, that we would not continue working during the shift unless we received an assurance that our grievance would receive attention. The stoppage had its effect. The regular works manager, a much more reasonable person, was telephoned at his home, and he gave the assurance that the overdue payment would be made. All this took time, but by midnight work had been resumed. This experience underlined to me that in some circumstances spontaneous strike action, after abortive negotiations, is not only effective but is justified.

Inside the factory all the political activity was in a left-wing direction. Because of the long hours of work the factory was not only the centre of trade union organisation but also of political interest. I do not recall anyone approaching me about the local Labour Party. I knew nothing of its existence, if indeed it did exist during the war years.

At the regular and frequent meetings of the shop stewards' committee there were political discussions about trade union rights, air raid precautions, the freedom of the press – particularly after the banning of the *Daily Worker* – the course of the war and the attitude of the British Government. There was also a well-attended regular discussion group around the communist monthly magazine, *Labour Monthly*.

At the end of 1940 and the beginning of 1941 there was much discussion among active trade unionists in the factory about the People's Convention. An appeal for support for the Convention was issued in the autumn of 1940, following a conference in July called by the Hammersmith Trades Council and Labour Party. The appeal was signed by 500 people drawn from all parts of the country and all walks of life. It included many prominent trade unionists. The initiating moves for what became the People's Convention were made in April 1940 when Chamberlain was still the British Prime Minister.

The appeal for the People's Convention said that the British Government represented the interests of the rich and privileged. Behind it were the men of Munich, the friends of fascism, whose policy had built up the power of Hitler. The Government, said the appeal, protected the war profiteers, placed all the burdens of war on the ordinary citizens, neglected essential measures for air raid protection, attacked civil rights and refused the demand of the Indian people for national freedom.

The appeal focussed attention on a number of main demands. They were that living standards and civil and trade union rights should be defended, that there should be adequate air raid precautions, that friendship should be sought with the Soviet Union, and that there should be a people's government with a people's peace to get rid of the causes of war. Critics of the appeal, including the Labour Party and the TUC, rightly pointed out that it was in substance an anti-war declaration. How was it possible, they asked, to obtain a so-called people's peace without first defeating fascism? The appeal reflected the policy of the Communist International, which had condemned the war as an imperialist conflict.

Nevertheless, the People's Convention attracted considerable support. When the Convention met in January 1941 more than 2,200 delegates were present, drawn overwhelmingly from working class organisations. Many shop stewards' committees were represented, including the committees from most of the big engineering factories in and around the London area. It was claimed that nearly 1¼ million workers were represented at the Convention.

In the Lagonda factory there was support for the Convention among many active trade unionists, and the stewards were represented at the conference in January 1941. I supported the sending of delegates, though I think now, with the benefit of hindsight, that the policy of the Convention was wrong. Certainly, some of the criticisms made of the British Government were valid, but the demands of the Convention took no account of the change represented by the replacement of Chamberlain by Churchill as British Prime Minister. Churchill was an imperialist of the traditional kind, but he was not an appeaser of Hitler and Mussolini. The only kind of 'peace' possible with Hitler would have been one which left him in possession of his conquests but with more time to prepare for further aggression.

Both my parents were by this time strongly critical of the war. Their anti-fascist convictions had throughout made them suspicious of Chamberlain. The collapse of the Western allies in Europe underlined their belief that among the rich and powerful there were many who were sympathetic to Hitler and Mussolini. My mother, in particular, felt that the Tory leaders around Chamberlain were more hostile to the Soviet Union than to Hitler. My father's view was that Churchill's accession to power in the early summer of 1940 meant that a fascist appeaser had been replaced by a reactionary imperialist. He deplored the manner in which India had been dragged into the war without any consultation with the real representatives of the Indian people. He supported the protests of the Indian National Congress and such leaders as Nehru and Krishna Menon.

In 1940 my mother wrote to me to express her pleasure that in a parliamentary by-election in Kettering a steel worker and local Labour councillor, who stood as a Workers' and Pensioners' Anti-War candidate, had secured over 6,600 votes, representing more than 27 per cent of the votes cast in the election. He gained this large vote despite being disowned by the Labour Party. The Kettering by-election result was an indication that my parents' views were probably shared by a much larger minority than it has been customary for commentators on the early stages of the war to acknowledge.

My mother was sympathetic to the People's Convention and wrote to me about a big meeting of Convention supporters which she had attended in Portsmouth. My father in one of his letters described his politics as the 'deepest red'.

Germany's invasion of the Soviet Union in June 1941 ended the controversy about the war among the active trade unionists in the factory where I was working. At the very outset there was some apprehension that Churchill would have reservations about helping the Soviet Union. These were almost immediately dispelled. I remember listening on the late shift, standing by my capstan lathe, to a broadcast by Churchill, relayed through the factory loudspeaker system. All machines were temporarily stopped to enable us to listen to the Prime Minister. Churchill made it clear, without a hint of hesitation or equivocation, that Britain would fight side by side with the Soviet Union until Hitler was finally defeated. From then onwards the more left-wing stewards and workers became the strongest supporters of the war effort and campaigned vigorously against anything which impeded production.

In the summer of 1941 the shop steward in the toolroom on the shift on which I was working enquired whether I wanted to become a toolmaker. I was then 20 years of age. This was the same steward who until a few weeks earlier had been the factory convenor. It was not, of course, within his authority to arrange for such a transfer, but he indicated that in view of my age he thought it probable that the management would respond to any representations he made.

I was excited at the prospect but felt that I should first consult the new convenor. This was Ken White, the disabled former International Brigader. He had an attractive personality, and I admired him. He was also a communist, and I had joined the Young Communist League. Ken White saw no objection to my going into the toolroom if given the opportunity, but felt that I should talk to another steward, David Michaelson, who worked on the milling section in the main machine shop where I was employed. David worked on the opposite shift.

When I spoke to David Michaelson he expressed opposition to my leaving the machine shop. He argued that it was better that I should remain on the section where already I had some influence as a trade unionist. I was very disappointed but reluctantly accepted the advice. David was also of the view that the approach by the toolroom steward was not motivated solely by concern for my future. It was no secret that David Michaelson and the toolroom steward had not seen eye to eye on a number of issues. David felt that if I moved to the toolroom I would be more directly within the sphere of influence of the former convenor and of a craft-conscious group who considered themselves a cut above the production workers in the machine shop.

Drawing Office

Some weeks later I was approached by the machine shop superintendent, who said that he had been asked by the chief jig and tool draughtsman to recommend a couple of youngsters about 20 years of age with machine shop experience to enter the drawing office. He proposed that I should be one of them. This was beyond any hopes or expectations that I had entertained. I again consulted David Michaelson, and again received the same adverse advice. This time, however, my mind was resolved. I did not accept that promotion from the machine shop to the drawing office at the age of 20 implied that I was deserting trade unionism or socialist principles. I felt that if I were to let go this second opportunity it would be unlikely that I would be offered a further chance to enter a more skilled occupation in the industry.

David Michaelson was as adamant in his point of view as I was in mine. He persuaded a substantial majority in the Communist Party group in the factory to condemn my action. He argued that as a shop steward I had succumbed to efforts by the management to remove me from the area where I had some influence. This ended for a number of years any relationship I had with him or with the shop stewards' committee, within which the Communist Party had substantial influence. In the future all my trade union activity was to be in the drawing office. The draughtsmen and planning engineers were not represented on the shop stewards' committee.

It is only fair to add that years later, when I had become a full-time trade union official and when David Michaelson had become the full-time editor of the unofficial shop stewards' paper, *The Metal Worker*, he acknowledged that his condemnation of my move from the machine shop to the drawing office had not been justified. He said that it had been narrow-minded but motivated by a desire to combat right-wing influence within the union.

Employment in the process planning section attached to the jig and tool drawing office was to me much more attractive than employment as a setter-operator on repetitive batch work in the machine shop. It called for a higher level of skill, and so I was aware that for years ahead I had much to learn. The working environment was also much pleasanter. There was no shift working, and the pay was better. The length of the basic working week was 41 hours, in contrast to 47 hours in the workshops, but no-one worked less than 15 hours overtime each week. Some, including myself, normally worked 2½ hours overtime each day, Monday to Thursday, 7½ hours on Saturday and, sometimes, but not regularly, 3 hours on Sunday mornings. When we were not working on Sunday mornings we were occasionally expected to attend Home Guard training sessions.

Employment in the drawing office opened to me a new and exciting world. Most of the draughtsmen and process planners were comparatively young men. Some of them had an aptitude for production engineering which I greatly admired. They were not reluctant to impart their knowledge. I quickly learnt that it was also essential to cultivate good and close relations with the supervisors and as many machine setters as possible in the machine shops. They had a fund of knowledge which could be of inestimable value to process planning engineers and jig and tool draughtsmen. Similarly, advice from toolmakers could help the drawing office to avoid mistakes in the design of jigs, tools, fixtures and gauges.

Nearly all the jig and tool draughtsmen and process planners had a working-class background. Typically they were the sons of skilled manual workers. They had entered the engineering industry either as craft or drawing office apprentices. A drawing office apprenticeship normally included workshop experience. Unfortunately at that time there were no women employed on process planning or jig and tool draughting, though there were a small number employed as tracers. There were also very few whose full-time education had continued beyond 16 years of age, though all had taken night school courses. Men with a much higher education were more likely to be found in the main product design offices and test laboratories rather than in the jig and tool design office, where much more emphasis was placed on workshop experience. Years later, with changes in the industry and the introduction of computer-aided design, the technical offices underwent a transformation and traditional drawing office techniques became almost a thing of the past.

Much to my pleasure I found that there were a number of people in the jig and tool drawing office with left-wing political views. They were not members of any political party but were aware of the failings of the policy of appeasement and of the imperialist views of Churchill. A number of them had read Left Book Club publications and the Penguin Specials, *Light on Moscow* and *Must the War Spread* by D.N. Pritt. The mood that there was need for radical change in post-war Britain had already taken root.

Nearly all the draughtsmen and process planners were members of a trade union, the name of which was new to me. It was the Association of Engineering and Shipbuilding Draughtsmen. For a period I was reluctant to join but maintained my membership of the Amalgamated Engineering Union. I needed to be convinced that the Draughtsmen's Association was a genuine trade union. There was no legitimate cause for my hesitation. I soon found that the AESD was a lively trade union which provided a very good service to its membership. It also had a democratic structure. At the heart of the organisation were the office committees elected by the membership. Each committee had a chairman and a corresponding member. It conducted negotiations with the management and circulated to the members all information received from the union.

One important service of the Draughtsmen's Association was the publication of technical booklets. About eight new titles were published each year. For many years the Association sold about 100,000 copies annually and claimed at the time to be Britain's largest technical publisher.

The draughtsmen at Lagonda's were members of the Weybridge branch of the AESD. The biggest factory in the branch was Vickers of Weybridge. Because of travelling difficulties and the blackout we were not able to attend branch meetings. Towards the end of the war we transferred our membership to the Feltham branch, where the biggest unit of membership was at General Aircraft.

Despite travelling difficulties, the office committee at Lagonda's maintained communication by telephone with AESD office committees in a number of big factories in the West Middlesex and Surrey area. After a period I was elected to the office committee and then discovered that draughtsmen were a well-organised group of workers in nearly every firm. In virtually all the big factories in the area there was left-wing influence on the office committees. For many years afterwards the district of the union covering West Middlesex remained a source of strength for the left.

The AESD committee at Lagonda's took part in the initiative to establish joint production committees in every department of the factory. This was an initiative that came from below. It was a response to the Nazi attack on the Soviet Union and the desire of trade union activists to strengthen the war effort. There was always a tendency for the management to focus discussion within the joint production committees on the failings of the labour force, including bad timekeeping and absenteeism. The union representatives accepted that these matters should be discussed, but also insisted on discussing other issues which fell within the responsibility of the management, including, for example, machine breakdowns, faulty tooling, the late delivery of components and facilities for training.

On one occasion the factory Home Guard unit was addressed by a high-ranking officer from the regional command. Hundreds were in attendance. It was intended to be a pep talk in which the importance of our factory security was underlined. In the course of the address, however, the high-ranking visitor made some derogatory observations about the Red Army. It evoked an immediate and loud protest from the assembled members of the unit. I and some other draughtsmen participated. The visitor was totally unaccustomed to this kind of protest. There was, however, nothing he could do except to claim that he had been misunderstood. It was not possible to charge with insubordination a considerable number of factory workers whose skilled labour was essential for the war effort. More to the point, it was the high-ranking officer and not the workers who had been wrong. We were justifiably suspicious of those in high circles who resented the new alliance with the Soviet Union and would have been content to stand aside whilst Germany and the Soviet Union weakened each other in combat.

In 1943 the Government released from detention the British fascist leader, Sir Oswald Mosley. It evoked a storm of protest. Most of it was directed against the Home Secretary, Herbert

Morrison, at that time one of the most prominent of Labour's leaders. When the news was received in the factories, protests poured into the Home Office. Almost every workshop at Lagonda's joined the protest. In the jig and tool drawing office nobody, as far as I recall, dissented from the view that the Government had made an error of judgment in releasing Mosley.

Young Communist League

Towards the end of 1941 I became an active member of the Hounslow branch of the Young Communist League. My wife, Renée, and I lived in Hounslow following our marriage in the early summer of 1941. Before long I became the branch secretary. The branch meetings took place on Friday evenings in the Hounslow Cooperative Hall and were well attended. We suffered a constant loss of membership because of conscription and evacuation, but we managed to keep going until some few months before the war ended, when bombing and further evacuation brought the branch to an end.

Because of the number of members working overtime the activities of the branch were confined almost entirely to weekends. At the branch meetings – at that time the branches of the YCL were known as clubs – we had speakers, table tennis, social activities and study sessions. Sometimes on Sunday afternoons from spring to autumn we went to the river or on a ramble. Occasionally on Saturday evenings a party was arranged to see a play at Richmond Theatre. An important part of the club's activity was to assist the war effort. There were three main activities: assistance with crops at Heston Farm, the collection of books for the armed forces, and assistance with engine cleaning at Feltham marshalling yards. All these activities took place on Sunday mornings. I was rarely able to participate because of overtime working, but I remember weeding in a very large field at Heston Farm.

In June 1943 I was a delegate to the Twelfth National Congress of the YCL held in the Beaver Hall, London. The congress was attended by about 300 delegates with an average age of 17½. I was then 22. At that time the YCL had about 20,000 members, of whom about 10,000 were serving in the armed forces.

The National Chairman of the YCL was Ted Willis. Ted opened the conference with a strong anti-fascist speech. He said it was a congress for the mobilisation of British youth against the common enemy. He pointed to the example of Soviet youth in the resistance to the Nazis.

The main report to the congress was made by the General Secretary of the YCL, Mick Bennett. He endorsed the anti-fascist call of Ted Willis and spoke of the YCL members who had already been killed in the British armed forces. He said that the immediate task of the YCL was to do everything possible to strengthen the war effort. He then called for a better future for youth in the post-war world. A manifesto adopted by the congress covering work and careers, health, education and leisure was printed in 60,000 copies.

I have never regretted my period in the YCL. They were years of inspiration; inspiration for the anti-fascist struggle and inspiration for the struggle for a better world. Nor did I find in the YCL the kind of intolerant and authoritarian sectarianism which I had encountered from some Communist Party members in the Lagonda factory. I also had an admiration for Ted Willis, the former Labour League of Youth leader, secretary of the Spanish Youth Foodship Committee and then YCL National Chairman.

My leaving the YCL was not the result of some great political conversion or recognition of 'the God that failed'. The Hounslow branch went out of existence in the 'doodlebug' bombing and because of conscription and evacuation. Moreover, the end of the war was approaching. The Communist Party appeared to favour a post-war coalition, possibly under Churchill. The Labour left, on the other hand, wanted to end the coalition. The voice and symbol of this challenge to a continuation of the coalition was Aneurin Bevan. In 1944 he was elected for the first time to the National Executive Committee of the Party. Only a few months earlier the parlia-

80

mentary and trade union leaders had threatened him with expulsion from the Party.

The majority of the Labour leadership finally came round to the view that at the end of the war the coalition should be ended and that Labour should put forward its own distinctive policy for post-war reconstruction, based on economic planning, the extension of public ownership, social security for all and full employment. I felt at the time that this was the right policy. In the union of which I was a member, the AESD, a ballot in 1944 had resulted in a huge majority for political action and affiliation to the Labour Party. This was a sign of the times. The Labour Party was springing into activity locally, and I rejoined after my lapse of the wartime years.

5

A Change of Direction?

The 1945 General Election was unlike any other I can remember either before or since. It seemed to present the electorate with a clear choice, likely to affect profoundly the lives and welfare of the people. Either we went forward with Labour to a new Britain or we went back to the conditions of the 1930s under the Conservatives.

At the time of the 1929 General Election, the first I remember, I was a schoolboy, but I recall that in Bradford all the four constituencies which then existed in the city returned Labour MPs. My parents voted for one of the successful Labour candidates, Norman Angell, but I do not think my father did so with any marked enthusiasm. His attitude was influenced by what he felt to have been the betrayal by some trade union leaders of the 1926 General Strike. The trade union leader he most disliked, because of his role in the defeat of the General Strike, was J.H. Thomas of the National Union of Railwaymen. Thomas was also the most prominent trade union leader in the Labour leadership.

My father's expectation of the likely failure of the 1929 Labour Government proved to be correct. The action of Labour leaders who went over to a coalition with the Tories in 1931 left him with a sense of disillusionment which influenced him throughout the 1930s. I remember his bitterness in the 1931 General Election.

At the time of the 1935 General Election I was living with my parents on the outskirts of Portsmouth, but for voting purposes our address was in the South Hampshire constituency. It was a safe Conservative seat, and the MP was Sir

Thomas Inskip. The Labour candidate was Robert Mack, a Portsmouth councillor and active member of the National Council of Labour Colleges. I helped with the delivery of leaflets. My parents voted Labour. My father was still without enthusiasm for Labour, but he was anti-fascist and he recognised that within the Tory Party there were many influential people who saw fascism as a bulwark against socialism and communism.

My parents were, however, condemnatory of the decision of the Labour Party to run a candidate in one of the Bradford constituencies against Fred Jowett who was standing for the ILP. Jowett was a pioneer of the socialist movement in Bradford. He was a textile worker who had been elected to the Bradford Council in the early 1890s and elected to Parliament from Bradford in 1906. He was a member of the minority Labour governments both in 1924 and 1929. When the ILP left the Labour Party Jowett remained with the ILP. He had always been on the left.

The split vote ensured that neither Jowett nor the Labour candidate was elected in 1935, though Jowett, much to my father's pleasure, received more votes than the Labour candidate. The unsuccessful Labour candidate was a young textile trade unionist named Wilfred Heywood. He was later to become the General Secretary of the Dyers, Bleachers and Textile Workers' Union (now part of the TGWU), a member of the General Council of the TUC and chairman of its Economic Committee. I was to work with him many years later when he and I served as full-time Board members of the National Board for Prices and Incomes.

The 1945 General Election was the first election in which I was able to vote. I was then 24 years of age. I shared with millions of others an enthusiasm, a determination and a hope for the election of a new kind of government and the building of a new Britain. I have never had the same intensity of feeling in any subsequent general election.

In 1945 there were a great many of us in the electorate who wanted far-reaching changes from the conditions of pre-war Britain. In broad outline, we were conscious of the changes that were needed. We wanted a Britain with full employment, rising living standards, decent housing and social security for all. We were convinced that these objectives would only be achieved through a planned economy in which the basic industries would be under social ownership.

In foreign affairs our view was that the wartime allies should continue to cooperate and seek to eradicate the roots of fascism throughout Europe. This meant that the anti-Soviet policies of the past should not return. In relation to the colonial world our sentiment was that the days of empire should come to an end. We sympathised with the striving of the colonial countries for their independence.

What was distinctive about 1945 was that millions of voters had a vision of a different kind of Britain. Although all the three main political parties had pledged themselves to full employment and social security, the millions who voted Labour had a consciousness that they were choosing something different and something new. That was why we not only voted Labour but we did so with such a strong sense of commitment. In this respect the 1945 General Election was unique; it was qualitatively different from any subsequent election.

Labour won the 1945 General Election by a wide margin of seats. Labour held 393 seats, the Conservatives 213 and the Liberals 12. It is important to note, however, that Labour did not secure a majority of votes. Labour's percentage share of the total vote was 47.8. The Liberals secured about 2¼ million votes and were significantly under-represented in Parliament. Labour won strong support among servicemen and among industrial workers. The size of the vote for the anti-socialist parties was partly a reflection of the prestige of Churchill as Britain's wartime leader and partly a reflection of the feeling among some of the electorate that the Tories and Liberals, no less than Labour, were pledged to full employment and social security. The post-war plans for social security were strongly linked with the name of Beveridge, whose political sympathies were with the Liberals rather than with Labour. The British press was also predominantly anti-Labour.

In every general election between 1950 and 1970 (seven

general elections in all), Labour secured more votes than it did in 1945, though only in 1951 and 1966 did it win a slightly higher share of the total votes cast. I participated actively in all these general elections and confirm from personal experience that the voting figures are misleading as an indication of the popular mood.

In 1945 the millions who voted Labour did so with inspiration for a better future. The 1950 and 1951 General Elections were in no way equal to the 1945 General Election. The inspiration had gone and had been largely replaced, even among strong Labour supporters, with a wish to keep out the Tories. This change in mood was not primarily the consequence of boredom with a government already in office for five or six years; it was the outcome in no small measure of the decisions taken by the Labour Government for rearmament, wage restraint and cuts in the social services, despite the many advances made after 1945.

In 1945 I lived in the Heston and Isleworth constituency, the centre of which was Hounslow, and worked in the Lagonda factory in the Spelthorne constituency, the centre of which was Staines. Both were in the mixed industrial and suburban belt of West Middlesex. Both seats were won by Labour by comfortable majorities. The successful Labour candidate in each constituency came from the trade union movement. In Heston and Isleworth the candidate was Bill Williams, a full-time official of the Union of Post Office Workers, and in Spelthorne it was George Pargiter, a member of the AEU, employed in the AEC factory at Southall, the factory that manufactured many of London's buses.

In the Lagonda factory all the activity was in support of George Pargiter, the Labour candidate. Election posters appeared on walls and machines in every workshop. It was as if it were a one-party election. No doubt there were some workers who did not vote Labour, but certainly there was no indication of any organised activity on behalf of other candidates. In the jig and tool drawing office the proportion of Labour to Conservative voters was probably about three to one. There were few arguments but plenty of discussion. It was

85

the Labour supporters who made the running and advanced the reasons for voting Labour. In the main the few who were less sympathetic to Labour did not respond with any vigour. They shared the majority view that changes were needed in Britain, but were more inclined to give their trust to Churchill in view of his wartime leadership. On the other hand, Churchill's attempt in the election campaign to frighten voters with the threat of a supposed Labour 'gestapo' badly misfired. It was an embarrassment even to those who were prepared to support him as a post-war leader. In the Spelthorne constituency Labour's majority was more than 8,000.

The Heston and Isleworth constituency was typical of West Middlesex. It was not an area of poverty, and even before the war it had low unemployment. There were a number of modern factories within the constituency and an even larger number within easy travelling distance. Many of the electorate lived in estates of semi-detached, owner-occupied houses built in the 1930s. There were also a number of council housing estates of reasonable standard. The industrial workers and their families lived side-by-side with a substantial population of white-collar workers. There was one part of the constituency consisting of large houses which was regarded as a safe Conservative area, but otherwise voters were not thought to fall automatically into either political camp. A fair proportion of the population of Heston and Isleworth had come to live in the constituency from other parts of Britain. In the event Labour won the seat with a majority of more than 6,000.

Most of the press seemed surprised at the result of the 1945 General Election. They had believed their own wrong assessment of the public mood and had underestimated the deep desire for social change and progressive advance shared by millions of the electorate, particularly among younger voters in the armed forces and industry. It seems also that the extent of Labour's victory surprised some of Labour's leaders. Ian Mikardo recalls in his autobiography that after he had successfully moved a resolution at the 1945 Labour Party conference, calling for the extension of public ownership, Herbert Morrison, who epitomised right-wing influence in the Labour leadership, said to him: 'You have just lost us the next election'. He could not have been more wrong.

There were many earlier indications of the changing political views of the British electorate. The result of the 1945 General Election was not a bolt from the blue. By-election results had shown, despite the political truce between the main parties, that the Tories could not count on holding seats which hitherto they had regarded as safe for their candidates. Gallup Poll figures through 1943, 1944 and 1945 suggested that the Conservatives were way behind Labour in popular support. In the armed forces the discussion circles around the Army Bureau of Current Affairs and the forces' parliaments were showing widespread support for social change. For those of us employed in industry there was the evidence of our own eyes and experience. In the West Middlesex factory belt and in London factories there was not only a high level of trade union and political activity, but in almost every medium-sized and large engineering establishment it was the left, including the communists, who were in the leadership.

In the union of which by then I was an active member, the Association of Engineering and Shipbuilding Draughtsmen, there was the persuasive evidence of a national ballot vote to establish a political fund and to affiliate to the Labour Party. The ballot was taken only a few months before the General Election. The result was as follows:

For political action   21,757
Against political action   9,288

The campaign for political action was conducted by a special national committee which consisted overwhelmingly of left-wingers. They were responsible for the circulation of leaflets to every drawing office. The message was radical. There were only two branches in the union, Newark and Dublin, that failed to return a majority in favour of political action, and even in Newark the majority against was only two votes.

It was particularly interesting to me that the five branches with proportionately the highest vote in Britain for political action were all in Yorkshire. They were Selby, with 13 votes to 0; York, with 40 votes to 4; Keighley, with 43 votes to 7; Wakefield, with 59 to 10; and Bradford with 213 to 39. The Leeds, Halifax, Dewsbury and Huddersfield branches also returned proportionately higher votes for political action than the national average. Significantly, most of the London branches secured proportionately higher majorities for political action than most of the branches on Clydeside and in the industrial belt of Scotland.

Ruskin College

In the spring or early summer of 1945 I read in one of our union's publications that the TUC were offering a number of scholarships for full-time adult education at Ruskin College, Oxford. I decided to apply. Applicants were required to set out their record of trade union activity and to give an account of their participation in workers' education, either through the classes and correspondence courses of the National Council of Labour Colleges, the Workers' Educational Association, the classes conducted by university extramural boards or the educational schools and courses organised by trade unions. By then I had completed about nine NCLC correspondence courses and participated in a number of weekend and day schools.

Applicants were also required to submit two essays, one from a choice of subjects related to the trade union and labour movement and one from a wider range of subjects. I do not recall my choice for the trade union essay, but for the wider range of subjects I chose to write on the extent to which the history and characteristics of a country are reflected in its fictional literature. It was an opportunity to write about the United States and its social novelists, particularly Upton Sinclair. During the war I had read many of Sinclair's novels, and I was a great admirer of his work. I often suggested to others with whom I worked in the engineering industry that they should read *Flivver King* because of its account of the bitter struggle for trade union organisation in the American automobile industry.

I was delighted when I was informed that I had been shortlisted for a TUC award at Ruskin. The shortlisted candidates were interviewed by a small panel of TUC General Council members. I was fortunate to be one of the first batch of six successful candidates for the post-war period. Two of the others were also from the Association of Engineering and Shipbuilding Draughtsmen. Some time later a further six awards were made by the TUC, and again three of the successful candidates were from the draughtsmen's union. At the time the AESD was overwhelmingly a union of younger people. At least a half of the members were under 30 years of age.

The TUC awards were funded from the profits of the TUC investment in the old *Daily Herald*. They provided for the payment of residential and tuition fees, subsistence for family dependents, a small amount of pocket money and a modest book allowance. As with so many other Ruskin students I regarded the offer of an award for full-time education as fortune beyond belief. Other students at the college were funded by local authorities, individual unions, the cooperative movement and educational foundations.

My excitement at the offer almost came to nothing. At that time the employment and movement of labour was still controlled under wartime regulations. I had been continuously in a reserved occupation – reserved, that is, from military service – and the age of reservation for jig and tool draughtsmen and process planning engineers was 18. In other words, none of us had been called up for the armed forces, and our employment was closely regulated. An official 'release' had to be obtained by an employee who sought to change his employer, even within the same occupation.

I applied for 'release' from my job to enable me to go full-time to Ruskin. My application was refused by the Ministry of Labour. I expect that the 'release' could have been secured by the union following representations to the Ministry of Labour, but it never reached that stage. The works manager at the factory where I was employed suggested that if I went to Ruskin the firm would keep me on their books as an employee and would guarantee to offer me renewed full-time employment when the Ruskin course was finished. The works manager asked in return that at the end of the course I should return to the group of companies responsible for the Lagonda factory. The Ministry of Labour were not informed of this suggested arrangement.

The offer was made with genuine generosity. I had been involved in a number of disputes in the factory which had reached the negotiating stage with the works manager, but he had never shown any personal animosity. On the contrary, he was progressive by sentiment and strongly in favour of higher educational opportunities for engineering workers. The Lagonda factory was also by this time part of a group of companies linked to Brush Electric of Loughborough, whose principal executive – perhaps he was also a substantial shareholder – was Alan P. Good, a well-known supporter of the leftish inclined Commonwealth Party, which on occasions had successfully challenged the wartime electoral truce. The works manager at Lagonda was true to his word about my going to Ruskin. He maintained his interest in my progress and later, after my return to employment, offered me a job in India to help in establishing a new and large engineering factory.

Ruskin was an exciting and enjoyable experience. In moments of reflection I found it almost unbelievable that I and other active trade unionists among the student body were being maintained, with subsistence for our family dependents, to listen to lectures, read books, write essays and engage in endless discussion on subjects which were at the very centre of our personal interest. I worked hard at Ruskin, primarily because it was all so stimulating and because I never thought of it as work in the sense in which that word is usually used. The Principal of the college was Lionel Elvin, a former Cambridge lecturer who had worked, I believe, for a time during the war at the British Embassy in Washington. He was also the son of a former trade union leader who had been president of the TUC. Lionel Elvin was a very able man and a good teacher who insisted on high academic standards. He was warmly respected by the students.

The principal history teacher at Ruskin was Stephen Schofield, who, in his lectures, regarded it as his special task to provoke those of us who had arrived with strong socialist convictions into thinking critically about our basic assumptions. Thus he would start a lecture with a statement such as: 'In the hungry forties of the nineteenth century the majority of the industrial working class had never had it so good.' He would utter this bombshell of an observation in a quiet voice and with a restrained manner, as though it were an obvious and commonplace truth. It made students recognise that conditions in the 1840s had to be compared not with 1945 but, say, with the period after the Napoleonic wars.

Inevitably Stephen Schofield's lectures were often followed by controversy. Nevertheless, he achieved his purpose of stimulating critical thinking, and he was always ready to provide evidence to support his most provocative statements. At a normal college of higher education Stephen Schofield's style might, perhaps, have been considered out of place because his observations were nearly always intended to disturb the assumptions of socialists. As I soon found out in tutorials he was not a reactionary, but experience with Ruskin students influenced his approach to teaching. At Ruskin he was rightly regarded as an asset. There were plenty of students ready and willing to take up the debate.

The principal economics teacher and the Vice-Principal of the college was Henry Smith. His views were similar to those of Joan Robinson of Cambridge. He encouraged students to study the theory of employment. His was a good influence and he related economics to the real-life experience of Ruskin students. He was interested in Marxian economic theory, but rejected the labour theory of value in relation to price determination. On the other hand, he thought that the Marxian concept of surplus value was a relevant tool of social analysis. He did not regard the labour theory of value as necessary for the theory of surplus value.

International affairs at Ruskin were taught by Dr Andrew
Martin, who later was appointed elsewhere to a professorial
chair. He insisted on the careful study of original documents
and texts. His message was that the serious student should
read the clauses of treaties and the speeches of statesmen and
not be misled by newspaper presentation. It was an important
lesson to provide to students.

A feature of Ruskin education was that there were many
special lectures from visitors, both British and foreign. Lionel
Elvin ensured that we were confronted with different points of
view. Quintin Hogg, later Viscount Hailsham, gave a vigorous
defence of the basic philosophy of conservatism. Emile Burns
outlined the Communist Party's version of Marxism. Dai
Grenfell spoke on the labour movement. All were subject to
close questioning and discussion. Quintin Hogg replied as
pugnaciously as some of his critical interrogators, and Emile
Burns demonstrated that courtesy could be effective when
dealing with hostile questions.

George Woodcock, later TUC General Secretary, and a
former Ruskin student and Oxford graduate, gave a series of
talks on trade unionism. They were of special interest because
of his distinctive approach. He was influenced by the social
philosophy of the Roman Catholic church, and he combined
this with his experience as a former textile worker and active
trade unionist. He was a highly intelligent man whose ability to
articulate ideas and to defend them could best be seen in a
committee or discussion group rather than at a mass rally or
conference.

Ruskin students were, and as far as I know still are, entitled
to use virtually all the facilities of the university. This was of
great advantage. In practical terms it meant the right of access
to lectures, seminars, libraries and undergraduate societies. I
attended a number of courses of lectures in other colleges, but
the lectures I particularly remember were by Professor G.D.H.
Cole at All Souls. What a great figure he was! He had lectured
in both philosophy and economics before his appointment to
the professorial chair in social theory. He thus embraced the
full range of politics, philosophy and economics, the subjects

for one of the most popular Oxford degrees. I was fortunate to have attended his inaugural lecture as the newly appointed professor at Oxford.

Cole was a consistent left-wing libertarian socialist. Among his generation he was one of the best-known Fabians, yet he was not typical of those who usually describe themselves as Fabians. His concern was not only to ameliorate conditions but to change the social order from capitalism to socialism. His conception of socialism was that the private ownership of industry should be replaced by social ownership, and that the anarchy, waste and unemployment associated with the pursuit of private profit should be replaced by economic planning. He argued that democracy should be extended to all forms of social activity, not least to the workplace. When many others were advocating the establishment of public corporations to run the newly nationalised industries, Cole, as much as anyone and far more than most, recognised that there would be serious problems with bureaucracy.

Cole was not a social democrat in the normal meaning of that description. Indeed, in the final chapter of his encyclopedic volumes, *A History of Socialist Thought*, he expressly repudiated for himself the denomination of social democrat. On the other hand, he was even further from being a communist of the kind identified with the Communist Party. He totally rejected the theory of democratic centralism for party organisation, and rightly pointed out that centralism submerged democracy to the point that it became dictatorship. Cole was deeply appreciative of the liberal, radical tradition, and his conception of socialism was inseparable from his support for democracy.

I attended every lecture and seminar that Cole gave during my period at Ruskin. He had an enormous range of knowledge, and his lectures on the history of political theory were unique. Among some academics there was an intellectual snobbishness towards Cole. He wrote for the citizen, it was said, rather than for scholars. The reality was that his ability to write so informatively and comprehensively for the general reader was one measure of his scholarship. He recognised that social theory should relate to social practice in which millions of citizens could participate.

The strongest of the political societies in Oxford immediately after the ending of the Second World War was the Socialist Club. It embraced all varieties of socialists. The main meetings were held on Sunday evenings during term. The Labour Club was much weaker and held its meetings usually on Sunday mornings. I belonged to both, and served as an officer of the Labour Club in Ruskin. I was, however, one of many who resented the idea that membership of the Socialist Club and the Labour Club should be regarded as incompatible. There was already a trend emerging which opposed any kind of joint activity with socialists who did not declare loyalty to the Labour Party. In my time this mainly meant opposition to joint activity with communists.

At Ruskin all the trade union students were socialists of one kind or another, but there were a number of students on local authority or educational foundation grants whose politics were less certain, though there were no Conservative or Liberal clubs within the college. The trade union students were divided in their political opinions into three main groups. Some were members of the Communist Party, though, from what I heard in later years, most of them went eventually in other directions. The second group were non-communist left-wingers, some of whom, but not all, were members of the Labour Party. The third group were more to the centre or right of the labour movement. Again, not all of them were members of the Labour Party. One of the advantages of Ruskin was that it provided so many opportunities for informal discussion on every aspect of social theory and practice.

One particular tutor I remember was a Mr Carritt at Queen's College. He set me an essay on Jeremy Bentham's utilitarianism, 'the greatest good of the greatest number'. The main thrust of my essay was that there was nothing wrong with 'the greatest good of the greatest number' as a guiding principle of political policy, but that it begged the question of what constituted the greatest good. I was brought up abruptly at my tutorial with Mr Carritt when he challenged my central

94

contention. He left me with the thought that 'the greatest good of the greatest number' was a principle compatible with dictatorship. Who was to judge what was the greatest good? Far better to defend the right of dissent. Dissent, he suggested, was essential for progress. Mr Carritt was, I believe, the father of Gabriel (Bill) Carritt, who I had met before the war in the British Youth Peace Assembly. Bill Carritt later worked for the Communist Party.

Employment with the TUC

Towards the end of my period at Ruskin I applied for and was offered an Oxford Extramural Board award. I was told that there would be a place for me at Balliol College. At about much the same time, however, George Woodcock, who was then the Secretary of the Economic Department of the TUC, asked the Principal of Ruskin if there was anyone who might be suitable and who would be interested to work in the Economic Department. I was fortunate to be suggested. This presented me with a dilemma. I wanted to take the place at Balliol, but even if I had completed the course the job which I most wanted was to join the TUC Economic Department.

I discussed my problem with George Woodcock, and his view was that I should go to the TUC. The experience, he said, would be unmatched and, in any case, I could apply for an award as a TUC evening student at the London School of Economics. I took his advice and mentioned that I had first to discharge my moral obligation to return to work for a short period at Lagonda Motors. This he accepted. The management of Lagonda's took an understanding view of my wishes and raised no difficulty. I left them for the TUC after only a few weeks back in the engineering industry.

I worked in the TUC Economic Department for about two years. Shortly after I started, George Woodcock was promoted to the post of Assistant General Secretary. Walter Citrine had resigned as TUC General Secretary to join the National Coal Board. He later became Chairman of the nationalised electricity industry. Vincent Tewson followed Citrine as TUC General Secretary.

When I started at the TUC I shared an office with Ted Fletcher. When Woodcock was made Assistant General Secretary, his place as head of the department was taken by Fletcher. A new recruit, Len Murray, many years later to become General Secretary of the TUC, was brought into the Economic Department, and he and I shared an office.

Woodcock and Fletcher did not find it easy to get on with each other, though both, in my view, were talented. Woodcock, in the best sense an intellectual, was also conscious of his working-class background and did not accommodate himself easily to people whose origins had been more privileged. Ted Fletcher was a Cambridge economics graduate and a chartered accountant. I was not sure of his social background, but there was no question of his sincerity and commitment to the labour movement. He had been active in Gloucestershire both in trade unionism and politics. Before the Second World War he had served in an ambulance unit on the side of the government in the Spanish war.

Fletcher did not have much sympathy with the Catholic social philosophy embodied in Woodcock's approach to trade unionism. When Fletcher was promoted, a few paragraphs about him were published in the TUC magazine, *Labour*. Woodcock deleted a reference to Fletcher's experience as a volunteer in the Spanish war. Fletcher, understandably, was offended by this incident.

George Woodcock was sometimes inclined to favour self-regulatory options by employers rather than direct state controls when dealing with industrial problems. This was not usually seen as the best way forward by Fletcher, who was particularly interested in promoting industrial efficiency and productivity by investment and training. Fletcher was later transferred to become head of a newly formed TUC Production Department. His relationship with George Woodcock was never satisfactory, and he later left the employment of the TUC to become an industrial consultant. I encountered his work on many occasions afterwards, and his influence on industrial relations was always helpful and enlightened.

Len Murray, with whom I worked closely for most of my period at the TUC, was a thoroughly competent, likeable and sincere colleague. I always maintained a warm regard for his contribution. He was a credit to the TUC. As General Secretary he conveyed to the public that the TUC had distinctive views to offer. He articulated the policies of the General Council with persuasive ability.

Among the other members of the Economic Department of the TUC at that time were Bert Turner and Don Bowers. I had known both of them from earlier activity in the movement. Bert Turner was a member of the Brixton branch of the Labour Party League of Youth when he was a student at the London School of Economics. He too was talented, and he too did not see eye to eye with George Woodcock on many issues of policy. He had a strong personality and stuck to his views in arguments with Woodcock. He later voluntarily transferred to the Education Department of the TUC and then left the TUC to become a lecturer at Manchester University. From Manchester, Bert was appointed to a chair at Leeds and then became Professor of Industrial Relations at Cambridge. Many years later I was to work closely with him again, when we were both Board members of the National Board for Prices and Incomes.

Bert Turner was always something of an iconoclast. He was an original and constructive thinker, and at various times produced well-documented publications to counter those who wanted to blame the trade unions for Britain's economic and industrial problems. He was not to be categorised as one of a particular group or school of thought. He was very much his own person. He did not agree with the Clegg-Flanders approach to industrial relations, which became identified with Oxford and Warwick universities. Turner did a lot of international work for the International Labour Organisation, the specialised agency of the United Nations. I maintained friendship with him and admiration for him, and occasionally visited him at Churchill College, Cambridge, where he held a fellowship.

Don Bowers came from a working-class background; his

father was a shipwright. Don went to Queen's College, Oxford, and developed left-wing views. He too did not share George Woodcock's approach to industrial relations and economic issues. He later transferred sideways and became the head of the International Department. This took place after I had left the TUC, and I heard that he fell into the disfavour of Arthur Deakin, the then General Secretary of the TGWU and Chairman of the International Committee of the TUC. Deakin was an obsessive anti-communist with a bullying style. Unfortunately, Bowers died in tragic circumstances whilst still a comparatively young man.

Much of my time in the TUC Economic Department was spent on the reports of the official tripartite working parties appointed by the Government to look into the problems of British manufacturing industries. The Minister responsible for this government initiative was Sir Stafford Cripps, who was then the President of the Board of Trade. The working party reports were informative documents on such sections of industry as cotton, wool and hosiery textiles, furniture, pottery and cutlery. George Woodcock gave me the task of reading and familiarising myself with all the working party reports. I had to summarise them for the Economic Committee, draw attention to the main recommendations and put forward the options for trade union policy.

The common theme of the reports was the need for modernisation, new equipment, capital investment and training. I became convinced that the necessary changes would not take place, at least in sufficient measure, without strong public intervention. Market forces would not provide the required investment, and even the encouragement of voluntary measures was unlikely to be adequate. The TUC and the Labour Party were, however, not committed to anything beyond the appointment of tripartite Development Councils to promote change. The Development Councils lacked any real power. They were appointed under the terms of the Industrial Organisation and Development Act, 1948.

The experience of dealing with the working party reports was a valuable one. It involved not only the study of the reports and of the problems of British manufacturing industry, but also meetings with trade union representatives in the industries concerned. At a later stage I was required to assist in preparing TUC views to the Government on the proposed enabling legislation for the appointment of Development Councils. My role was not in any way influential in policy-making, but I observed that the employers were resistant to any kind of effective public intervention. I also accompanied TUC delegations to Ministers to discuss these industrial problems. My job was to help in preparing briefs and in the reporting of discussions.

George Woodcock also asked me to help in the work of a committee concerned with public ownership. I remember this particularly because it involved on two occasions accompanying TUC delegations to meet the Prime Minister, who was joined by a number of Cabinet Ministers. The representations concerned, first, compensation for workers displaced or made redundant as a result of a change of ownership and, second, proposals for steel nationalisation.

One of the leading members of the TUC delegation when steel nationalisation was discussed was Lincoln Evans, the General Secretary of the main steel union, the Iron and Steel Trades Confederation. He gave the impression that he was not an enthusiast for steel nationalisation. His point of view seemed to be that he favoured the price-fixing arrangements operated by the big steel firms because it gave stability to the industry. The industry's wage fixing arrangements enabled the workers to share in the prosperity of their employers. Any rapid expansion of capacity might be followed in a recession by an even more rapid contraction. It would then be the workers who would carry the burden. He was concerned that in any transition to public ownership the need for future stability should be kept clearly in view. His critics felt that these arguments could easily be translated into support for price-fixing by an oligopoly of private firms and the limitation of capacity.

George Woodcock had, I felt, some sympathy with Lincoln Evans' contentions whilst not going against TUC and Labour

Party policy. Woodcock had no strong belief in the beneficial effects of competition. The benefits had always to be balanced against the unnecessary costs of an unregulated and unplanned expansion and contraction. In an industry, such as iron and steel, where very heavy capital investment was involved, the disadvantages of unregulated expansion were particularly obvious and might result during a future recession in a wave of unemployment among steel workers. This would then affect other industries and could have disastrous consequences. Hence the issue before the labour movement was not whether under public ownership the steel industry could be more rapidly expanded to cater for an existing unsatisfied demand, but how to regulate the industry in a manner which balanced the long-term need for stability and continued employment for the workforce with the need for expansion. Self-regulation by the big steel firms, with machinery for consultation with union representatives, was preferable to unrestrained competition. Nevertheless, George Woodcock's view was, I think, that public ownership offered the option most likely to succeed.

When the TUC representatives met Clement Attlee and his Cabinet colleagues, I was present as part of the TUC secretariat. My most vivid recollection is of a clash of opinion between Lincoln Evans and Aneurin Bevan. Bevan was present as a leading member of the government, even though, as Minister of Health, he had no departmental responsibility for the steel industry. He did, however, as MP for Ebbw Vale, have a strong constituency interest. Bevan's contention was that the big steel firms had for many years operated as an oligopoly and had disregarded the public interest whenever it appeared to conflict with the profits and continued domination of the big firms. They had protected inefficiency and thwarted new developments when their profits and domination were threatened. He cited examples to illustrate his argument.

What I found of special interest was the manner in which the Prime Minister permitted, even encouraged, Bevan to put his point of view and to take the initiative in the exchanges. He was less indulgent towards some of the other Ministers who were present and who were rather more cautious than Bevan in meeting head-on the arguments of Lincoln Evans. I enjoyed the meeting. My sympathies were with the views of Aneurin Bevan.

Another of my tasks at the TUC was to help in servicing the Scientific Advisory Committee. This consisted of a small number of members of the General Council, together with three prominent scientists chosen from among names put forward by the Association of Scientific Workers. During my time the three scientists included Professor P.M.S. Blackett, Professor Newitt and Sir Robert Watson-Watt. Much of the time of the committee was spent considering the future of atomic energy. A deputation was received by the Prime Minister in December 1947. The TUC representatives, who included Professor Blackett, urged that priority should be given to research into the industrial applications of atomic energy as against its military applications. The TUC representatives also expressed concern about health hazards to workers employed on atomic energy projects.

The Prime Minister stated, in reply, that research was being conducted in all branches of atomic development, including industrial, military and medical applications. The possibilities of the industrial applications of atomic energy were constantly being considered. The Minister of Supply, who accompanied the Prime Minister, assured the TUC delegation that everything possible was being done to protect the health of workers employed on atomic energy projects.

The 1947 report of the General Council of the TUC contained a section on the development of atomic energy. I helped in the drafting of the section. Read now with the benefit of hindsight it was rather too optimistic, but the TUC was more realistic than many other commentators. It argued for the peaceful application of atomic energy, stringent health precautions, full public control and the need for vigilance about the consequences of excessive secrecy. The TUC also urged the need for a coordinated national fuel policy.

Another of my tasks at the TUC was to prepare a draft of a pamphlet on equal pay for equal work between men and women. The pamphlet took the form of a series of questions and answers. I had a number of interesting discussions with George Woodcock about the principle of equal pay. As a former cotton weaver, George Woodcock was familiar from experience with an occupation where the principle of equal pay had been established. Even at that time, however, it was clear that one of the most difficult tasks would be to establish not only equal pay for equal work but equal pay for work of equal value. In many occupations pay has been depressed because the job has been traditionally regarded as 'women's work'. Very few, if any, men were (or are) employed on 'women's work'. Thus a direct comparison cannot be made with men's wages. Nevertheless, the skill and diligence required in many jobs regarded as 'women's work' are not less than that required in many occupations traditionally carried out almost exclusively by men. This problem still remains, years after the formal establishment of the right of equal pay for equal work.

Pay and Prices

In February 1948 the Prime Minister made a statement to the House of Commons calling for restraint on incomes and prices. A White Paper was then issued on 'Personal Incomes, Costs and Prices'. The argument put forward by the Government was that any further increase in the general level of incomes without any corresponding increase in the general level of output would lead only to an increase in the inflationary pressure on prices. Higher prices would make British goods and services less competitive in foreign markets and the problem of the balance of payments, which was already acute, would become even worse. This would lead to unemployment and falling living standards.

The Government asked everyone as a general principle to accept a temporary halt to further increases in personal incomes from whatever source they were obtained. Very limited exceptions were accepted for groups of workers in exceptional circumstances.

This statement of Government policy and the request for

restraint was considered at length by the trade union movement. In the Economic Department of the TUC work was concentrated on assisting the General Council to prepare its response. There were two dominant considerations. The first was whether the broad economic argument of the Government about the danger of accelerated inflation should be accepted. The second was the need to reflect the particular circumstances of groups of workers as expressed through the claims put forward by their unions.

The outcome was a statement adopted by the General Council setting out a series of recommendations to affiliated unions. The key recommendations were as follows:

'... the principles of the White Paper relating to wage movements are acceptable to the trade union movement to the extent that they:

a) recognise the necessity of retaining unimpaired the system of collective bargaining and free negotiation;

b) admit the justification for claims for increased wages where those claims are based upon the fact of increased output;

c) admit the necessity of adjusting the wages of workers whose incomes are below a reasonable standard of subsistence;

d) affirm that it is in the national interest to establish standards of wages and conditions in under-manned essential industries in order to attract sufficient manpower; and

e) recognise the need to safeguard those wage differentials which are an essential element in the wages structure of many important industries and are required to sustain those standards of craftsmanship, training and experience that contribute directly to industrial efficiency and higher productivity.'

The recommendations of the General Council were put to a conference of trade union executive committees and were adopted by 5,421,000 votes to 2,032,000.

The conference that took this decision was held at the

Central Hall, Westminster in March 1948. It was attended by 1,550 delegates, approximately half as many again as normally attend the annual TUC. Most trade union executive committees were present in full strength. This was an indication of the importance of the subject under debate. Questions about incomes policy continued to be central to trade union thinking for many years.

I was present at the special conference, but only to listen to the debate as a member of the staff of the Economic Department of the TUC. Staff members were, however, called upon both before and after the conference to speak to trade union branches and trades councils in support of TUC policy. For the first time since working for the TUC I felt uncomfortable about the role I had to play.

I accepted the argument that accelerated inflation would damage Britain's economic prospects and I recognised that the purchasing power represented by wages formed part of the total demand on national resources. I supported also the continued existence of a Labour Government and I wanted it to complete its programme of social reform.

On the other hand, I felt that the TUC recommendations interpreted the White Paper in a manner which the White Paper never intended. The White Paper did not envisage that wage increases would be justified based on increased output, a reasonable standard of subsistence, the need to attract manpower to undermanned industries and the need to safeguard differentials to sustain craftsmanship. Nearly every union could justify its claims under one or more of these criteria.

The TUC criteria were realistic but the White Paper, in calling for the acceptance of the general principle that there should be a temporary stop to further increases in personal incomes, was not. Unfortunately, it was not the TUC criteria, but the White Paper, which would influence employers.

Moreover, there was no effective way in which the Government proposed to exert similar control over profits. Restraint in the distribution of dividends was not the same as the control of profits. Undistributed profits were no less the property of shareholders than distributed dividends. Profits were rising more rapidly than wages.

The recommendations of the TUC called for the endorsement of the policy of general stabilisation as set out in the White Paper 'on condition that the Government pursues vigorously and firmly a policy designed not only to stabilise but to reduce profits and prices'. I felt this to be so unrealistic that its purpose was to persuade trade unionists to accept Government policy in the false belief or expectation that profits and prices would be reduced.

By the spring of 1948 it was also becoming evident that the Labour Government was exhausting its reforming zeal. A policy of severe wage restraint might have been acceptable in conditions of economic difficulty if the Government had given the impression that it was determined to press ahead towards the kind of changed society advocated in 1945. This was no longer the case. At home there were already arguments for 'consolidation' within an economic system that was still predominantly capitalist, and in foreign policy Britain had become increasingly involved, under US leadership, in the restoration and strengthening of the capitalist system wherever it had influence. There was no better example of this than in Greece, where the British Government supported the forces of reaction in military conflict with the resistance forces that had helped to liberate the country from fascism in the Second World War.

During my period at the TUC I was an evening student at the London School of Economics. I joined the trade union course on an award from the TUC. The course lasted for three years and was hard work, involving attendance at the LSE for three nights a week and additional time for reading and the writing of essays.

The L.S.E.

At the LSE there was not the same opportunity as at Ruskin for endless discussion with other students over meals and late into the evening. Ruskin was a community, whereas the LSE

105

was a teaching establishment. Nevertheless, some of the teaching was of a very high standard. The lectures on employment law by Otto Kahn-Freund, who many years later was to become a distinguished member of the Donovan Commission on Trade Unions and Employers' Associations, were magnificent. I remember too the fascination of lectures by Harold Laski who, when dealing with the history of political theory, somehow managed always to relate his theme to current problems. He was not an admirer of the policies of Ernest Bevin, Labour's Foreign Secretary.

The lecturer in charge of the trade union students was a Mr Bassett. His subject was politics, but his views were very different from those of Harold Laski. One of his main contentions was that the things on which the Conservative Party and the Labour Party had similar views were more important than the issues which divided them. Mr Bassett approved of this fundamental unity of purpose. It was a view which did not commend itself to the majority of the trade union students, but it made us think about the likely consequences of the support given by the majority of Labour leaders to the United States' foreign policy. Would this ideological alliance with the USA ultimately have a more lasting influence on Britain than the social reforms introduced by Labour?

One of the trade union students on the LSE course was Ron Huzzard, a draughtsman who for many years was active in the draughtsmen's union. Ron is a Yorkshireman who came to London after early employment with an engineering firm in Hull. He has been a member of the Labour Party throughout his politically active life, and he is also a Quaker. He was elected to the parliamentary panel of the draughtsmen's union and, though he fought elections, he was, unfortunately, not elected to Parliament. He served with distinction as a councillor in the Conservative stronghold of Bromley. Ron Huzzard probably did more than anyone, over a very long period, to help in shaping the progressive policy of the draughtsmen's union on international issues.

During his membership of the Labour Party Ron has held many offices, and was for a period the secretary of his constituency Labour Party. He is still the voluntary national secretary of Labour Action for Peace. He is the most hardworking voluntary secretary any national organisation could wish to have. Ron Huzzard and his wife Rosalie have given many years of exemplary service to the labour movement. Ron was deservedly given a TGWU peace award – in the memory of Frank Cousins – in 1991. He is for me an enduring symbol, in views and in activity, of the generation of young Labour supporters who in 1945 were striving for a change of direction.

6

Trade Union Official

In the late summer of 1948 an opportunity arose for me to move from the employment of the TUC to that of the union of which I was a member, the Association of Engineering and Shipbuilding Draughtsmen, which at that time had about 45,000 members. One of the national officials of the union, George Thomson, was in poor health and was due to retire. George Thomson came from Glasgow and, as a shipbuilding draughtsman, had been active in the union from its early days in the First World War.

As a young man Thomson, like a number of the pioneers of the union, had been drawn to trade unionism because of his support for socialism. He had been influenced by the radical movement on the Clyde both immediately before and during the 1914–18 war. He was a strong supporter of guild socialism, later to be associated with the name of G.D.H. Cole. He was elected to the Executive Committee of the union in 1917 and became a full-time official in 1920. In 1935 he was elected to the General Council of the TUC, and in 1947 presided over the annual TUC.

George Thomson's principal tasks in the AESD were to edit the union's monthly journal, to serve as a member of the Executive Committee of the union, to act as secretary to a number of executive sub-committees and to represent the union in a number of other organisations. In the 1920s Thomson's influence was strongly on the left of the movement, and there were regular complaints at the annual conference that the monthly journal was 'too socialist'. These complaints never secured majority support among the delegates. The tradition was established that the editor should have discretion in the conduct of the journal and should be responsible for its contents, not to the Executive Committee, but to the annual conference. It was felt to be important that the journal should be maintained as a free platform for the expression of the views of the members. The editor was required to have regard to the policies of the union in his expression of editorial views, but this was always interpreted liberally, providing that other views were not suppressed.

In the 1930s and 1940s George Thomson moved politically towards the mainstream of opinion in the trade union movement. In the early 1930s he opposed the Morrisonian idea that publicly owned industries should be run as public corporations, which he predicted would become bureaucratic institutions controlled by the former captains of private industry. He wanted much more direct involvement by workers and trade unions. In other respects, however, his views became less radical. It is probable that he was influenced by his antipathy to the undemocratic centralism of communism and the bitter exchanges in the years following the 1926 General Strike. By the time I knew him, he was regarded by left-wingers in the union as being well on the right of the movement.

When George Thomson announced his intention to retire I was approached by a number of union members in the London area, mainly activists on the left, to become a candidate. I agreed. The advantage was, as I saw it, that I would be able once again to participate more freely, than in employment at the TUC, in debates about policy and, perhaps, to exert some influence in the Executive Committee and at the annual conference of the union. The prospect of writing regular articles for the union's journal, with considerable editorial discretion, was particularly attractive.

The method of choosing full-time officials of the AESD was stipulated in the rules. The lay delegates at the annual conference elected a selection committee, consisting entirely of lay members. Vacant posts were advertised, and only members of the union were eligible to apply. At that time full members of the union had to have at least eight years' experience in the engineering or shipbuilding industries. The selection committee drew up a shortlist, interviewed the shortlisted candidates and then voted for their choice. The report of the selection committee was subject to endorsement or rejection by the annual conference.

Supporters of this system of choosing full-time officials argued that it combined lay control and democracy with a procedure for the detailed examination of candidates. It also, so it was argued, eliminated the bias in favour of older candidates with long experience and candidates drawn from large branches, inevitable under a system of electing officials by rank-and-file ballot. The issue of how to choose full-time officials had been debated on a number of occasions at conferences of the AESD, but the delegates had always rejected any proposal, usually supported by the left, for ballot votes in which every member would be eligible to participate. It was felt that such a system, though having the appearance of democracy, was less democratic in substance than the system of selection, after interview, by a selection committee of lay members elected by the lay delegates at the annual conference.

In the election for the selection committee the left and right tendencies in the union competed for places. In the selection committee for a new national official to replace George Thomson, neither the left nor the right had a decisive majority. It was not possible to predict whom they might choose.

I was put on the shortlist, and I regarded it as fortunate that, following the interview, each shortlisted candidate was asked to write on the same day an essay of about 1400 words on an issue of general trade union interest. The candidates were not given notice of this request except at the interview, and the essay had to be completed in about five hours. Certainly, my experience at Ruskin, the LSE and in the Economic Department of the TUC, gave me an advantage in writing such an essay at short notice. I was selected for the vacant post.

The selection, however, did not go unchallenged. At the Executive Committee one of the most influential of the lay members, whose views were on the right of the movement, sought, on a technical interpretation of the rules, to defer the

110

whole process of selection. The Executive Committee, with strong support from the then General Secretary, James Young, did not accept that the process should be deferred. I started work with the AESD as a national official in the middle of September 1948.

James Young was an interesting trade unionist. He worked as a draughtsman at John Brown's shipyard, Clydebank, before the First World War, and he was in at the formation of the union in 1913. He was utterly dedicated to the union, and worked long hours and almost every weekend in its service. He worked for many years as a full-time organiser and did not become General Secretary until his late fifties. He followed another Glaswegian, Peter Doig, who was the first full-time General Secretary of the union and who remained in office for many years. Doig was a man of considerable ability who had been influenced by the radicalism of the Clyde during the First World War, and who remained more on the left than on the right of the movement throughout his life. I had a number of long discussions with him. His interests were very wide and ranged through politics, sport and astronomy.

A number of young full-time officials of the union, including myself, were fortunate to enjoy the goodwill of the General Secretary, James Young. He had an unusual attitude. He was a strong supporter of Ernest Bevin and his views were generally on the centre-right of the movement. On the other hand, he was personally sympathetic to younger officials who had left-wing views. He seemed to take the view that there was something odd about any young official who had already arrived at a right-wing point of view.

Two of the younger officials, George Doughty and I, both firmly on the left, received strong support from the General Secretary. The majority on the Executive Committee of the union at that time were on the right, but with James Young as General Secretary, both George Doughty and I were never in trouble. This goodwill also extended to another young official, Reg Silverthorne, who was a member of the Communist Party. Reg was more erratic in his behaviour, but he had boundless enthusiasm and optimism. When the General Secretary

111

thought it necessary to criticise or even reprimand Reg, because he did not always observe the requirements of the national negotiating procedure agreement with the engineering employers, he did it in a way that displayed generosity rather than animosity.

George Doughty, who was later to become a very successful General Secretary of our union, was already making his mark as a highly competent official. He kept closely in touch with the active membership in the West Midlands area where he was the divisional official, gained the confidence of members whose claims he pursued, observed the requirements of the negotiating procedure agreement and made sure that the rules of the union were upheld. He did all this in a manner compatible with his reputation for trade union militancy.

Wages Policy

When I became a member of the Executive Committee of the AESD in the autumn of 1948 there was growing criticism of the policy on wages of the Government and the TUC. These criticisms were voiced in the Executive Committee, not only by those who had been critical when the policy of restraint had been introduced, but also by some who had supported it. They reflected the views of the majority of the membership of the union. The members, nearly all of whom worked in privately owned engineering and shipbuilding firms, could see for themselves that, whilst they were expected under Government and TUC policy to exercise wage restraint, the profits of their employers were rising steeply. There was also in many firms an acute shortage of suitably qualified and experienced technical staff. Drawing office staff and associated technicians were conscious of their contribution towards higher productivity. There was thus a widespread feeling that the union's claims for higher wages were justified.

The economic situation was made worse by rearmament. In the November 1948 issue of *The Draughtsman* I wrote an editorial emphasising that the rearmament programme had serious and damaging economic implications. A sound national economy, the article said, was the first line of defence, and 'we may question the wisdom of increasing the size of the armed forces when our most essential industries are still seriously undermanned'.

At the 1949 annual conference of the AESD a resolution was carried expressing dissatisfaction with the policy of the Government on wages, prices and profits. This modified a decision of the previous conference in support of TUC policy towards the White Paper on personal incomes, costs and prices. This, in turn, determined the attitude of the draughtsmen's delegation towards incomes policy at the 1949 TUC.

The General Council of the TUC put forward a resolution pledging continued support for 'the greatest possible measure of restraint in seeking to increase personal incomes and expenditure unrelated to increased productivity.' There was a resolution of opposition to the policy of wage restraint from the Electrical Trades Union, and a composite amendment to the General Council's resolution, calling for 'detailed plans designed to achieve the necessary increased production at lower costs, the required expansion of exports and the effective control of prices and profits'.

The draughtsmen's delegation decided to support the composite amendment, and I was asked to second it in the debate. It was moved by Bryn Roberts, the General Secretary of the National Union of Public Employees. Bryn argued that it was not sufficient to call for restraint. More effective policies should be pursued to deal with the underlying problems. In seconding the amendment I drew attention to the inconsistencies in the General Council's attitude towards prices and profits. In 1948 they had secured support for the policy of restraint on condition that the Government pursued vigorously a policy designed not only to stabilise but to reduce prices and profits. This had not happened. In 1948, in comparison with the previous year, profits had risen by 17 per cent and directors' emoluments by 36 per cent. These increases were much higher than the increases in wages.

In the 1949 TUC debate on incomes policy most of the big

113

unions supported the General Council. Arthur Deakin, on behalf of the TGWU, was totally supportive of Government policy; Tom Williamson of the General and Municipal Workers' Union pointed out that the General Council's policy should not be interpreted as supporting a wage freeze; and Jack Tanner of the AEU said that although his union had been critical of the wage restraint policy, the AEU delegation felt that the General Council was doing everything possible in the circumstances to achieve trade union objectives. In the vote the General Council won support for their policies with overwhelming majorities.

This largely uncritical attitude towards the Government's policy on wages, prices and profits proved to be shortlived. In the second half of 1949 Britain's economic situation deteriorated. The Government decided to devalue sterling in an attempt to improve the balance of payments. The accompanying speculation was described by Aneurin Bevan as 'the obscene plundering in Throgmorton Street'. Devaluation gave an upward thrust to prices, and the Government appealed for continued severe restraint on wages. Capital investment was cut, but arms expenditure was substantially increased. Profits continued to rise at a much faster rate than wages.

Trade union criticism was growing in face of this worsening situation, and in January 1950 the General Council convened another special conference of trade union executive committees to consider a report on the economy. I again spoke on behalf of the draughtsmen's union in opposition to the General Council's recommendations which, in effect, endorsed the Government's policy. The General Council asked unions to reconsider their existing wage claims, and went so far as to ask unions with cost-of-living sliding scale wage agreements to hold wage rates stable up to a specified limit for higher prices.

An important indication of the loss of popular support for Government policy and TUC recommendations was provided by the result of a coalfield ballot conducted by the National Union of Mineworkers. The National Executive Committee of the NUM and a conference of delegates recommended support for TUC policy. In a ballot, however, it was overwhelmingly rejected. The NUM was only one of a number of unions which switched from support to opposition to Government and TUC policy on wages, prices and profits. At the January, 1950 special conference the General Council's recommendations were carried by the much reduced majority of 657,000 votes. The voting was 4,263,000 to 3,606,000.

At the annual conference of the draughtsmen's union, held in the spring of 1950, the Executive Committee led the delegates in opposition to the Government's policy. I was given the task of speaking on their behalf. I pointed out that the major share of the rewards of increased productivity since the introduction of the policy of wage restraint had gone to the employers. Profits had risen substantially. The delegates expressed opposition to any reduction in workers' living standards. They also opposed the cuts that had been made in the housing programme and in investment for the re-equipment of British industry. They contrasted this to the rise in military expenditure to a figure substantially higher than the 1949 Budget estimate.

Opposition to Government policy continued to grow, and at the 1950 TUC the General Council's report dealing with wages was narrowly defeated. A resolution from the ETU opposing wage restraint was also carried by a small majority.

Rearmament

These debates about wage restraint were a reflection of a deeper division about the whole trend of Government policy. The Labour Government had increasingly identified itself with the attitude of the United States in the Cold War between East and West. The left in the trade union movement sought to oppose the effect of this policy on the living standards of the working people. Identification with US policy meant support for a rearmament programme. Such a programme could be carried through only by holding down living standards, curtailing the social services and reducing investment for peaceful industrial purposes. At that time there was very little slack in the economy which could be put to work on rearmament without cuts in other directions.

In August 1950 the Labour Government published the text of a memorandum on defence which contained the following revealing sentences:

'His Majesty's Government in the United Kingdom have been requested by the United States Government to inform them concerning the nature and extent of the increased effort, both as regards increases in forces, and increases in military production which His Majesty's Government are willing and able to undertake, as well as information concerning additional military production programmes which could be initiated with United States assistance.'

The memorandum stated that the British Government welcomed the initiative of the USA. A programme for substantial rearmament was put forward. The Minister of Defence, Emanuel Shinwell, said that Britain had no alternative but to consider the defences of the Far East, the Middle East, Europe and particularly Britain. Russian or Russian-inspired aggression had to be resisted.

The report of the General Council to the 1951 TUC assessed the effect of rearmament. It said that the most important development in the economic situation had been the large increase in the defence programme from about £780 million in 1950–51 to about £1,300 million in 1951–52 and to about £4,700 million in the years 1951–52 to 1953–54. Such an increase inevitably meant some reduction in the standard of living. The Government, said the General Council, had adopted a policy which placed the emphasis on a rise in prices rather than on a rise in taxes. Worldwide rearmament had also led to raw material shortages and big rises in prices. The amount of civil investment in Britain was being cut and would fall further in 1952 and 1953.

There were some in the trade union movement who believed that rearmament and the accompanying sacrifices were necessary. I did not. I put my point of view in an article in *The Draughtsman* in September 1950. I argued that it was a mistake

116

to attribute every outbreak of social unrest in any part of the world to Soviet penetration or instigation. Where millions of people were living in poverty and were being exploited, social change was inevitable. The basic motive force for unrest was indigenous and not imported. The 1939–45 war, with its resistance to fascism and the development of national liberation movements, had shaken to their foundations the social structures in many countries liberated from enemy occupation.

I also argued that regard had to be paid not only to Soviet policy but also to US policy.

'In international affairs America has employed her great power and influence on an unprecedented scale since 1945, but her assistance to Chiang-Kai-Shek and the recent moves regarding Formosa (Taiwan) illustrate that she has not been averse to supporting unworthy causes in pursuit of her policy in the more backward areas of the world where the impetus for social change is being strongly felt. The hysteria of sections of US opinion and the desire to extend American influence against Russia even, if necessary, to the point of attempting to arrest inevitable social changes in other countries, is an important factor in international relations.'

My article also referred to the figures for Soviet armed strength quoted by the Minister of Defence. I pointed out that in proportion to population the Soviet armed forces and tank strength were approximately on a par with those of Britain. In addition, of course, there were the atomic weapons possessed both by the USA and the USSR. (By then the Soviet Union had broken the monopoly of atomic weapons possessed by the USA.) My article added:

'What, at least, is clear is that rearmament leads always to competitive rearmament without necessarily altering the proportions in which weapons are possessed by the competing countries.'

The experiences of subsequent years served to confirm the views which I had already formed in the late 1940s about the Cold War and rearmament. The attempt by the USA for many years to thwart the recognition of the communist government of China within the United Nations, and, in later years, the atrocious war conducted by the US Government against Vietnam and the support given to reactionary governments and forces in Latin America, notably in Chile, Nicaragua and Cuba, all led me to reject the notion that the Cold War was a struggle between totalitarianism and the 'free world'.

This did not imply blindness towards injustices in the Soviet Union or the countries of Eastern Europe where the communists held power. There were many such examples of injustice. One of the earliest after the Second World War was the refusal or, at best, the procrastination of the Soviet authorities in granting exit permits to Soviet women who married British men. There was the ridiculous so-called 'doctors' plot' against the life of Stalin. There was the equally ridiculous intolerance towards views which in any way differed from those of the biologist, Lysenko. These infamous episodes were accompanied by acts of persecution.

In the countries of Eastern Europe there was the enforced absorption of social democratic parties into parties dominated by communists. The ruling communist parties were required to accept the Soviet Union as the model of socialist construction. Any significant deviation was regarded as treason. Yugoslavia was thrown out of the Eastern European communist alliance because Tito and his colleagues had their own ideas about building socialism. The most incredible allegations were then made against them. Tito and others were said to have been recruited by fascist agents. Similar charges were also made against a number of leading communists in other East European countries. Some were executed, as in Czechoslovakia and Hungary, and some were sentenced to long terms of imprisonment. They were all fabricated charges. By 1953 mass protests took place in parts of Eastern Europe, notably in Poznan and Berlin.

Many of us on the left, though appalled by these injustices, did not want, in the circumstances of the Cold War, to join an anti-Soviet crusade. We felt that we would be giving encouragement to the reactionary designs of the USA. There was

118

nothing I wrote in the late 1940s or 1950s which could be interpreted as supporting the injustices and crimes of Soviet power. Nevertheless, I now recognise, with the benefit of hindsight, that I was among those whose response was for a period more muted than it should have been.

China

The Chinese revolution and the coming to power of Mao Tsetung in 1949 was the most significant of social changes following the Second World War. I supported the new government because I felt that it would help in the struggle of the Chinese people against feudalism, against imperialist intervention and for economic development. I joined the British China Friendship Association, was elected to its Executive Committee and became its national Vice-Chairman. The Chairman was Stanley Mayne, who was the General Secretary of one of the larger civil service unions and who later, after retirement, became a Labour member of the London County Council. He was a very able man.

Unfortunately my membership of the BCFA led to my exclusion from the Labour Party. The Labour Party National Executive Committee decided to proscribe the BCFA. This meant that membership of the BCFA was regarded as incompatible with membership of the Labour Party.

I felt that the decision to proscribe the BCFA was politically mistaken. Of course, the organisation included communists, but it also included many who were not. More importantly, it stood for friendship with the most populous country in the world which, after many years of intervention and exploitation by foreign powers, was setting out on a new course. Its new government was being unjustifiably prevented, because of the influence of the USA, from taking China's seat in the United Nations. In no sense was the new China the creation or puppet of the Soviet Union.

I decided not to resign from the BCFA and to inform my constituency Labour Party accordingly. I was at the time an

119

active member of the General Management Committee of the Heston and Isleworth Labour Party. I anticipated that this would lead to my exclusion from the Party. I very much regretted such a possible exclusion, but I felt that the proscribing of the BCFA was a Cold War gesture for which there was no justification.

On 9 April, 1953, the Hounslow Cooperative Party, which I represented on the General Management Committee of the Heston and Isleworth Labour Party, was informed that I could no longer attend General Management Committee meetings. The letter concluded with the following paragraph:

'It is regretted that this decision had to be made in view of the fine work which Mr Mortimer has done for the Movement. I therefore ask you to appoint a new delegate to the General Committee.'

The Heston and Isleworth Constituency Labour Party also wrote to me personally. The letter said that my continued membership of the British China Friendship Association was incompatible with membership of the Labour Party. The letter added:

'The Executive Committee regret that such a decision had to be taken and wish to express their appreciation of the work you have done for the Party, and your honesty of purpose in disclosing your intention to continue your membership of that Association.'

I was at the time the voluntary secretary of the Hounslow branch of the Cooperative Party. I retained this job for about seven years and played an active part in Cooperative affairs. This experience was helpful when years later I was elected to the Board of the London Cooperative Society. The London Cooperative political organisation had a lively structure, and I regularly attended its conferences as a branch delegate. I was also a regular attender at the quarterly sectional meetings of the LCS held in Hounslow. These were usually very well-attended meetings where there was keen controversy between left- and right-wing trends.

I remained outside the Labour Party until 1958. By that time the British China Friendship Association had been affected by differences between China and the Soviet Union. My personal sympathies in the early controversies were more with China than with the Soviet Union. I felt that the Soviet Union were seeking to dictate their policies to China, and I had already reached the conclusion, as a result of events in Eastern Europe, that the Soviet Union regarded their allies not as equals but as subordinates. Khrushchev was erratic in his policies and behaviour, and was prepared to use military force to maintain the subordination of other countries where the communists were in power. Such policies could not succeed against China.

Eastern Europe

Towards the end of 1956, after the unrest in Poland and the uprising in Hungary, I expressed my criticism of Soviet policy in strong terms. I wrote an editorial for *The Draughtsman* which stated:

'In Eastern Europe the common people of Poland and Hungary demanded the democratisation of their social system, the ending of the appalling crimes of the secret police, and the assertion of the sovereign equality of their State, particularly in relation to the Soviet Union. These demands embraced millions of people, including the industrial working class, from which any government claiming to be socialist ought to find its strongest support.

'The responsibility for the conditions which gave rise to these demands rests primarily with the Soviet Union...'

The article went on to point out that the Twentieth Congress of the Communist Party of the Soviet Union had revealed in the most macabre detail that, simultaneous with substantial economic progress, a political tyranny had developed which

121

had been responsible for the murder of many thousands of people, including many whose lives had been devoted to the labour movement, the deportation of national minorities during the war and the stifling of any kind of independent criticism, even from those sympathetic to the socialist system. These conditions had been reproduced in the countries of Eastern Europe. In Hungary in particular, the military intervention of Soviet troops was a criminal act of suppression. Soviet troops, urged the article, should be withdrawn immediately and unconditionally.

Towards the end of this article I drew attention to commentators whose only desire was to discredit everything about socialism but to say nothing about colonial injustices. They made no protest about the hundreds of Africans hanged in Kenya or the tens of thousands held without trial in detention camps. Nor did they protest about the many thousands killed by the French army in North Africa, or the use of British armed forces to overthrow the elected government of British Guiana. Those who protested about the injustices of colonial rule were in the strongest moral position to protest against Soviet intervention in Hungary.

The article also quoted the words of Rosa Luxembourg: 'Freedom is always freedom for the person who thinks differently.' She added that freedom loses all its virtues when it becomes a privilege. My own observation was that the demand for freedom of thought and expression does not arise abstractly; on the contrary, it is an essential requirement for social progress. Without the clash of ideas, wrong policies, abuses and even crimes will go unchallenged. It was Marx who stated that 'to leave error unrefuted is to encourage intellectual immorality'.

7

Trade Union Activity

In 1955 I moved from the Heston and Isleworth to the Twickenham constituency. I helped there in the General Election of that year. In the ward to which I had moved there was no Labour Party organisation, even though at one time there had been Labour councillors. I was urged by a number of active members in the Twickenham Labour Party to rejoin the Party.

Disagreements within the BCFA helped me to make up my mind. In 1958 I rejoined the Party and helped to re-establish the Party organisation in the ward where I was living. I became ward chairman and subsequently fought unsuccessfully as Labour candidate in Borough Council and County Council elections. I also served on the General Management Committee of the Twickenham Labour Party.

Though I felt strongly about the political circumstances which had led to my exclusion from the Labour Party, the focal point of my interest throughout the 1950s was in trade unionism and in the effort, in which many colleagues shared, to ensure that the draughtsmen's union should be an effective force in its members' interests and a progressive influence in the wider movement.

For many years it had been the practice in the draughtsmen's union for active members of left-wing commitment to consult collectively from time to time, with a view to extending their influence on policy. This radical socialist influence had existed from the very beginning of the union in the period of the great industrial unrest before the First World War. Many of the pioneers of the union were influenced by the ferment of

123

socialist ideas in the shipyards and engineering factories of Clydeside.

I was drawn into a left-wing consultative group when I was a rank-and-file member of the union, years before I became a full-time official. The groups expanded during and after the Second World War. Opponents usually described the left groups as 'communist', 'communist-inspired' or 'fellow travellers'. They were mistaken. Communists formed part of the left groups, but throughout the period in which I was active they did not dominate them, particularly at national level. Most of the influential members of the groups were in the Labour Party, though some were not members of any political party.

The really remarkable feature of the left-wing influence in the draughtsmen's union was the extent to which it drew on the support of an extensive network of members, the great majority of whom were under 40 years of age. The typical left-wing member of that period was the son or daughter of a working-class family who had reached the drawing office, either following or as part of an engineering apprenticeship, and had spent considerable time at night school gaining technical qualifications. His or her commitment to the left was derived not only from experience but also from some familiarity with socialist publications.

There were a number of main issues around which the left were broadly united. They were in favour of a vigorous policy on wages and conditions and of close collaboration with other engineering and shipbuilding unions, both at workplace level and within the structure of the Confederation of Shipbuilding and Engineering Unions. They wanted to preserve the sovereignty of the membership within the union and the supremacy of the rank-and-file branch delegates within the annual conference. They were opposed to any kind of political discrimination within the rules which might affect the right of members to stand for office.

The left favoured political action and affiliation to the Labour Party by the union. It argued for public ownership and other forms of public control for sections of the engineering and maritime industries. It did not accept the arguments, both of the Conservative and Labour leaderships, in favour of Cold War strategies and heavy military expenditure.

This brief summary of the issues around which the left found it possible to unite does not imply that there were no differences. At a later period some of the differences became more important and certainly affected me personally. Nor does it imply that others in the union were consistently opposed to the views which the left promoted. Far from it. The left would not have been able successfully to extend its influence without winning or sharing the support of a large number of members on main issues of policy.

A New General Secretary

In 1952 the union's General Secretary, James Young, was due to retire at the age of 65 years. The new General Secretary was to be elected by vote of the branch delegates at the annual conference. The existing Assistant General Secretary, who was not on the left, was regarded as a strong contender for the vacant post.

The left groups in the union consulted among themselves about the possibility of running a candidate. It was decided that our candidate should be George Doughty, who at that time was still a full-time official in Birmingham. It was a wise choice. George had achieved national prominence as an advocate for a vigorous wages policy before his election as a full-time official. He had a reputation as a competent and responsible official. He came from an area where it was essential that a left candidate should win support if he was to have any chance of being successful in a national vote of branch delegates. George was on the Labour left, but his main impact in the union had always been on collective bargaining. In the West Midlands there was a strong group of Labour Party members, a number of whom were or became magistrates, who were supporters of George Doughty and whose views were generally on the left. They could be depended upon to win support for George Doughty in the branches in the area. There

125

were virtually no prominent communists in the union in the West Midlands.

In the discussion on the choice of a left candidate, my own name had also been put forward for consideration. I opposed the suggestion and argued strongly for George Doughty. George was approximately ten years older than I was – I was then 30 years of age – and he had a better and longer record in the union, even though I was then a national official and he was a divisional official. He was certain of almost unanimous backing in the West Midlands, whereas support for any other left candidate would have been more doubtful. In the area from which I came, West London, nearly all the branches could be expected to support any chosen left-wing candidate. Of particular importance was George's high reputation in collective bargaining.

George was reluctant to be drafted as a candidate. He was a Birmingham citizen by birth and experience and happy in his location. It was far from certain that he would win if he stood for the General Secretaryship. He was a modest person, and his reluctance to stand was understandable.

The person who more than anyone else convinced various active members, myself included, that victory was within our grasp if we worked energetically for it, was Reg Silverthorne, the union's full-time official in the West London area. Reg was a communist, but it was his personal sense of commitment which was infectious. The retiring General Secretary, James Young, who was usually a conventional Labour supporter in political matters, was also known to favour the election of George Doughty as his successor. He recognised George's qualities in collective bargaining, his ability to win support among members and his sense of responsibility towards the negotiating procedural obligations of the union.

At the conference at which the election for a new General Secretary was to take place I shared a room with George Doughty. He was a close colleague of mine, and I had been asked by many who were supporting his candidature to persuade him against any last-minute withdrawal. I also indicated that, together with two other full-time officials, I intended to enter the debate at the conference about the candidates in favour of him. This I did. I do not think that the intervention of three full-time officials swung the debate, but the knowledge that we were prepared to do it strengthened the campaign for our candidate.

George Doughty won the election for General Secretary by a comfortable margin. He remained in office until his retirement. He served for many years on the General Council of the TUC and the Executive Council of the Confederation of Shipbuilding and Engineering Unions. He was a good general secretary, always competent in the area of industrial relations, responsive to the wishes of the membership, loyal to their interests and a consistent supporter of progressive causes. His interests were centred on collective bargaining and, though a supporter of the Labour left, I do not think he ever found much inspiration in the Labour Party conference.

The majority of the lay members on the Executive Committee of the AESD were not pleased with the outcome of the election for a new General Secretary. They made their displeasure apparent in a number of ways during the following two or three years. Some of them felt that, as a national official, I should not have entered into the campaign in support of George Doughty and that I should not have spoken in the conference debate.

Nevertheless, the momentum of events was now flowing in favour of the policies advocated by those who had supported the election of the new General Secretary. This was particularly true in respect of the industrial policy of the union. A vigorous attitude was taken in support of members' claims on pay and conditions. There were national claims affecting all members employed in constituent firms of the employers' federations, but even more important were the claims which were submitted at factory level. These claims were pressed through the negotiating procedure. Usually concessions were won which were accepted by the membership. If a satisfactory settlement was not secured, it was open to the members to seek official support for strike action.

There was no shortage of such requests, and when official

127

support was given a generous rate of strike benefit was paid. The union had an extraordinary record of success in such disputes. They often lasted a number of weeks because at the outset the employer felt that his production was not seriously affected by a drawing office strike. A feature of nearly all AESD official strikes was that they were very effectively organised, with disciplined peaceful picketing, sympathetic support from other members of the union and well-produced posters.

Throughout the 1950s I was acting as the secretary of the national publicity committee of the union, and I was often called upon to speak at strike meetings or to help in publicising the efforts being made by members. The union's journal, *The Draughtsman*, which I edited, carried regular reports of disputes in which members were engaged.

Among the strikes which I particularly remember during this period were those in the London area. They included strikes at Duple's, which lasted for 17 weeks, at Bechtel-Wimpey in the City of London, which lasted for nearly 5 months, at Middlesex Tool and Gauge, which lasted for 5 weeks, at Handley Page, from early November 1953 to near the end of February 1954, at Technicolour and at all the factories of the De Havilland group of companies. The De Havilland dispute led to the appointment by the Minister of Labour of a court of enquiry. There was also the campaign around the national one-day engineering stoppage in 1953 and a campaign of mass meetings for the recognition of the AESD on behalf of drawing office workers in the iron and steel industry. There were many other disputes during the 1950s, but my memory of some of them is less clear.

In the Handley Page dispute there was an efficiency of organisation of the highest standard. It was largely due to the influence of the leading personality in the strike, Bill Court. There were regular rotas for picketing, for the provision of refreshments, for the preparation of posters, for publicity efforts and for cleaning the strike headquarters. Regular mass meetings of the strikers were held so that everyone was kept informed of developments. The strike led to a satisfactory settlement. Bill Court was an active left-wing member of the

Labour Party and stood unsuccessfully as a Labour candidate in the 1955 General Election. He was also elected to the Executive Committee of the union. He later emigrated to one of the newly independent African states.

The De Havilland dispute centred on a claim for increased holidays. It embraced all the De Havilland factories in different parts of Britain. I was allocated by the union to work with the members at the engine factory at Edgware. There was a high level of trade union organisation among the technical staff, and there were no problems in making the strike effective. I was with the members almost every day during the dispute and was impressed by the manner in which the strike was conducted.

It was during the De Havilland dispute that I first met Reg Birch, who was a prominent member of the AEU. He was at that time a shop steward in the toolroom at the De Havilland engine factory. He was later to become a full-time Executive Council member of the AEU. He stood unsuccessfully for the Presidency of the AEU, but in his time he was considered to be one of the most influential members of the rank-and-file policy-making body of the AEU, the National Committee. I was to know him for many years afterwards, particularly when I was chairman of ACAS. He died some years ago during his retirement.

Reg spoke with a strong London accent and there was no mistaking his working-class background. He was unexcitable in manner and courteous in his personal dealings. Beneath this cool and courteous style there was a very sharp mind and strength of purpose. He was at one time a member of the Communist Party, but then disagreed with his communist colleagues on matters concerning trade unionism and on international issues. He broke away and was associated with a small group sympathetic, for a period, to China and Albania.

Plan for Engineering

Throughout the 1950s the Confederation of Shipbuilding and Engineering Unions advocated what was known as the Plan for Engineering. This had its origin in the late 1940s, and the thinking behind it was that public intervention was necessary in parts of the engineering industry if a high level of efficiency were to be attained. The required level of investment and structural change would not, it was said, be secured if the industry were to be left dependent on private ownership and market forces. Support for the introduction of economic planning into the industry, including a measure of public ownership, came from the Amalgamated Engineering Union, the main union in engineering, and from a number of other unions based mainly on skilled workers.

The basic ideas behind the Plan for Engineering were also strongly supported by the General Secretary of the CSEU, Gavin Martin, and the President, Harry Brotherton of the Sheet Metal Workers' Union. Gavin Martin had the responsibility to develop the ideas of the Plan and to ensure that they were put forward as a draft. He was a former official of the Boilermakers' Society who had earlier worked in the Caledon Shipyard in Dundee. He could be best described as a 'responsible militant'. He had little sympathy for the right-wing leadership of the Labour Party, and I gained the impression that as a young man he had been influenced by the Socialist Labour Party, one of the organisations which had helped to form the Communist Party. He disapproved of the existence of the Communist Party, which he regarded as a breakaway political organisation, though he was not hostile to individual communists to be found among the leaders of the engineering unions. When he was given a cigar at a social function he sometimes said that he would pass it on to Harry Pollitt, the Communist Party leader. Pollitt, like Gavin Martin, was a former boilermaker. Gavin knew him well from the days when they were both active in the union. He had a high regard for Pollitt's abilities and capacity for leadership, but he felt that he had wasted these talents when he became a full-time worker for the Communist Party. I think Gavin was of the view that if Pollitt had remained within the mainstream of the movement he would have been a strong candidate to become General Secretary of the Boilermakers' Society.

In the late 1940s and the early 1950s Gavin Martin, with the consent of the AESD, asked me to prepare draft documents for the Plan for Engineering. I was a delegate to the quarterly meetings of the CSEU – the General Council, to give it its formal title – and I was elected and re-elected for a number of years to the Standing Orders Committee of the CSEU. I spent many hours with Gavin Martin talking about the problems of the engineering and shipbuilding industries. There was no doubt that his was the guiding hand in the development of the Plan for Engineering.

The Plan for Engineering was drafted and re-drafted over a number of years. It consisted of a collection of documents. They were later published both by the CSEU and, as a booklet, by the AESD. Many thousands of copies of the AESD booklet were sold, including bulk orders for other unions. The main recommendations of the Plan for Engineering were that the air-frame, aero-engine and machine tool industries should be brought under public ownership. The Plan pointed out that aircraft manufacture was heavily dependent on State funding but that the existing competing firms were too small to keep abreast of world competition. The options were that there should be either a larger private monopoly or public ownership. The Plan was in favour of public ownership.

In relation to the machine tool industry the Plan pointed to its importance for the future of the entire engineering industry. Engineering firms were dependent upon machine tool manufacturers for their productive equipment. Unfortunately, far too many British machine tool manufacturers were small and lacked the necessary funds to specialise in advanced equipment. The Plan urged that selected firms in the industry should be brought under public ownership and should develop both standard ranges of machine tools and specialised equipment. In the final stages of the Plan much of the work on the machine tool industry was carried out in the research department of the AEU, where the head of research was George Aitken, one-time prominent member of the International Brigade in the Spanish War. His son, Ian Aitken, who became a well-known journalist, was a research worker for a period with the CSEU.

The Plan for Engineering also examined the problems and prospects of a number of other sections of the industry, including heavy electrical equipment, agricultural machinery, builders' castings and metal fittings, coal mining machinery, locomotive and wagon manufacture and repair, motor vehicle manufacture, radio manufacture, textile machinery and founding. It made various recommendations, short of public ownership, to strengthen these sections of industry. All the recommendations required public intervention.

Closely related to the Plan for Engineering were the proposals of the CSEU for the maritime industries: shipbuilding, ship repair, marine engineering and shipping. Gavin Martin took a strong interest in the development of these proposals and drew on his extensive knowledge of the problems of the maritime industries. I drafted most of the documents under the guidance of Gavin and, at an earlier stage, of Sir John Stephenson, who at that time was the General Secretary of the Plumbers' Union. John Stephenson was a former Tyneside shipbuilding worker who later became a chairman of a regional Gas Board. At a later date both Ted Hill and Danny McGarvey, as principal officials of the Boilermakers' Society, took a strong interest in the proposals for the maritime industries. Ted Hill was a former ship repair worker from London, and Danny McGarvey a shipbuilding worker from Clydebank.

The CSEU's proposals for the maritime industries outlined the main problems facing shipping and shipbuilding. These problems included the growth of world shipbuilding capacity, the demand for giant oil tankers, 'flags of convenience', subsidies of various kinds in different countries, the changing techniques of ship construction and the need for more space in shipyards for modern methods of construction. It was argued that the violent fluctuations from year to year in shipbuilding activity could not be overcome unless some stability could be achieved in the flow of orders received from shipowners. Replacement orders, said the CSEU, should be based on long-term requirements and not on short-term considerations. The

CSEU urged that the maritime industries should be brought under public ownership.

Unfortunately, the Plan for Engineering did not win the support of the wider trade union and labour movement, particularly in the earlier years. Its strongest opponent was Arthur Deakin, the then General Secretary of the Transport and General Workers' Union. He denounced it in abusive terms. I think it fair to comment that his opposition was not based upon reasoned argument but on his perception of insidious left-wing influence within the engineering and shipbuilding unions. After the death of Arthur Deakin the TGWU took a much more sympathetic attitude towards the proposals of the Plan for Engineering.

Throughout the 1950s I spoke with others at CSEU annual conferences, at the TUC, and at many weekend schools and branch meetings in favour of the Plan for Engineering. Eventually the wider movement supported the proposals for the public ownership of the aircraft and shipbuilding industries. By that time, however, the problems had grown.

In retrospect, the Plan for Engineering, so fiercely denounced at the time by Arthur Deakin and opposed by most of the right-wing leaders of the movement, was a very modest set of proposals. It should have been more radical and more ambitious. The failure to tackle many of the problems of the engineering industry contributed to the decline of British manufacturing in the 1980s and to the growth of the balance of payments deficit.

Wider Interests

The draughtsmen's union was affiliated to an international organisation known as the International Federation of Commercial, Clerical and Technical Employees. At one of the international meetings it was decided to establish a committee to gather information about pay and working conditions in the participating countries of Western Europe. I was nominated to serve on the committee.

133

It proved to be, from my point of view, one of the most productive committees on which I have ever served. We met in rotation in the capitals or main cities of the participating countries. This itself was very helpful because we were able to use the opportunity to visit big industrial establishments. Even more important was the large amount of comparative information which we were able to assemble. It was an eye-opening exercise.

I do not now remember the details of our findings, but I recall the main impression that they left with me. It was that Britain was being overtaken by a number of other countries, and that the Scandinavian countries, particularly Sweden, were already well ahead. Britain's workers were not as well off, in comparative terms, as was often assumed. The British press had contributed to a widespread but largely false assumption that working conditions in Britain were better than in the other leading industrial countries of Western Europe.

My visits to Sweden, both then and subsequently, influenced my outlook. When I first went to Scandinavia I was sceptical of the praise always given to the Swedes, Danes and Norwegians by the then General Secretary of our union, James Young. I soon learnt otherwise. His complimentary observations were justified. In each of the Scandinavian countries there was and is a high level of trade union organisation among technical staff, relatively good conditions, and many employment laws and practices which seemed to me to be in advance of Britain.

A colleague on some of these European visits was Clive Jenkins. I had known him from the time when he was a very young trade union official. He is a person with exceptional talents. He was always capable of seeing opportunities in situations where most of us see only problems. He had a flair for publicity during his many years as a trade union leader and set himself the most ambitious objectives. He enjoyed pursuing them. Some trade unionists criticised his style. I certainly would not deny that his style was unique in the trade union movement, but I always felt that on fundamentals he had strong socialist convictions which he put forward quite fearlessly.

Clive and I collaborated in writing two books, both published by Robert Maxwell's Pergamon Press. I do not think Clive would object to my claiming that I did most of the drafting, but he had the talent to introduce certain vivid passages which illuminated my more pedestrian style. In subsequent years he made an outstanding contribution to the growth of the Association of Scientific, Technical and Managerial Staff. Our early visits to other countries, and to Sweden in particular, influenced our thinking about trade unionism and the rights of working people.

Another committee on which I served which had a significant outcome was one established by an organisation then known as the National Federation of Professional Workers. This organisation was badly named. It was in reality an organisation of white-collar trade unions, the overwhelming majority of whose members were employed persons. They were neither self-employed nor members of the traditional liberal professions. The NFPW did not exist in opposition to the TUC; most of its affiliated unions were also affiliated to the TUC. I served later for a period as the President of the NFPW on the nomination of the AESD.

The NFPW established a committee to examine the economic arguments surrounding the suggestions then being made that the minimum age at which the standard rate of retirement pension became payable should be increased. A recommendation to this effect was put forward by an official committee of enquiry appointed by the Government to review the economic and financial problems involved in providing for old age. The official committee of inquiry recommended that the minimum age for men should be increased to 68 for men and to 63 for women. They also urged that tax relief should not be granted to occupational superannuation schemes with lower minimum pension ages than those fixed for the purpose of National Insurance.

The reason put forward for these recommendations was that over the following 25 years the number of elderly people in the

135

community would rise rapidly. Ever more resources, it was said, would be necessary to maintain them at a satisfactory standard of living. The weakness of this argument was that it took no account of the likely growth in the national income over this same period. The growth in the output of goods and services would not only provide for the growth in the number of pensioners at the existing standard of living but would be sufficient to provide rising living standards for the whole community.

Another argument which seemed to me to be relevant was that any compulsory extension of the length of working life might increase the future level of unemployment. I did not share the view of those, whether in the Conservative Party or the Labour Party, who assumed that the problem of unemployment within capitalism had been solved for all time. I wrote an editorial article for *The Draughtsman* which pointed out that if the capitalist system lurched into another slump, as it had always done periodically in the past, there would be widespread unemployment, and 'it would be ludicrous to flood the labour market with tens of thousands of men and women over 65 and 60'. I concluded that if the recommendations of the official committee of inquiry in favour of increasing National Insurance retirement ages were implemented it would represent 'an unwarrantable and extremely serious attack on the social services'.

At the 1954 TUC the draughtsmen's union put down a motion recognising that 'in certain circumstances and subject to safeguards employees should be permitted to work beyond the normal retirement age providing they are fit and willing to do so'. The motion went on, however, to affirm that any general move by employers or the State to extend the age of retirement should be opposed. I moved the motion on behalf of the union. Surprisingly, the General Council of the TUC decided to oppose the motion and put up Miss Godwin, the General Secretary of the Clerical and Administrative Workers, to speak on their behalf. She said that I had brought a nineteenth-century mind to a twentieth-century problem. We were now past the time, she added, when 'hard work, long hours and low wages made a man old in his fifties'. Men and women should have the right to continue in employment while they had the capacity and the desire to do so.

When replying to the debate, I again drew attention to the wording of the motion. It did not urge compulsory retirement in all circumstances but insisted that citizens should have a right to expect to retire at not later than 65 years of age. This expectation should be coupled with an expectation of retirement in reasonable comfort. The motion was carried against the recommendation of the General Council by 5,156,000 votes to 2,794,000.

In a subsequent debate in the House of Commons the attitude of the Conservative Minister of Pensions and National Insurance, Mr Osbert Peake, was rather better than that of the main Opposition speaker, Dr Edith Sumerskill. The Minister said that his study of the question had made him more and more sceptical about any gain to the national economy by raising the minimum retirement age. Dr Sumerskill was much less definite in her views. Fortunately there were other participants in the debate, notably Mr Ellis Smith MP, who emphasised that the Labour Party should not agree to any increase in the retirement age.

In August 1957 the Conservative Government established a Council on Prices, Productivity and Incomes. It was sometimes known as the 'Three Wise Men' or, more properly, as the Cohen Council, after its Chairman, Lord Cohen. It was to report on movements in the national economy with a view to encouraging a policy of restraint. It had no statutory powers to intervene in collective bargaining. It reported early in 1958.

In a front page statement in *The Draughtsman* I said that, in effect, the report of the Cohen Council had argued that there should be no interference with profits and dividends but that wage earners should accept a cut in living standards. Their thinking was that nobody should be shocked by a rise in unemployment and that the economy could not work efficiently without a margin of unemployment. There should be no price control, subsidies should be abolished and rent restrictions

137

should go. I said that these dangerous conceptions were now fashionable among the ruling circles in Britain.

The General Council of the TUC strongly criticised the Cohen Council report. It said that its conclusions were one-sided and partisan. The Cohen Council report urged wage restraint while, at the same time, encouraging higher dividends. The TUC did not cooperate with the Cohen Council.

I was active in the Labour Party both in the opening years and the closing years of the 1950s, but my exclusion from the Party in 1953 led me to concentrate my political activity in other directions. I remained as secretary of the Hounslow branch of the Cooperative Party and, as the representative of the draughtsmen's union, played an active role in the Union of Democratic Control.

International Issues

When the Korean war started in June 1950 I opposed it. I did not support Britain's participation in a war which, it was claimed, was in support of a United Nations' decision to condemn and resist aggression by North Korea against South Korea. In my view, the decision of the Security Council had not been taken in accordance with the requirements of the UN Charter. It did not receive the concurring votes of the five permanent members of the Security Council, as required by the Charter. The Soviet Union had absented herself from the proceedings, and China was supposedly represented not by the government in effective control of the country but by a defeated rump in Taiwan protected by the USA.

Of equal importance were the circumstances surrounding the outbreak of the war. Throughout the Far East, following the end of the Second World War, there was popular pressure for social change. This movement embraced China, Korea, Malaya, the Philippines, Indonesia and the countries of Indo-China, including Vietnam. It extended throughout Asia, above all into India and Burma. Where the old imperialist powers considered themselves strong enough, they resisted the changes or sought to accommodate them within a political framework acceptable to their interests. In India the Labour Government had the good sense to recognise the inevitable and to agree to self-government.

Korea had been occupied by Japan. It had provided a launching base for the Japanese invasion of China in the 1930s. US influence had prevented the kind of social change in South Korea which had taken place in North Korea. Soviet influence had helped to sustain a communist dictatorship in North Korea. In other words, the events in Korea could not be considered in isolation from the broad sweep of historical change in the Far East and in Asia.

When, in the course of the Korean war, the US President alluded to the possibility of using atomic weapons, the British Prime Minister, Clement Attlee, flew to Washington to seek assurances that they would not be used. When UN troops – under the command of the very reactionary General Douglas MacArthur – crossed into North Korea the Chinese intervened with military force. The war did not end until the summer of 1953. It achieved nothing. Tens of thousands of lives were lost. It was a costly military episode to be set within the context of the social changes in the Far East, US resistance to the recognition of the new China and the Cold War between the USA and the Soviet Union. My attitude to the war throughout was influenced by the policy of India, which pressed constantly for negotiations to stop the fighting.

In 1952 the annual delegate conference of the AESD carried a resolution calling for the ending of hostilities in Korea, Indo-China and Malaya. It also urged the Executive Committee to support organisations working for the ending of the Cold War. One consequence was that the union became affiliated to the Union of Democratic Control in which I began to play an active part as the union's representative. The UDC had existed for many years and was originally associated with the name of E.D. Morel, a one-time Liberal who later became a Labour MP. The UDC had a record of exposing the injustices of the imperialist powers in colonial countries. Morel, who died in 1924, did more than anyone to draw world attention to the atrocities of the Belgian colonialists in the Congo. He formed the Congo Reform Association in 1904.

At the time of my election to the Executive Committee of the UDC, the Chairman was Elwyn Jones MP. Many years later he became Lord Chancellor. Others who were actively associated with the UDC at various times in the 1950s were the MPs Fenner Brockway, Harold Davies, Tom Driberg, John Freeman, Leslie Hale, Walter Monslow, Ben Parkin and Reg Sorensen. Ritchie Calder, Dorothy Woodman, Preston Benson, Maurice Lichtig, Dr Guy Routh and Lt-Commander E.P. Young also served on the Executive Committee. Two other long-serving members of the EC were Barbara Drake and Catherine Marshall. Their support for progressive causes went back to the early days of the UDC. The Secretary of the UDC, and an author of many of its publications, was Basil Davidson. His speciality was Africa, on which he became a world authority. He was succeeded as Secretary by Audrey Jupp, whose untiring efforts helped to maintain the UDC for some years despite mounting financial problems caused by the declining market for pamphlets and the impossibility of producing them at low prices.

The UDC was mainly a pamphleteering organisation. It published usually about six pamphlets each year, with a total sale of about 60,000. These were the years when it was still possible economically to arrange for the regular publication and sale of pamphlets within the labour movement. All the pamphlets were on international issues, including African problems, the Far East, the Arab world, German rearmament, British Guiana and Greece. The UDC also provided speakers for about 120 local meetings each year. In the middle 1950s I became the Chairman of the UDC and the editor of its publications.

In 1954 the UDC launched a petition against proposals for the rearmament of Germany. The sponsors included Aneurin Bevan, Lord Boyd Orr, Professor G.D.H. Cole, the Rev Donald Soper, Harold Wilson and the General Secretary of the AESD, George Doughty. Many thousands of signatures

140

were collected, including signatures from members in almost every branch of the AESD.

In 1954 and 1955 I argued strongly against German rearmament in a succession of editorial articles in *The Draughtsmen*. The monthly circulation of the magazine had by then risen to just under 65,000. In February 1954 I said that behind the new German armed forces stood the same reactionary, nationalist and big business interests that prepared the way for Hitler and provided the main support for fascism. Why was it that the House of Krupp had been restored? The article continued:

'Despite its support for Hitlerism, despite its worldwide reputation as a merchant of death, and despite its employment of thousands of slave workers during the war, it is again a powerful force in the German economy.'

Herr Alfred Krupp had been convicted as a war criminal at the Nuremberg trials.

A statement issued in support of the UDC petition against German rearmament put forward an alternative policy. It said that none of the Great Powers should seek an ally in German militarism. Instead, neither East nor West Germany should be allowed to rearm or enter into military alliances. Agreement should be sought for the unification of Germany on the basis of free elections and the withdrawal of all occupation troops. The Great Powers should then guarantee the integrity of the frontiers of a united Germany as well as the frontiers of Germany's neighbours. Germany should be allowed a limited national force subject to UN inspection and control.

At the TUC and the Labour Party conference in 1954 the main issue was that of German rearmament. The majority of the leaders were in favour of German rearmament, arguing that it was essential to build up the defence forces of Western Europe, with a controlled contribution from West Germany. Support for German rearmament, with what it was claimed were safeguards against the re-emergence of German militarism, was carried by narrow majorities.

In the late summer of 1954 Ron Huzzard and I represented

the AESD at a conference in Germany on the social and economic foundations of peace. One of the speakers at the conference was Harold Wilson. Delegates were present from 13 countries. Many Germans were also present. We reported to our union that, almost without exception, the Germans to whom we had spoken expressed concern at the re-emergence of strongly right-wing elements in German public life. They attributed this not only to the influence of the Adenauer Government but also to the encouragement given by the United States' occupying authorities. The Germans at the conference wanted the reunification of their country. They opposed the system of political control in East Germany, but supported many of the social and economic measures in the East, including the break-up of the big private estates and the introduction of welfare schemes.

Ron Huzzard and I brought back to Britain examples of reactionary military magazines which we had bought on German bookstalls. We also reported on a rally of the Steel Helmet organisation which had taken place whilst we were in Germany. It had been addressed by Field Marshal Kesselring, who a few years earlier had been condemned to death as a war criminal but was subsequently released. Kesselring attacked the Soviet Union, praised the USA and claimed that Germans were the finest soldiers. He predicted that German power would become the basis for new policies in Europe.

In 1953 I went for the first time to the Soviet Union and acted as the chairman of a delegation of trade unionists drawn from different unions. We visited Moscow, Stalingrad (now Volgograd), Rostov-on-Don, Sochi on the Black Sea and Gagri in Georgia. We had an interview with Shvernik, the President of the Soviet Union. We travelled nearly 5,000 miles and visited a number of factories.

My general impression of the Soviet Union was that the standard of living was lower than in Britain, but in all the places we visited there were signs of progress. A great amount of construction was being undertaken, although there was still an acute housing shortage. There was an impressive effort to develop social service facilities and cultural activities, centred often on large factories. The standard of the shops was much below that of Britain. In making these comparisons, the backwardness of Tsarist Russia and the destruction caused by war had to be kept in mind. As events many years later were to prove, however, the burden of armaments and the absence of effective democracy brought to a halt the social progress which had been made. The system disintegrated under these pressures and failings.

My exclusion from individual membership of the Labour Party gave some of my opponents in the union an opportunity to prevent my standing in an election for a national committee to recommend the selection of candidates for the union's parliamentary panel. Up to that time I had been successful for a number of years in being elected to the committee. At the 1954 annual conference of the union another full-time official of the union moved from the floor, and without notice, that only individual members of the Labour Party should be eligible to stand in the election. I rose immediately on a point of order. Such a proposition, I said, was contrary to the rules. No decision of the conference could take away from a member the right which he possessed under the rules to stand for office. The President of the union did not accept my point of order. The motion was duly put and carried. I was excluded from the election.

Later in the same conference the President of the union made a personal statement to the effect that, though he had given his ruling in good faith, he now felt that there was some element of doubt about it. He was therefore going to ask the Executive Committee to look at the matter during the forthcoming year. In the following months the Executive Committee sought Counsel's opinion on the issue. The opinion was clear: under the rules as written, the right of members to stand for election could not be taken away on political grounds, providing they were otherwise eligible for election. My right to stand in such elections was restored, and in subsequent years I was again successful in being elected to the selection committee for the parliamentary panel. I was also able to point out – though it did not affect my right under the rules – that I was not a member of any political party that ran candidates in opposition to the Labour Party. The Cooperative Party, of which I was a member, had an electoral agreement with the Labour Party.

The C.S.E.U.

In 1957 the General Secretary of the Confederation of Shipbuilding and Engineering Unions, Gavin Martin, retired from office. He had been a very good trade union official, but in his final years had been handicapped by illness. He died in 1958. I wrote an obituary article about him which pointed out that no-one had ever been in any doubt as to where he stood. He was a champion of the interests of the working class. His experience had given him a belief in the effectiveness of workshop action, but he acted with a sense of responsibility towards the interests of workers. He would not agree to the dissipation of their energies in a fruitless struggle. He knew what it meant for a worker's family to go short of the means of life.

Gavin Martin and Harry Brotherton, the President of the CSEU for many years, did much to enhance the prestige of the organisation. Engineering and shipbuilding were important for the British economy, and the unions were influential. Unlike the TUC, the CSEU had a negotiating role with employers on the pay and conditions of hundreds of thousands of workers.

Five candidates were nominated to follow Gavin Martin as General Secretary of the CSEU. Each affiliated union, and there were more than 30 of them, was entitled to make a nomination. The five nominated candidates were Maurice Kidd, the Assistant General Secretary, George Barratt of the AEU, Danny McGarvey of the Boilermakers' Society, Harry Urwin of the TGWU, and myself from the AESD. Each union was entitled to cast a vote equal to its affiliated membership. If no candidate secured an outright majority on the first ballot, the top two were to go to a second ballot.

The block voting system for the CSEU was probably as fair

144

as any system likely to be devised. Unions with the largest affiliated membership had the largest vote. This meant in reality that the AEU, because of its large affiliated membership, had to win the support of only one other medium-sized union to carry the day. Indeed, the AEU deliberately affiliated on less than its total membership so that it did not totally dominate the voting.

The result of the first ballot was:

Barratt (AEU)	500,000
Kidd (Assistant General Secretary)	315,688
Mortimer (AESD)	184,867
McGarvey (Boilermakers)	140,000
Urwin (TGWU)	104,000

George Barratt, the AEU nominee, secured the vote of only his own union in the first ballot. Nevertheless, it was sufficient for him to top the poll. Three of the candidates, McGarvey, Urwin and myself, were all regarded as being on the left.

In the second ballot nearly all the unions swung behind Maurice Kidd, the Assistant General Secretary of the CSEU. It was not, however, sufficient to give him victory. One other medium-sized union voted with the AEU. The result was:

Barratt (AEU)	626,867
Kidd (Assistant General Secretary)	617,688

The candidate who secured the least number of votes in the first ballot, Harry Urwin, went on to become in later years the Assistant General Secretary of the TGWU and one of the most prominent leaders of the TUC. He was a trade unionist of outstanding ability.

I was sorry not to have succeeded in the election for General Secretary of the CSEU. I had never been much motivated by personal ambition, but of all the elections in which I have stood, both before and since, this was the one I would have preferred to win. I had a strong interest in the pursuit of trade unionism in engineering and shipbuilding.

I had earlier been repeatedly defeated in elections for the General Council of the TUC. I was nominated by the AESD each year between 1950 and 1957, but never came anywhere near to being elected. These were years when it was almost impossible for a left-wing candidate from a relatively small union to succeed. In 1958 the AESD, quite rightly in my view, changed its nomination to George Doughty. George's point of view was similar to my own on many issues, but he was the General Secretary of the union. George was finally elected to the General Council, ten years later, in 1968, when there had been a change in influence in the TUC. A new trade group was created for electoral purposes, and it covered technicians. George Doughty won this new seat.

Within the Wider Movement

After rejoining the Labour Party I became active not only as chairman of the ward organisation and as a delegate to General Committee of the constituency Party where I lived, but also in a national organisation of Labour Party members known as Victory for Socialism. I served on the Executive Committee of this organisation. The main purpose of VFS was to reaffirm in contemporary terms the case for socialism and to seek to influence the Labour Party to take a more socialist direction. Among its prominent members were a number of Members of Parliament, including Sidney Silverman, Fred Messer and Stephen Swingler. Some of the members of the Executive Committee were also prospective parliamentary candidates and later were elected to Parliament.

VFS played a modest but important role in demonstrating that the domination of the right, around Hugh Gaitskell and a number of trade union leaders, had not eliminated more radical thinking within the Party. The control exerted by the right was formidable, and it was not exercised with generosity towards those who took a different view. Aneurin Bevan, for example, had the Whip withdrawn from him for a period by the Parliamentary Labour Party, and narrowly avoided expul-

146

sion from the Party. It was a measure of the strength of right-wing influence among the unions that at the 1955 annual conference of the Labour Party, Hugh Gaitskell defeated Aneurin Bevan for the treasurership of the Party by a more than four to one majority. The voting was 5,475,000 to 1,222,000. The election of Frank Cousins as General Secretary of the TGWU in 1957 was, however, an indication of changes to come.

Within the constituency organisations of the Labour Party the right were not dominant in the 1950s. In the elections for the constituency section of the National Executive Committee of the Party, candidates associated with the views of Aneurin Bevan were more successful than candidates from the right of the Party. In the Parliamentary Labour Party, on the other hand, supporters of Bevan were always in a minority. After the resignation of Attlee in the mid-1950s as leader of the Party, Gaitskell was elected to succeed him. In a vote of the Parliamentary Labour Party he won by a comfortable margin over both Bevan and Morrison. At that time only members of the Parliamentary Labour Party were eligible to vote in the election for the leader, but it was also known that Gaitskell had the support of the majority of the leaders of the big unions. The argument advanced by those who supported the right was that their policies were essential to make Labour electorally attractive. Yet at the 1955 General Election the Conservative Party secured the highest proportion of the total vote – 49.7 per cent of any party in any General Election since 1945. In the 1959 General Election the Conservative Party were returned with a substantially increased majority over Labour, even though their total share of the national vote declined marginally. There was a sharp increase in the Liberal vote. Labour's very 'moderate' policies and the Party's move towards the centre did not bring success. They served to confirm the prejudices of marginal voters against Labour, whilst simultaneously dampening the enthusiasm of many Labour Party members.

The death in 1959 of Professor G.D.H. Cole took from the British labour movement a man for whom I had the greatest

147

admiration. He was more than an outstanding scholar and teacher; he was also an active participant on behalf of progressive causes. I was fortunate, as recorded in an earlier chapter, to have been able to attend his lectures and seminars whilst I was a student at Ruskin College. When I became an official of the AESD I reviewed a number of his publications in *The Draughtsman* to try to encourage members to read his work. When Cole died I wrote an editorial article for *The Draughtsman* which paid tribute to his immense contribution to the cause of socialism.

Throughout the 1950s I took an active part in the work of the Labour Research Department, and served for a period as its Chairman. I was elected to the Executive Committee of the LRD as the nominee of the AESD. The LRD is an independent research organisation, funded almost entirely by affiliated trade unions. It is not part of the Labour Party. For a period it faced difficulty because it was proscribed by the Labour Party. This was later lifted. The AESD was one of the first unions to affiliate to the LRD after the 1914–18 war, and the affiliation continued throughout its existence. The LRD does a valuable job for trade unionism and deserves the wide support it now receives.

Part of my job as an official of the AESD was to act as secretary of its National Technical Committee. This committee was responsible for publishing technical booklets to assist draughtsmen and other technicians in their work. About eight new titles were published every year, and they achieved a wide circulation. For a number of years the annual sale of AESD technical booklets was about 100,000. The union claimed at the time to be the largest technical publisher in Britain. It was a self-financing project, even though the booklets were sold at prices much below normal commercial levels. The union was able to use its organisational structure, with its network of office committees in almost every engineering factory and shipyard in Britain, to provide a very economical chain of distribution. Many years later this technical publishing activity declined and was finally discontinued. Some manufacturers began to issue free technical publications about their own products and their engineering applications.

My main recollection of the 1950s is one of intense activity. For most of the period it was a difficult time for the left. The difficulties reflected the impact of the Cold War on Britain and the British labour movement. It was not until towards the end of the decade that a change of mood in the dominant top leadership of the TUC and the Labour Party began to develop. Despite some of the unfavourable external pressures, the left was able, nevertheless, to strengthen its influence inside the AESD. This was not due to any small group of individuals, and even less to any particular leader. It was attributable to the work of a substantial number of members in many parts of Britain whose views and experiences inclined them to the left. The policies which they advocated found a response among many thousands of rank-and-file members.

I estimate from my engagement diaries for the period, most of which I still possess, that during the 1950s I spoke at approximately 1,500 meetings, or roughly three per week. They included branch meetings of various unions, mainly of the AESD, union recruitment meetings, strike meetings, weekend schools, conferences of various kinds and meetings of political organisations. In 1959 my first full-length book was published, *A History of the Association of Engineering and Shipbuilding Draughtsmen*.

I was one of thousands in the 1950s who continued to argue for socialism and vigorous trade unionism and was not swept along in support of the Cold War. It is a role which I do not regret.

149

8

A Policy for Change

In the first half of the 1960s the main task of the left was to strive for a change in the economic and political direction of Britain. This had to be conducted on more than one front. The 1950s had been the years of Conservative rule. The Tory leaders claimed that the people 'had never had it so good'. Living standards for the great majority of the people had risen, but Britain's underlying problems had not been overcome.

Britain's rate of industrial expansion was among the worst in Europe in the 1950s. If Britain had kept pace with the rest of Europe, living standards could have been very much better than they were. The stop-go economic policy led to intermittent periods of stagnation and increased unemployment. Imports exceeded exports, and problems with the balance of payments and currency crises continued to dominate economic policy.

The Conservative view was, fundamentally, that the 'free market', based predominantly upon private ownership and the pursuit of profit, should be left to itself. Public spending should be kept strictly in check and direct taxation, particularly on the better-off, should be reduced. The lower the rate of direct taxation, so it was argued, the greater the incentive for the profit-seekers, and it was they who stimulated wealth creation.

The Conservative Government also spent billions of pounds for military purposes. Immense resources were allocated to the development of missiles and to nuclear weapons. Other West European countries, particularly West Germany, and Japan in the Far East, were specialising much more in civil production. If these Conservative policies were to be changed radically, it

150

was necessary also to shift to the left the policies of the labour movement. In 1951, when the Conservative Party came to power, there was a widespread feeling that, although Labour had secured a record number of votes, based upon fear of a return to Tory policies, the Party had run out of constructive ideas. It favoured 'consolidation'. This was later developed, by some leading Labour politicians, into theories about contemporary capitalism which appeared to accept that the problem of unemployment could be resolved by economic management but without any significant change in the pattern of industrial and commercial ownership. Socialism, they suggested, was not so much about ownership but about democracy and equality. Soon after the 1959 General Election Hugh Gaitskell, who was then the leader of the Labour Party, suggested that Clause IV of the Party's constitution, which called for the common ownership of the means of production, distribution and exchange, should be amended.

Thus the task of the left was not only to expose the deficiencies of Conservative rule but to affirm the need for and win support for effective economic planning, particularly to increase industrial investment, to extend public ownership, to improve the social services and to cut military expenditure, including the ending of the pretence that there was, or should be, an 'independent British nuclear deterrent'. Without such policies or, at the very least, moves in their direction there was no possibility that Britain would surmount its fundamental economic problems. Nor was there much likelihood of a Labour Government. Fortunately, in the years between 1959 and 1964 some progress was made in shifting the labour movement to the left. This shift was not dramatic, and there were reverses as well as advances.

All these issues were discussed and argued about inside the Draughtsmen's Association. The debate was constant, but throughout the period the left won the votes of the majority of the delegates on most issues at the annual conferences of the union. The point of view of the union was then projected into the debates of the wider trade union and labour movement. I played a part in this effort.

In the June 1960 issue of *The Draughtsman* I used the occasion of a review of a new pamphlet, *Socialism for the 1960s* by John Hughes, published by *Tribune*, to argue against the attempt by Hugh Gaitskell to revise the Party's constitution. In supporting the views of John Hughes, the review said that the real question was not whether Labour should nationalise every pub and cigarette shop but whether public or private ownership was to be dominant in the economy. Was our society to be run first and foremost by reference to real social needs, on the basis of economic planning and the public ownership of the more important industries, or was its functioning to be determined by the profit-making considerations of private ownership?

The review went on:

'The case, then, for a socialist policy in the 1960s is not just a question of listing more industries for public ownership. It is primarily one of re-shaping our economic system so that effective economic planning for social needs, with the subordination of private profit, becomes possible. For this, the social ownership of the commanding sections of the economy is essential. Only then can we plan for social need; provide for a sustained and balanced growth of the economy without the lurchings that are all too characteristic of capitalism; pay proper regard to social costs and social benefits that do not enter into the accounts of private firms; develop research on a much more extensive scale; overcome the great inequalities between earned and unearned income which exist because of the private ownership of industry; and provide for the real democratic participation of workers in the control of industry.'

There were many other trade unionists who spoke out in defence of Clause IV. They saw it as symbolic of the socialist commitment of the Labour Party. Hugh Gaitskell and those who supported his view on the need to amend the constitution were surprised at the opposition which they had aroused. They dropped their proposal.

Nuclear Disarmament

In 1960 there was another reverse for the leadership of the Labour Party. The Party conference carried a resolution in favour of unilateral nuclear disarmament. The decisive factor was the swing of trade union votes, led by the Transport and General Workers' Union. At the 1960 TUC a similar decision, rejecting 'any defence policy based on the threat of the use of strategic or tactical nuclear weapons', was carried by 4,356,000 votes to 3,213,000. The Congress also carried, however, by a majority of 690,000, a statement from the General Council of the TUC which argued that whilst in future the British contribution to the Western armoury should be in conventional weapons, the provision of the Western strategic deterrent should be left to the Americans. The statement also opposed the establishment of Thor missile bases in Britain and said that the West should never be the first to use the H-bomb.

Hugh Gaitskell spoke strongly against the commitment to unilateral nuclear disarmament and promised to 'fight, fight and fight again' to reverse it. He succeeded, and in 1961 both the Labour Party conference and the TUC accepted Britain's possession of nuclear weapons. Support was given to a joint declaration made in February 1961 by the General Council of the TUC, the National Executive Committee of the Labour Party and the Parliamentary Labour Party, stating that the West could not renounce nuclear weapons so long as the Communist bloc possessed them, that Britain should remain a member of NATO, and that, as a loyal member of the NATO alliance, Britain could not oppose on principle the establishment of Allied bases on her territory. The statement also called for negotiations for disarmament and no first use of the H-bomb.

The Draughtsmen's Association was consistently in support of the renunciation of nuclear weapons. This policy was endorsed by the delegates at successive annual conferences of the union. The General Secretary, George Doughty, spoke in the TUC debates both in 1960 and 1961. In an editorial article in the January 1961 issue of *The Draughtsman* I asked why it was that every Conservative newspaper in Britain was on the side of Hugh Gaitskell and his supporters in their fight against the 1960 Labour conference decision on defence and nuclear weapons. The answer, the article said, was not because they wanted a Labour Government but because they wanted no effective challenge to Tory policy.

At trade union branch and CND meetings, and in articles in *The Draughtsman*, I spoke and wrote in favour of unilateral nuclear disarmament. My point of view rested on a number of main propositions. The first was that nuclear weapons were intended for the mass annihilation of the civil population. In a nuclear war millions of people would be killed in the most horrific manner, without any pretence that they constituted a military target. I could not conceive of circumstances which could justify the use of such weapons. Secondly, if there were any case at all for the mutual deterrence of nuclear weapons it applied only to the then two superpowers, the USA and the USSR. The case could not be extended to other powers, including Britain. It was hypocritical for Britain to argue for its own nuclear weapons but to press for non-proliferation in relation to others.

Thirdly, there was no effective defence for Britain in nuclear war. Her highly congested population made her the most vulnerable of targets. Hence, any threat by Britain to use nuclear weapons against the Soviet Union was, in reality, a threat to commit national suicide. Fourthly, Britain's claim to possess an 'independent nuclear deterrent' was a pretence. Britain was a nuclear weapons base for the USA. The nuclear warheads for the missiles based in Britain were in full US ownership, custody and control. Fifthly, the evidence was that the Soviet Union was determined to exercise its domination in the areas where the Red Army was in occupation following the defeat of fascism, but it did not seek military conquest in Western Europe. It was Aneurin Bevan who observed that communism constituted not a military threat to the West but a social challenge.

Finally, Britain's heavy expenditure on armaments and the development of nuclear weapons had contributed in no small

154

measure to her economic weakness. Resources which should have been used for civil production were instead being employed for military purposes. Britain was falling behind other industrialised countries.

Although the policy of unilateral nuclear disarmament had been reversed by the Labour Party and the TUC, the debate succeeded in raising the issues in public consciousness and strengthening the challenge to the bipartisan policy of support for NATO, for US policy and for American bases in Britain. This was reflected in the Labour Party's manifesto for the 1964 General Election. Labour challenged the very notion of an 'independent British deterrent'. Britain, said Labour, would be utterly dependent on the USA for the supply of Polaris missiles. The 'deterrent' would not be independent, it would not be British, and it would not deter. Labour also undertook to put forward proposals to stop the spread of nuclear weapons, to establish nuclear-free zones in Africa, Latin America and Central Europe, to stop the private sale of arms and to work to bring Communist China into its proper place in the United Nations.

Industrial Issues

The active struggle of the Draughtsmen's Association on wages and hours of work reached a new level of intensity in the first half of the 1960s. At every meeting of the Executive Committee requests were received for support from members in different engineering firms and shipyards for official strike action following the exhaustion of negotiations. For every dispute which reached this stage there were very many more where a negotiated settlement had been concluded.

Many thousands of members took part in one-day strikes in February and March 1962 in support of a national wage claim. A little later the members voted by 25,900 to 17,470 against a national strike. The alternative which was favoured was that the union should pursue its claim factory by factory and shipyard by shipyard. The significance of the voting figures for a national strike was that a higher proportion of AESD members voted for strike action than manual workers in a similar ballot of unions affiliated to the Confederation of Shipbuilding and Engineering Unions. The strategy of pursuing separate claims at individual establishments did much to stimulate rank-and-file activity and to increase the rate of recruitment to the union, even though in the majority of factories and shipyards the AESD already had a high density of membership.

In March 1960 the AESD concluded an agreement with the Engineering Employers' Federation for a reduced working week. Those previously employed on a 40-hour week had their hours reduced to 38½. There was then a scale of reductions for members whose working week was less than 40 hours. The effect of the agreement was that nearly everyone covered by AESD agreements in federated engineering firms had their basic week reduced to between 38½ and 37½ hours.

To coincide with the campaign for a reduced working week I wrote a pamphlet, published by *New Left Review*, entitled *The Forty Hour Week*. It carried a foreword by Ken Alexander. The pamphlet recalled that the claim for a 40-hour week went back to the 1880s. A strike for an 8-hour day in the United States had inspired the international labour movement to choose 1 May as a day of demonstrations for a shorter working week and for solidarity.

In Britain the unions succeeded after the First World War in establishing a basic 47- or 48-hour working week for most manual workers. Many white-collar workers had a shorter basic working week. In engineering drawing offices the usual basic working week was 41 hours. After the Second World War the basic hours of work for many manual workers were reduced first to 45 or 44, then to 42½ or thereabouts, and later to 40. There was then a movement to reduce hours below 40. In the late 1980s the engineering unions campaigned vigorously and successfully for a further reduction.

Despite the successes of the campaign for a shorter working week, the average hours worked in Britain for manual workers continued to be among the highest in Europe. The reason for this was the prevalence of regular overtime. Unfortunately, in Britain the employers usually resisted any attempt to establish the joint regulation of overtime. Instead they insisted that the control of overtime was a 'managerial prerogative'. The reality was that regular overtime working became in too many cases a cloak for inefficiency.

For the 1963 TUC the Draughtsmen's Association tabled a motion expressing support for the campaign for a shorter working week and longer holidays, and drawing attention to the progress being made in many other countries. This motion was composited with others on the same subject. The composite was moved by the Amalgamated Society of Woodworkers and seconded by the AESD. I spoke on behalf of the draughtsmen's delegation and emphasised that the development of the campaign required both effective arguments in presentation and rank-and-file pressure to achieve results. I recalled that the ILO had adopted its 40-hour week Convention as long ago as 1935, and in 1961 had accepted a further recommendation in favour of a shorter working week.

I referred also to the campaign for a shorter working week in other countries. In the USA progress was being made on claims for a working week of less than 40 hours. In the Soviet Union average hours of work were about 39½. In West Germany, despite her defeat in the war, agreement had been reached before Britain for a 40-hour week in engineering. In France the basic 40-hour week had been established under the Popular Front Government before the Second World War. Moreover, in most industrial countries the annual holiday entitlement of workers was better than in Britain. The campaign for a shorter working week expressed the common interests and solidarity of workers in all countries. The motion was carried without opposition.

In November 1963 I was included among a delegation of three from the Draughtsmen's Association to visit Sweden at the invitation of the Swedish Union of Clerical and Technical Employees. During the visit we went to an Ericsson telecommunications manufacturing factory, the Volvo plant near Gothenburg and two shipyards. The experience confirmed the favourable impression of Swedish conditions which I had formed in earlier visits. The delegation prepared a report stating that the standard of living of design staff in Sweden was significantly higher than in Britain. We also noted that a very high proportion of the workers in Swedish industry and commerce, including design staff, were trade union members. The Swedish Union of Clerical and Technical Employees in Industry was highly efficient, and the statistics which it produced were of great assistance in collective bargaining.

The pensions of salaried employees in Swedish industry were paid partly by the State and partly through a supplementary scheme negotiated through collective bargaining. The details of the scheme were complicated, but the net effect appeared to be that pensions were equivalent to 65 per cent of salary for salaried male employees of 65 years of age and salaried women employees of 60 years of age. An important provision was that pension rights were preserved on a change of employment from one firm to another. Pensions were automatically adjusted to keep in step with the cost of living.

In the autumn of 1964 the Draughtsmen's Association became involved in a bitter strike concerning the pension rights of members employed at Vickers-Armstrong (Shipbuilders) Ltd, Barrow. The dispute started with a claim for wage increases. The claim was taken through all stages of the negotiating machinery without agreement being reached. The union then gave notice of official strike action. The members withdrew their labour, and the firm then sacked them and terminated their membership of the pension scheme. The members were told that when they returned to work they would have to rejoin the pension scheme. Under the terms of the pension scheme a broken period of employment, even if only for a few weeks, could result in a much lower pension for a long-service employee than if continuous employment had been maintained.

The Draughtsmen's Association protested to the Shipbuilding Employers' Federation and made it clear that under no circumstances would they agree to a settlement which would prejudice the pension rights of members on strike. The

158

union pointed out that under the Contracts of Employment Act continuity of employment was not broken when a worker participated in an industrial dispute of which proper notice had been given. Members in other firms were asked not to work on drawings, contracts or components for Vickers-Armstrong (Shipbuilders).

The threat to pension rights in an industrial dispute was seen as a national issue by the membership. The response to the call for solidarity action was immediate and widespread. Members employed at Vickers-Armstrong (Shipbuilders) Ltd, Walker-on-the-Tyne, withdrew their labour in protest and demonstrations took place in other shipyards. Vickers' shipbuilding work was boycotted elsewhere in drawing and technical offices.

The strength of the protest movement against the threat to pension rights had the desired effect. The threat was withdrawn by Vickers-Armstrong (Shipbuilders) Ltd. Talks took place in London, and a settlement was reached. All-round pay increases were granted, together with assurances about pensions and bonuses.

The full-time divisional organiser of the AESD covering the Vickers shipbuilding dispute was Ken Gill. He was already showing the qualities of leadership which later led to him being elected as the General Secretary of the union. After the amalgamation of TASS with ASTMS Ken became the Joint General Secretary of MSF, and later, after the retirement of Clive Jenkins, he became the sole occupant of the office of General Secretary. Ken Gill served for many years on the General Council of the TUC and became the President of the Congress. He was one of the outstanding trade union leaders of his generation.

In an article on the Vickers' shipbuilding dispute Ken Gill asked: 'What would be the future if our members could be bludgeoned into docility by a threat to their future retirement?' He pointed to one of the important lessons of the dispute. It was that when there was solidarity the isolation of Barrow was shown to be a myth. Victory was secured after 14 weeks of strike action.

Rookes versus Barnard

In the first half of the 1960s the AESD was involved in a legal case, Rookes versus Barnard, which made trade union history. Damages were awarded against three members of the union for 'conspiring by unlawful means to induce British Overseas Airways Corporation to terminate the employment of a former member of the AESD, Mr D.E. Rookes.' The three members of the union were respectively the corresponding member (office steward) in the drawing office of BOAC at London Airport, Mr J. Fistal; the chairman of the local branch, Mr A.J. Barnard; and the full-time divisional organiser in West London, Mr R.J. Silverthorne.

Douglas Rookes was originally an active member of the AESD. Indeed, he was one of the representatives of the union who, in accordance with the established procedure, met BOAC to notify them that 100 per cent membership had been secured by voluntary action. The Corporation agreed that no action would be taken by them to prejudice this position.

In the second half of 1955 Douglas Rookes resigned from the union, not because it was too militant, but because he was dissatisfied that the union had not pursued vigorously enough a grievance concerning conditions in a new building to which the members had been transferred. He pressed for 'more direct action'. The union, with the support of the divisional organiser and the majority of the members, was seeking to negotiate a settlement. Douglas Rookes sought to persuade other members to join him in resigning from the union.

Efforts were made to persuade Douglas Rookes to accept the majority decision of the members and not to resign from the union. He refused. The members then carried a resolution to inform the employer that unless he was removed from the office by a given date there would be a withdrawal of labour. BOAC removed Douglas Rookes from the office but kept him on the payroll for a period. In March 1956 he was given notice that his employment was to be terminated. He then took legal action against the three named members of the union.

The case was heard in the Queen's Bench Division of the

160

High Court, and judgment was given against the three union members. Damages of £7,500 were awarded to Douglas Rookes. In his judgment Mr Justice Sachs referred to an agreement between the employers and the unions on the National Joint Council for Civil Air Transport, under which there were to be no strikes. The AESD was part of the National Joint Council. The judge held that the terms of the agreement were part of the individual contract of employment of each union member employed in the design office at London Airport. Threats to act in breach of the agreement were held to constitute intimidation if they were likely to harm the plaintiff and were followed by reasonable foreseeable damage.

The conclusion of the judgment was that the defendants were not, as had been argued by the union, protected by the Trade Disputes Act 1906. This Act granted protection against certain liabilities to any person acting in contemplation or furtherance of a trade dispute. One was to induce a breach of contract. Another was to interfere with the trade, business or employment of another person. Without such protection a range of trade union activities would be unlawful. Hence the 'immunities' of the Trade Disputes Act 1906 were intended to have the same practical effect as positive rights in other systems of law.

The union supported its members in an appeal against the High Court judgment. The Court of Appeal unanimously upheld the appeal and gave judgment to the effect that the action of the members, and of the officials who had acted on their behalf, was protected by the Trade Disputes Act 1906. This, however, was not the end of the saga. Douglas Rookes appealed to the House of Lords, and they reversed the decision of the Court of Appeal. They did, however, refer the question of damages to a further trial. Mr Rookes had, nevertheless, won his case before the highest court in the land.

The effect of the House of Lords ruling was, in the words of Counsel in the Court of Appeal, to drive a 'coach and four through the Trade Disputes Act 1906'. The wrongful act, it had been decided, was to threaten to strike in breach of contract. This constituted 'intimidation'. The argument of the union that the members had 'interfered with trade, business or employment' in contemplation or pursuit of a trade dispute, and that this was expressly protected by the Trade Disputes Act 1906, was rejected.

The union was advised that it could not legally pay the damages awarded against its members. As much as it could do under the rules was to give to each of them the maximum benevolent grant of £500. All the savings and the houses of the defendants were at risk. In the circumstances the union launched an appeal to the membership to assist the three defendants and to offset the very heavy legal costs. The response was extremely good. Many other unions also contributed to the appeal.

Unfortunately one of the defendants, Reg Silverthorne, the union's full-time official in West London, died at the early age of 48, on 3 November, 1961. He left a young son, who in the space of four months lost both his mother and father. Without doubt the early stages of the legal case took a heavy toll on Reg Silverthorne. He never for one moment accepted that he had done anything wrong in the dispute at London Airport. He was convinced that he had acted in the interest of trade unionism.

Reg had been one of my earliest friends among the left-wing active members of our union. He was an unforgettable character. His father, an unemployed Welsh miner, came to the Home Counties with his family before the Second World War in search of work. Reg was one of the most class-conscious trade unionists I have ever met, and he was always ready to give advice and support to members.

In an article in *The Draughtsman* in April 1964 I gave support to the demand of the union for new legislation to repair the damage to trade union rights done by the House of Lords' judgment in the case of Rookes versus Barnard. I argued that new law, damaging to the unions, had been made not by Parliament but by the judges. They had interpreted the Trade Disputes Act 1906 in a manner which had not been contemplated by Parliament and which greatly reduced the protection given to trade unionists in the course of industrial disputes.

My personal preference at that time, which I expressed in the article, was for a system of positive legal rights, including the right to organise, to bargain collectively, to conduct union activities at the place of work and to strike. Not one of these rights, I pointed out, was guaranteed by British law.

In the tradition of British industrial relations most trade unionists accepted the lack of affirmative legal rights because they believed that they also had few legal liabilities for actions normally taken – that is, non-criminal actions – in pursuit of industrial disputes. On balance, most trade unionists took the view that this lack of legal rights and obligations was preferable to any alternative system under which unions might have both rights and liabilities. It was felt that it helped to keep the courts out of industrial relations.

In an article in *The Draughtsman* I suggested that the Rookes versus Barnard judgment had changed the situation. It had reduced the rights of trade unionists and had greatly increased their liabilities. The article cautioned against any assumption that it would be necessary only to introduce new legislation to restore to trade unionists the protection which they previously thought they possessed under the 1906 Trade Disputes Act. The article pointed out that it had never been established that the 1906 Act gave protection to trade unionists who break their contracts of employment in pursuit of a trade dispute. The protection, according to the Act, was for inducing a breach of contract. In practice, legal action had rarely been taken by employers when employment contracts had been broken. They were more concerned to find a settlement to the dispute. This, however, did not imply that trade unionists were legally protected.

In 1968 I joined with Clive Jenkins in writing a book entitled *The Kind of Laws the Unions Ought to Want*. It argued for more legislation to protect trade union rights and to establish improvements in minimum labour standards. The experience of the Rookes versus Barnard case influenced the contents of the book. Today, in the light of later experience with ACAS and trade union recognition, I would amend some of the suggestions Clive and I then made.

The Draughtsmen's Association conducted a vigorous campaign throughout the trade union movement for new legislation to overcome the damage done by the Rookes versus Barnard judgment. Other trade unions were not slow to recognise that, in the words of the General Council's report to the 1964 TUC:

'In any situation such as that existing in the Rookes versus Barnard case, it was now impossible to make any threat of a strike without running the risk of incurring legal action; to minimise that risk it was certainly necessary to see that no overriding agreement excluded the right to strike.'

The 1964 TUC carried a resolution, moved by George Doughty on behalf of the Draughtsmen's Association, calling for a change in legislation to give trade unionists the protection 'that the 1906 Act intended'.

The legal position for the unions was made worse by another case, Stratford versus Lindley, affecting the Watermen, Lightermen, Tugmen and Bargemen's Union. The House of Lords reversed a decision of the Court of Appeal and granted an employer in the London docks an injunction restraining the union from taking industrial action against the company. Both the Lightermen's Union and the Draughtsmen's Association pressed for a radical reform of the law and said that they did not agree that 'a mere amendment of the Trade Disputes Act would be sufficient to restore the position'. They suggested that the tort of intimidation – the threat to break a contract of employment in the course of a trade dispute – should be abolished; that wider protection should be given to unions by extending the definition of a trade dispute; and that protection should be given to unions against actions for conspiracy to commit breaches of contract in pursuit of a trade dispute. The TUC were not persuaded of the need for more radical amending legislation.

As a result of the October 1964 General Election a new Labour Government came into office. Unlike the previous Conservative Government, it was sympathetic to the view of the TUC that the law should be changed by a relatively simple Bill to attempt to redress the situation created by the Rookes versus Barnard judgment. A new Trades Disputes Bill was passed by the House of Commons but was amended, against the Government's wishes, in the House of Lords. The House of Commons rejected the Lords' amendments, and this time the Bill became law. It stated that an act done in contemplation or furtherance of a trade dispute shall not be actionable as a civil wrong on the ground only that it consists of a threat to break a contract of employment or to induce someone else to break a contract of employment.

Controversy

Towards the end of 1960 there was a by-election in Bolton East in which the Labour candidate was Bob Howarth, a member of the parliamentary panel of the Draughtsmen's Association. Bob had all the attributes to make an attractive candidate. He was youthful, intelligent, of good appearance, fluent and he had good political and trade union experience. He was an active member of the union, who had been consistently associated with the left in his trade union activity. Bolton East was regarded as a marginal seat. At the 1959 General Election, when there had been a local alliance between the Conservative Party and the Liberal Party, the Conservative candidate had been elected with a majority over Labour of 2,732.

In the by-election in 1960 the Conservative Party held the seat with a majority of 641 over Labour, but a Liberal candidate received over 10,000 votes. There was also a 'New Conservative' candidate who polled 493 votes. The combined Conservative, 'New Conservative' and Liberal vote exceeded the Conservative vote in the previous General Election, whereas the Labour vote fell by more than 8,000.

The by-election was not fought in support of the Labour Party's policy of nuclear disarmament. Initially, the impression was created that the issue was being avoided. *The Times* wrote:

'Mr Howarth boxed so cleverly to avoid the question that it began to look as if the poll would take place without his being forced to declare himself.'

Later, Bob Howarth was reported to have said that he would have supported the rejected policy statement of the National Executive Council of the Labour Party and opposed the successful resolution of the TGWU on unilateral nuclear disarmament at the 1960 annual conference in Scarborough. This, however, was not all. Prominent members of the Labour Party who were also MPs for Lancashire constituencies and members of the NEC of the Party, but who were known either to support or respect the Scarborough conference decision, were excluded as speakers from the Bolton by-election. They included Harold Wilson, Anthony Greenwood and Barbara Castle. Fred Lee, a Lancashire MP who had been an engineering worker, was also not used. It was made clear by those responsible for the election campaign that full-time officials of the Draughtsmen's Association who were known as supporters of the Scarborough decision, including the local full-time official, John Forrester (later to become a member of the NEC of the Party), would not be required for factory gate, street or indoor meetings.

In an editorial article in the December 1960 issue of *The Draughtsman* I condemned the conduct of the Bolton by-election as deplorable. It was not fought on the policy of the Party but on the policy favoured by the Gaitskell leadership. Until the time of the election it was thought by most, and perhaps all, active union members who had supported Bob Howarth's inclusion on the parliamentary panel of the Draughtsmen's Association that he was a supporter of the policy of unilateral nuclear disarmament, which was the official policy of the Party as decided at the Scarborough conference.

The following issue of *The Draughtsman* carried an article from Bob Howarth replying to this criticism. He said that at a time when the Labour Party was beset by internal controversies it was not easy for a Labour candidate in a marginal seat to achieve a successful result. The main requirement in Bolton was for the candidate to give a lead to supporters to look outwards for a contest with the Tories and their past allies, the Liberals. The Bolton branch of the union was of the view that it was no mean achievement to come so close to success.

Bob Howarth accepted that there were justifiable grounds for criticising organisational aspects of the campaign, such as the selection of public speakers. He said that he had made these criticisms on numerous occasions to the election agent. It was most unfair to blame the candidate. The full-time regional organisers of the Party had taken over, 'and they were determined only to present a platform which generally represented a certain point of view'. Short of a public row, said Bob Howarth, it became abundantly clear that, 'try as I may ... I could not change this'.

In his article Bob Howarth said that he did not attempt to avoid the defence issue, but because he had certain reservations about the Scarborough decisions he did not make it his main campaign point. He continued:

'... as far as I know the only aspect of the Scarborough decisions on defence and nuclear weapons which I do not accept, is that I am opposed to Britain leaving the Western Alliance. I do not accept that neutralism is a practical alternative for our country. I do believe in collective security. I believe we could play a greater role in influencing Western policies, particularly American, by remaining a member of NATO.'

Significantly, his article went on to suggest that Britain could give 'an outstanding moral and practical lead by renouncing nuclear weapons and attempting, through the UN, to form a non-nuclear club, excluding initially the two great Powers'. Such action, said the article, together with Labour's proposals for an area of disengagement in Central Europe, including both halves of Germany, would contribute immeasurably to a more peaceful atmosphere.

If the by-election campaign in Bolton had been fought on the lines outlined by Bob in his article it would have been consistent with Labour Party policy, and there would have

167

been no grounds for criticism. I have no doubt that Bob Howarth was right when he indicated that it was the regional organisers of the Labour Party, acting in conformity with the wishes of the leadership of the Party, who exerted pressure for the course that was taken.

In its report to the annual conference of the Draughtsmen's Association the Executive Committee reported that they deplored the direction of the Bolton by-election campaign. The union had agreed on 5 November:

'subject to Mr Howarth taking a firm stand in the matter, to make immediate representations to Transport House (Labour Party head office) for national speakers who would not only reflect the Labour Party policy as determined at the 1960 Scarborough conference but who would be more suitable as platform figures and as representing northern constituencies. However, the approval of Mr Howarth to this course was not forthcoming.'

The reference back of this section of the Executive Committee report was moved at the annual conference of the union, but was defeated.

Later in 1961 Bob Howarth was readopted as prospective candidate for Bolton East. He was subsequently elected to Parliament.

At the same annual conference of the Draughtsmen's Association that discussed the Bolton by-election an emergency resolution was carried calling for the restoration of the Whip to a number of members of the Parliamentary Labour Party from whom it had been withdrawn because they had voted against the military estimates. They included Michael Foot and Sidney Silverman.

Trade Union Cooperation

In 1958 the annual conference of the Draughtsmen's Association had adopted a resolution stating that experience in the conduct of disputes 'dictates that amalgamation with other engineering unions should be genuinely sought...' The resolution also called for the union to initiate discussions with other unions 'which organise technicians employed in the engineering and allied industries with a view to strengthening cooperation between staff and manual workers...'

Responsibility for implementing this decision of the annual conference was given to a sub-committee of the Executive Committee, of which I was the secretary. I was strongly in favour of the policy decision of the conference, and set out my ideas in an article in *The Draughtsman*. I recalled that the Draughtsmen's Association had been involved in previous amalgamation discussions in the periods 1918–20, 1925–27 and 1943–46, but all had proved abortive. In each case the AESD had eventually withdrawn because it was not able to secure sufficient autonomy to deal adequately with the distinguishable interests of drawing office staff and allied technicians. Nevertheless, the entire experience confirmed that the conditions of drawing office staff could not be isolated from those of other workers in the engineering and shipbuilding industries.

The essential problem was, therefore, as I saw it, to devise a trade union structure which would provide for the common interest of all workers in the engineering industry whilst simultaneously enabling design technicians to protect and serve their special interests. The answer, I suggested, might lie in the creation of a virtually autonomous technicians' section of a broader industrial union. The core of such an industrial union would, of course, have to be the AEU.

My article pointed to some of the probable impediments to amalgamation with other unions catering for technicians. The Society of Technical Civil Servants was involved in the civil service negotiating machinery. Civil service staff negotiations were conducted exclusively by civil service organisations. The Association of Scientific Workers embraced members in different areas of employment. Only a minority were employed in engineering. The Association of Supervisory Staffs, Executives and Technicians had an established place in engineering, and more recently had organised a growing number of technicians. On the other hand, ASSET had a different approach to the organisation of supervisors. The Draughtsmen's Association took the general view that supervisors should be members of their appropriate craft or industrial union, whereas ASSET had a tradition of organising workshop foremen. ASSET also had a substantial membership in non-engineering areas of employment.

The possibility of a wider trade union amalgamation continued to occupy the attention of the Draughtsmen's Association for a number of years, and aroused controversy. There were some members who saw no reason for change. They regarded the Draughtsmen's Association as a well-organised, relatively well-off union with a clear occupational identity. They did not deny the need for cooperation with other engineering unions, but felt that this could be achieved within the Confederation of Shipbuilding and Engineering Unions. Others were more sympathetic to the idea of a white-collar amalgamation with the Association of Scientific Workers and ASSET. Another group, of which I was a member, saw the future in an engineering amalgamation with a trade group structure.

In the outcome – some years later – the proposals for an industrial union based around the AEU did not find favour. The fundamental problem was the incompatibility of the traditional structure and practices of the AEU with the requirement of the Draughtsmen's Association for sufficient autonomy to preserve its distinctive characteristics. Similarly, the engineering orientation of the Draughtsmen's Association did not at that time rest easily with the broader orientation of both the AScW and ASSET.

ASSET and the AScW eventually came together in an amalgamation known as the Association of Scientific, Technical and Managerial Staff. In 1961 the AESD changed its name to the Draughtsmen's and Allied Technicians' Association, to take account of the widening occupational basis of the membership. More and more technicians were being employed in engineering whose functions were related to design, production and quality control, but who were not employed on drawing boards.

Years later DATA entered into a loose amalgamation with the AEU, the Foundry Workers and the Constructional Engineering Union and became known as the Technical, Administrative and Supervisory Section of the Amalgamated Union of Engineering Workers. This, unfortunately, was not successful and was later dissolved. TASS, after amalgamating with a number of other unions including the Sheet Metal Workers, the Tobacco Workers, the Patternmakers, the Metal Mechanics, and the Gold, Silver and Allied Trades, then entered into an amalgamation with ASTMS to become the Manufacturing, Science and Finance Union, more usually known as MSF. The membership of MSF is spread over many industries and service occupations, with large concentrations of members in insurance and other financial institutions, the National Health Service, the universities, a variety of organisations in the voluntary sector and in different manufacturing industries. The majority of MSF members are not employed in engineering, though the union has a substantial membership throughout the industry.

Long before the amalgamation between TASS and ASTMS there was often close cooperation between the Draughtsmen's Association and ASSET and the AScW. One of the areas of this cooperation was parliamentary lobbying on occupational issues of concern to white-collar employees. ASSET, in particular, had an effective Parliamentary Committee consisting of Labour MPs who were members of that union. The committee met monthly and ASSET, on the initiative of Clive Jenkins, invited the Draughtsmen's Association to send a representative. I was elected as the representative and attended the committee regularly for a number of years.

My recollection of the ASSET Parliamentary Committee is of the range of its work and, frequently, the influence it was able to exert. Among its regular attenders during my period as a member were, in addition to Clive Jenkins, Ian Mikardo, Jack Diamond (later Lord Diamond), Harold Wilson and Sir Leslie Plummer. The combination of talent which they brought

171

to bear on any issue on the agenda was formidable. They were also often joined by Muriel Turner (now Baroness Turner and an active member of the Labour group in the House of Lords), who was an official of ASSET and is one of the most able women the trade union movement has produced. In earlier years her views were generally on the left of the labour movement, but in more recent times she has, I think, moved more towards the centre.

Ian Mikardo, who died some years ago, was an attractive figure. I still find it incredible that he did not hold office in any of the Labour governments during his many years as an MP. He had the ability to reduce complex issues to their bare essentials but without distorting reality. I know of no-one else who within one minute in a broadcast interview could make a point so succinctly and in a manner which could be so readily understood by listeners. Throughout his parliamentary life and during his years on the National Executive Committee of the Labour Party he was a consistent supporter of progressive causes. My views on Israel did not coincide with his, but even on this issue I always listened with respect to what he had to say.

On the ASSET Parliamentary Committee Harold Wilson was a tower of strength. This was where I first had the opportunity to see him at close quarters. He was always extremely sharp to pick up a point and to suggest a way forward. My impression at that time was that he was consistently to the left of centre in the labour movement.

Following the unexpected death of Hugh Gaitskell at the beginning of 1963, Harold Wilson was elected Leader of the Labour Party. He had challenged Gaitskell for the leadership in 1960 and had been defeated. George Brown had been elected Deputy Leader and was the candidate favoured by many on the right to follow Gaitskell. There were three candidates to become Leader following Hugh Gaitskell's death: Brown, Callaghan and Wilson. Wilson led in the first ballot – then confined to members of the Parliamentary Labour Party – and James Callaghan was eliminated. In the second ballot Wilson defeated Brown by 144 votes to 103. After Harold

Wilson had been elected Leader, Clive Jenkins organised a small dinner party of trade unionists, with Harold Wilson in attendance, to celebrate the occasion. I was present, and all who were there looked to the future with hope and with some optimism. We felt that both in the TUC and the Labour Party there were important signs of change and that, at long last, after years of Conservative rule, an effective and more radical challenge would be mounted to bring about a change of government.

I also represented the Draughtsmen's Association on a Joint Parliamentary Scientific Advisory Committee, in which the leading trade union role was taken by the Association of Scientific Workers. The committee concerned itself with issues which had a significant scientific content and included representatives from a number of trade unions. My main recollection of the committee was of the helpful and consistently progressive attitude of the late Judith Hart MP.

The Common Market

In 1961 the British Government decided to apply for membership of the European Economic Community. The Common Market, as it was more usually described in Britain, was established by the Treaty of Rome in 1957. The original participating countries were West Germany, France, Italy, Belgium, Holland and Luxembourg. Britain did not join at the outset because it was felt that many of the features of the Treaty of Rome were objectionable. The provision of a common external tariff was seen as incompatible with Britain's system of trading preferences with Commonwealth countries. There was also some feeling that the Common Market, under pressure from the French and to some extent the Germans, would pursue an agricultural policy likely to lead to higher food prices. Britain finally joined with the Scandinavian countries, Switzerland, Austria and Portugal, to form at the beginning of 1960 a much looser trading arrangement known as the European Free Trade Area.

The British Government's decision to open negotiations with the European Economic Community with a view to joining was prompted both by political and economic reasons. Politically, there was pressure for a united instead of a divided Western Europe. The British Government saw such a united Western Europe as the strong ally of the USA. The French, however, saw it more as an independent group, friendly, perhaps, to the USA but certainly not under American leadership. Economically, Britain was continuing to experience difficulties whilst West Germany and France were making progress. In 1963 the French Government under General de Gaulle vetoed Britain's application to join the Community.

Opinion in the British labour movement was divided. Probably the majority at that time were either opposed to Britain's application or sceptical about the claimed benefits that would follow from British membership of the EEC. A minority were in favour, and were influenced by what they saw to be both the political and economic advantages of a more united Western Europe.

I tried to get as much information as I could about the Treaty of Rome and the operation of the Common Market. I depended not only on information to be found in newspapers and TUC reports, but I went on a number of occasions to reference libraries to read, as they say, the 'small print'. The more information I accumulated, the more persuaded I became that Britain should not accede to the Treaty of Rome. I expressed my views at meetings of the Executive Committee of the Draughtsmen's Association and in a number of articles. I also participated in debates at the CSEU and the TUC on behalf of the Draughtsmen's Association.

My objection to the Treaty of Rome was both political and economic. I saw it as a framework for the dominance of capitalism in Western Europe. Within this framework, German big business would be the principal beneficiary. Living costs in Britain would rise because of higher prices. Dearer foodstuffs would be imported from Europe at the expense of Commonwealth products, which would have to surmount tariffs designed to protect the less efficient peasant farmers of France and Germany. In the trading area of the EEC it was more likely that Germany, France and Italy would benefit in trade in manufactured items. Britain would probably move into deficit on her balance of payments.

The Treaty of Rome, it seemed to me, would seriously prejudice the power of the British Government to plan the economy. The Treaty was based on the belief that the free market should prevail. True enough, the Treaty of Rome contained many qualifying clauses to provide for public intervention, but the main thrust was to serve the dominant economic interests of private ownership within the confines of the EEC. Because of Britain's traditional trading relations with non-EEC countries, the Common Market, I felt, would require Britain to impose more restrictions on her international trade than it would remove. Furthermore, because of the Common Market agricultural policy Britain would become a net contributor to the EEC funds. In other words, Britain would be paying for subsidies to Continental farmers.

The arrangements of the Common Market, I was persuaded, were also likely to threaten the economic progress of underdeveloped countries. These arrangements discriminated against their industrial products and, in effect, the EEC regarded the underdeveloped countries as permanent producers of raw materials and tropical or semi-tropical foodstuffs. This would condemn them to economic backwardness. It was a facade for neo-colonialism.

The majority of the top leaders of the trade union movement were slow to reach a decision about Britain's application to join the Common Market. In a special report to the 1961 TUC the General Council expressed support for the opening of negotiations for British entry. They said:

'The TUC insists that the real test of European economic unity is whether it will promote full employment, economic growth and better living standards. The General Council have urged that any agreement should require Governments to define their full employment aims and state the methods which they would adopt individually and collectively to attain full employment.'

At the 1961 conference of the Confederation of Shipbuilding and Engineering Unions and at the 1961 TUC I moved motions on behalf of the Draughtsmen's Association, opposing British entry into the Common Market. At the CSEU conference some of the bigger unions were reluctant to take a decision before the anticipated debates later in the year at the TUC and the Labour Party. The motion was remitted to the Executive Council.

At the TUC the critical motion expressed the view that 'entry into the Common Market by Britain on the basis of the Treaty of Rome would be injurious to our national interests'. The motion went on to emphasise the importance of developing trading relations with the Commonwealth and underdeveloped countries. It called for the development of international trade, compatible with the maintenance of full employment, and for the reduction of trade barriers, the continuation of Commonwealth preferences and the retention by the British Parliament of adequate powers to maintain full employment and economic expansion.

In moving this motion I argued that the Treaty of Rome would require Britain to impose more new trade barriers than it would remove. It would also require the free circulation of capital which, in the event of a serious balance-of-payments problem, would necessitate deflation and unemployment. Physical controls on luxury imports or on the export of capital would not be permitted. The power of a British Government to plan the economy would be restricted. In the debate the opponents of the motion ranged from those who were sympathetic to the purpose of the Common Market to those who, like Frank Cousins, were critical of the Treaty of Rome but who wanted to negotiate about the terms of a possible British entry. The seconder of the critical motion, Richard Briginshaw of NATSOPA, claimed that the main purpose of the Common Market was political and not economic, and that the driving force was the United States.

Britain's position, he argued, would not be strengthened by entry. It would be weakened.

In replying to the debate on behalf of the General Council, Sir Alan Birch referred to the similarity of some of the views expressed both by supporters and opponents of the motion. He did not think that Britain could go into the Common Market on the exact terms of the Treaty of Rome, but he also did not think that Britain should commit itself to opposition. Congress should reserve the right to make a judgment when the results of the negotiations were available. The General Council's policy carried the day.

At the 1962 TUC the subject of Britain's proposed entry into the Common Market was again debated, and again I moved the main composite motion of opposition on behalf of the Draughtsmen's Association and a number of other unions. Many unions participated in the debate but, as in the previous year, the majority were in favour of awaiting the outcome of the negotiations before making a judgment. The issue for the time being was deferred when in 1963 General de Gaulle made it clear that he would not accept any significant concessions to the points put by the British Government.

David Kitson

In June 1964 a member of the Draughtsmen's Association was arrested in Johannesburg, South Africa, and imprisoned under the South African Detention Law, which gave the police the authority to hold suspects in solitary confinement and 'incommunicado' for 90 days. His name, David Kitson, was to become familiar to thousands in the trade union and labour movement in the years to follow. Following his arrest Kitson, according to information received by the Draughtsmen's Association, was interrogated for four days and nights and was not permitted to see a lawyer. After the interrogation he was put in solitary confinement. He was detained without charges being made against him. After three months of solitary confinement, Kitson was again detained for a further 90 days.

177

David Kitson was a white South African by birth. He gained an engineering degree at the University of Natal. In 1947, when he was 28 years of age, he came to England, found a job with the De Havilland Company and joined the Draughtsmen's Association. He quickly became an active member. In 1952 he won the Association's scholarship to Ruskin College and remained there for two years. After Ruskin he worked for the British Oxygen Company. He was offered promotion on condition that he would give up being a union representative. He refused. He was later sacked and blacklisted by other firms. In 1959 he returned to South Africa, together with his wife Norma, who was also South African and whom he had married three years earlier.

The Sharpeville massacre, when South African police fired upon Africans demonstrating against the Pass Laws, killing 69 people and wounding 188, proved a turning point not only for the African National Congress but for David Kitson personally. The ANC ceased to rely solely on non-violent demonstrations and agreed to support armed resistance to gain civil rights for all South Africans and to bring apartheid to an end. Armed action was to be carried out by a new organisation, known – in English translation – as 'Spear of the People'. In 1962 Kitson joined the new organisation and became involved in its activities.

In November 1964 Kitson, together with four others, was brought to trial, charged with sabotage, recruiting others for military training and receiving money to finance their campaign. The five were charged with conspiring to commit acts of sabotage, and Kitson was accused of serving on committees of the High Command of the resistance organisation.

From the moment that information was received of the arrest of David Kitson, the Draughtsmen's Association did what it could to assist. It made representations to the South African authorities in London, requesting that either charges should be made against Kitson and his colleagues or that he should be released from detention. Money was made available to assist with legal representation.

A Kitson Committee was formed with representatives from divisional councils of the Association. The chairman was Des Starrs, the chairman of the Finance and General Purposes Committee of the union, and I acted as secretary. The committee, with the full support of the union, conducted a vigorous campaign to ensure that publicity was given to the Kitson case throughout the British trade union and labour movement. Thousands of pounds were raised in voluntary contributions to assist the campaign, to help with legal representation and to provide financial support for David Kitson's family. Resolutions were tabled for the TUC and Labour Party, and demonstrations were held in London. Staff and students at Ruskin College also joined the campaign and established their own Kitson Committee.

David Kitson was given a 20-year sentence at his trial. Milton Mkwayi, a leading figure in the ANC, was given life imprisonment. The other three defendants were given 18, 15 and 12 years respectively. At his trial David Kitson conducted himself with great courage and dignity. He said that after Sharpeville he could either run or stand. He continued:

'So I stood. It was natural, in view of my past, to find a home in the South African Communist Party. At least my participation would show that I stood alongside the Africans and their fellows. It showed the world that another white had chosen the side of humanity.'

When David Kitson was in prison he was never forgotten by the union. Each Christmas the union encouraged members to send cards to him at his prison address. He did not receive them, but he heard about the hundreds who had written to him. He said afterwards that when he was in solitary confinement it was 'a wonderful uplift for my morale.' Deputations were organised to the South African authorities, and a number of Members of Parliament were particularly helpful.

At the beginning of his sentence David Kitson was allowed one letter and one visit every six months. The union pressed for more humane treatment, not only for David but for other political prisoners. He was later given a different grading and allowed a letter and a visit every month. Some of the money collected by the union was used to buy extras for the political prisoners. One particular request was that Kitson and other prisoners should be permitted to take courses of study. This request was eventually granted. During his imprisonment David Kitson took more than 50 courses and secured degrees in economics, political science, and applied mathematics, a diploma in datametrics and a pass in a university course in Zulu. All this was in addition to his original degree in mechanical engineering.

One particular lay member of the union, Des Starrs, deserves special mention for his consistent support for David Kitson. From the formation of the Kitson Committee to the time of David's ultimate release, 20 years later, Des Starrs was tireless in his efforts. Both George Doughty and Ken Gill, as successive general secretaries of the union, were always ready and available to help. Norma Kitson was constantly in the forefront of the campaign.

My own active involvement in the Kitson Committee ceased in 1968, when I left the employment of the union, though I remained in touch with its activities and did what I could to assist. I attended the reception party when David finally came back to Britain after his release from prison.

Some years before David Kitson's release the union, in an effort to secure a remission of sentence, made it known to the South African authorities that a fellowship for him could be funded at Ruskin College. This offer was made after consultation with Ruskin College. Unfortunately, it did not evoke a response from the South African authorities. Nevertheless, the offer still stood when David was released from prison. He took up a fellowship at Ruskin.

Some time later there was a sad development. The union's financial support for a fellowship was for a limited period. By that time David Kitson was beyond the normal age of retirement. There was also a disagreement between Kitson and the African National Congress. Some felt that the union should have maintained the fellowship, but the majority supported the

Executive Committee in the view that in the circumstances the funding of the fellowship should not be extended beyond the commitment which had been given.

My personal view was one of sympathy for David Kitson, but I resented the criticism being levelled against the union by people who were not members and who, in many cases, were unaware of the efforts made on behalf of David Kitson for more than 20 years. I was conscious that in the allocation of funds the union had to observe its own rules. I made no pretence to judge the disagreement between David Kitson and the ANC.

Nothing can take from David Kitson the inspiring memory of his example. As a white South African, with an education and experience to assure him a comfortable life, he decided instead to identify himself with the movement for African liberation. When brought before the court, he defended his views with great courage and dignity. He served to the full the long sentence of 20 years' imprisonment. In the early period the conditions of imprisonment were inhumane. He never capitulated. He emerged from imprisonment with an undimmed conviction that apartheid was wrong. In the long history of the Draughtsmen's Association no member suffered more for his beliefs than David Kitson, and none has done more to provide a living example of the power of humanitarian ideals.

More Controversial Issues

Another international issue in which I had a strong interest in the first half of the 1960s was the extending rift between the Soviet Union and China. My basic sympathy with the declared intention of both countries to build a new kind of social order remained, and I did not share the view that either represented an aggressive force threatening Western Europe or the USA. On the other hand, both seemed to be embracing unrealistic assessments of their own problems and potentialities.

At its Twenty-second Congress, held in October 1961, the

Communist Party of the Soviet Union adopted a new programme which appeared seriously to overestimate the strength of the Soviet economy. The programme predicted that in the decade 1961–70:

> '...the Soviet Union, in creating the material and technical basis of communism, will surpass the strongest and richest capitalist country, the USA, in production per head of population; the people's standard of living and their cultural and technical standards will improve substantially; everyone will live in easy circumstances; all collective and state farms will become highly productive and profitable enterprises; the demand of Soviet people for well-appointed housing will, in the main, be satisfied; hard physical work will disappear; the USSR will have the shortest working day.'

The new programme stated that: 'The main economic task of the Party and the Soviet people is to create the material and technical basis of communism within two decades.' This task was to be achieved by 1990. By then, the programme predicted, 'Soviet society will come close to a stage where it can introduce the principle of distribution according to needs...' Thus goods and services would, in the main, no longer be distributed among citizens according to their earnings. There would be such abundance that people would be supplied with whatever they needed. This, it seemed to me, did not qualify as serious political and economic analysis. It was nothing less than a portrait of an unrealistic dream-world.

Similarly in China, the so-called 'Great Leap Forward' was supposed to make it possible for China to catch up with Britain in total output in 15 years and with the USA in 50 to 70 years. China overestimated its own ability to achieve very rapid economic growth, particularly after the withdrawal of Soviet technicians, and underestimated – with its misleading talk of 'paper tigers' – the strength of the USA.

The illusions of both the Soviet Union and China, and the accompanying bitter exchanges between them concerning, for example, China's nuclear ambitions, different interpretations of

182

'peaceful co-existence', differences about the significance of the anti-imperialist struggle in the Third World and differences about the way forward to socialism in different countries, would have had little direct impact on the Draughtsmen's Association except that some on the left in the union were influenced by them and sought to translate their ideas into what others of us regarded as 'ultra-left' activities. In the second half of the 1960s these differences led to sharp controversy within the union. I came under considerable personal criticism because of my resistance to what I felt were 'ultra-left' views.

In 1961 and 1962 the related issues of economic planning and incomes policy again came to the fore. The Government sought the cooperation of employers and unions in coordinating longer-term economic policies and in the work of a proposed National Incomes Commission.

The Government put forward its ideas for a National Economic Development Council in the second half of 1961. The TUC were cautious in their response and sought clarification as to the Government's intentions. Early in 1962 the General Council decided to join the NEDC. They said:

'In deciding whether to accept the Chancellor's invitation the General Council considered whether they would best serve the interests of the Movement by doing so. They were well aware that the Government's proposal to set up the NEDC did not prove that the Government was committed to economic planning as Congress understands it. Nevertheless, the General Council eventually decided that they should put to a practical test the question whether participation would give them a genuine opportunity of influencing the Government's policies in ways which would help trade unionists.'

The General Council said that they recognised that the NEDC would not be an executive body. Its purpose would be to guide the work of an expert planning staff and to recommend for adoption by the Government, and, where appropriate, for

183

acceptance by employers and unions, plans for securing economic growth.

The proposal for a National Incomes Commission was put forward by the Government only a few months later. The Government said that it wanted to establish a more realistic relationship between the growth of incomes and productivity. This, it was argued, was a major prerequisite of achieving faster economic growth. The Government acknowledged that it had been found difficult to achieve simultaneously full employment, a favourable balance of payments, stable prices, a strong currency and economic growth.

The reality was that, despite the claim that the British people 'had never had it so good', the problems of the British economy had not diminished. During the preceding ten years British output had been growing more slowly than that of almost any other industrialised country in the world. Of her European neighbours, only Belgium had a poorer record. In an article which I wrote early in 1962 I pointed out that the Government could not escape responsibility. Instead of stimulating production by planned investment and expansion in key sections of the economy, it had alternated between policies which led to an indiscriminate free-for-all and policies which slowed down the wheels of productive industry. It had also committed Britain to a consistently high level of military expenditure; much higher than in West Germany.

The General Council of the TUC rejected the Government's invitation to support the proposed National Incomes Commission. They said, in effect, that they recognised the problems which the Government had described, but that the National Incomes Commission would make no contribution to solving them. Its objective was merely the restriction of wages.

In the Government's view the work of the NEDC and of the National Incomes Commission were related. The Draughtsmen's Association accepted that this was the Government's view, and decided not to support either the NEDC or the NIC. In an editorial article for *The Draughtsman* in June 1962 I wrote that, despite all the talk about 'planning', the National Economic Development Council would have no real power to plan the economy. To expect a Conservative Government to endow it with such powers was 'about as unrealistic as expecting water to flow uphill'.

At the 1962 TUC the Draughtsmen's Association moved a composite motion calling upon the TUC to withdraw from the NEDC. Our spokesman was George Doughty. George Woodcock, on behalf of the General Council, said that whilst it was too early to laud the NEDC, it was much too early to condemn it. The composite motion was defeated and the General Council's policy supported.

These issues were again debated at the 1963 TUC. This time, a resolution submitted by the Boilermakers' Society, opposing wage restraint, was carried by 4,283,000 to 3,902,000. Another resolution, submitted by the Association of Scientific Workers, expressing concern at statements in a report of the NEDC which urged that incomes should rise substantially less than in the past, was carried by just over 6 million votes to just over 2 million. A report on economic development and planning prepared by the General Council was accepted by 7,474,000 votes to 629,000. The Draughtsmen's Association voted for the two successful wages policy resolutions and voted against the General Council's report on economic development and planning.

The report on economic development and planning had to be amended from its original draft form to secure adoption by Congress. As originally drafted, it accepted the view that money incomes should rise substantially less than in the past. It became known that this would not be acceptable to many union delegations and that the report would probably be rejected. Almost at the last moment, the report was amended to make it clear that an expansion of purchasing power was a necessary factor in economic growth.

My own view on the General Council's report on economic development was that it was unrealistic. In an article which I wrote at the time, I pointed out that the view of the General Council was that the success of planning would depend on the extent to which both workers and employers would be 'prepared to make their attitudes and actions conform to the needs of the community as a whole, as expressed in an agreed plan'.

This meant that in the view of the majority of TUC leaders the success of planning would depend upon a policy of collaboration between the existing Conservative Government, the employers and trade unionists. The essential measures for Britain's economic recovery, I argued, would not be taken by a Conservative Government. In Britain over 80 per cent of industry was privately owned, and the dominating motive of economic activity was the pursuit of private profit. Decisions were taken in industry not according to social needs and priorities but according to considerations of profitability. Only rarely were the most profitable projects also the most socially needed. A policy of collaboration between a Conservative Government, the employers and trade unions would be on terms dictated fundamentally by those who regarded private profit as the mainspring of economic activity. My critical views on the report of the TUC General Council were shared by a majority of the draughtsmen's delegation but by only a minority of TUC delegates.

My point of view did not rule out the possibility of effective economic planning under a Labour Government committed to economic expansion and the achievement of full employment. Moreover, I accepted, in an article which I wrote for *The Draughtsman* in October 1963, that 'it would be necessary to ensure that changes in incomes were in broad conformity with the requirements of a national economic plan. The whole purpose of the policy would be to give a better standard of life to the ordinary people and to bring about a massive redistribution in wealth and power to the advantage of workers.' This acceptance of the possibility of some kind of incomes policy under a Labour Government committed to planning, expansion, full employment and the redistribution of income and wealth, brought me into conflict with some on the left of the Draughtsmen's Association. They felt that there was no likelihood of such conditions ever being fulfilled.

At the 1964 TUC I moved a composite motion on behalf of the Draughtsmen's Association, calling for a planned economy and cooperation between the unions and a Labour Government. The motion envisaged the possibility of an 'acceptable incomes policy, taking into account all forms of income including rent, interest and profit'. The motion was seconded by Les Cannon on behalf of the Electrical Trades Union. He spoke at some length on what was meant by an acceptable incomes policy and expressed support for the view of Harold Wilson, the Leader of the Labour Party, that there had to be 'purposive planning based on social justice and that account must be taken of all forms of income'. Frank Cousins, he recalled, had put forward the admirable proposition that there should be a planned growth of incomes. The motion was carried without a recorded card vote. One or two speakers in the debate expressed reservations about an 'acceptable incomes policy', but the overwhelming majority of delegates were sympathetic to the idea that there should be a planned growth of real incomes and that this necessitated an incomes policy.

At the 1964 annual conference of the Draughtsmen's Association a resolution was carried expressing opposition to trade union participation in the National Economic Development Council and in the National Incomes Commission under a Conservative Government. An amendment was, however, carried, which I supported in the debate, stating that under a strong Labour Government trade union participation in a 'socialist equivalent of NEDC and NIC would be in the vital interests of members, trade unions and country'.

In the early 1960s a number of members of the Draughtsmen's Association began to gain a new prominence. Ken Gill, who was later to become the General Secretary of the AUEW-TASS and then of MSF, was first elected as a full-time official. Ken quickly made his mark by his qualities of leadership.

When Tony Benn was campaigning for the right to renounce an inherited peerage and to remain a Member of Parliament for a constituency for which he had been elected, one of his active supporters was Ted Bishop, a member of the Draughtsmen's Association. Ted was the Vice-President of the Bristol South-East constituency Labour Party and President of the

Bristol Labour Party. Tony Benn was the MP for Bristol South-East.

When Tony Benn was not allowed to remain as member for Bristol South-East, it was Ted Bishop and another member of the Draughtsmen's Association, George Sale, who moved and seconded that Tony Benn should be the Labour candidate at the enforced by-election. The campaign for the right of electors to choose their parliamentary representative and for the right of an hereditary peer to renounce his peerage was successful.

George Sale was the union's full-time official for the Bristol area. A former draughtsman from Derby, he was one of the most hard-working and popular officials in the history of the Draughtsmen's Association. He was on the left of the Labour Party, and he would almost certainly have become a national official of the union but for his unfortunate premature death.

Ted Bishop was a member of the parliamentary panel of the Draughtsmen's Association and was elected to Parliament as Member for Newark in 1964. He later became a Minister. He died before his full potential was realised.

At the 1964 General Election, eight members of the Draughtsmen's Association stood as Labour candidates and three were elected. The successful candidates included Will Howie, who stood for Luton, Ted Bishop, who stood for Newark, and Bob Howarth who won the seat in Bolton East which he had earlier contested in a by-election. Will Howie first won the Luton seat at a by-election before the General Election of 1964. He was the first member of the union to become a Labour MP. He later became a Labour Whip and later still went to the House of Lords.

One of the unsuccessful candidates in 1964 was Albert Booth, who was a very active member of the union on the North-East coast. He later became the MP for Barrow and served as Secretary of State for Employment and as a member of the Cabinet in the late 1970s. For a period he was the National Treasurer of the Labour Party. When he was defeated at Barrow the Labour Party lost one of its best people. Sincerity and modesty were his outstanding characteristics. He too has always been on the left of the movement. He is still active at rank-and-file level in MSF and in his constituency Labour Party.

Working with Others

In the first half of the 1960s a group of left-wing trade unionists, of whom I was one, launched a discussion magazine entitled *Trade Union Affairs*. The initiative came from Clive Jenkins, who was the editor, and among the members of the editorial board were Geoffrey Drain, who later became General Secretary of the large public service union, NALGO, Hugh Jenkins of British Actors' Equity, who later became an MP and then a member of the House of Lords, Paddy Leech, who served for many years as a national trade union official in the entertainment industry, Ernie Roberts, who was Assistant General Secretary of the Amalgamated Engineering Union and then a Labour MP, A.C. Torode, who for many years was the General Secretary of the Sign and Display Trades Union, and myself.

The purpose of this publication was to encourage trade unionists, and particularly full-time officials, to write in some depth about problems facing the movement and their personal experiences when dealing with these problems. We felt that it was not sufficient to be guided by pragmatic considerations. The movement needed to understand what it stood for and where it was going. It was a good idea, and was an example of Clive Jenkins' initiative at its most constructive. We maintained the publication for a number of issues, without any kind of external subsidy, but then because the circulation was limited we ceased publication. Despite the problems, *Trade Union Affairs* attracted a wide span of writers, many of whom in later years played a distinguished part in the trade union and labour movement.

Another publication with which I was associated was the *International Socialist Journal*. I was invited to participate by Ralph Miliband. It was a left-wing socialist magazine with editorial offices in Milan. The British sponsors, in addition to

Ralph Miliband, were Frank Allaun and Michael Barratt Brown. Other sponsors came from Italy, France and Belgium. Ken Coates, now a Member of the European Parliament, and I were the British members of the editorial board of the journal. Our editorial meetings were normally held in Paris. This was when I first became acquainted with Ken Coates, who, from a working-class background became a tutor in higher education. He is not only talented but extraordinarily energetic. His political stamina is the equal of anyone I have ever met. Years later, together with Tony Topham, he wrote two very good volumes of the history of the unions that formed the TGWU. More volumes on the history of the TGWU are to follow.

The *International Socialist Journal* must have been expensive to publish. Much of the money came from Italy. One of the leading Italian supporters was Lelio Basso, a former Secretary General of the Italian Socialist Party. The journal was published, as far as I recall, in Italian, French and English. The journal lasted for a number of years, but I was always surprised that, with such heavy expenses, it lasted as long as it did.

I continued also as a member of the Executive Committee of the Union of Democratic Control and as the editor of its publications. We continued to publish pamphlets on a range of international issues. In 1963 we published a booklet written by Philip Noel-Baker on *The Way to World Disarmament – Now*. It carried a foreword by Harold Wilson. Philip Noel-Baker won the Nobel Peace Prize in 1959.

In 1963 Audrey Jupp, the Secretary of the Union of Democratic Control, resigned to take an appointment with one of the newly independent countries of Africa. Her departure was a serious loss to the organisation. Moreover, it coincided with the decline in the sales of political pamphlets, which was affecting not only the UDC but also other political organisations. Citizens were increasingly looking towards television documentary and discussion programmes as a source of information on political issues.

During the first half of the 1960s I was writing for or assisting in the publication of a number of trade union journals, including at various times the magazines of one of the printing unions, the Fire Brigades Union, the Heating and Domestic Engineers' Union, the Constructional Engineering Union and ASSET. This was in addition to my work on *The Draughtsman* which I continued to edit and which gave me considerable scope for the expression of a radical view on a wide range of trade union, industrial, economic and political issues. The importance of trade union journalism has often been underestimated in the labour movement. The publications of the unions offer a modest counter-influence to that of the daily newspapers owned by wealthy proprietors, most of whom have little, if any, sympathy with trade unionism.

I also wrote for a publication then known as *The Statist*, for *Personnel Management* and for *Tribune*. For a period, Clive Jenkins and I shared a questions and answers column in *Tribune* dealing with problems at work.

I also served as the chairman of a rules revision committee for the London Cooperative Society. It was an interesting exercise, because the fundamental problem was how to maintain democratic interest and control in a large trading organisation which was facing increasingly strong competition from supermarket chains.

A Labour Victory

In the 1964 General Election the Labour Party gained a narrow victory, even though its total vote was slightly less than in the 1959 General Election. The Conservative Party, however, lost nearly 1 million votes in comparison with 1959, and the Liberal Party increased its vote from 1,638,571 to 3,092,878. The new Labour Government had a working majority of four in the House of Commons.

Labour's manifesto for the 1964 General Election emphasised the need for economic planning to modernise industry, secure full employment, obtain a faster rate of economic growth and find a solution to the problem of the balance of payments. It argued for the mobilisation of the resources of

191

technology. The manifesto said that public ownership would make a vital contribution to the national plan. Labour called for a national incomes policy which would not be unfairly directed at low paid workers but would provide for the planned growth of incomes broadly related to the annual growth of production. The incomes policy was to apply to all forms of income: to profits, dividends and rents as well as wages and salaries.

Labour's working majority following the 1964 General Election was so small that another election was widely regarded as inevitable. In 1966 Labour went to the country with an appeal for a renewed mandate, but with a bigger parliamentary majority, to fulfil the programme started in 1964. The appeal was centred on the need for planning. The electorate responded and gave the Labour Party a comfortable majority of seats. Labour increased its national vote by nearly 860,000 in comparison with 1964. The Conservative Party lost about 580,000 votes and the Liberal Party about 765,000 votes. Because of the distortion of the British electoral system, Labour's comfortable parliamentary majority was secured with 47.9 per cent of the total vote. Though the Liberal Party's national vote declined, they ended up with 3 more seats than in 1964, but they were still very much under-represented in proportion to the total vote they received.

The second half of the 1960s was to provide the answer to the claims put forward by the Labour Party in 1964 and 1966.

Steel man rocks the fence

TUC Conference Blackpool

EXPRESS TEAM REPORTING

ANTI-SIX JIM COLLECTS OVER 2,000,000 VOTES

By
JOHN GRANT, RICHARD O'SULLIVAN and RONALD BOYLE
Blackpool, Thursday

Robert Willis   Jimmy Jarvie   Richard Briginshaw   Jim Mortimer   John Newton

LABOUR WEEKLY JUNE 7 1985

Two militant leaders want law reform to protect unions

BY OUR LABOUR STAFF

Policies must meet the gravity of the problems facing Britain

TO STEP into retirement – in reality more a transfer of activity than a withdrawal from active backwaters. Yet the real justification for an occasional retrospective glance at the labour movement is to seek guidance for the future and confidence from progress already made.

It is now more than 50 years ago since I attended my first branch meeting of the Labour League of Youth and nearly 50 years ago since I started and nearly shop fitter apprentice and joined a trade union. In these 50 years the world has changed at a pace unprecedented in world history. It is perhaps impossible to recall that throughout this long period...

Mortimer looks back at... in the struggle for...

Life at top was tough for Jim

By Jack Foster

ONE of the toughest jobs in politics in General election and that of the Labour Party General Secretary of the Labour Party's National Executive Committee...

When it comes to a tough job, Jim's our Kissinger

THE MAN who occupies what must be...

Jim Mortimer 'Socially useful'

Gentleman Jim leaves the fray

By Jack Foster

THE General Secretary of Labour Party is as tough a job as any in politics.

For a start your paymaster is the fractious National Executive Committee.

Its meetings were "purgatory" for Jim Callaghan. If ever a party leader falls ill, voting on whether to send a get well card is contested on factional lines – or so the joke goes.

When Jim Mortimer took over the job three-and-a-half years ago, with his air of personable, reasonable... people warned him it was like becoming gaoler in the Lusitania.

And when he retires early next month and hands over to Larry Whitty of David Basnett's boilermaker's union he will know it has been a storm-tossed voyage.

Every so often Labour has looked like running aground on Michael Foot's leadership, the Tatchell by-election, Militant Tendency and Scargill's strike.

Order

"It is," says Jim Mortimer, a man who bankers after order and stability. "The most difficult job I have had."

This from the man who chaired ACAS...

Jim Mortimer: Bids farewell to the Labour Party

me newspaper perceptions of
e author; not necessarily
ecting his own views!
ntinued overleaf)

Draughtsmen do not favour Socialism

DIFFICULTIES facing leaders of the Association of Engineering and Shipbuilding Draughtsmen in attempts to win converts to Socialism among their 63,000 members are given prominence in a history of the association published to-day.

Mr. J. E. Mortimer, the author, a member of the Association's executive and an official for 12 years, refers to the "backward attitude of some of the members.

The Association probably maintains a higher prop... unions of m... adhere...

majority of A... craft-con...

2 HOME NEWS

Labour ponders a bill of rights for trade unionists

Repealing the union laws of the Tories is not enough, says Mr Jim Mortimer (right).

Patrick Wintour examines the options for reform

---

14 FINANCIAL GUARDIAN

Teams welcome a new ref

John Torode says goodbye to Jim Mortimer of ... d greets ... oversial ... r as ... n, ... s strong Lowry

OUT ... Mortimer   IN ... Lowry

DAILY MAIL TEAM AT BLACKPOOL—LESLIE RANDALL, KEITH McDOWALL, PETER WHALEY

It's shaky on the fence

FENCE - SITTING T.U.C. chiefs were definitely slipping after a two-hour Common Market debate at Blackpool yesterday.

One in four trade unionists is now known to be against joining Europe.

The man who gave the sharpest tug at the T.U.C. General Council's coat tails, trying to bring it down on the side of the anti-marketeers, was journalist Mr Jim Mortimer.

Best - ever

A backroom boy for the up - and - coming 70,000 - strong Draughtsmen and Allied Technicians, he received a half-minute ovation for a brilliant speech.

Mr. Mortimer sounded an alarm, to which many speakers responded, that the movement might not get another chance to decide its attitude. By the time the T.U.C. next meets, Britain may be permanently linked with Europe.

Some Congress veterans claimed last night that his calm analysis of the complicated Treaty of Rome added up to the best-ever speech from the floor of Congress.

Because the big unions had decided their attitude beforehand, Mr. Mortimer had no chance to win, but so skilfully did he marshall his facts that he won the backing of many smaller unions.

Voting by card was 2,022,000 to 5,945,000, a majority for the platform's "wait-and-see" policy of 3,823,000.

Unenviable

Among Mr. Mortimer's supporters were the 317,000-strong National Union of Railwaymen, one of the "big six," the Electrical Trades Union (253,000), the Boilermakers, the printing unions, furniture operatives, and many others.

The big boys, like the Transport Workers, Engineers, General and Municipal, Miners, and Shopworkers, all backed the General Council.

The man with the unenviable task of asking the impatient delegates to postpone the key decision, was steelworker leader Mr. Harry Douglas.

HEFTY TUG ROCKS CONGRESS LEADERS

JIM ... Brilliant sp...

chairman o... Economic Com...

A known... found is ha... impartial, and colleagues later to "walking on...

Mr. Douglas...delegates — "T... will be affected... we like it or no... have to live with... T.U.C. fence-sitting. The... preferred to think... cautiously opening a door... what was behind it.

"This Congress is in... nature of a grand inquiry... is the wisdom or unwisdom... going into the Common Market... Do not reach a verdict before... you hear all the evidence.

To join, however, necessarily solve problems. It was wand.

"We shall really try for economic trouble if... upon entry as a sort of... for all our economic... comings," warned Mr. L...

He was fed up with... T.U.C. fence-sitting. The...

The Draughtsmen's spoke... man demanded Britain shou... not join on the basis of the... Treaty of Rome and that th... final decision should be decided by a General Election.

"The Treaty of Rome is not in the interests of the British working people," he said. "But

IN SPITE of the inherent impracticality of the idea, there is no doubt that Mrs. Thatcher's proposal for... a referendum in the event of another miners-style confrontation with a future Conservative Government has alarmed the moderate trade union movement.

While they contemptuously dismiss the plan in public, they privately concede much is to lose... Their own chest of... against the threat of substantial... tie of those millions in... proportion of those millions in... were to be canvassed. If a government... trade union weakness.

Indeed it has occurred to... that it could really happen...

He is a man of flinty integrity — his unfashionable belief in incomes policy as an essential part of the battle against inflation and a central ingredient in socialist planning took him on to the PIB when his natural allies on the Left were busily denouncing it as a capitalist plot.

From time to time before the election Mrs Thatcher encouraged those around her to have a bash at ACAS. There was even talk that

board seldom, if ever, split on union/management lines and some of the most controversial ACAS board decisions had been unanimous. "How do you know?" the politico is alleged to have replied, rudely. "Because I am a member," came the devastating reply.

Now, Jim Mortimer is retiring, to be replaced by Pat Lowry, the industrial relations boss of British Leyland throughout the traumatic period when Edwardes "took on" the unions.

Remember the secret hal... with consummate... undermine the mili... both the shop floo... gional offices." Re... he sacking of "Red... acking of the... the Commu... yard"? Remember... is with which the... relations polici... eyland were de... ... icular by Leh... ... ion "the Trans...

... it be that union leaders ... e an honest

... man who ... as good ... e other th... outlined it... dustrial rela... ... s column on... hat Lowry... he Commu... taker wa... he union... AS board.

... hat union ... an honest ... ould it be... n public... s accept... ... the ... trade ...

Labour Party meets in Brighton, PETER PATERSON

The Labour Party meets in Brighton calls for a new truce on the industrial relations front

Why the unions must give peace a chance

JIM MORTIMER: Expert stresses

Forward looking after 50 years

JIM MORTIMER, who yesterday retired as general secretary of the Labour Party, talks to David Whitfield.

Jim Mortimer as the first chairperson of the arbitration and conciliation service ACAS, flanked by Jack Jones (left), and Moss Evans.

JIM MORTIMER retired yesterday, after just over three years as general secretary of the Labour Party, more concerned to look forward to the next election rather than reminisce about his few remarkable decades in the labour movement.

From 15-year-old apprentice ship fitter and engineering unionist through to retiring general secretary, Jim Mortimer has earned the reputation of an able administrator with strong political views — tempered by a balance and intellect that has frequently won the respect of the right, as well as the left, and along with it unity.

When ex-general and municipal union head of research Larry Whitty moves into the general secretary's small office in Labour's Walworth Road headquarters on Monday morning he will take over more than an organisational machine at last under firm financial control after years of decline.

He will move into an office, which under Jim Mortimer, has become respected by the party's leadership as much for its political guidance as its attention to administrative detail.

Aspirations

This week Jim Mortimer told the Morning Star what the party needs to do not just to win the next election, but then to "ensure that we meet the legitimate aspirations of the working people."

His firm conclusion is that there should be no retreat from the programme spelled out in the Labour Party's democratically decided conference policies and the left's alternative economic strategy.

"It is very important we do have a Labour government," he said spelling out the profound difference with this Tory government "... we want to ensure that the Labour government is successful and is able to represent the views of the British people."

"We have to deal with the people that will react against the policies of the Labour government. We have to explain to the Labour voters what the alternatives are.

These are the lessons that this that the retreat from socialist reduction will only cause a spiral in the wrong direction. The views of the party in power on this he says state...

words is to emphasise his life-long commitment to the left of the movement.

Jim Mortimer had and still has a close political friendship with leader Michael Foot. But it is known he has not always seen eye to eye with Neil Kinnock, particularly over the handling of the miners' strike and the so-called oneperson, one-vote on reselection.

But for Jim Mortimer there is no doubt that "those essential points need to be firmly tackling unemployment and reversing the attack on the trade union and Labour government trade union the movement...

SDP as a prime cause of "very considerable electoral difficulties."

Aided by what he calls "the distorting mirror" of the media, the disillusionment caused by failings in policy and the alienation caused by disunity and splits has been directed at the party itself — not those guilty of splitting or the prominent party spokesmen who attacked party policy during the election campaign.

The answer now is not to shirk problems toward the position of the Labour-SDP Alliance.

"We have to address ourselves to the real seriousness of Britain's economic position."

If unemployment is to be tackled that also means tackling the decline in Britain's manufacturing industry — "importing manufactured goods than exporting them" running backwards for British industry. "Getting back to train people in the skills necessary" — plus

British capitalism is in deep trouble. And it has been getting worse for many years.

"One has to advocate radical policies — but to do it in a way that is never sectarian, to work within the broad movement and to seek to influence and not to be discouraged by difficulties or occasional defeats.

"The central problem of British Socialism is how best to work and to participate in the broad stream of the movement and at the same time to advocate policies which will meet the real needs of the situation."

With his modest, down-to-earth manner, summing up complex problems in simple clear language, Jim Mortimer has become renowned for his ability to painstakingly pick a path through disagreements to unity.

Plagued by Labour's financial crisis — the party owed its workers £400,000 in unpaid wages when he arrived four years ago — Jim Mortimer admits the job of general secretary of the Labour Party has been particularly difficult.

Deterioration

Inadequate resources have been at the centre of all his work — "all we have is old furniture" — as well as accommodating the inputs from the constituency parties, the conference, the executive and parliamentary party as well as the trade unions. Today the deterioration has been halted.

Much now depends on the outcome of the union political fund ballots. "The unions have conducted a good campaign aimed at the workplaces and designed to show why members need a voice in Parliament to represent and further their occupational interests."

Jim Mortimer started as an apprentice at Ruskin, to work for retirement, was 20

Has Jones recruited a Trojan Horse?

BY STEPHEN FAY

WITHIN 24 HOURS of the reve... ome of Jim Mortimer from the ... creasing observation ... creative abnormality a journal of ...

The quiet man who can put Labour in a conciliatory mood

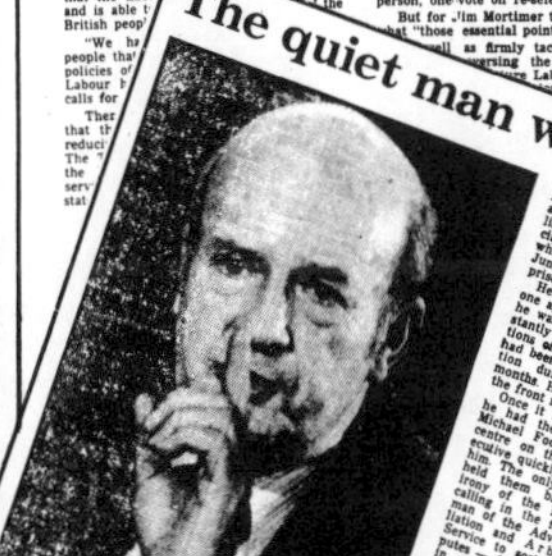

WHEN the name of Mr Jim Mortimer was mentioned as general secretary...

[text continues]

ACAS for his sensible ability...

FACE TO FACE WITH FOSTER

JACK FOSTER, our man at Westminster, talks to Labour's retiring general secretary, Jim Mortimer, and also assesses the party's General Election chances.

The stormy voyage of 'Lusitania' Mortimer ...

GENERAL secretary of the Labour Party is as tough a job as any in politics. For a start, your paymaster is your National Executive Committee. In meetings of the party's party member is aimed at a specific national lines or so he does...

he took over the job three years and a lot of personal with his own personable Yorkshire vanity welcomed him from the Lusitania coming barrel on the...

he retired and

Labour's powder point at the end of...

Jim meant in his fiercely loyal way, but it also sees as one of the gaffes of the campaign, behind the strength arrival, the party chief...

more rapid than many people realised, there will

Jim Mortimer — quiet worker for harmony

by ANNE CADWALLADER

ANYONE who retires as a troubleshooter in the thorny field of industrial relations with the praise of both Michael Foot and Jim Prior ringing in his ears must be a remarkable person.

And Bradford-born Jim Mortimer (pictured right) who retires today aged 60 as chairman of ACAS, the Advisory, Conciliation and Arbitration Service, certainly fits the bill.

From lowly beginnings in Girlington Road, Bradford, Jim Mortimer rose to play a unique role in ACAS as its first chairman after a long and distinguished career in industrial relations.

ACAS is the "pig in the middle" of British industry. It was set up by the Labour Government in 1974 to help industry solve its problems without the disruption of strike action.

When both sides stop talking to each other and words like "strike action,"

"picket" and "lockout" start being used, ACAS is there to help.

Jim Mortimer, as first chairman, had to face considerable criticism from the trade unions (who saw it as a way of limiting their power) and businessmen (who saw it as a barrier to sharper management).

But despite the formidable prejudice against it he has successfully carried it over rough ground, including bakery, steel and Leyland strikes as well as the Grunwick episode.

Now both sides are concerned with him at his retirement. Mr. Mortimer is no publicity seeker. While others may trumpet their wares he has quietly got on with the job.

His father and grandfather worked from Bradford Exchange as engine drivers none of their working lives and were active in ASLEF. His mother was one of the last "hand loaders" — at 12 she worked half a day in a Bowling textile mill and

good deal to his personal contribution."

And Prior's implacable enmity on the other side of the House of Commons. Michael Foot, Leader of the Opposition, said: "I think that when I read the Day of Judgement it will be my appointment of Jim Mortimer to ACAS that will save me. He was undoubtedly the right man for the job and has saved the country millions of pounds. He's done a marvellous job.

Despite the high praise showered on him at his retirement, Mr. Mortimer is no publicity seeker. While others may trumpet their wares he has quietly got on with the job.

His father and grandfather worked from Bradford Exchange as engine drivers none of their working lives and were active in ASLEF. His mother was one of the last "hand loaders" — at 12 she worked half a day in a Bowling textile mill and

spent the other half at school.

His father was also a newsvendor for the York shire Observer. His staid was on the corner of Lloverb Road and Heaton Road, outside Lister's Mill. When Jim was a young boy his father introduced him to the legendary W. H. Drew, leader of the Manningham Mills strike — "He seemed a little bad tempered to me," remembers Jim now.

The family split up and left Bradford to find work when Jim started work in the Portsmouth Docks, leaving for London and a job as engineering draughtsman. His interest in the union lead him to a TUC-sponsored scholarship at Ruskin College, Oxford and the London School of Economics.

He worked for the TUC, sharing a room with Len Murray. The next 12 years from 1948 were spent working for the Draughtsmen and Allied Technicians Associa-

tion. Barbara Castle invited him to work for the Prices and Incomes Board until its demise in 1971 when he joined the board of London Transport as director in charge of industrial relations.

Then in 1974 came the call from Michael Foot to join ACAS as its first chairman, the culmination of a respected career.

Along the line he has written seven books, including, with Clive Jenkins, a history of the Draughtsmen's Union. He is an honorary fellow of Bradford University.

Jim Mortimer is married with two children, a physicist and an air stewardess. He lives in Richmond but pays regular visits to Bradford to see his mother who still lives in Kensington Street, Girlington, the next door street to where Jim was born.

His main achievement is that he kept the confidence of the unions while taking

jobs that should have lead to conflict with them.

He remained a confirmed friend of the trade union movement, while others taking up similar state positions have been called, with some reason, "turncoats".

But back in 1968 he came in for a salvo of abuse for accepting a £8,500 salary working for the Prices and Incomes Board, compared to his previous £2,250 with the Draughtsmen's Association.

At the time he said he had previously looked for its role in holding down wages, "because I believe it is doing an essential function by subjecting important price rises to scrutiny."

Despite union reservations when he accepted the post he was welcomed by them on taking over as chairman of ACAS.

He's always been against using the law in industrial relations. "Persuasion should be our only weapon," he says.

NATIONAL UNION OF MINEWORKERS

ST. JAMES' HOUSE, VICAR LANE,
SHEFFIELD, SOUTH YORKSHIRE S1 2EX

President A. SCARGILL   Secretary P. E. HEATHFIELD

Telephone: 0742 700888X 766900

Please quote our reference in reply:

Your Ref:

Our Ref: NOII/RW/HS/87

16th February, 1987.

Mr. J. Mortimer,
31 Charleston Street,
LONDON,
SEI7 IRL

Dear Mr. Mortimer,

HONORARY MEMBERSHIP OF THE NUM

It is my great pleasure to inform you that the National Executive Committee of
this Union has agreed to confer upon you Honorary Membership of the NUM.

This decision has been made in recognition of, and tribute to, your dedicated services
to the NUM and its members, particularly throughout the period of the 1984/5 strike
and subsequently in relation to our victimised members.

An Honorary Membership Card is enclosed and I shall be pleased if you will confirm
your acceptance of admission to Honorary Membership in accordance with the
Rules of the Union of which a copy is enclosed.

May I take this opportunity of congratulating you upon your admission to Honorary
Membership and thank you on behalf of all our members, for the support you have
given to this Union through some of its most difficult days. I trust that your
association with this Union will continue for many years.

Yours sincerely,

Pete

P. E. Heathfield,
Secretary.

Encs

HM

NATIONAL UNION OF MINEWORKERS
MEMBERSHIP CARD
HONORARY MEMBER

The Union has agreed to confer upon
the following named person
Honorary Membership
of the
National Union of Mineworkers.

NAME   Mr. J. Mortimer

DATE ISSUED   16.2.87

Printed by Macdermott & Chant Ltd. (TU), London and Welshpool

9

Prices and Incomes Policy

The big issue for the trade union movement in the second half of the 1960s was incomes policy. In December 1964 the Government, the TUC and the principal employers' organisations issued a Joint Statement of Intent on Productivity, Prices and Incomes. It argued that the economic objective was 'to achieve and maintain a rapid increase in output and real incomes combined with full employment' and that the social objective was 'to ensure that the benefits of faster growth are distributed in a way that satisfies the claims of social need and justice'.

It then urged that vigorous action should be taken to raise productivity and that the increases in total money incomes should be kept in line with increases in real national output. The Government indicated that it would prepare and implement a plan for economic development, providing for higher investment, improving skills, industrial modernisation, balanced regional development, higher exports and the sustained expansion of production and real incomes. It also said that it would set up machinery to keep a continuous watch on the general movement of prices and money incomes of all kinds. The Government undertook to use their powers or 'other appropriate means' to correct any excessive growth in profits as compared with the growth of total wages and salaries.

The TUC and the principal employers' organisations expressed their support for these major economic objectives and agreed to cooperate with the Government in the proposed machinery for the review of general movements of prices and of money incomes of all kinds. They agreed with a proposal that there should be an examination in particular cases, 'in order to advise whether or not the behaviour of prices or of wages, salaries or other money incomes is in the national interest as defined by the Government after consultation with management and unions'.

Thus it was that the National Board for Prices and Incomes came into existence. Its chairman was Mr Aubrey Jones, a former Conservative Cabinet Minister. The Board included a small number of full-time members and a number of part-time members. The members were drawn from management, the trade union movement and from persons with an academic background. The Board had its own staff of economists, accountants, statisticians and persons with experience of industrial relations. The Government assumed responsibility for referring for examination to the Board particular price movements and claims and settlements affecting pay and conditions of employment

A White Paper issued in April 1965 put forward 'a statement of considerations' to be taken into account in prices and incomes policy. These same considerations were also intended to guide the National Board for Prices and Incomes in its work. It was argued that enterprises should not raise their prices except in circumstances which were specified under four main headings. The exceptions were designed to permit price increases where a pay increase in accordance with the criteria could be justified but it was not possible to make offsetting reductions in costs; where there were unavoidable increases in non-labour costs which could not be offset by reductions in costs; where there were unavoidable increases in capital costs per unit of output; or, if after every effort to reduce costs, the enterprise was unable to secure the capital required to meet the demand for its products. The nature of these permitted exceptions to price stability pointed to the extreme difficulty, and, perhaps, impossibility, of exercising effective price control in a capitalist economy with strong inflationary pressures.

In relation to incomes, the White Paper put forward a

'norm' of 3 per cent to 3½ per cent. It said that this 'norm', indicating the average rate of annual increase of money incomes per head, would be consistent with stability in the general level of prices. This was based upon an assumption that there would be an average rate of growth in output per head of something approaching 3½ per cent.

In the same way that the White Paper put forward exceptional grounds for price increases, it also outlined exceptional circumstances for increases in wages and salaries above the 'norm'. It emphasised, however, that exceptional increases would need to be balanced by lower than average increases to other groups.

The grounds for exceptional pay increases included more exacting work or a major change in working practices, resulting in higher productivity. Even in such cases some of the benefit, it was stressed, should accrue to the community in the form of lower prices. Other grounds for exceptional pay increases were where a change in the distribution of labour – or the prevention of a change – was essential in the national interest; where wages and salaries were too low to maintain a reasonable standard of living; and where the pay of a group of workers had fallen seriously out of line with pay for similar work and needed in the national interest to be improved.

The grounds for exceptional pay increases, like the criteria for price increases, were open to differences of interpretation even among those who supported the prices and incomes policy. In the subsequent years of its existence the National Board for Prices and Incomes developed what, in effect, became a 'theology' for the interpretation not only of the original guidelines but of amendments made from time to time, to take account of changes in the economic situation, in the Government's policies and in the guidelines themselves.

The Government's proposals for a prices and incomes policy and, more particularly, their proposals for machinery for implementing it and the associated guidelines on prices and pay were put to a special conference of trade union executive committees on 30 April, 1965. The conference was addressed by George Brown, the Minister for Economic Affairs, who said that the issue was one of order or chaos, of planning or anarchy. He pointed out that the proposals for a productivity, prices and incomes policy, on which there was agreement between the Government, the employers and the TUC, had been reached after months of intense discussion. The policy, he said, was in favour of order and planning. The National Board for Prices and Incomes was not intended to replace collective bargaining machinery, but would work alongside it.

The policy was commended to the conference by George Woodcock, the General Secretary of the TUC. He spoke on behalf of the General Council and, as always, in a persuasive manner. He made no exaggerated claims for the proposals. He said that the word 'plan' and even the word 'policy' were too grandiloquent for what was being put before the delegates. An incomes policy had to be accepted as something sensible in its own right and not something drawn artificially out of loyalty to a political party. The 'norm' would not be a 'rigid law'. The real object was to get sufficient control over prices and costs so as to enable Britain to have a fair chance in competition in foreign markets. The guidelines attempted to create a standard of conduct, but there would be no attempt to impose sanctions.

When the report of the General Council was thrown open to discussion by the delegates, I was the first to speak. I opposed the proposals on behalf of the Draughtsmen's Association. I disputed the proposition that incomes had risen disproportionately faster in Britain than in other countries. In the previous five years hourly earnings and hourly earnings per unit of output had risen faster in France, Western Germany and Italy than in Britain. On the other hand, since the Joint Statement of Intent had been signed, distributed dividends, after tax and depreciation, had risen by 20 per cent.

I suggested that the emphasis on incomes policy tended to divert attention from the real economic problem facing Britain. This problem was not wages but the misdirection of resources. There was an inadequate level of investment in British industry, and too much was being spent for military purposes. The level of overseas investment was also too high. The pull of market forces, the very essence of capitalism, had distorted the

200

economy. Economic planning meant that the social will had to override market forces.

In the debate, some unions gave strong support to the proposed policy whilst others expressed misgivings but felt that the policy had to be given a chance to work. John Boyd, on behalf of the AEU, expressed confidence that the incomes policy would be successful. Harry Nicholas of the TGWU suggested that an attempt was being made to introduce an incomes policy without an economic plan. Clive Jenkins, on behalf of ASSET, said that the analysis presented by George Woodcock was irrelevant to the needs of the economy. British labour costs were too low, and this had encouraged low capital investment. There was no proper planning of the economy, and the unequal distribution of wealth had been 'frozen for decades'. Danny McGarvey of the Boilermakers' Society said that the incomes policy would do harm to the trade union and labour movement, and would lead to disillusionment. Strong support for the policy was voiced by Harry Douglass of the Iron and Steel Trades Confederation. He called upon the unions to work with the Labour Government. Support was also given by USDAW and the Foundry Workers.

The report of the General Council was carried by a large majority. The voting was:

For the report   6,649,000
Against the report   1,811,000

Almost immediately following the April 1965 conference of trade union executive committees, five affiliated unions representing the great majority of organised technical staff decided to issue 'A Declaration of Dissent' as an answer to the Joint Statement of Intent. The five unions were the Cinematograph and Television Technicians, ASSET, the Scientific Workers, the Technical Civil Servants and the Draughtsmen and Allied Technicians (The AESD had changed its name to the Draughtsmen's and Allied Technicians' Association). The five unions asked me to prepare the draft of the declaration. The draft was adopted with very few amendments of substance,

201

though Clive Jenkins introduced a number of characteristic phrases to enliven the text. The declaration was circulated as a pamphlet in many thousands of copies. The Draughtsmen's Association sent copies to every drawing office. It was thus circulated to almost every engineering factory and shipyard in Britain.

'A Declaration of Dissent' said that scientific and technical staff were in favour of planning, but Britain was still predominantly an unplanned society. The guidance given by the Government and the National Economic Development Council did little more than indicate the probable pattern of development in the years ahead, but the main consideration affecting economic decisions in private firms remained the desire to maximise private profits.

The Declaration pointed out that there was a vital difference between wage restraint and dividend restraint. A wage claim that was abandoned or diminished meant that purchasing power was foregone for ever. In contrast, dividend restraint implied no more than the transfer of profits to reserve or increased investment. The real assets of the shareholder would thereby be increased, and this would be reflected in the future in either higher dividends and/or a higher share price.

Another section compared British wages with wages in other leading European manufacturing countries. Recently published statistics suggested that British wages were not the highest but the lowest among these countries. Hourly earnings, including social benefits, were higher in Western Germany, Italy, Belgium, France and the Netherlands.

The Declaration argued that the pull of market forces within the British economy and the heavy burden of military spending had led to a misdirection of resources. The need was for more effective economic planning. The Declaration also followed the example of the TGWU in asking a number of practical questions about the interpretation of the 'norm', the utilisation of productivity savings for lower prices and the transfer of benefits to lower-paid workers.

At the 1965 TUC the debate on incomes policy was renewed, but it was becoming increasingly clear that profits, pay and prices were increasing at a faster rate than desired by the Government. The Draughtsmen's Association seconded a motion from the Boilermakers' Society, reaffirming support for a planned economy based upon the public ownership of the basic industries, and rejecting the Government's productivity, prices and incomes policy. It was comfortably defeated by 6,131,000 votes to 2,212,000.

Nevertheless, an attempt by the Amalgamated Union of Building Trade Workers to refer back the General Council's endorsement of the Government's proposal to give the National Board for Prices and Incomes limited statutory powers received rather more support, even though it was defeated. The move to refer back the General Council's report received 3,003,000 votes. The number against the reference back was 5,738,000. The General Council's report was then adopted by 5,251,000 votes to 3,312,000. The result was a clear indication of growing unease in the trade union movement.

In 1966 the situation became more difficult. A non-statutory 'early warning' system had been introduced late in 1965, under which notification had to be given of any claims and settlements affecting pay and conditions of employment. The 'early warning' also applied to proposed increases for certain prices and charges. At the end of 1965 the Government indicated that they intended to introduce legislation to provide for a statutory 'early warning' system. It was also to be coupled with provisions for a compulsory standstill whilst a proposed pay claim or price increase was investigated by the National Board for Prices and Incomes. A Bill designed to give effect to these changes was introduced early in 1966.

'Severe Restraint'

When Parliament was dissolved for the purpose of the 1966 General Election, the Bill lapsed. With the return of the Labour Government with an increased majority, the Bill was reintroduced in the summer of 1966. By then the economic situation had worsened. The balance of payments was heavily in deficit, inflationary pressures were strong and, according to the Government, incomes were rising at a far faster rate than could be justified by increasing production. The Government introduced a prices and incomes standstill to be followed by a period of 'severe restraint' in which the incomes 'norm' was to be regarded as zero. Under the legislation, employers were protected from legal proceedings if and when, in response to the Government's request for a standstill, they withheld pay increases to which an employee was entitled under his contract of employment. The Cabinet also introduced a number of deflationary measures.

In a number of articles during 1966 I expressed opposition to the Government's policy. I argued that it was unnecessary, unfair, punitive and destructive of trade union rights. At the 1966 annual conference of the Draughtsmen's Association I moved, on behalf of the Executive Committee, a successful motion calling for more effective economic planning, increased industrial investment, a reduction in military spending, and measures designed to bring about a substantial redistribution of wealth and income in favour of wage and salary earners. The motion rejected the Government's incomes policy. One of the many branch delegates to speak in support of the motion was Joe Ashton, who was later elected to Parliament.

The articles against the Government's policy put forward a number of main arguments. The incomes policy and the wage freeze, it was suggested, did not deal with the real sources of Britain's economic difficulties. These were excessive military spending, inadequate investment in industry, and deflationary policies which had the effect of cutting back production. The incomes policy was unfair because it perpetuated the gross inequalities of British society. It was dishonourable because the Government had assumed power to compel people to break agreements and had given employers legal immunity for so doing. It was punitive because it introduced new criminal liabilities for workers who sought to persuade an employer to pay a wage increase forbidden by the Government. It was destructive of trade union rights because it had suspended the right of workers to settle their terms and conditions by collective bargaining with their employer.

In the early summer of 1966 there was a national strike of seamen. The claim of the National Union of Seamen was for a 40-hour week. They were seeking no more than had already been established in many other industries, including engineering. The seamen also asked for an easing of the harsh disciplinary code imposed by the penal clauses of the Merchant Shipping Acts. They said that they had been promised a reform of the law for some 20 years.

The strike was denounced by the Prime Minister, Harold Wilson, in the most severe terms. He sought to persuade the public that the strike was the outcome of a left-wing conspiracy. He did not address himself to the grievances which had caused the dispute, but made clear the Government's determination to try to defeat the seamen. Fortunately, he did not succeed. The strike was eventually settled on terms which brought a significant improvement in conditions for seamen.

The Draughtsmen's Association supported the struggle of the seamen. A national donation was made to the dispute fund, and an interest-free loan was offered to the NUS. Collections to assist the strikers were made in the drawing offices of many engineering firms and shipyards. I wrote an editorial article for *The Draughtsman* which said:

'Where do we stand on the dispute between the shipowners and the seamen? There can be no doubt about the answer. We are on the side of the seamen; not partially or mainly, but wholly on their side.'

In July 1966 Frank Cousins resigned from the Cabinet, in protest against the restrictive legislation on incomes policy. A national economic plan, which had been produced and published in 1965, looked increasingly unrealistic. The object of the plan was to achieve a substantial increase in national output in the years up to 1970, to put right the balance of payments and to promote prosperity. The plan, however, was more an expression of hope than a mechanism for the control and allocation of resources.

At first there was some improvement in the economic situation, but in 1967 all the old problems returned but in aggravated form. The 'early warning' system and the standstill were followed by a period of 'severe restraint'.

The TUC convened another conference of trade union executive committees for 2 March, 1967. A report was presented to the conference by the General Council which said that a progressive incomes policy must make a contribution to planned economic expansion. The report, however, was more cautious in its attitude to Government policy. It said that Government intervention in incomes could never be a substitute for economic policy. It went on:

'By exaggerating the direct contribution that incomes policy can in the short run make to improving the balance of payments, the Government has laid on that part of its policy a burden that it cannot carry.'

In the subsequent debate, I spoke on behalf of the Draughtsmen's Association. I pointed to the contrast between the reality of the economic situation and the economic framework which the General Council had suggested for an acceptable incomes policy. The General Council had called for an effective social and economic plan, but the National Economic Plan which had been published bore no relationship to the existing British economy. Full employment had been sacrificed. Unemployment had been created as a deliberate part of the Government's policy of deflation. There was economic stagnation, not expansion. Investment had been cut, but this was the long-term determinant of productivity. Living standards were not rising, and there was no movement towards a more equitable distribution of income and wealth.

Clive Jenkins, on behalf of ASSET, also opposed the acceptance of the General Council's report. He pointed out that in the preceding months production had fallen and unemployment had risen, yet the unions were 'about as aggressive as hamsters'. Free collective bargaining, he said, had never caused unemployment. The rise in the number of jobless had been created by Government deflationary measures.

Despite these criticisms, most of the unions supported the General Council's report because they saw it as a choice between a voluntary and a compulsory incomes policy. The TUC were in favour of a voluntary policy of restraint. If this were rejected, the Government would be almost certain to continue statutory restrictions. The report was approved by 7,604,000 votes to 963,000.

The Government, nevertheless, did not abandon its statutory intervention on incomes. New legislation was introduced and passed by Parliament, to extend by Government order the periods of standstill on certain prices and pay awards, and to give legal protection to employers who had withheld certain pay increases. This policy aroused substantial opposition within the trade union and labour movement. A number of Labour MPs abstained in the vote in the House of Commons. At the annual conference of the Draughtsmen's Association the delegates carried by a very large majority a resolution deploring the policy of the Government. The resolution was moved by the General Secretary, George Doughty. In a subsequent editorial article in *The Draughtsman* I expressed the hope that the TUC at its annual congress would make clear its opposition to the Prices and Incomes Acts.

The 1967 congress of the TUC registered a sharp change in the mood of the trade union movement. A composite motion, moved by the TGWU, expressing opposition 'to restrictive and negative incomes policies' and expressing support for 'a high wage, high efficiency policy', was carried without a card vote. Another successful motion, moved by the Boilermakers' Society and seconded by George Doughty on behalf of the Draughtsmen's Association, said bluntly that the Prices and Incomes Acts had been detrimental to the interests of trade unionists and should be repealed. A motion which expressed qualified support for a prices and incomes policy, 'in moving towards a planned economy', was defeated on a card vote by 4,277,000 to 4,109,000.

The severity of the prices and incomes policy did not prevent the worsening of the economic situation. The deficit in the balance of payments increased, and in November 1967 the Government devalued the currency. Credits were secured from the International Monetary Fund, but on condition that home consumption was cut. A series of measures were introduced, designed to reduce or, at best, to hold down living standards and the social services.

Disillusionment

By this time disillusionment with the policies of the Labour Government was widespread within the trade union movement. Joe Gormley of the National Union of Mineworkers, and at that time a member of the National Executive Committee of the Labour Party, was widely reported as saying that unless there was a change in the thinking of the Labour Party leadership, the miners and others might be forced to consider forming a new party. In the Draughtsmen's Association a proposition was put forward at the annual conference – with support from what I regarded as the 'ultra left' – that the union should disaffiliate from the Labour Party. It was given support by a prominent member of the Executive Committee of the union, Michael Cooley, who said that the Labour Government had attacked the workers in a manner without precedent. It had grovelled to the gnomes of Zurich and supported an American war of aggression in Vietnam. Michael Cooley was one of a group whose influence in the leadership of the union was growing. Much of their criticism, I felt at the time, was directed against my own view, expressed both at meetings of the Executive Committee and in the union's journal, that socialists should remain within the Labour Party and should not leave it to the domination of those who supported the policies of the Government.

I expressed my views on the relationship between the unions and the Labour Party in an editorial article in the December 1967 issue of *The Draughtsman*. I described at some length how the Labour Party had come into existence primarily to defend trade union interests. The case for independent labour representation in Parliament was as strong as ever. To translate dismay with the record of the Labour Government into desertion of the Labour Party would be to surrender the struggle to those responsible for the present troubles. Nor was it an acceptable alternative to put up candidates supporting left-wing policies in opposition to Labour candidates. Over the years the politically conscious working people of Britain had come to regard the Labour Party as the instrument through which to seek political representation. The alternative to the Labour Party was seen to be the Conservative Party. I ended by urging that it was more than ever essential for trade unionists to work inside the Labour Party.

My relationship with the 'ultra-left' group on the Executive Committee of the union was becoming increasingly strained. The group was not drawn from any one political party. A couple were lapsed members of the Communist Party, two or three others were or had been individual members of the Labour Party, and one was sympathetic to the International Socialists (later to become the Socialist Workers' Party). They were not the majority on the Executive Committee, but they had considerable influence, and the circumstances of the time gave a certain validity to the bitterness of their criticisms. Unfortunately, this also expressed itself in personal relationships. I found it a difficult experience, not least because my defence of membership and activity in the Labour Party was sometimes misinterpreted as a defence of the policies of the Government. This was made more acute because I continued to argue that there could be circumstances under a Labour Government, if it were moving in a progressive direction, when a productivity, prices and incomes policy would be necessary in the interests of the community, including trade unionists.

The year 1968 was one of difficulty and disillusionment for the labour movement. There was no improvement in the economy, and the Government carried through their deflationary policy with cuts in spending and increased taxation. At the 1968 annual conference of the Draughtsmen's Association, resolutions were carried condemning the Government's economic policies and opposing the incomes policy legislation. Another successful resolution called for an effective prices policy but was silent on the relationship between prices and incomes.

At the time of devaluation, the General Council of the TUC had issued a statement generally sympathetic to the Government. The statement declared that the immediate aim of devaluation was to stop the run on sterling. The way forward, said the General Council, was to use the spare capacity of British industry to promote an expansion and a massive increase in exports. The General Council added:

'In these circumstances a prices and incomes policy, designed as part of an overall strategy for full employment and the strengthening of Britain's economy, which alone can yield higher and rising living standards, takes on added importance.'

Yet another conference of trade union executive committees was convened, this time at the end of February 1968. It approved by the narrow margin of 4,620,000 to 4,084,000 an economic review prepared by the General Council.

In the early summer of 1968 new legislation was introduced, to prolong the duration of certain provisions of the Prices and Incomes Acts 1966 and 1967 and to extend the period for which standstills in prices and changes in pay and conditions could be enforced. The Government said in a White Paper that for pay settlements that satisfied specified criteria there should be a ceiling of 3½ per cent. The criteria were set out at length in the White Paper, but provision was made for exceptions to the ceiling for agreements which raised productivity and efficiency sufficiently to justify a pay increase above 3½ per cent. On the other hand, the White Paper stipulated that pay increases based on a rise in the cost of living were not justified under the criteria and were not to be conceded. These various conditions, and the difficulties of interpretation, became part of the 'theology' of the National Board for Prices and Incomes in the subsequent period.

At the 1968 TUC opinion was overwhelmingly against legislative restrictions on wages. A resolution to this effect, moved by Frank Cousins on behalf of the TGWU, was carried by 7,746,000 to 1,022,000. It said that the legislative restrictions on wage and salary movements had hindered legitimate trade union activity, economic expansion and improvements in industrial efficiency. It called for the repeal of the legislation.

Another resolution was carried, however, to indicate that the majority of the trade union movement – though by now a very slender majority – was still in favour of a voluntary incomes policy. It was moved by the National Union of Dyers, Bleachers and Textile Workers. It pledged full support to the TUC's voluntary incomes policy and said that it was the only feasible alternative to growing legislative interference in wages negotiations, and was the fairest way of removing anomalies and injustices inherent in the wages structure. It was carried by 4,266,000 votes to 4,232,000. A much more emphatic expression of support for a prices and incomes policy, moved by the EETPU, was defeated by a very heavy majority. The General Council's report on incomes policy, which gave cautious support to voluntary arrangements, was adopted by a majority of just over 750,000 votes.

Industrial Disputes

The arguments about incomes policy had significant practical implications for the Draughtsmen's Association. There was no period in the second half of the 1960s when members were not engaged in struggles for higher pay, shorter hours or other improvements in conditions. At every meeting of the Executive Committee requests were considered from members at various firms for official support for strike action. Not all requests for strike action were sanctioned. The union was concerned to ensure that it had a reserve of adequate funds in the event of a big dispute, and it sought always to resolve problems, wherever possible, by negotiations. Nearly every dispute was ended on terms which represented improved conditions for the members involved.

The union was particularly vigilant to protect its office representatives against victimisation by employers. Unfortunately, it was rarely possible to protect victimised representatives without strike action or the threat of strike action. No employer admits to victimising a representative. He always advances some other plausible reason for his discrimination.

Without doubt, the most effective way to defend a victimised representative is for the members in the office or workshop to demand immediate reinstatement. If this demand is not met, it should be supported by strike action. Any delay through the negotiating procedure reduces the possibility of a successful outcome.

In my view, it is not a breach of the procedure to strike in support of a victimised representative, because the initial breach is in the act of victimisation. The need for an immediate response against victimisation is one reason why the Labour Party's commitment, introduced during the 1980s under Neil Kinnock's leadership, to obligatory ballot votes before all strikes, was wrong. Procrastination makes it more difficult to protect a victimised representative.

In early 1965 the Draughtsmen's Association conducted major official strikes at AEI, Larne in Northern Ireland, English Electric in Liverpool, at the Scottish factories of Rolls-Royce, the manufacturer of aircraft engines, at Hopkinson's of Huddersfield, at Distington Engineering of Workington, at AC Delco of Liverpool, and at Harland and Wolff of Belfast. In April 1965, as a result of a national agreement concluded with the Engineering Employers' Federation, the basic working week for members of the Draughtsmen's Association was reduced to a maximum of 37½ hours. This was the third such national agreement for reduced hours of work negotiated since the end of the Second World War in 1945.

In the summer of 1965 a dispute with the Shipbuilding Employers' Federation about a minimum pay scale led to the setting up of an official Court of Enquiry by the Minister of

Labour. The claim of the union had been presented to the employers in October 1964. The employers made an offer, but it was rejected by the union. A national overtime ban was imposed, and a one-day token strike took place in federated shipyards in April 1965. This was followed by prolonged strike action at a number of shipyards, to which the employers replied with the threat of national lockout to begin on 5 May. The Minister of Labour then intervened. A suggestion that the claim should be considered by the National Board for Prices and Incomes was rejected by the union. A Court of Enquiry was appointed, and its report led to the reopening of negotiations. The settlement reached represented a significant step forward for the union. It was followed by a similar agreement with the Engineering Employers' Federation.

In the summer of 1965 there were strikes of DATA members at Trico-Folberth, Frigidaire, Bonar-Long in Dundee, and at Workington Iron and Steel. A long strike for higher wages at Locker Industries, Warrington, was settled in the early winter on terms favourable to the union.

In the early months of 1966 the union was involved in a major dispute with the English Electric Company, covering its Whetstone and Rugby factories. Some 500 members took part in a strike which lasted for nine weeks and was eventually settled on favourable terms. The dispute concerned the employment of contract labour, so called 'self-employed' staff and the impending redundancy of permanent staff. The issue was of national importance because of the growing practice of firms to employ agency staff as a substitute for their own staff.

By the closing weeks of 1966 the Draughtsmen's Association was feeling the effects of the Government's incomes policy. At Parsons of Newcastle the employers argued that a claim of the union for longer holidays should be rejected because of the 'freeze'. This led to a lengthy strike by approximately 125 members of the union. Improvements were secured.

Some time later the Government intervened, with the intention of prohibiting a negotiated wages settlement at another large firm in the North-East, Clarke Chapman of Gateshead.

Following further representations by the union, it was agreed that the increases should be paid from 1 July, 1967. A strike for higher wages at Bord-na-Mona in Ireland lasted for many months. The biggest dispute in 1967 was in shipbuilding. It started with a wages claim at Swan Hunter, and went through all stages of the negotiating procedure. The employers made a final offer, but subject to 'Government permission'. The Shipbuilding Employers' Federation then resorted to a national lockout to force the submission of the union. Thousands of DATA members took part in demonstrations of support for the shipbuilding draughtsmen, and token strikes of solidarity took place in a number of engineering firms. After ten weeks the national lockout was called off. The DATA members remained completely solid throughout the dispute. The original dispute at Swan Hunter was settled with an agreement for increased wages. The strike at Swan Hunter lasted from the end of February 1967 until 16 May.

All these disputes were publicised in *The Draughtsman* and I participated in a number of the demonstrations and meetings of members. All the full-time officials of the union were called upon to speak at meetings.

Another dispute in which I spoke at a demonstration of strikers was at CBR Jersey Mills, Brighton. This was a dispute involving members of the National Union of Hosiery and Knitwear Workers. The management were opposed to trade union recognition, and a number of workers associated with the union's claim had been dismissed. The working hours were said to be 72 per week. The Draughtsmen's Association made a donation to the strike fund and asked members in other firms not to work on machinery or contracts for the strike-bound plant.

A campaign was initiated in 1967 to secure national recognition for DATA for draughtsmen employed in the iron and steel industry. Recognition had been secured in a number of individual steel companies, but there was no agreed national procedure. Together with other officials, I spoke at a number of large meetings of members employed in the steel industry. The campaign was successful.

Towards the end of 1967 and in the early months of 1968, the Draughtsmen's Association conducted a very vigorous campaign for wage increases at factory and shipyard level. This was a partial answer to the 'official' incomes policy of the Government. It was intended to win improvements, certainly in the initial stages, outside the framework of a national agreement. It proved to be highly successful.

During this period the Draughtsmen's Association was involved in a strike lasting more than 18 weeks at Plessey, Liverpool. It was in support of a wage claim. The final settlement provided for substantial increases. The leading lay member in the strike was Len Formby, who later became a full-time official of the union. It was Formby who, in response to a complaint that 'working to rule' was in breach of the negotiating procedure, said that the members were 'working without enthusiasm'. It was a saying which later gained wide currency.

Vietnam

Another big issue in the second half of the 1960s was the Vietnam War. At the 1965 annual conference of the Draughtsmen's Association a resolution was carried, expressing concern at the intensification of US military action in Vietnam and calling for an international conference to end the fighting. In July 1965 I wrote an article for the union's journal urging members, branches and divisional councils to make known to all concerned the union's call for an end to the war. The article pointed out that the US Government had always opposed elections in Vietnam if such elections were likely to lead to a government under communist leadership or with communist participation.

By this time I was playing an active part in the national protest movement against the Vietnam War and the support given by Britain to the United States' military intervention. Paradoxically, it was because of the strength of this protest campaign, the vigour of the Movement for Colonial Freedom and the campaign in support of David Kitson that it was decided to wind up the Union of Democratic Control, of which I was the Chairman. The single-issue campaigns had gathered momentum, and it was felt that the objectives of the UDC could best be pursued by the separate campaigning organisations.

At the 1966 TUC I spoke on behalf of the Draughtsmen's Association in support of a successful resolution calling for a negotiated peace in Vietnam and for the ending of the bombing of North Vietnam by the USA. Among other speakers in support of the resolution were Terry Parry of the Fire Brigades' Union, who moved the resolution, Lawrence Daly of the NUM and Jack Jones of the TGWU.

At the 1967 TUC the Draughtsmen's Association sponsored a more strongly critical resolution on the Vietnam War. It called upon the British Government to dissociate itself from American policy in Vietnam and to press for the ending of the war, with the withdrawal of foreign troops and nation-wide elections as envisaged in the 1954 Geneva Agreement. The DATA delegation asked me to move the resolution on behalf of the union. I welcomed the opportunity, and spoke in terms condemnatory both of American and British policy.

The General Council of the TUC opposed the resolution, but when put to the vote it was carried by 4,686,000 to 3,319,000. It was the last occasion I was to speak at the TUC as a union delegate. I remember the outcome with satisfaction. The American military intervention in Vietnam was an outrage and the support given to it by Britain's Labour Government a disgrace.

At the 1967 TUC I also spoke in criticism of the channelling of millions of pounds from the Central Intelligence Agency of the USA under the cover of the international trade union movement. I quoted at length from American sources in support of these charges. The money was being used to support the objectives of the US Government. George Woodcock replied by stating that he could not speak for the various international trade union secretariats, but there was no evidence that any money had been received by the Interna-

216

tional Confederation of Free Trade Unions from anywhere other than a trade union source.

This was one occasion where I think George Woodcock did not give proper regard to the available evidence. Clive Jenkins and I were persuaded from our own experience in the international movement that money was being directed from the CIA through American organisations, with a view to strengthening US international influence.

The campaign in support of David Kitson continued throughout this period. John Forrester spoke at the TUC on behalf of the union about the imprisonment of Kitson. At the 1966 TUC I spoke in support of the South Africa Defence and Aid Fund, and referred to the large sum of money raised by the members of DATA to assist David Kitson and his family. Regular features were published in the union's journal about South Africa and the imprisonment of Kitson and his colleagues. In January 1967 *The Draughtsman* published an article on the conditions in the Central Prison Pretoria, where David Kitson had been held. The author, himself a former political prisoner, described it as being amongst the most notorious prisons in the world. Regular executions of political prisoners took place.

10

The Prices and Incomes Board

In the summer of 1968 I was invited to join the National Board for Prices and Incomes as one of its two full-time trade union members. The Minister then primarily responsible for the prices and incomes policy and for the work of the NBPI was Barbara Castle. As Secretary of State for Employment, she had taken over this responsibility from George Brown, the Minister at the Department of Economic Affairs.

At a meeting with Barbara Castle I said that I was prepared to do what I could to achieve the proclaimed objective of the policy, namely the planned growth of incomes together with effective price control, but that I did not support the legislative restrictions on collective bargaining. I indicated that I would have voted with the minority of Labour MPs against these restrictions if I had been in Parliament. Barbara Castle did not agree with my objections, but appeared satisfied that I would help to strengthen the influence of trade unionism in the work of the Prices and Incomes Board.

I had first met Barbara Castle in 1937 – she was then Barbara Betts – at the London conference of the Socialist League. I was then 16 years of age, and I remembered her clearly. She had no reason to remember me. I did not know her closely in subsequent years, but in the post-war period we had sometimes been active in the same left-wing campaigns and organisations. Her outstanding attribute was her sense of commitment and enthusiasm for any cause to which she gave her support. She was able to inspire others with this same enthusiasm. Of her commitment to the cause of labour and socialism there was never in my mind the slightest doubt. She ran into considerable criticism because of the prices and incomes policy and because of her proposals affecting trade unions in the White Paper, 'In Place of Strife', but, in my view, her motivation was never reactionary. Indeed, in conversation her strongest criticisms were always reserved for the right wing in British politics, whether in the Conservative Party or in the labour movement.

Before I started work at the National Board for Prices and Incomes there was a slight problem regarding 'security'. I do not now recall how it arose, but I became aware of it. It was, of course, based on the usual unjustified assumption by those responsible for so-called security that left-wing trade unionists are a potential risk. It was not the first time, nor was it to be the last, that I came up against this invisible and insidious influence. Whenever I have had the opportunity I have affirmed in the most vigorous terms that, far from operating in a covert way, I have sought since my youth to proclaim my views and openly to influence others. I was never a 'Cold War warrior' and did not identify myself with the interests of American capitalism, dressed up as the 'struggle of the free world'. The way forward to social progress, colonial liberation and socialism is through economic and political struggle, and the main instrument in this struggle is the labour movement.

It would, of course, be ridiculous to deny the existence of espionage networks operating on behalf of all the principal powers in the world, but I have never come across any examples of espionage operations within the left wing of the trade union movement. In contrast, on a number of occasions I have encountered activities designed to embrace active members of the trade union movement, which were almost certainly financed from the United States' Central Intelligence Agency.

My decision to join the National Board for Prices and Incomes came in for much criticism from colleagues who shared my general political and trade union views. The more generous of my critics said that I had made an error of judgment; the less generous, that I had betrayed the ideas for which I had stood. A minority of left-wingers supported my action, but few of them were to be found in the union of which I was an official. I spent an unhappy period listening to criticisms at the final meeting I attended of the Executive Committee of the Draughtsmen's Association. I had been a member of the Executive Committee for approximately 20 years.

My critics argued that, whatever my personal intention to bring a trade union influence on prices and incomes, the NBPI was an instrument of a policy that was directed against working people. Its purpose was to hold down wages, and it was backed by legal measures which included the breaking of agreements and penal sanctions. They pointed out that I had been a public opponent of this policy, both as a speaker at the TUC, in numerous articles which I had written and as the author of 'A Declaration of Dissent'. My decision to accept the invitation to join the NBPI was described as an act of desertion which would disillusion many active trade unionists.

I did not dismiss as unfounded a single one of these criticisms. On the other hand, I was conscious that there were strong arguments in the opposite direction. Our union, which was on the left, and I personally, had advocated the election of a Labour Government. The logical implication was that left-wingers should seek to maximise their influence and should not leave all public appointments to individuals on the right wing of the movement. My views were unchanged, and I would do whatever was possible to influence the NBPI in favour of its stated objectives at the time of its formation. Moreover, the prices and incomes policy and the establishment of the NBPI had been supported by the majority of the trade union movement.

There was also an important ideological point on which I differed from many other opponents of the prices and incomes policy. I had never rejected the contention that in conditions of full employment or near full employment there was likely to be an inflationary problem unless there was an effective public policy to deal with the relationship between the allocation of resources, public spending, productivity, prices and incomes of all kinds. Inflation expressed either the conflicting pressures of different demands on limited available resources or the determination of employers to maintain their profits in conditions where ineffective competition enabled them to increase prices without a corresponding fall in sales.

Hence, with a Labour Government the task was to ensure that the public policy for dealing with these problems should be directed to serve the interests of working people. The cutting edge of my criticism was that this was not being done. I had no illusions as to the extent of my own limited influence, but if a Labour Minister gave me the opportunity to exert some influence I did not intend to reject it.

I was also influenced by disagreements within the leadership of the Draughtsmen's Association. A group around Michael Cooley was growing in influence, and I regarded them as 'ultra-left'. They had little sympathy with the Labour Party. At the 1968 annual conference of the Draughtsmen's Association some of these disagreements were expressed in a debate on a Labour Party report on industrial democracy. I supported the report, but some on the 'ultra left' were very critical and suggested that there could be no real answer short of workers' control.

Board Members

The Chairman of the NBPI was Aubrey Jones, a former Conservative Minister, a former Chairman of Staveley Industries and an economist with a particularly sharp mind. During my period as a member of the NBPI, I had a number of discussions with him in which he explained his point of view.

As I understood his views he believed that capitalism, with the motivation of private profit, provided the best framework for human progress, but that public intervention in many areas was essential to overcome problems arising from the free play of market forces. One such area was employment policy. Left to itself, the economic system led to periodic unemployment and the under-utilisation of resources. It was, therefore, the task of the state to stimulate demand from time to time, to

221

maintain a high level of employment. It was necessary also for the state to promote competition, as a preventive measure against monopolistic or oligopolistic abuse. His attitude towards the public ownership of industry was pragmatic. He preferred competitive private ownership, but if it could be demonstrated that a privately owned industry was in a state of decay or in need of investment which only the state could provide, he did not object to public ownership, providing that the industry concerned was providing a service or products needed by the community. There were also certain natural monopolies, such as water supply, which satisfied his criteria for public ownership.

Central to Aubrey Jones's standpoint was his conviction that in an economy with a high level of employment, a productivity, prices and incomes policy was essential for combatting what would otherwise be inevitable inflationary pressures. Employers occupying a dominant market position were able to pass on in higher prices any increase in costs which they had to sustain. The alternative, as he saw it, was to introduce arrangements, preferably voluntary but, if necessary, backed by statutory force, for restraint on both prices and incomes. Increases in incomes should represent real increases in living standards and should reflect the real growth of the economy. Hence, pressure to improve efficiency and a national policy for economic growth were essential parts of the policy he advocated.

The other full-time members of the NBPI when I joined it were Lord Peddie, Ralph Turvey and Wilfred Heywood. Lord Peddie was from the cooperative movement, a Labour supporter and a former director of the CWS. Ralph Turvey was an academic economist who had gained industrial experience as Chief Economist with the Electricity Council. Wilfred Heywood had a trade union background, and had served as the General Secretary of the National Union of Dyers, Bleachers and Textile Workers. He was at one time the Chairman of the Economic Committee of the General Council of the TUC and a member of the Restrictive Practices Court. The secretary of the NBPI was Ken Clucas, an able and

222

unflappable administrator, who was later to reach the top flight in the civil service as a Permanent Secretary.

Lord Peddie was particularly helpful to me in my early days at the NBPI. He had a friendly attitude and was always ready to provide the kind of information and advice without which it is difficult to settle into a new environment. Ralph Turvey was rather more remote, but was also helpful whenever I had occasion to consult him. Both Ralph and Professor Brian Reddaway, who was then a part-time member of the Board, emphasised the importance of competition for price restraint.

Wilfred Heywood viewed my appointment, I suspected, with some displeasure. He did not direct this at me personally, but I do not think he felt that the appointment of someone from the left of the trade union movement was wise. Wilf was the personification of a particular kind of trade union official more frequently to be found in earlier years than in modern times. Much of his formative experience had been gained in the years before the Second World War, and he was cautious in his approach. He was certainly not a trade union militant. He had considerable natural ability, and formed his own opinions about particular claims largely on the basis of his discussions with the employers and the union representatives. He was probably more sceptical than any other member of the Board about the value of the enquiries made and reports prepared within the NBPI by the various groups of specialists on industrial relations, marketing, operational research, accountancy and statistics. I think he also felt that Aubrey Jones was inclined to seek an unnecessary level of sophistication in enquiries and reports.

I had strong reasons for my interest in the personality of Wilf Heywood, and I think he reciprocated this interest in my own background. We both came originally from West Yorkshire and both had been influenced by the culture of religious Nonconformity. We were both conscious of the part played by the ILP in the development of the early labour movement in West Yorkshire. Wilf's father had been an active trade unionist in the textile industry, and Wilf had stood as Labour candidate in the 1935 General Election in Bradford against Fred Jowett, the ILP pioneer who first won a parliamentary election in Bradford in 1906. I told Wilf of my father's bitterness at the decision of the Labour Party in 1935 to run against Fred Jowett. Despite these differences, I formed an understanding with Wilf Heywood and an appreciation of his qualities.

When a price or income reference was received from the Department of Employment it was customary for the Chairman, Aubrey Jones, to allocate it for detailed examination to a couple of members of the Board, usually one full-time member and one part-time member. The Board members who had been given this responsibility then interviewed the parties directly involved. After that the specialist staff of the Board conducted their investigations and prepared papers setting out their findings and conclusions. A draft report was prepared, usually by a member of the staff allocated for this purpose. This was then considered by Board members responsible for the reference and ultimately by the full Board. Any amendments were made by senior staff attached to the Board and by Aubrey Jones himself.

Wilf Heywood advised me shortly after I arrived at the NBPI to give particular importance to the preliminary interviews with the parties directly involved, to form my own judgment based upon these interviews and my own industrial experience, and not to be easily influenced by the suggestions put forward by the specialist staff of the Board. He felt that the specialists were too ready to tell employers and unions how to conduct their affairs, without a full appreciation of the constraints which they had to face. For many references it was sound advice, but there were occasions when the specialists uncovered facts and figures of which the employers and unions were unaware or, for various reasons, were reluctant to acknowledge. Aubrey Jones, in contrast, was always ready to make investigations by specialists, even when these investigations were not welcomed by the parties involved.

Of the part-time members of the NBPI, the one whom I had known longest was Professor H.A. Turner of Cambridge. We were both office-holders of the Brixton Labour Party League of Youth in the late 1930s, and we both served in the Economic Department of the TUC under George Woodcock. Bert Turner could not be placed into any particular school of thought, but his ideas were always stimulating.

Bert and I were given the responsibility for the enquiries and preparation of the report of the NBPI on hours of work, overtime and shift-working (Report No 161, Command 4554, December 1970). The report revealed that the length and pattern of working hours had increasingly departed from any basic standard set by collective agreements. Substantial overtime was regularly worked by male manual workers, shift-work had increased rapidly, and there was an increasing number of workers, particularly women, in part-time employment.

Bert Turner and I had a difference of view about the control of overtime. Bert was more ready to accept that the existing arrangements gave flexibility to suit the needs of both employers and workers. To employers, overtime provided a means of increasing the use of available manpower and equipment. To workers, it offered an opportunity to obtain higher earnings.

My view was that persistent overtime was often associated with inefficiency and with rates of basic pay that were lower than they should have been. Traditionally in Britain, the employers had regarded the control of overtime as a managerial prerogative, but in reality had often abdicated any effective control. Overtime had become an alternative to higher efficiency and higher basic pay. I favoured a system of joint control of overtime.

There was much in the report on which both Bert and I were in agreement, and both sides of the argument on the difference of emphasis between flexibility and control were reflected in the final draft. The report was, in my view, an informative document and its suggestions were constructive. I doubt, nevertheless, whether it had much practical effect.

Another part-time member of the NBPI with whom I was called upon to work closely was Admiral Sir Desmond Dreyer. The NBPI produced a number of reports on the pay of the armed forces. I was not involved in the early enquiries, but I participated in some of the later enquiries. Later still, I was appointed to the Armed Forces Pay Review Body.

Admiral Dreyer was a man of considerable charm and, rather unexpectedly to me, he held progressive views. He had been a junior officer at the time of the Invergordon naval mutiny in the early 1930s, and the experience had helped to shape his opinions. He was sympathetic to the grievances of the naval ratings who participated in the mutiny, and I had a number of conversations with him about the collective representation of members of the armed forces in the determination of pay and conditions. He left me with the impression that he would not have been opposed to something similar to trade union representation.

My work on the pay of the armed forces gave me an opportunity to hold meetings with members of the armed forces at various levels, to discuss their grievances and their pay and conditions. It was an enlightening experience. Nearly all these discussions were held without the presence of senior ranks and were often held within a working environment. I remember holding one such meeting in the cramped conditions of a submarine.

The most striking feature of these meetings was how little most members of the armed forces understood of the pay structure, including the various allowances to which they were entitled and the deductions for which they were liable. This was one important consideration which led the NBPI to recommend the introduction of a military salary, under which married and single persons would be remunerated equally for similar work, that there should be a comprehensive basic rate of pay for each rank and trade, that earnings should be known and that there should be a system of job evaluation.

My lasting impression of the meetings in the armed forces was of the number of grievances which existed but without anyone feeling that there was much possibility of resolving them. There was, in this respect, no sense of joint responsibility for conditions. Always the complaint was that someone else was taking a decision which could not be influenced. I regarded this as less satisfactory than in a workplace, where there is effective collective bargaining and where trade union representatives exercise a responsibility for understanding and upholding agreed conditions.

There are of course special features of service life which make it impossible to establish a strict parallel with collective bargaining in civil employment. Nevertheless, my experience in dealing with the pay of the armed forces strengthened rather than weakened my conviction that some kind of collective representation would be beneficial. One of its biggest advantages would be to increase the sense of participation, and hence of responsibility, of the members of the armed forces in the determination of their pay and conditions.

Experiences

One of the disadvantages of separate pay review bodies is that they may be tempted to become the advocate for, rather than the judge of, the group for whom they are responsible. Each separate review body is likely to feel that it wants to be as generous as the other review bodies. It becomes persuaded of particular grievances without being called upon to make comparisons with the grievances of others. The advantage of the NBPI was that it had to take account of the wider implications of its recommendations.

Soon after I arrived at the NBPI I became involved in discussions about busmen's pay. The Department of Employment made a number of separate references to the NBPI on agreements or proposed agreements in the road passenger transport industry. These references did not, in my view, reflect credit on the Government's interpretation of the prices and incomes policy. Road passenger transport workers were an easy target for attack. The industry did not directly affect exports, and any disruption caused by dissatisfaction on the part of the workers would be felt mainly by other working-class citizens, who were dependent on public transport.

My view was that the pay of road passenger transport

workers should not, in fairness, be considered solely in the light of the criteria set out in the official guidelines for incomes policy, but should take account of pay movements elsewhere and the manpower problems faced by many road passenger undertakings. I recall that amendments were made to one of the draft reports to try to take account of my views, but I nevertheless regarded the bus reports as among the least satisfactory of those published by the NBPI. The reports contained a number of proposals designed to encourage efficiency in the industry. Some were sensible, as, for example, that more women bus crew should be recruited and trained. Others seemed to me to be less commendable. There was, for example, scope on some routes for the introduction of driver-operators (the elimination of a conductor), but the NBPI did not, in my view, give adequate weight to the disadvantages of driver-operators in busy urban areas.

A pay reference in which I was closely involved concerned workers in the clothing industry. One of the main issues to emerge was the relationship between the arrangements for voluntary joint negotiations and the statutory Wages Councils. The industrial relations specialist staff of the NBPI were strongly in favour of recommending that the Wages Councils should be abolished. They argued that though one of the original intentions of the Wages Councils was to foster the development of collective bargaining, the practical effect was the reverse. The very existence of the Wages Councils was said to discourage membership of the main union in the industry.

There was evidence to support this view but, on the other hand, the Wages Councils provided a measure of protection for the lowest paid workers, who might otherwise be the victims of severe exploitation. This danger would increase with the growth of unemployment. Moreover, I felt that one of the reasons for the desire to abolish the Wages Councils was that they were allegedly being used to secure industry-wide wage increases based on voluntary agreements reached between the biggest employers' association and the principal union, the National Union of Tailors and Garment Workers. Such industry-wide wage increases were said to be incompatible with

228

the low pay criterion of the incomes policy guidelines. My view was that increases in minimum rates would inevitably affect differentials, and that it was neither fair nor realistic to expect otherwise. I did not regard the wages of workers in the clothing industry as a threat to the British economy.

The NBPI recommended that the Wages Council system should be eventually phased out of the clothing industry and replaced by joint voluntary negotiating machinery at industry and plant level. I went along with this recommendation because it was made in the context of strengthening collective bargaining, but I remained sceptical as to whether it would bring about the desired result.

An interesting experience that I had whilst working on the clothing industry reference was to visit the main factory of Burton's in Leeds. At that time Burton's were large-scale manufacturers of men's suits, and they had a number of factories employing thousands of workpeople. The managing director was Sidney Jacobson, who, I seem to recall, had joined the firm when it amalgamated with Jackson's. Sidney's brother became, I think, the chairman of Burton's.

Sidney Jacobson was a most unusual employer. He told me at our first meeting that his views were not typical of most clothing employers and that he believed in 'progress faster than evolution'. He suggested that industrial efficiency depended, above all, on the contribution of management, and that effective management should not rest on labour exploitation. He recounted to me his earlier experiences as a worker in the clothing industry in London. He had, at the time, supported a militant group among the trade unionists of the industry, and he remained committed to the idea of strong trade unionism. When I met the stewards in the factory, they confirmed that this was his view and that he acted in a manner compatible with his beliefs. I was impressed by the arrangements I found in the factory. Sidney Jacobson was also particularly considerate of the welfare of immigrant workers. He remembered that his father had once been an immigrant worker when he arrived in Britain from Eastern Europe.

Burton's later went through a difficult time because of the

229

changes in men's fashions. Later still, they were often in the news because of a very different management. Nevertheless, my own experience with the management style of Sidney Jacobson provided an example – confirmed in later years with other experiences – that good management is often associated with an enlightened attitude towards labour relations.

A reference which I found particularly interesting concerned the pay and conditions of workers at Smithfield meat market in London. The main conclusion to emerge from the enquiries was the need to modernise the operations of the market. Meat was still being handled in much the same way as it had been 100 years earlier. There were many different groups of workers, both employed and self-employed, but there was little coordination between the various interests. There were two employers' associations, representing market tenants and carriers, but the intensely competitive conditions encouraged a fragmented state of industrial relations.

Those who argue for the breaking down of industry-wide collective agreements often overlook the problems that can arise from fragmentation. The Smithfield reference pointed to the need for a comprehensive agreement under which the pay of each group of workers could be considered in relation to the pay of all other sections. Effective collective bargaining to provide for such a comprehensive agreement had to rest on strong trade union organisation and the readiness of employers to negotiate together, despite their competitive differences.

Of the price references in which I was particularly involved, there were two which I have special reason to recall. The first concerned a proposed price increase of about 9 per cent for viscose yarn. It was produced in four factories of Courtaulds. About 40 per cent of production was exported at an average price one-third below prices in the UK market. Demand had fallen, and there was a world surplus of productive capacity.

My work on the viscose yarn reference brought me into discussions with Frank Kearton (later Lord Kearton), then the head of Courtaulds. He was a man of strong character who gave the impression of being completely familiar with the economics of the business with which he was entrusted. By the normal standards of big business, his personal views were unusual. He was, according to my standpoint, progressive and not averse to the kind of influence which the NBPI was seeking to exert on prices. At the same time he was thoroughly realistic about the purpose of business within a market system. If the proposed price increase were withheld, it appeared likely that Courtaulds would bring forward the closure of one of its factories in Northern Ireland and might stop production at another factory in North Wales. The problem, therefore, was to balance price stability against the possibility of unemployment. It was also doubtful whether, if the factories ceased production of viscose yarn, it would be possible to employ the resources in other ways. There were thus complex problems of the relationship between different prices in export and home markets, the average costs and marginal costs of production in different factories, and the balance between prices and employment. Frank Kearton presented the options with clarity and he was conscious of the political implications of whatever decision might be taken. A settlement was finally reached for a price increase of about 5 per cent instead of the original proposed 9 per cent.

The other price reference of special interest to me concerned ice cream. The NBPI were asked to examine costs, prices and profitability in the ice cream manufacturing industry. I was pleased when Aubrey Jones asked me to take responsibility for the initial enquiries and work on the reference.

I acknowledge that I approached the reference with some initial ideas. I have always had a strong liking for ice cream, and my limited experience of holidays or visits to other countries had left me with the impression that ice cream was one of the manufactured commodities where Britain, taking into account quality, price and availability, was competitive. On the other hand, the leading manufacturers had increased prices on three occasions within a period of six months before the reference was made to the NBPI. The two leading manufacturers, Wall's (a Unilever company) and Lyons, together accounted for over 75 per cent of the total value of the market.

The two leading manufacturers had both in previous years substantially increased the range of their ice cream products. There was also a similarity in the kind of products offered to the public. On investigation it was found that there were also other similarities, including recommended retail prices and the arrangements for the supply and maintenance of refrigerated cabinets for the storage and display of ice cream.

When I visited the factories where the ice cream was manufactured I was favourably impressed by the methods employed, the resources put into the development of the industry and the managerial style. The industry is highly seasonal and, even within the different seasons, has to take account, often at very short notice, of marked fluctuations in the weather. The return on capital of the two principal ice cream manufacturers was no more than reasonable, and there was no evidence of excessive profits. There were no important cost savings which they had failed to achieve. The conclusion of the NPBI was that the manufacturers' need for additional revenue through price increases had been established.

In addition to its reports on particular references concerning proposed increases in prices or incomes, the NBPI also published a number of general studies on, for example, productivity agreements, payment by results, job evaluation, salary structures, hours of work, overtime and shiftworking, and problems of low pay. The main value of these reports was in the extensive information they contained. I participated in the preparation of a number of them.

These general studies were, however, not without their problems. The reports on productivity agreements were particularly important because of their relevance to the way in which the prices and incomes policy, under the influence of the Government and its official guidelines, was being interpreted. In two early reports, prepared before I became a member of the NBPI, it had been argued that there was a strong case for encouraging the spread of proper productivity agreements in which higher pay for increased productivity could be justified in the light of the Government's policy for 'severe restraint'. Guidelines were suggested by the NBPI against which proposed productivity agreements might be tested for acceptability. These guidelines were adopted by the Government for the application of its incomes policy, and were then used by the NBPI in assessing new productivity agreements.

Productivity agreements became very fashionable. In a number of occupations the measurement of productivity presented no great difficulty. In others, the task was, in my view, almost impossible. I recall one rather macabre discussion in which a union representing funeral workers was seeking to establish productivity criteria under which its members might secure a wage increase. There were many other occupations in which the measurement of work done could not sensibly be confined to quantity. Quality was often more important than quantity. How, for example, could productivity criteria be fairly applied to instrumentalists in an orchestra or to designers in an engineering drawing office?

Even for occupations where productivity measurement could realistically be made, there was a formidable problem of interpretation regarding the contribution made by workers. Under the official guidelines it was stated that, in order to qualify for exceptional pay increases:

'It should be shown that the workers are making a direct contribution towards increasing production by accepting more exacting work or a major change in working practices.'

I did not agree with this guideline, though it was not within my power to do other than work within it and to interpret it as realistically as possible. The crux of the difficulty was that workers expect, justifiably in my view, to benefit from increased productivity, irrespective of the circumstances which have led to the increase. Thus in many cases the major contribution to higher productivity comes from better tools and equipment, improved organisation or long production runs. Sometimes these changes may be accompanied by 'more exacting work or a major change in working practices', but sometimes they may not. Indeed, my own experience in

233

engineering led me to believe that part of the task of a jig and tool designer is to provide for less exacting work on the part of a machine operator. If the result is an increase in productivity, it should be reflected ultimately in the wages of the workers.

The official guidelines on productivity agreements called for 'clear benefits to the consumer through a contribution to stable prices'. It was a worthy sentiment but very difficult to enforce. Indeed, if effective price competition is absent it may remain no more than a pious wish. It would be unfair to penalise workers because of the failure of an employer to act with proper regard to the public interest. Wage restraint in such circumstances would do no more than contribute to higher profits.

In a later report on productivity agreements, the NBPI shifted its emphasis to some extent. It spoke of the need for agreements which would help enterprises to move towards the goal of continuous adaptation to changing technology. The underlying aim should be constantly to raise efficiency within a context of negotiated agreements embracing workers of all kinds, including manual and non-manual workers, supervisors, technicians and managers. The NBPI suggested that the new agreements should be known as 'efficiency agreements' and that the guideline concerning the contribution of workers should be amended to read:

'It should be shown that the workers are contributing towards the achievement of constantly rising levels of efficiency. Where appropriate, major changes in working practice or working methods should be specified in the agreement.'

This wording was an improvement on the earlier wording, and was closer to my own point of view.

The NBPI was finally brought to an end in 1971 by the Conservative Government elected in the previous year. During its approximately six years of existence it produced 170 reports, 79 on pay, 67 on prices, 10 on both pay and prices, 9 general studies and 5 general reports.

Success or Failure?

The NBPI did not achieve the objective for which it was established, namely to assist the planned growth of real incomes by curtailing inflationary pressure in an expanding economy. The control of inflation was regarded as essential for maintaining a high level of employment and for securing a favourable balance of payments. The responsibility for this failure rested primarily on the continuing weakness of the economy. The Government's policy, though it included many useful measures, was inadequate to deal with the deep-seated problems of British capitalism. Despite all the talk of planning, there was no real attempt to plan the economy. Market forces and private profit motivation remained dominant.

Economic growth during the period of the existence of the NBPI was no more, on average, than about 2 per cent per year, instead of the 3 ½ per cent which had been anticipated by the Government. Unemployment rose steadily over the whole period. Net real incomes of the median wage earner, married with two children, rose by no more than an annual average of about 1 per cent, after taking account of tax and social insurance deductions. A worker whose wages had been tied to the official 'norms' of the incomes policy would have suffered a fall in his living standards. That most workers did not suffer such a fall was due not to the official incomes policy, but to their defiance of it.

Nevertheless, the existence of the NBPI was not a futile experiment. It sought, despite the failings of the Government's economic policy, to deal in a serious manner with a fundamental problem, namely inflation, which will always face a progressive government seeking to combine economic growth, full employment, price stability, a balance of international payments and independent collective bargaining. It developed methods of enquiry which were both speedy and effective and focussed attention on problems, the resolution of which could contribute to greater efficiency in industry and commerce.

The work of the NBPI demonstrated also some of the real problems of applying a prices and incomes policy within capitalism, even with a government pledged to progressive social change. A productivity, prices and incomes policy cannot be divorced from the general effect of economic policy. If prices are rising faster than anticipated, workers will seek to defend their living standards by pressing for correspondingly higher pay increases.

The NBPI did not accept comparability as a strong argument in wage claims. Comparability, it was suggested, was inflationary. There is clearly some truth in this contention but it was, nevertheless, often unrealistic. Arguments about comparable wage levels are very relevant both to employers and workers.

Similarly, the NBPI did not give weight in wage claims to supporting arguments about movements in the cost of living. Such arguments, it was contended, were circular. Cost of living increases prompted wage claims, and higher wages prompted higher prices. Again, this contention was not without some substance, but it had to be applied with caution. The potentialities for productivity improvements varied widely from one occupation to another. Moreover, productivity agreements did not provide an infallible formula for pay increases. Care had to be exercised to ensure that those who had already achieved a high level of efficiency were not penalised in comparison with other groups, who might claim higher pay on the grounds that they were eliminating existing inefficiencies.

The NBPI encouraged the wider application of the techniques of job evaluation and work measurement. Both these techniques can be of benefit, but it is essential, as the NBPI usually emphasised, that they should not be regarded as 'scientific' and they should certainly not be seen as in any way excluding collective bargaining. Job evaluation and work measurement rest ultimately on the subjective judgments of others. Job evaluation, by whatever method, is a way of seeking fairness in assessing the relative 'weight' of a range of different jobs. The assessment depends on opinion, which may reflect fact, prejudice and historically conditioned attitudes. Work measurement includes, among other factors, an assessment of effort rating. This is often highly subjective.

In relation to profits there is no way, in my view, that satisfactory total control can be exercised, but this does not mean that nothing can be done. Dividend control is not the same as profits control. Profits which are not distributed still remain the property of the shareholder, and may be ultimately reflected in the growing capital value of the assets of the company. The value of the assets may be realised in a takeover bid.

The NBPI was inclined, when considering a proposed price increase, to consider whether increased revenue was required by a company to provide for needed capital investment and an average return on capital employed. This was full of problems. Sometimes, but by no means always, the assessment of needed capital investment was fairly straightforward. On other occasions, account had to be taken of very obvious risks and uncertainty. To calculate an average return on capital employed depended, in turn, on the valuation of the capital assets. Should the valuation be based on historic costs, current valuation or replacement costs? In a period of rising prices, a different basis of valuation can result in widely different rates of return on the capital in the business. I remember one such price reference, where a company suggested that the annual increase in site values for its premises represented an increase in the capital employed. Hence a price increase could be justified, irrespective of any increase in costs. The return on capital, it was argued, had to be maintained.

Perhaps the best that can be said on the role of the NBPI in the control of profits is that it exercised vigilance, it opened the affairs of a number of companies to scrutiny, it made many helpful recommendations to promote efficiency as a means of offsetting increases in costs, and it embodied the idea that the control of inflation implies much more than the control of wages.

11

Law and the Labour Movement

In 1965 the then Labour Government appointed a Royal Commission on Trade Unions and Employers' Associations. The decision to appoint such a Commission was taken largely in response to press and Conservative agitation against the unions and against unofficial strikes. It was claimed that Britain's strike record was much worse than that of most other advanced industrialised countries and that this was a principal cause of Britain's poor economic performance.

The reality was, as the Royal Commission subsequently demonstrated in its report and as was shown even more emphatically in an informative paper, 'Is Britain Really Strike Prone?', by Professor Turner of Cambridge, that Britain was not uniquely stricken by costly industrial disputes. According to working days lost in relation to numbers employed, Britain's record was about average in comparison with other industrial countries; it was worse than some but better than others.

Some on the left felt that the appointment of the Royal Commission was a mistake and that it would lead to new anti-union legislation. They saw it as an act of appeasement towards those who were campaigning against the unions.

My personal view was less critical. I felt that the Royal Commission would have the opportunity to show that trade unionism and collective bargaining were essential for the effective functioning of democracy and that they should be strengthened by a combination of voluntary and legal measures. The membership of the Royal Commission included a number who could be expected to argue strongly and persuasively for trade unionism and collective bargaining, including

George Woodcock, the TUC General Secretary, Harold Collison of the National Union of Agricultural Workers, Hugh Clegg, the distinguished scholar of industrial relations, and Otto Kahn-Freund, whom I remembered as an outstanding lecturer on the law of industrial relations when I was a student at the London School of Economics. Some other members of the Royal Commission were less sympathetic to trade unionism. The chairman of the Commission was Lord Donovan, whose record suggested that he would be understanding of the purpose of trade unionism and collective bargaining.

The Draughtsmen's Association decided to give evidence to the Royal Commission, and the Executive Committee asked me to prepare a draft. The draft, which ran to about 26,000 words, was accepted with a number of minor amendments. It was submitted to the Royal Commission and widely circulated as a booklet to members of the union.

The evidence submitted by the Draughtsmen's Association set out a strong defence of trade unionism. It argued that trade unionism promoted the interests of its members and accelerated the social and economic advance of the nation. It pointed out – and argued the case in detail – that trade union recognition by many employers fell far short of a desirable standard. Under British law trade unions were not privileged as some of their opponents alleged; they were underprivileged.

At the time of the appointment of the Royal Commission the Draughtsmen's and Allied Technicians' Association had approximately 70,000 members, drawn exclusively from engineering and shipbuilding design staff and related technicians. It was a union of white-collar workers – but with a difference. Nearly all of them had workshop experience, either as apprentices or as adult manual workers. Many members of the union had started their working lives as engineering or shipbuilding craft apprentices.

The Draughtsmen's Association was formed in John Brown's shipyard, Clydebank, in 1913. It had gained recognition from the Engineering Employers' Federation in 1924, following a succession of drawing office strikes. Recognition

239

was gained at a later date in the shipbuilding industry and in a number of other industries where engineering draughtsmen were employed.

DATA's evidence explained that the union had always attached great importance to a 'status quo' clause in its negotiating procedure agreements. Such a clause stipulated that no alteration in wages, the length of the working week or recognised working conditions should be introduced without negotiations. Too many unions suffered the disadvantage of a negotiating procedure which permitted the employers to make certain changes without negotiations.

A distinction was drawn between formal recognition, as provided in a negotiating agreement, and real recognition of trade union rights at workplace level. Real recognition implied not only that union representatives should be able to negotiate on claims and grievances, but that they should be consulted on all issues affecting the employment of the members they represented, including terms and conditions of employment, health, safety and welfare at work and the prosperity, efficiency and progress of the establishment and industry in which they were employed. Real recognition also required that the management should recognise the right of a workplace union committee to meet regularly in working time, to have simple facilities for typing and the preparation of notices, to display union notices within the workplace, to collect subscriptions, to distribute official union literature and to hold occasional meetings of all members within the workplace.

The evidence also called for time off for union activities for lay members who were branch officers or members of district, regional or national trade union committees. Employers should not discourage employees from joining a trade union and should not discriminate against active trade unionists. DATA's evidence said that whilst formal recognition existed in the overwhelming majority of firms where DATA members were employed, real recognition in the majority of firms fell short of a satisfactory standard. It was pointed out that it was commonplace for active members of DATA to be advised informally by their employer or supervisor that it would be better for their prospects if they were not so active in the union. Victimisation could take many and varied subtle forms. There were probably hundreds of cases of victimisation of some kind or another affecting DATA members every year.

DATA drew attention to its technical publishing programme as a contribution to engineering design and technology. The scale of the service, it said, was unique in the trade union movement. Approximately 100,000 technical booklets and data sheets were produced by the union and sold each year. This programme was started in 1919. For many years the union was one of the largest, if not the largest, technical publisher in Britain.

The collective bargaining arrangements of DATA at national, district and workplace level were described in detail in the evidence. The policies pursued by the union, it was explained, were determined democratically at an annual conference of lay branch delegates. The Executive Committee of the union consisted entirely of lay members, except for three full-time national officials who participated in the proceedings but without a vote.

Employers, it was pointed out, had frequently sought to limit the scope of collective bargaining. Thus in the engineering industry they had not been prepared to enter into negotiations about transferable pension arrangements, though this was of vital interest to almost every technician in the course of a career. Similarly, some employers had been reluctant to enter into discussions about arrangements to deal with redundancy. They regarded these issues as 'managerial prerogatives'.

DATA pointed out in its evidence that probably more than 99 per cent of all grievances and claims affecting its members were resolved by negotiation. Nevertheless, sometimes further action was felt to be necessary. The right to threaten strike action sometimes helped to resolve disputes, and the right to take strike action was essential for effective trade unionism. When DATA was unable to reach a satisfactory settlement by negotiation it was the normal practice to consult the members as to their wishes for any further action. If the members were in favour of strike action, and if the Executive Committee were satisfied that the issue was of sufficient importance in the light of the union's wider commitments, approval was given for strike action. Between 1951 and December 1964 official strikes of DATA members took place at 238 firms. The number of members involved was 15,157. The total amount paid in dispute benefit was more than £900,000. These figures did not include the national one-day token strikes called officially by the Confederation of Shipbuilding and Engineering Unions, in which thousands of DATA members participated.

It was explained in the evidence that DATA had very little difficulty with unofficial strikes. The Executive Committee received more requests for strike action than it authorised, but when requests were turned down the members nearly always accepted that the Executive Committee had a general responsibility to take into account all the requests for strike action and to determine an order of priority. There was no feeling in the union that the Executive Committee was holding back because of any lack of sympathy with the members' interests.

DATA's evidence surveyed at some length the provisions of the law relating to trade unionism in Britain. It argued that the law was defective in a number of important respects. All workers, it said, should have the right to join a union and to participate in trade union activities without any kind of constraint from their employers. DATA referred in this connection to Conventions of the International Labour Organisation, the specialised agency of the United Nations, on freedom of association, the right to organise and to bargain collectively.

There was a strong case, it was suggested in DATA's evidence, to protect positively by law the right to organise and to bargain collectively. These affirmative legal rights did not exist in Britain, even though many lawyers and other commentators often spoke of the legal position of the unions as though they enjoyed special privileges. This, the evidence explained, arose from the manner in which the legal position of the unions had evolved. Without immunity from certain common law liabilities, trade unionism would have no legal protection for its essential functions and activities. The so-called immunities in British law appeared in other systems of law as positive rights.

DATA's evidence recognised, nevertheless, that it would still be desirable, as far as possible, to keep industrial relations issues out of the normal courts. It suggested a number of possible different procedures to achieve this objective.

These views on the need to strengthen the legal rights of trade unionists were elaborated in a book, *The Kind of Laws the Unions Ought to Want*, which Clive Jenkins and I wrote and which was published by Pergamon Press in 1968. The purpose of the book was to argue the case for more legislation to protect trade union rights and to establish or bring about improvements in minimum labour standards. The main issues covered in the book included the right to organise and to bargain collectively, complaints under ILO Conventions, security of employment and protection against unfair dismissal, transferable pensions, the control of working hours and a minimum wage. There was a concluding final chapter that put the case against a statutory incomes policy.

It has sometimes been said to me in later years that *The Kind of Laws the Unions Ought to Want* urged that a legal right of trade union recognition should be based upon a balloting system of the kind contained in the Employment Protection Act, and that my then advocacy of such a system was in contrast to my later scepticism about it. The fact is that the book did not advocate legal recognition based upon balloting. It discussed the advantages and disadvantages of such a system, and concluded that it was a method 'which occasionally might be suitable in circumstances decided by an Industrial Court consisting of experienced people'. The book put forward other suggestions but emphasised that: 'If certain basic trade union rights were to be protected by law it would still be desirable, as far as possible, to keep disputed issues out of the normal courts'. A favourable reference was made to the constructive suggestions put forward in a report of a Labour Party working party in 1967. This was published under the title, 'Industrial Democracy'. The working party proposed various measures, other than balloting on recognition, to strengthen and extend trade union representation.

The Donovan Report

The report of the Royal Commission on Trade Unions and Employers' Associations was published in June 1968. It drew heavily on the experience of a number of manufacturing industries, particularly engineering, and on construction. It said that Britain had two systems of industrial relations: a formal system based on trade unions and employers' associations responsible for industry-wide collective agreements, usually establishing certain minimum conditions of employment and a negotiating procedure; and an informal system at workplace level, embracing managers and workers' representatives, responsible for negotiating pay and other conditions above the minimum levels. The Royal Commission said that the informal system was often at odds with the formal system.

The Royal Commission report pointed out that over the previous 30 years there had been a decline in the extent to which industry-wide agreements determined actual pay. The widening gap between agreed rates in industry-wide agreements and average earnings was attributable to piecework or incentive earnings, company or factory additions to basic rates and overtime earnings. All these elements were strongly influenced by negotiations and behaviour at workplace level. This bargaining was, to use the words of the industrial relations scholar, Allan Flanders, 'largely informal, largely fragmented and largely autonomous'.

These characteristics of collective bargaining, it was said, provided the explanation for the pattern of strikes in Britain. Although the number of working days lost in strikes had remained relatively low, the number of strikes had risen. Official strikes, that is strikes authorised and supported by the unions concerned, accounted for only 5 per cent of the total. Over the previous three years each unofficial strike involved on average about 300 workers and lasted a little over 2½ days.

244

The decentralisation of collective bargaining, the Royal Commission said, had 'taken place under the pressure of full employment, which has been almost continuous since 1938.'

According to the Royal Commission the overriding need was for a reconstruction of voluntary collective bargaining. The central defect was 'the disorder in factory and workshop relations and pay structures promoted by the conflict between the formal and the informal systems.' It put forward a number of suggestions, all designed 'to promote the orderly and effective regulation of industrial relations within companies and factories...'

The report of the Royal Commission related the reform of industrial relations to the requirements, as they saw it, of an incomes policy. Rising or full employment, the report said, was almost always accompanied by increases in pay which outstripped any rise in productivity. This led to higher costs, higher prices and economic difficulties. The proposals put forward by the Royal Commission, it was claimed, would 'assist the working of incomes policy' and help to bring under control the unregulated tendencies of the existing system.

When the Royal Commission report was published, my attitude to it was generally sympathetic. I recognised the realism of its description of the collective bargaining arrangements in engineering. I was pleased that it argued for trade unionism and for the extension of collective bargaining. The opening sentence of its fifth chapter expressed a sentiment which I hoped would be widely endorsed:

'Properly conducted, collective bargaining is the most effective means of giving workers the right to representation in decisions affecting their working lives, a right which is or should be the prerogative of every worker in a democratic society.'

The report put forward proposals for the development of collective bargaining.

There were, however, a number of observations in the Royal Commission report which were more ominous. It entertained the possibility of imposing penalties on trade unions or workers responsible for stoppages in breach of agreements. It spoke of the need not only to recognise the part played by shop stewards, but also to define and control their role. It contemplated the possible legal enforcement of procedure agreements where 'the strike situation makes it necessary'. It was imperative, said the Royal Commission, that the number of unofficial, and especially of unconstitutional, strikes should be reduced, and reduced speedily.

These various observations were all made within a context calling for the development of collective bargaining within a regulated system. They were not put forward, ostensibly, as anti-union proposals. On the other hand, they gave currency to suggestions for new legal restrictions.

As the report recognised, many so-called unofficial stoppages took place because some industry-wide agreements, particularly on wages, bore little relationship to reality. The workers had learnt by experience to depend on their own organised strength in the workplace. Moreover, many so-called unofficial disputes were caused by employers unilaterally altering established conditions or piecework arrangements without first seeking a negotiated settlement. These disputes were unofficial in the sense that they were not authorised in advance by the union, but equally they were not condemned by the union. Some were later made official. In many cases the grievances were resolved by subsequent negotiations. Unofficial strikes often helped to 'lubricate' the negotiating machinery.

With hindsight, I think my initial reaction to the report of the Royal Commission was too generous. I was impressed by its expression of support for trade unionism and collective bargaining, but gave insufficient weight to what I think was one of its fundamental purposes, namely to suggest ways of curtailing trade union militancy at workplace level in conditions of a high level of employment in a capitalist society.

Following the publication of the report of the Royal Commission, Barbara Castle entered into consultations with various groups about the possible shape of new legislation on industrial relations. I attended two such private consultative sessions. They were held at the Civil Service College, Sunningdale, and were informal. As far as I recall, no-one was there in a representative capacity. Those present included trade union leaders, prominent employers, academics, lawyers and civil servants. The discussion centred around proposals for a new Commission on Industrial Relations, its functions, employment rights, industrial relations at workplace level and trade union recognition. I do not remember any significant exchange of views about possible new legislative sanctions against trade unions.

'In Place of Strife'

When the Government published their proposals in the White Paper, 'In Place of Strife', the trade union movement was surprised and deeply concerned to find that it was intended to take powers to impose statutory financial penalties in certain circumstances on trade unions and workpeople. The objections of the TUC were set out in a report prepared by the General Council.

'The proposals to which the General Council object in particular are those that would empower a Minister to impose a 28-day "conciliation pause" where in his opinion this is required, and to enforce it by the Industrial Board imposing fines on workpeople who do not comply with an Order to return to work; would give a Minister the right to force a union – again where he decides that it is necessary and again under the threat of financial penalties – to conduct a ballot before calling an official strike, and, moreover, to conduct the ballot on the basis of a question finally decided not by the union but by the Minister; would give an outside agency (the Industrial Board), acting under an Order that a Minister has in his opinion judged to be necessary, the power to impose financial penalties on a union which refused to comply with a recommendation that it should, in the case of an inter-union dispute over recognition, be

247

excluded from recognition; and would, again under threat of a financial penalty, compel trade unions to register their rules and to include in those rules provisions that would have to be approved by an outside agency (the Registrar). The General Council also dissent from the Government's view that the Industrial Board should operate as the Government's agent for the purpose of imposing financial penalties on individuals and trade unions, and should oversee relations between trade unions and their members.'

The General Council noted that the proposed new Industrial Board should, according to the Government, include trade union members. The General Council said that they did not believe that any trade union representative would be prepared to serve on a body which was responsible for deciding that trade unionists should be fined for industrial activities.

The view put forward by the trade union movement was that industrial relations should be improved and collective bargaining strengthened by, essentially, voluntary means. This did not imply indifference to the need for change and development, but these changes could best be made on the basis of voluntary action. This was the foundation of free trade unionism, and was an essential prerequisite if trade unionists were to accept such changes willingly. The TUC believed that this was also a central message of the report of the Royal Commission.

There were a number of other proposals in the White Paper which were intended to be helpful to the achievement of trade union objectives and workers' interests. They included, for example, the establishment of a Commission for Industrial Relations, proposals to assure workers of the right to join trade unions and to obtain trade union recognition, proposals to afford greater legal protection in some respects for trade union activities, and proposals against unfair dismissal, and for the provision of information for more effective collective bargaining.

During this period I received a number of invitations to speak at meetings of trade unionists on 'In Place of Strife'.

There was no doubt of the strong feeling against the Government's proposals. Discussion at these meetings was confined almost entirely to the objectionable features. My own observations relating to those parts of the White Paper which the trade union movement might, in principle, find helpful were received either coolly or were largely ignored.

The TUC conducted a very vigorous campaign against those parts of the Government's proposals to which they were opposed. In the spring of 1969 the Government announced that they intended to expedite the introduction of legislation. It was to be interim legislation and was to include penal clauses. The General Council then convened a special TUC – the first such special Congress since 1920 – to give affiliated unions the opportunity to express their views on the Government's policy.

By an overwhelming majority the special TUC approved a recommendation stating that the trade union movement was 'unalterably opposed' to the proposal that the Government should take powers to impose statutory financial penalties on workpeople or trade unions, in connection either with industrial disputes or with the compulsory registration by trade unions of their rules. The special TUC also approved recommendations affirming that some of the other proposals of the Government could, in principle, be helpful, and empowering the General Council to take further action, including proposals for rule changes, to improve procedures for the settlement of disputes.

Within two weeks of the holding of the special TUC it became clear that the campaign of opposition mounted by the TUC to the proposed legislation, with its penal clauses, had been sufficient to persuade the Government to change course. Following a meeting with the Prime Minister, Harold Wilson, on 18 June, 1969, the General Council of the TUC gave a 'solemn and binding undertaking' to take further steps – which were set out in detail – to help to resolve disputes involving, directly or indirectly, large bodies of workers. In return the Government gave an assurance that they would not proceed with interim legislation on industrial relations, and would not include the so-called penal sanctions in the legislation to be introduced in the following session of Parliament or in any legislation during the lifetime of the existing Parliament.

The trade union movement rightly regarded this agreement with the Government as a victory for good sense in industrial relations. Many commentators interpreted it as a defeat for the Government and a triumph for trade union militancy. The settlement was to be short-lived.

A New Government

In the early summer of 1970 the Labour Government was brought to an end by defeat in a General Election. The Conservative Party secured nearly 1,000,000 votes more than Labour and won 330 seats in Parliament, as against 287 for Labour.

The Labour Government had a good record on many issues. It improved a wide range of social security benefits very quickly after its election. It secured the passing of the Redundancy Payments Act, and it set up training boards in a wide range of industries. It improved conditions of employment on the docks. It brought the steel and the shipbuilding industries under public ownership. For the first time, more than 400,000 houses were built in a single year. It helped to develop public transport.

On the other hand, although the Government introduced various measures to stimulate industrial change, it could not be claimed that it challenged the capitalist control of the dominating heights of the economy. Military expenditure was maintained at a high level, and the Government gave support to American policy in Vietnam, though it resisted appeals for the despatch of British troops to Vietnam.

It was, however, Labour's economic record which was to prove the undoing of the Government. None of the basic problems of the economy had been put right. There was a succession of sterling crises, and the currency was devalued. The Government's interpretation of the prices and incomes policy had caused disillusionment among some of its most active working-class supporters. The Government narrowly avoided outright confrontation with the unions on proposals for new legislation affecting trade unions.

The new Conservative Government abolished the National Board for Prices and Incomes and introduced new legislation on industrial relations. The Industrial Relations Act was strongly opposed by the trade union and labour movement.

Among the more important provisions of the Industrial Relations Act was the creation of a new court, the National Industrial Relations Court, and the introduction of a list of 'unfair industrial practices' which could lead to legal action. Although the list was drawn up ostensibly to establish equal liability for employers, employers' organisations, workers and trade unions, the cutting edge of the legislation was directed against trade unionism and trade unionists. In particular, it sought to penalise sympathetic industrial action by trade unionists, where the purpose was to persuade an employer not to supply goods or services to another employer involved in a dispute.

It was felt by the trade union movement that the outlawing of sympathetic action of this kind was a threat to the whole conception of trade union solidarity. The readiness of workers in certain circumstances voluntarily to suffer a loss of earnings in support of others but without benefit to themselves was seen by the trade union movement as behaviour to be commended rather than condemned.

The National Industrial Relations Court was also empowered, 'in emergency situations which threaten the economy or public safety and health', and in response to a request from the Secretary of State for Employment, to order a suspension of industrial action, a so-called 'cooling-off' period of up to 60 days, to enable further efforts to be made to reach a peaceful settlement. This provision was borrowed from the American Taft-Hartley Act, where its record was less successful than the more flexible arrangements existing in Britain for the resolutions of disputes. The 'cooling-off' period was sometimes regarded as a 'hotting-up' period, to be taken into account by the parties when, as was often the case in the USA but not in Britain, collective agreements were due to expire on fixed dates.

251

The Industrial Relations Act also empowered the National Industrial Relations Court to order a ballot, in response to a request from the Secretary of State, 'if there is doubt whether a majority of the workers concerned support industrial action which threatens the livelihood of a substantial number of workers', or if 'there is doubt whether the workers have had an adequate opportunity to express their views.' A compulsory ballot was subsequently ordered in a railway dispute. It went overwhelmingly in favour of the unions.

The new Act also established the presumption that any written collective agreement reached after the Act came into force was intended to be legally enforceable unless it contained a statement to the contrary. This reversed the traditional concept of voluntary collective agreements in industrial relations, drawn up not by lawyers but by practitioners who used everyday language for the purpose, and interpreted agreements in the light of the practical requirements of the employment relationship. It was felt, not only by the unions but also by many employers, that the new legal presumption would provide much more work for lawyers and would have the effect of damaging rather than helping industrial relations. In the event, most unions and employers 'contracted out' of the presumption of legal enforceability.

Some of the other provisions in the Act were less objectionable, and some introduced improvements in workers' rights. Nevertheless, the main thrust of the legislation was to introduce legal sanctions into industrial relations, directed primarily against trade unions and trade unionists. I shared fully the view of the trade union movement that the new legislation was intended to weaken trade unionism.

The new legislation was finally defeated by the mining dispute of 1973–74 and the outcome of the General Election in February 1974. The Prime Minister, Edward Heath, decided to call a General Election on the alleged issue of 'Who governs Britain: Parliament or the unions?'

It was a false issue because the mining dispute concerned wages. In 1973 there was an oil crisis following military conflict between Israel and Arab states. In Britain successive governments had run down the coal industry and had increased the nation's dependence on oil. The miners claimed that their wages, in relation to earnings in other industries, had suffered. The Heath Government insisted that the miners' pay claim should be settled within the limits of the then pay policy. The dispute led to a three-day working week in many areas of employment. The nation became conscious of the vital importance of fuel supplies, and many felt that the main need was to find a settlement in the mining dispute.

In the February 1974 General Election the Conservative Party lost more than 1¼ million votes in comparison with the 1970 General Election, despite an increase in the total poll from 72 per cent to 78.7 per cent of the electorate. Even so their total vote – though not the number of elected MPs – was still more than 200,000 higher than that given to Labour. The Liberals increased their total vote from 2,117,000 to 6,063,000. Labour formed a new minority Government.

12

Some Other Issues

The shape of the trade union movement is always changing.
There are many reasons for the changes. Some industries
decline and others expand. Shipbuilding, coal-mining, railway
and dock employment, textiles and iron and steel manufacture
have all contracted. At one time these industries provided the
bulk of trade union membership. In contrast, other fields of
employment have expanded, particularly in the provision of
services of various kinds. They provide opportunities for the
growth of trade union membership.

It is not only industries which decline or expand; the same is
also true of particular skills or occupations. In the engineering
industry old craft divisions have been undermined by changes
in technology. Today, computer specialists are employed in a
wide range of industries and services. Industrial boundaries
also shift from one period to another, with the development of
new materials, manufacturing processes or methods of distribution. Plastics are used in many different processes, and developments in information technology find application in almost
every kind of industrial and commercial activity. All these
changes affect trade union organisation.

In periods of falling trade union membership, notably in the
1980s as a consequence of the growth of unemployment, there
is a further strong reason for changes in trade union structure.
Some unions run into financial difficulty and look round for an
amalgamation with a financially stronger organisation. In more
recent years, some amalgamations have also been encouraged
by ideological sympathies between the leaders of separate
unions. When considering possible options, both leaders and

254

active members of unions seeking an amalgamation have looked with sympathy in the direction of unions with a similar outlook on the main industrial and political issues of the day.

In my final years as an official of the Draughtsmen's and Allied Technicians' Association, much attention was given to the possibility of amalgamating with one or more other unions. My personal preference was for an amalgamation with the Amalgamated Engineering Union, but within a structure which would provide for the representation of the identifiable and distinguishable interests of technicians in the engineering, shipbuilding and related industries. I argued strongly for such a policy, and drafted policy statements on amalgamation which were adopted with few amendments both by the Executive Committee and the annual conference of the union.

One of the most compelling reasons for an amalgamation with the AEU was that the members of DATA were employed, overwhelmingly, by the same employers as the members of the AEU. The two unions negotiated with the same employers' organisations, and agreements negotiated by the Confederation of Shipbuilding and Engineering Unions and the AEU affecting hourly paid workers influenced the negotiations conducted by DATA. Moreover, in my view, the drawing together of the AEU and DATA would provide a structure in which each could contribute to the other something from its traditional strength. The AEU was based on an important section of the traditional industrial working class, whereas DATA represented an expanding body of white-collar technicians, most of whom came from working-class families and many of whom had workshop experience as craft apprentices. DATA was a union with an unusually large minority of articulate and politically conscious trade unionists.

There was, however, another option open to DATA. It was to amalgamate with other white-collar unions which included technicians among their membership. At one time it was considered that the most suitable such union was the Society of Technical Civil Servants. This was a union consisting predominantly of design staff in the civil service. One of the constituent founding organisations of the STCS had been the Association

255

of Civil Service Designers and Draughtsmen, which was an offshoot of the Draughtsmen's Association formed after the General Strike. Under the terms of the Trade Disputes and Trade Unions Act 1927, civil servants were forbidden to belong to any union or federation of unions not consisting wholly of state employees. This Act was repealed by the Labour Government elected in 1945. The ACSDD was formed in 1927, and consisted at the outset of members of the Draughtsmen's Association employed in the civil service.

For many years the Draughtsmen's Association maintained a close relationship with the civil service draughtsmen and, in the post-war years, with the Society of Technical Civil Servants. The General Secretary of the STCS was a very able trade unionist, Cyril Cooper. Ultimately the STCS decided to join forces not with the Draughtsmen's Association but with the Institute of Professional Civil Servants. This was a disappointment to the Draughtsmen's Association but was, nevertheless, an understandable decision. It made sense in collective bargaining terms for the civil service design staff to be associated with other civil service technical and professional staff.

Another possibility was for the Draughtsmen's Association to amalgamate with the Association of Scientific Workers. The two unions had much in common. The AScW had a significant membership among technicians in manufacturing industry and some of them, as, for example, stress technicians in the aircraft industry, were in areas of employment very close to or even overlapping those of design staff in the Draughtsmen's Association. Their negotiating procedure agreement with the Engineering Employers' Federation gave them negotiating rights for a wider range of technicians among their members. Moreover, the policies of the Draughtsmen's Association and the AScW on many issues were very similar. The AScW also had a number of able officers both among its lay members and full-time staff.

There were, however, problems about a possible amalgamation. One of the most important was that the AScW membership was not confined to manufacturing industry. It also had

256

important groups of members in the National Health Service and in the universities. Thus if an amalgamation were to take place with the AScW, with the majority of AScW members employed outside the engineering industry, would it be compatible with an amalgamation between the Draughtsmen's Association and the AEU? On both sides the majority view at that time was that it would not be compatible. The amalgamation discussions with the AScW came to an end.

Shortly afterwards the AScW amalgamated with the Association of Supervisory Staffs, Executives and Technicians to form the Association of Scientific, Technical and Managerial Staff, and the Draughtsmen's Association entered into a loose form of amalgamation with the AEU, the Foundry Workers and the Constructional Engineering Union. The new union was known as the Amalgamated Union of Engineering Workers.

Unfortunately, the new union eventually broke apart. The foundry section and the construction section became more closely integrated into the new structure, but the technical, administrative and supervisory section – in reality the old Draughtsmen's Association, but with amended rules giving it wider scope for recruitment – did not find it possible to reach a satisfactory arrangement within the amalgamation.

There are different views as to the cause of the breakdown in the AUEW. By the time it took place I was no longer actively involved, but it seemed to me at the time to have been caused by differences about trade union structure. The engineering section of the AUEW – in reality the old AEU – was proud of its long traditions and what it felt to be its very democratic structure. As by far the largest constituent section of the new union, it expected the technical, administrative and supervisory section, by then known as TASS, to shape its structure very much on the lines of the engineering section. TASS was prepared to go some considerable way in this direction, but wanted to preserve certain features based on its own tradition. The relationship was not helped by differences between the two sections on some trade union and political issues. It became clear that the amalgamation was little more than a formality.

257

There was no compelling reason for TASS to remain in the amalgamation. It was financially strong, had recognition for negotiating purposes from the main employers, and its density of membership in its main area of recruitment, among the design and related technical staff of the engineering and shipbuilding industries, was high. For all practical purposes the amalgamation came to an end, but the title AUEW-TASS was retained.

In the 1980s TASS sought to attract other unions, not only in the engineering and allied industries but also in other manufacturing industries. It did not confine its appeal to staff employees, but also sought mergers with unions catering predominantly for hourly paid skilled workers. In 1981 the National Union of Gold, Silver and Allied Trades, with a membership of rather more than 1600, merged with TASS. Towards the end of 1983 a significant merger was made with the National Union of Sheet Metal Workers, Coppersmiths and Heating and Domestic Engineers. The NUSMWCHDE was one of Britain's oldest and best-organised trade unions. Its membership at the time of the merger was approaching 58,000. In the engineering industry the Sheet Metal Workers' Union had always played a prominent role, a reflection of its very high density of membership among those eligible to join.

In the following year, 1984, another long-established craft union, the Association of Patternmakers and Allied Craftsmen, with more than 7,500 members, merged with TASS. Two years later another engineering union, the National Society of Metal Mechanics, with 27,000 members, joined the merger. In the same year, 1986, TASS went way outside the engineering industry and merged with the Tobacco Workers' Union, with nearly 13,500 members.

The argument used for the mergers in engineering was not only that staff technicians and craftsmen were employed by the same employers, but that the former clear distinction between staff technicians and craftsmen had become blurred and was being increasingly eliminated by technological change. The argument for the extension of the union into other manufacturing industries was that all were being affected by new

258

technology. This technology did not have rigid industrial boundaries.

TASS was also extending its recruitment among administrative staff. Here, too, old distinctions between technicians and clerical workers were of less relevance. The application of computers was having a profound effect not only in drawing and technical offices, the traditional areas of strength for TASS, but also in offices where hitherto most of the work had been done by clerical workers.

In 1988 TASS entered into a new amalgamation, this time with the Association of Scientific, Technical and Managerial Staffs. The new union took the title of Manufacturing, Science and Finance. It became generally known as MSF. At the time of the amalgamation TASS claimed to have 241,000 members and ASTMS 390,000. The two general secretaries of the former amalgamating unions, Clive Jenkins and Ken Gill, became the joint General Secretaries of the new union. Later, Clive Jenkins retired prematurely and Ken Gill was elected unopposed as sole General Secretary. Ken Gill retired in 1992 and was succeeded by Roger Lyons, a former ASTMS national official, who, in a ballot, defeated Barbara Switzer, a former national official of TASS.

The case for the amalgamation between TASS and ASTMS was a strong one. In the engineering and related industries the two unions each had a large membership, sometimes working in similar or even the same occupations. ASTMS, however, also had a substantial membership in insurance companies, the universities, the National Health Service, the voluntary sector, including voluntary organisations of many different kinds, and sections of manufacturing other than engineering.

In the years following the amalgamation the balance of the membership changed with the decline of engineering, shipbuilding and other manufacturing industries. Many of the traditional areas of strength of the former TASS diminished or, in some cases, disappeared. In the London area, for example, engineering technical employment was reduced to but a fraction of its earlier size. In addition, with the development of new computer-aided design techniques, draughting in the traditional manner, with the use of drawing boards, T-squares and set squares, became almost an obsolete skill.

In the light of these developments, it is relevant to ask whether I was right or wrong in the 1960s to press for an amalgamation with the AEU and to oppose an amalgamation with the AScW. My view remains that it would have been preferable to establish, if it had been possible, an all-embracing engineering union. That it did not prove possible was due, above all, to differences which, in my view, should have been surmounted. This is not to direct criticism against any one union or group. All who were involved reflected the strength of their traditional loyalties.

On the other hand, I have no doubt on reflection that I underestimated the speed of contraction of the engineering industry, particularly during the years of Conservative Government following the 1979 General Election, and the extent to which draughting would be overtaken by new technology. The application of computers and word processors in so many different industries and services strengthened the case for a trade union amalgamation whose scope extended beyond engineering. When MSF was formed I supported the view that, in the circumstances of the time, it was the proper course for TASS to take. Those who had not agreed with my advocacy of an all-embracing engineering union or who had argued that it was an unrealisable objective, held that my earlier opposition to an amalgamation with the AScW had merely contributed to a delay in the eventual formation of a wider union on the lines of MSF.

Some two years before I resigned as a full-time trade union official to join the National Board for Prices and Incomes, I received an invitation to deliver a lecture in Dublin on the life and ideas of James Connolly. The occasion was the fiftieth anniversary of the Easter Rising in 1916. After the defeat of this attempt to establish an Irish Republic a number of leaders were executed by the British, among them James Connolly. Connolly, who had been injured in the fighting and had a foot amputated, was too weak to stand for his execution and he was shot seated in a chair.

In preparation for this lecture I read as much as I could of the works of Connolly and about his life, including the four volumes of his collected works, published in Dublin with the support of the Irish Transport and General Workers' Union. Though Connolly's name will always be associated with the struggle for Irish independence, he was not born in Ireland. He was born in Edinburgh on 10 June, 1868, of Irish parents. By any standard of measurement he was among the greatest socialists of working-class upbringing the world has produced.

Connolly served in the British Army and worked in various manual jobs. He played a leading part in the development of the socialist movement in Ireland and was also active in the United States. When he returned to Ireland he became a leader of the Irish Transport and General Workers' Union. In the Easter Rising he served as the Commandant-General of the Republican forces in Dublin.

Connolly was not only an activist of the labour movement, he was also a thinker of outstanding quality. His books and essays are of the highest standard in the history of socialist theory. His understanding of the relationship between the struggle for national independence on the part of subject nations and the struggle for socialism was unequalled. As the essayist Robert Lynd once wrote in a foreword to the works of Connolly:

'...In the evolution of civilisation the progress of the fight for national liberty of any subject nation must, perforce, keep pace with the progress of the struggle for liberty of the most subject class in that nation...'

I regarded as an honour the invitation to give the Connolly lecture in Dublin. I was conscious that I was an Englishman and that I was not a Roman Catholic. It was my opportunity to record that in England, as in Ireland and in many other countries, the life and teachings of Connolly continued to inspire and enlighten many who were active in the labour movement.

The meeting was well advertised by the Dublin Trades

Council, and the large hall in which it was held was packed on the evening of the lecture. At the end of the lecture I was presented with a full-scale replica of the flag of the Irish Citizen Army. I was also introduced to a surviving relative of James Connolly. It was for me a memorable occasion.

I intended, following the Dublin meeting, to travel to Belfast, where the Draughtsmen's Association had a large membership. I now, however, had a new problem. I had to carry the full-size replica of the flag of the Irish Citizen Army. It was, if I recall rightly, about nine or ten feet high. No doubt I could have wrapped the flag around the flagpole, but it would have been a strange incident if the flag had unfurled whilst I was in Belfast. My colleagues suggested that I should return first to London and then proceed to Belfast. I accepted their advice. The flag thereafter stood in my office at the headquarters of the Draughtsmen's Association. It was eventually returned to Ireland.

Problem about a Visa

During my period as a member of the National Board for Prices and Incomes, I visited the United States for the first time. Aubrey Jones received an invitation to attend a conference on industrial relations to be held in Atlantic City and to give one or two lectures to selected audiences. For reasons which I cannot now remember, he was unable to attend the conference and he asked me to deputise for him. The conference was to be attended mainly by American academics with a specialist interest in industrial relations and labour law.

When I applied for a visa to enter the USA I was asked to answer the then usual questions about membership or association with the Communist Party or organisations which, in the eyes of the US authorities, might be regarded as 'front' organisations for the Communist Party. Though I regarded these questions as improper and prompted by the wish of the US authorities to pursue the Cold War and to harass anyone who might question US policy, I decided that my best course was to provide a full list, as far as I could remember, of the many organisations of which I had been a member. The list was lengthy, starting with a Methodist boys' club and extending in subsequent years through many organisations of the labour movement.

The official who interviewed me at the US Embassy seemed to be more interested in my one-time membership of the British China Friendship Association, of which I had been National Vice-Chairman, than of my membership many years earlier of the Young Communist League. My attitude was that when I joined an organisation it was because I was in agreement with its objectives. I was not deterred by the presence of members of the Communist Party.

Moreover, as I explained, I was in sympathy with the proclaimed economic objective of the Russian and the Chinese revolutions to build a new kind of society based upon the social ownership of the main means of production. Their respective political systems reflected their history and the circumstances at the time of revolutionary change. There was no tradition of representative democracy. My views as to the way forward in Britain were influenced by British experience and the inextricable link between the efforts of the trade union movement for social improvement, the extension and strengthening of democracy and the struggle for socialism.

I did not regard it as acceptable that I should distinguish, for the benefit of the US authorities, between organisations which were or were not in my view influenced by members of the Communist Party. I am sure that I left no doubt in the mind of the official who interviewed me that I was not a supporter of the policy of the US Government in the Cold War. This, however, as I saw it, was no reason why I should be refused a visa. My proposed visit to the USA was in no way a threat to security, and I was not anti-American. On the contrary, there was much in American history which I admired, including, for example, the struggle for independence from Britain and the role of Thomas Jefferson. I regarded Franklin D. Roosevelt as one of the outstanding statesmen of modern times.

It was made clear to me that I would probably not be

granted a visa. My application would be referred to Frankfurt, which I was given to understand was the headquarters of US security in Western Europe. I recall that I had to pay for a telephone call made by the US Embassy from London to Frankfurt, perhaps because I wanted a decision quickly if I were to be in time to attend the industrial relations conference in Atlantic City.

Shortly afterwards I received a letter from the US Embassy, stating that I had been found ineligible for a visa under the terms of the Immigration and Nationality Act. I could, however, apply for 'defector status'. To establish my eligibility for a visa, it would be necessary for me to demonstrate that I had conclusively dissociated myself from all connection with any kind of communist activity for a period of at least five years before the date of my next visa application, and that for the same period of at least five years I had acted in a fashion to indicate my active opposition to communism.

The US Embassy asked for documentary evidence of such anti-communist activity, including writings, speeches and 'similar manifestations'. Three copies of any such documents were to be submitted. I was also asked to present evidence – again in three copies – if I had joined any 'reputable anti-communist organisations' and of the extent of my participation. I was asked to submit a personal affidavit indicating that I had been consistently anti-communist for at least five years. This declaration had to be corroborated by sworn affidavits from others. Simple letters of recommendation attesting to good character were, I was warned, not sufficient. The affidavits, the Embassy insisted, must address themselves to the specific point of my anti-communist attitude and activities. In addition, a brief biography had to be submitted on each person writing a testimonial on my behalf. A special biographical information form would also be given to me for 'any affiants whose residence or nationality is American'. All this information had to be submitted as a unit and not piecemeal, and I was advised that if it were 'deemed adequate several months may elapse before a decision is reached and you are informed of it.'

My reaction on receiving this information was a mixture of anger, contempt and amusement. I was angry because it was an example of 'witch-hunting' intolerance. The attitude of the US authorities was in stark contrast to the attitude of the Soviet authorities when I had visited the USSR. The Soviet immigration authorities had not asked about my political opinions or the organisations to which I had belonged. I felt contempt for the US authorities for suggesting that I could apply for 'defector status' and all the humiliating servility and hypocrisy that went with it. I was amused because it was almost unbelievable that the world's foremost power should go to such ridiculous lengths in pursuit of the prejudices of its rulers.

I had the opportunity during a visit to the US Embassy almost immediately after I had received this letter, to express my views to a senior official. I do not know what other moves were made, but there was a satisfactory anticlimax to this sequence of events. I received very quickly a visa, strictly for the duration of my proposed business in the USA. I was told, but I do not know with what truth, that the visa was issued by delegated authority under what was described as a 'Presidential waiver'.

When I arrived in New York I was met by an official of the British Embassy and, to his surprise, went through a special entry procedure. All went well, and I heard nothing more of the earlier problem. Some years later, when I again went to the USA to visit the National Labour Relations Board in Washington, there were no difficulties about entry. I told the US Embassy in London of my earlier experience and their response, in good humour, was that 'things had changed'.

I much enjoyed my short visit to New York and Atlantic City, even though the conference I attended was a disappointment. Nearly all the participants were professional academics from American universities, and many of the papers presented for discussion were ostentatiously theoretical. My impression was that theories were being constructed about every kind of sequence of events in industrial relations and the behaviour of employers and employees, but without any real social analysis of conflicting class interests. It appeared to be fashionable to illustrate these theories by mathematical statements or equations. Much of it, I thought, was very artificial and avoided discussion of many real controversial issues. In personal and private discussion, some of the participants had a well-informed and lively appreciation of the problems of the American trade union movement, of the effect of the existing labour legislation and of the hostility to collective bargaining of many US employers. This, however, did not find much expression in official sessions of the conference.

During my days in New York I was taken into various districts of the city. I was struck by the contrast between the glamour of the fashionable areas and the rather run-down appearance of some other areas. The sight of apartment, office and workshop blocks with external metal fire escapes and the presence of water hose stands in some of the older streets in poor areas reminded me of scenes from American films during my boyhood. A few districts were in a state of dilapidation and degradation with burnt-out buildings, extensive squatting and a serious problem of drug-taking and drug-dealing. I felt that the tasks facing the local authorities were even more formidable than in some of the inner areas of British cities.

My other main impression was of the friendliness of the great majority of the people I met, and their democratic attitude. One gained the feeling that people genuinely regarded themselves as citizens who, in important respects, had equal rights. The USA has, of course, the social privileges that go with wealth and economic power, but my impression was that citizens were less deferential than would be customary in Britain.

London Cooperative Society

During my final period with the Draughtsmen's and Allied Technicians' Association, and during most of the time that I was a member of the National Board for Prices and Incomes, I was also a lay member of the Management Committee of the

London Cooperative Society. The Management Committee was the directing board of the LCS.

I had for many years been active in the Cooperative movement. I regularly attended the members' quarterly meetings in my own district, had been elected to and served on the District Committee in Hounslow and had held the office of Cooperative Party branch secretary in Hounslow for a number of years. On a number of occasions I attended as a branch delegate the annual conference of the London Society's Political Committee. My original interest in the Cooperative movement was aroused by my mother, who had always been a keen cooperator. She believed strongly that Cooperative products had the stamp of good value and reliability, that if anything was less than satisfactory the Coop was receptive to complaints, and that Cooperative business was conducted with a sense of social responsibility. She was a member of the Cooperative Women's Guild.

Before being elected to the Management Committee of the LCS I had been elected to a rules revision committee, charged with the task of revising the rules to strengthen, if possible, the democratic participation of members in the affairs of the Society. I was elected to be the chairman of this committee. We held many meetings and took evidence from individuals and gatherings of cooperators in different areas covered by the LCS. It was an opportunity to learn about the participation of members in the LCS.

There were no easy answers to the problem of how to increase democratic participation in an organisation covering the vast geographical area and business activities of the London Cooperative Society. There were a number of different considerations to be reconciled. In the first place, there was the imperative requirement to conduct a successful business. This required a high standard of management and a readiness to take decisions to keep abreast of the most efficient methods of distribution. Secondly, account had to be taken of the interests of staff. They too were entitled to participate in the control of the direction of the Society. Indeed, their participation had to be encouraged. Thirdly, it was fundamental to provide for the active participation of as many as possible of consumer members. Account had to be taken of the many voluntary Cooperative organisations, particularly the Women's Guild, which already attracted many participants. In the end, the success or failure of cooperative enterprise is determined by the response of consumers.

I was elected to the Management Committee of the LCS as one of the candidates of an electoral organisation, embracing consumer and employee members. The Society was just emerging from a difficult and controversial period when John Stonehouse was the President. He had been replaced, and the Management Committee were determined to try to restore the fortunes of the Society. A new Chief Executive Officer had been appointed. At the time the LCS had about 20,000 employees.

There were two basic problems, as I saw it, confronting the LCS. The first was that it had too many small shops, particularly in the East End of London, where the population was declining. The premises were usually unsuitable for expansion. Hence there was a high labour cost and management expense in relation to turnover. These small shops, even when converted into self-service stores, could not compete effectively with the much larger supermarkets and hypermarkets being built by competing chains on a limited number of selected sites, usually with facilities for car parking.

The growth of supermarket trading with car parking facilities did not exclude the need for smaller shops catering for the local needs of a neighbourhood. These smaller shops, however, could usually be run more economically by small traders who either owned or leased them and often lived on the premises. The functions of management, shop assistant, cash till operator and cleaner were combined in the proprietor and his immediate family. Moreover, small traders often adjusted their hours of business to suit what they perceived to be local needs. This frequently involved long hours of work with which the cooperative movement could not and would not wish to compete. Extended hours of opening in larger stores had to be met by shift working arrangements on the part of the employees.

The London Cooperative Society recognised the necessity to

268

shift its resources from small shops to larger stores and to introduce the most up-to-date methods of self-service trading. Nevertheless, it was not a policy that could be pursued ruthlessly by disregarding the views of traditionally loyal cooperators in working-class areas or the interests of the affected staff.

The second major problem facing the LCS concerned management. Modern distribution demands a high standard of management. There is not an unlimited supply of good managers and, at that time, they had either to be trained in special schemes or recruited from other well-known chains of successful stores.

I enjoyed my three years on the Management Committee of the LCS, and it gave me an insight into the business problems of the cooperative movement. The task of combining business efficiency, democratic accountability and proper regard for the interests of staff is one which will remain central to the building of a socialist society.

At the end of a three-year term of office, members of the Management Committee had to stand for re-election. I was defeated; the only candidate to lose a seat on behalf of the left-wing electoral organisation with which I was associated. My friends said that I lost my seat because by then I had become a member of the National Board for Prices and Incomes. The NBPI was not popular among the voters on whose support I depended.

Another project with which I was associated before I became a member of the NBPI was an abortive attempt to launch a new Labour daily newspaper. Others who were involved included Tom Driberg MP, Norman Buchan MP, Lord Willis and George Elvin, who was then the General Secretary of the Association of Cinematograph, Television and Allied Technicians. The moving spirit in this endeavour was a former executive of one of the big newspaper chains who, it was said, was friendly with Harold Wilson. Those of us among the supporting group who were actively engaged in the trade union and labour movement gradually became apprehensive that we were being encouraged by the former newspaper executive to enter into a project that owed more to enthusiasm than to a feasible and realistic assessment of the possibility of launching a financially viable newspaper.

We eventually drew back when we found that commitments were being contemplated which we considered to be beyond our resources. We were faced with legal problems, and I remember that finally we were assisted by Harold Lever MP. We were grateful to him. This experience underlined to me the need for caution when considering the possibility of a new Labour newspaper. Ours was neither the first nor the last abortive project.

Court of Inquiry

In December 1970 I was appointed by the Secretary of State for Employment to be a member of a Court of Inquiry into a dispute in the electricity supply industry. It was a three member inquiry under the chairmanship of Lord Wilberforce, who at that time was a member of the judicial bench of the House of Lords. The third member of the inquiry was Raymond Brookes, who was then the Chairman of Guest, Keen and Nettlefolds Ltd.

In September 1970 the unions represented on the National Joint Industrial Council for the Electricity Supply Industry presented a claim for substantial increases in pay and improvements in shift allowances, overtime rates, holidays and a reduction in the hours of the standard working week. In October a further item, relating to the pay of apprentices, was added to the claim. The employers made offers which the unions regarded as unacceptable. In December 1970 the negotiations broke down and the unions called for a ban on overtime, a work to rule and the complete withdrawal of all cooperation. The negotiating procedure agreement for the electricity supply industry provided for arbitration on any unresolved issues. The unions made it clear that they were not prepared to submit their claims to arbitration, despite the provisions of the agreement.

The dispute was specially significant because of the importance of electricity supply for the whole economy. Any disruption in supply could affect every other industry and service and the well-being and convenience of domestic consumers. It had further significance because the dispute had developed during a period of rising and high inflation. The Government was seeking to reduce inflationary pressure by a progressive reduction in the level of pay settlements, particularly in the public sector. At that time electricity supply was under public ownership and was thus part of the public sector.

The crux of the case put by the unions was that their members' wages, even after taking into account the offer made by the electricity employers, were lower than the average level of wages in other industries for comparable levels of skill. The electricity supply industry, it was argued, had an outstanding record of improvements in productivity. Under a series of agreements the workers had cooperated in increasing efficiency. In a number of White Papers published on incomes policy, it had been emphasised that workers who cooperated in such effective agreements could expect wage increases higher than the 'norm'.

The employers, in reply, stated that their offers went much of the way to meet the claims of the unions. They accepted that the industry had a very good record of improvements in productivity, but pointed to the importance of technological developments brought about by heavy capital investment. They deplored the refusal of the unions to observe the terms of the agreement which provided for arbitration on unresolved issues. The employers had been willing to submit the dispute to arbitration.

An unusual feature of the proceedings of the Court of Inquiry was that it received, by invitation, a memorandum of evidence from the Treasury. Oral evidence was given by the Permanent Secretary, Sir Douglas Allen, and by the Chief Economic Adviser, Sir Donald MacDougall. The Treasury evidence drew attention to the high and still rising level of inflation. The Treasury memorandum said that:

271

'A continuation of this rate of inflation would have grave economic and social consequences, and it would frustrate rather than promote the objective of increasing the real standards of living of the community.'

The Treasury also commented on the arguments often put forward to justify pay increases. In relation to productivity they suggested that 'an indiscriminate approach which ignored the causes of increased productivity would be seriously inflationary'. Account had to be taken of the input of capital. In relation to claims based on the cost of living, the Treasury suggested that if this resulted in settlements being above the rise in productivity, it was likely that prices would increase. In relation to claims based on wage comparability, the Treasury said that if the pace of inflation was to be slowed, the circle of increases had to be broken somewhere, even if this meant that previous relativities were not maintained.

The report of the Court of Inquiry said that these general principles had to be related to the particular case under examination. There should be scope for recognition of specific arrangements for relating the pay of particular groups to the acceptance by workers of changes in the organisation and methods of work in order to improve productivity. On the relevance of the cost of living, the report said that it was unrealistic to suppose that, in the then climate and pattern of wage settlements, pay could be negotiated without regard to the rise in the cost of living. On comparability the report pointed out that if wages in the electricity supply industry got out of line, beyond a certain degree with pay for similar jobs elsewhere, workers would be lost or not recruited.

As the Chairman of the inquiry, Lord Wilberforce conducted the proceedings with fairness and skill. A great amount of evidence was taken on the rise in productivity in the industry and was set out clearly in the report. One of the key witnesses was Derek Robinson, Senior Research Officer at the Oxford University Institute of Economics and Statistics. He agreed that Britain was in a state of serious and accelerating inflation, but emphasised that workers in one industry could not be expected to accept a moderation of their wage claims merely on general arguments about inflation, particularly in the absence of some convincing assurance that action was being taken to control prices.

The third member of the Court, Raymond Brookes, had a reputation as a strong-minded employer. I found him to be a modest man who felt more at home talking privately to other employers and union representatives than conducting proceedings with considerable national publicity. He brought to bear his long industrial experience, and he was determined to reach his own conclusions. My impression was that he attached importance to productivity and believed that people who contributed to it should be correspondingly rewarded. Although he had a reputation for toughness and rigour in business affairs, he supported the concept of good pay for good performance.

The three of us found no difficulty in reaching agreement on our recommendations. We concluded that over a period of years the workers had cooperated in major changes in working practices which had facilitated a heavy capital investment programme and a reduction in the industrial labour force. Their earnings, however, particularly for skilled workers, had not kept pace with weekly earnings in many other industries. Our recommendations were that basic rates aud certain allowances should be increased beyond the offers made by the employers, and that the introduction of certain incentive bonus schemes should be speeded up. We deplored the action by the unions in avoiding a reference to arbitration in accordance with their agreement with the employers. If the unions did not wish to be bound by arbitration, they should have proposed a suitable amendment to the constitution of the National Joint Industrial Council for the Electricity Supply Industry.

I added to the report a note of reservation concerning the relationship between the electricity supply industry dispute and the national economy. This note was published together with the agreed report. In my note of reservation I said that it was not possible to deal fairly with the problem of one dispute within a general formula, on the lines put to the Court by the

Treasury, which required that in a series of pay agreements there should be a progressive reduction in the level of settlements. Such a formula was too crude for justice even within the private sector and was likely, in practice, to discriminate against the public sector.

The note of reservation accepted that there was a serious inflationary tendency in the British economy, but said that this could not be explained solely in terms of high wage claims. Other important factors were the slow rate of growth in the economy, low capacity utilisation with the consequential upward pressure on costs, the use of market power to put up prices by firms in sheltered conditions, and the impact on costs of various deflationary measures. Prices had also been pushed up by devaluation and increased taxation.

In the note of reservation I argued for a counter-inflationary policy which aimed to stimulate growth and dealt with the links between expansion, productivity, prices and incomes of all kinds. A policy which was directed mainly at wages with accompanying deflationary pressures on the economy was more likely to lead to increased unemployment.

Some of these arguments are still relevant to the British economy.

13

London Transport

Towards the end of my period at the National Board for Prices and Incomes, and after it had already been announced that the Board was to be abolished, I one day received a telephone call from Sir Richard Way, the then Chairman of London Transport. He indicated that it might be useful if we could meet. At the time I assumed that the discussion would be about proposals on bus operations made in a number of reports prepared by the Prices and Incomes Board. When we met he asked whether, subject to acceptance by the Greater London Council, I would be interested in joining London Transport as the board member for personnel and industrial relations.

I was surprised to receive the invitation but I replied, without enquiring about the pay or other conditions of the appointment, that I would be very pleased to join London Transport. It seemed just the kind of job in a public enterprise that I would enjoy doing.

The procedure apparently was that the Chairman made suggestions for board members for the consideration of the GLC, which under the terms of the Transport (London) Act 1969 had been given responsibility for the policy and financial control of London Transport. The transfer of control from the Minister of Transport to the GLC took place on 1 January, 1970. The board members constituted the London Transport Executive. The Executive consisted of a chairman and five full-time members, responsible respectively for the buses, the railway system including the underground, engineering operations, finance and personnel. There were also a small number of part-time Executive members drawn from other walks of life.

I was interviewed both by the then leader of the GLC and the leader of the opposition party. All went well, and so I began work in a job which for approximately three and a half years gave me a great deal of satisfaction. Sir Richard Way was an extremely good Chairman. He was a former civil servant, and one of the very few who had risen from the ranks to become a Permanent Secretary at a comparatively young age. He did not join the civil service in the administrative grade. He left the civil service long before the normal age of retirement, to take over a large engineering firm.

Sir Richard Way's style of chairmanship was, in my view, admirable. He gave his full-time board colleagues plenty of scope to do their respective jobs in their own way, but he was always available for consultation. He was decisive when decisions had to be taken. In personal style he was friendly and cheerful. No-one was in doubt that he was the ultimate commander, but he exercised his leadership with a light touch. When from time to time I asked for his advice on a matter within my own area of responsibility, his usual reply was that I should first exercise my own judgment after taking account of the views of colleagues, but that if difficulties then ensued I should consult him again.

In 1971 London Transport had about 60,000 employees. At one time the figure was over 100,000, but the bus fleet had subsequently been much reduced. My responsibility was for industrial relations and for all aspects of the personnel function. I had to work in close cooperation with the other board members responsible for transport and engineering operations, and with the board member responsible for finance.

There were many different negotiating machines in London Transport. For the buses, for example, there were separate negotiations for the bus crew, the supervisory and administrative staff and the workers employed on bus maintenance in the garages. There were also separate negotiations for the bus maintenance factories at Chiswick and Aldenham. On the railway there were negotiations for the operating grades, for the booking clerks and the technical and administrative staff, and for the engineering workers employed in a main factory at

Acton, in other maintenance workshops and on the permanent way. There were also negotiating arrangements covering employees in the many staff restaurants and canteens of London Transport, a food factory, building and works maintenance, power stations and power distribution, lifts and escalators, ticketing and display, medical services, sports and recreation facilities, various professional groups including doctors, lawyers, journalists, architects and technicians of various kinds, the administrative staff in the main headquarters and senior officers.

The negotiations conducted through these different arrangements were, of course, often related to each other, and certainly a settlement reached for one section of staff could be expected to have repercussions in other directions. To the outsider it might seem that there was a strong case for a sweeping rationalisation of the negotiating machinery. If everything could have been started anew, I have no doubt that the machinery could have been simplified. On the other hand, negotiations are not only concerned with major claims affecting wages and the main conditions of employment; they also embrace initiatives of the management and grievances which concern only a small group of workers. It is preferable to settle these grievances as near as possible to their point of origin. On the railway in particular, great emphasis is placed upon the wage structure covering many different grades and the effect that changes affecting one small group may have on pay differentials or in creating new anomalies. The railway unions show great competence in dealing with these problems. Their negotiators are very well briefed, and their documentation on the evolution of the wage structure is nearly always reliable.

One particular problem in a large complex organisation covering many different occupations is that internal consistency in pay differentials is not always compatible with external comparisons, particularly when there are changes in market forces affecting a particular occupation. In my time an ever-present problem was the need to attract and retain staff to maintain the transport system in accordance with the statutory

277

obligations imposed on London Transport. The demand for different kinds of skill changes from one period to another and account has to be taken of external pressures in the labour market. Thus, for example, when computers are being installed new staff have to be recruited and existing staff have to be trained to acquire new skills. The pay structure has to take account of this kind of pressure.

In railway employment London Transport was always compared with British Rail, yet for many of the staff the two organisations did not operate in the same labour market. London Transport came under pressure from time to time from government departments not to conclude agreements which, it was argued, could prejudice negotiations between BR and the railway unions. This pressure was, of course, usually exerted in a diplomatic manner. We would be asked to provide information on our negotiating intentions, but there was no doubt about the purpose of the exercise. The effective reply to this pressure was that London Transport had to discharge its statutory duty to provide an effective transport system in London, and that it could not do this unless it could attract and retain staff. Moreover, London Transport was responsible to the Greater London Council. This did not imply that London Transport had no interest in the wider ramifications of its settlements, but it could not be expected, at the expense of its own legal obligations, to have overriding regard to whatever incomes policy for BR was favoured by the Government. I recall explaining this problem on a number of occasions to senior civil servants and to more than one Minister of Transport.

Our relations with BR were, in any case, good. My immediate opposite number on the board of BR was Bert Farrimond. We kept each other informed of our main objectives. We sought to avoid unnecessary problems in parallel negotiations whilst recognising that there were often significant differences in the circumstances surrounding the issues to be negotiated.

My responsibility for industrial relations gave me the opportunity to influence the conduct of collective bargaining in the direction which I thought it should take. This did not call for any sharp departure from existing policy. London Transport had a good record, and my predecessors had developed a worthy tradition. My board colleagues responsible for the buses, for the railway and for engineering operations were all committed to the need for collective bargaining. The industrial relations department of London Transport was headed by Bill Mallet, who had many years of experience and a fund of invaluable knowledge about earlier negotiations.

A Commitment to Collective Bargaining

I tried to set an example of strong commitment to the value of collective bargaining. It was, as I saw it, an important aspect of democracy, expressing the right of employees to join in the regulation of their pay and conditions of employment. It also enabled the management to initiate change, with a constant striving for greater efficiency, in a manner that would take account of the interests of employees, tap and utilise their experience, and ensure as far as possible that changes were introduced as smoothly as possible with benefit to all concerned, including the travelling public.

I did not take the view that disputes were caused by agitators. In any workplace there are not only common interests but conflicts of interest. Articulate representatives will not find support unless there are grounds for the grievances which they ventilate. By ventilating grievances they help to ensure that problems are not 'swept under the carpet' and become worse because they are not resolved. Conflicts are not unnatural, and the task of negotiators is to resolve them. Most settlements last only for a limited period. Change is constant in the conduct of any organisation, particularly if it is trying to keep ahead of developments in technology, and industrial relations must reflect the pressure for and consequences of change.

Negotiating procedure agreements and arrangements are of special importance in industrial relations. They set out the voluntary obligations, rights and responsibilities of the parties.

In my view, and I sought to influence London Transport in this direction, no subjects should be regarded as managerial prerogatives and outside the scope of discussion. If an issue is causing concern to employees, it is better that it should be discussed. Sometimes issues of concern are based on nothing more than inadequate information. To provide the necessary information is to help the effectiveness of the enterprise. If an issue of concern is based on substance it should, as far as possible, be resolved in a manner which takes account of realities and the various interests involved.

An important principle in negotiating arrangements is that changes should not be imposed unilaterally on workers without discussion and, if necessary, negotiations. This does not mean that change is impossible. On the contrary, a vital responsibility of management is to initiate improvements in techniques, to plan for capital investment, to employ people effectively, to train and promote suitable candidates and to identify new opportunities for the product or service which is being offered. Changes nearly always affect industrial relations, and so the initiative in the negotiating procedure should rest much of the time with management. It is quite wrong to sit back and await the next pay claim or grievance but to introduce changes without discussion and negotiation and in a manner likely to maximise discontent.

This does not imply that every change sought by management is subject to veto by employees acting through their unions. The obligation on the management is the same as on the unions when changes are being sought. Agreement must first be sought through the negotiating procedure. If this does not produce a settlement, then either side is free to take such action as it thinks appropriate.

There are occasions when it suits the purpose of a trade union not to reach agreement on a proposed change, but to accept the management's right to introduce it after exhausting the negotiating procedure. This is not necessarily an unfair ploy on the part of a trade union. Their task is to represent the interests of their members, and management should accept that the responsibility for decisions which may create problems cannot always be shared by a collective agreement. The essential requirement, however, is that unions should have the opportunity to put their point of view through the negotiating procedure.

In most of the industrial relations arrangements of London Transport a distinction was made between negotiating machinery and consultative machinery. It was not a distinction I favoured, though I did not feel sufficiently strongly about it to seek changes. It was mainly a matter of choice for the unions.

The argument for separate machinery for negotiations and consultation rests on the contention that there is a clear distinction between issues which are suitable for joint regulation through collective agreement and issues which are the subject of management decision, but on which the views of the unions ought to be heard. My view was that there is such a distinction, but that it is a constantly shifting frontier. Furthermore, consultative issues often give rise to issues which need to be negotiated. Conversely, negotiated issues may give rise to managerial problems on which the unions may choose to express a view but, legitimately, do not want to accept the joint responsibility of an agreement. There are thus occasions when it is a fair response from a union when it says: 'We note what you say and reserve the right to raise any consequential grievances, but the problem is for the management to resolve.'

Similarly, I was never enthusiastic about the separation of grievance procedures from negotiating procedures, though if such a formal separation were requested there was not much point in opposing it. Grievance procedures are usually intended to deal with complaints made by individual employees. It is, nevertheless, important that where separate grievance procedures exist they should be integrated into the normal negotiating arrangements. If the grievance cannot be resolved at the level of the workplace, the normal negotiating machinery at a higher level should not be bypassed. Above all, grievance procedures should not be regarded as some kind of alternative to the normal arrangements for trade union recognition and collective bargaining.

281

A commitment to collective bargaining also requires of management a belief in the value of trade union representation. A trade union representative at workplace level is performing an important function; he or she is not a 'pain in the neck' who has to be tolerated because it is the policy of the top management to recognise trade unions. A commitment to collective bargaining is incompatible with the victimisation of an employee for trade union representation and activity. This does not mean that a trade union representative is not subject to the same requirements as other workers, except to the extent necessary for trade union functions, but if the management feel that a charge should be brought against a trade union representative care should be taken to ensure that it is done in the presence of another senior trade union representative and, if possible, a full-time official. The old adage must be observed that not only has justice to be done, but it has to be seen to be done.

The commitment to collective bargaining also has implications for the recruitment policy of an enterprise. It is wrong for an employer to discriminate against a would-be recruit on grounds of his or her trade union activity with a previous employer. This also constitutes victimisation, but it is much more difficult to identify and prove than when an existing employee is discriminated against because of trade union activity.

During my period at London Transport there were at least two occasions when suggestions were made by other employers that we would be unwise to employ a particular applicant for a job because the applicant was an active and militant trade unionist. The suggestions were not accepted. My view was that applicants should be considered solely on their suitability for the job for which they were applying. The two applicants concerned, one a member of the AEU and the other of the TGWU, proved subsequently to be capable members of the workforce and contributed to the effectiveness of the collective bargaining arrangements.

The personnel function at London Transport, as distinct from the industrial relations function, was extremely wide-ranging. The two functions cannot be rigidly separated; the one affects the other, but for administrative purposes the two functions were organised in separate departments. Each had its own chief office responsible to the board member for personnel.

The personnel function covered recruitment, training, a staff college, welfare, including the welfare of orphaned children of former members of the staff, pensions, homes for pensioners, sports facilities, including the upkeep of a number of sports grounds, staff records and assessment, voluntary clubs of various kinds and the organisation each year of Christmas parties in various parts of London for the children of London Transport employees. Closely related to the work of the personnel function was the work of the medical department, with its own chief medical officer and a number of doctors.

I very much enjoyed every aspect of this work, and it provided me with many interesting and instructive experiences. On recruitment, for example, I learnt that young employees in certain occupations were not always the most suitable. Among bus drivers, for example, London Transport's extensive records, going back for many years, revealed that accident-proneness tended to decline with maturity of age. Thus bus drivers of, say, 50 years of age were on average less prone to traffic accidents than drivers of 21 years of age. Similarly, up to a certain age employees were inclined to have more short spells of sickness. The trend was then reversed after the age of about 50. These interesting findings influenced our recruitment policy and our readiness to accept older workers.

During my period at London Transport we had a serious shortage of bus crew, reaching at times into many thousands. Both the board member responsible for the buses, Ralph Bennett, and I argued strongly that special measures were needed to attract and retain staff, including assistance with housing. It was pointless to recruit would-be bus crew from other areas of Britain, only then to find that they could not afford to buy a house in London or had no priority on local authority housing lists. We had the support of the board on the need for special measures, including higher wages, but our

283

initiatives were not always welcomed by the Government because they considered them inflationary.

A Helpful Enquiry

A very helpful enquiry on behalf of London Transport was conducted by Professor Dorothy Wedderburn into an acute shortage of bus crew at one of our largest garages, in an area where there were some hundreds of men and women registered as unemployed. The enquiry confirmed that very few of the unemployed would have made suitable bus crew. Indeed, the requirements of the job demanded a highly selective recruitment policy.

In the first place, bus crew have to be physically fit. But driving is not a healthy occupation. A driver is confined to a driving seat for hours on end, often in stressful conditions. The stopping and starting bell constantly rings for his or her attention. A driver has to have good eyesight, and must be prepared and able to work irregular hours with a pattern of seven-day working. He or she has to have a special driving licence and a calm and rational approach to the many provocations and exasperations to be experienced on the road in the course of a working day. A driver is responsible for the safety of passengers. He or she must be able to get to the garage in the morning to drive a very early bus and to return home without dependence on public transport when the last bus is driven into the garage at night. A driver must understand running schedules and, as far as possible, keep to a timetable. Regrettably, a driver will be called upon from time to time to help deal with obstructive or even violent passengers.

The requirements for bus conductors were in many ways similar to those for drivers. A driving licence was not necessary, and the responsibility for safety was of a different kind. On the other hand, conductors have a physically demanding job and on London's double-decked buses have to climb and descend the stairs on a moving vehicle many times during each working shift. They are also at the sharp end of any abuse from passengers or expressions of frustration when buses are late, irregular or arrive in convoy. These problems are rarely the fault of staff, but are usually due to traffic delays and congestion.

Both Ralph Bennett and I were in favour of the recruitment of women as bus drivers and, later, as one-person bus operators. The TGWU cooperated in this initiative. Today, women bus drivers are a familiar sight in London.

London Transport had already started to introduce one-person operation on many bus routes before I arrived. The driver combined his duties with that of the conductor. The pressure for this change was entirely economic, not least because of recommendations made earlier by the National Board for Prices and Incomes in its reports on bus operations. The direct labour cost of one-person operation was much less than for a crewed bus, even though a driver-operator received a higher rate of pay than a driver of a crewed bus.

I was, nevertheless, not an enthusiast for one-person operation on buses, particularly in inner London. They cause delay whilst passengers queue to pay or show their passes, and the presence of a conductor is often reassuring to older passengers. The cost of traffic delays caused by one-person operation of buses is a social charge which is not revealed in the accounts of London Transport.

The bus fleet in London is much less than it was in earlier years. In my time, before privatisation, London Transport was required to operate economically, which, in reality, meant that its calculations were often made by disregarding social costs and social benefits. It led to misleading conclusions and bad policies. This, however, was not the fault of London Transport but was the consequence of the policies determined by those who set the guidelines for public transport in London.

For many years the London Underground system was not very different in shape from what it was immediately before the First World War. Only in more recent years have new lines been developed. Even today the system is lopsided: North London is better served than South London.

The Underground system provides a very effective rapid means of transport for millions of passengers. Much of the

285

so-called Underground system runs on the surface, particularly in outer London. It is a criticism of Britain that it failed adequately to develop the system in London after a promising and early start. This criticism, however, cannot be confined to public transport. It applies equally to many other industries.

The problem, fundamentally, is one of lack of investment. Too few of Britain's resources have been devoted to industrial modernisation and expansion and to the development of the infrastructure. Instead huge sums have been invested abroad because of the prospects of higher profits, and, in the years since the Second World War, resources have been used for military purposes far beyond the economic capacity of the country. Britain's military spending has been consistently higher than the average for NATO European countries. In particular, the two countries that have provided the strongest industrial competition, Japan and Germany, have spent proportionately less on arms than Britain. By seeking military strength, Britain has produced economic weakness. Britain has also concentrated on its financial services at the expense of its industrial base.

The misdirection of much of Britain's investment capital was brought home to me vividly during my time at London Transport. For a period I was chairman of one of the principal pension funds of London Transport employees. There were millions of pounds to invest. I shared the view of the unions that London Transport pension funds should, compatible with reasonable security, be invested in projects which would promote industrial development in and around the London area. The prosperity of London Transport was bound up with the prosperity of the London region.

We were told by our professional financial advisers that discriminatory investment based on social considerations would probably be regarded as illegal if challenged. Our responsibility was to maximise the return on investments, compatible with security, for the sole benefit of existing pensioners and contributors. The result was that we sought investments not only in Britain but in foreign property development.

Shortly after my appointment to London Transport Executive the Chairman, Sir Richard Way, asked me to take board responsibility for the catering services. At that time London Transport had about 130 staff restaurants and canteens, a food factory and nearly 1,000 staff employed in the catering department. If I remember rightly, the department was providing about 100,000 meals, snacks and refreshments every day. The catering service, although run as a separate department with its own chief officer, was closely related to the personnel function. The service was providing meals and refreshments for employees.

In asking me to assume board responsibility for the catering service the Chairman was, I think, of the view that it would give me some direct experience of departmental management, as distinct from functional responsibility for industrial relations and personnel throughout the organisation. Day-to-day management was under the control of a Chief Officer who was a specialist in catering and who had spent his working life in catering organisations. My responsibility was to answer to my board colleagues on catering investment and on the strategic direction of our catering services.

I found this experience quite fascinating. One of the problems which exercised the board members responsible for the buses, the railway system and the engineering operations was that many of our canteens were not particularly attractive and that too many of them were untidy. This was not just a problem of management. The culture associated with canteen feeding in many British factories and other industrial establishments was that whilst the food was good, the kind of service provided was at best utilitarian. Tables were often left in an untidy state.

I accompanied colleagues on visits to one or two other countries, to ascertain whether this culture of canteen feeding was universal or whether it could be improved. The conclusion very firmly was that it could be improved. Both in Sweden and Germany there were examples of a much higher standard of accommodation and service.

In cooperation with board colleagues and the Chief Officer for catering, it was decided to embark on a long-term programme for the upgrading of canteens. The aim was to provide staff restaurants which would provide not only good food but would be inviting to all who attended. This would require cooperation from all concerned, particularly in keeping tables tidy, with the prompt removal of used crockery and bottles.

The formula introduced for the new regime was that London Transport would be responsible for the initial investment for modernisation, but that each year a sum of money would be made available to the representatives of workpeople to spend as they wished on restaurant facilities. This could include, for example, special furniture, decorative ware or a television set. In return the workers' representatives were asked to share in the responsibility for maintaining the cleanliness and tidiness of the restaurant. It was a costly programme, and the intention was that it would be spread over a number of years. Two or three such restaurants were created during my period at London Transport, and I recall that they were very attractive. I do not know what further progress was made because I left London Transport whilst the programme was still in its early stages.

Another interesting experience with the catering service concerned the appointment of canteen or restaurant managers. The policy of the department was not to discriminate on grounds of gender, but to appoint either a woman or a man according to her or his suitability. My own conclusion was, however, that in the small number of garage canteens where there had been friction between bus crew there was an advantage in having a woman manager of mature years. Men involved in argument are less likely to abuse a woman in front of other men than they are to abuse another man. Thus a woman manager could often intervene successfully when the intervention of a man might be less effective.

A Public Service

The main responsibility of London Transport Executive was:

'to provide such public transport services as best meets the needs of Greater London, in accordance with principles approved by the Greater London Council and with due regard for efficiency, economy and safety of operation, subject always to the requirement that at the end of an agreed period the aggregate of the net balance of its consolidated revenue account and that of the general reserve is such as may be approved by the Council for that period.'

The Executive had constantly to weigh both commercial and social considerations but, in the ultimate, a commercial target had to be met. The commercial target was affected by the changes affecting London's traffic. Most people use public transport to travel to and from central London and to move from one point to another within central London. There is a high demand for the use of private cars even within inner London, but it would be impossible to satisfy London's transport needs if everyone tried to use a private car. As it is, the congestion in London's traffic is caused overwhelmingly by the minority who use private cars to get from one point to another.

In the suburbs there are different traffic conditions. There is less congestion, and in some suburbs a high proportion of the population depend on private cars for transport other than for travel to and from work. The decline of cinema attendance has also affected the demand for public transport in the evenings. The harshest impact on services, if regard were paid only to commercial considerations, would be in the outer suburbs. Yet it is in these areas that the Conservative Party has its strongest support. If London Transport had failed to take into account social considerations based on social costs and benefits – as often suggested by the most rigorous of 'free market' advocates – it would have been the Tory areas that would have suffered most.

It does not need a business genius to run buses commercially in peak times in inner London, particularly if measures are taken, such as the widespread introduction of bus lanes, to facilitate the movement of buses. The problem of 'uneconomic' routes is more likely to arise in outer areas.

Another serious problem for public transport in London is that the demand for its services is spread very unevenly over the day. There are peak periods in the morning and in the late afternoon and early evening, corresponding to the length of the working day for millions of commuters. The provision of many extra services can be expensive. Additional vehicles and staff have to be employed to provide the passenger capacity for relatively short periods. Labour costs represent a high proportion of the day-to-day working expenses.

If London Transport had to meet its own capital costs, including the enormous sums required for the development of the Underground system, fares would have to be increased to an even higher level than at present. It would be a self-defeating exercise. Fares in London are already higher than in many other capital cities, and further substantial increases would reduce passenger traffic. There would be increased road congestion, and social costs would rise. Thus commercial considerations must always be modified by social considerations. Public transport organisations should be permitted to take into account social costs and social benefits.

When I left London Transport I did so with sadness. It was a challenging and very enjoyable job.

Some years later, when Ken Livingstone was the leader of the Greater London Council, I was approached as to whether I might wish to be considered for the chairmanship of London Transport. At the time I was a candidate for the post of General Secretary of the Labour Party. I decided, with some reluctance, that, from my personal point of view, the Labour Party job, though considerably less paid, might provide a bigger task. I am certain that if I had opted for London Transport and if I had been selected, I would have enjoyed the job immensely. The policy of the then GLC towards transport in London was one with which I was in total sympathy.

The Labour-controlled GLC, under the leadership of Ken Livingstone, believed in the development of public transport and pursued a policy designed to attract more passengers and to improve the services. The policy of reducing or holding down fares achieved its objective, and the introduction of free passes for senior citizens was a much-needed social reform.

Labour's transport policy in London was partially thwarted by subsequent legal action, when the courts placed themselves above the democratic will of London's voters. The left-led GLC was highly popular, and would have been returned with a substantial majority if the electorate had been permitted to vote. Transport policy was central to Labour's appeal. The Government of Mrs Thatcher regarded the prospect of a continuing GLC, with a vigorous and radical policy, as unacceptable. The GLC was abolished. It was a disgraceful decision by the Conservative Government and left London as the only capital city in Europe without a capital-wide local authority.

Unfortunately, as I was later able to confirm from my personal experience at the headquarters of the Labour Party, Ken Livingstone was almost as unpopular with some influential people in the Labour Party when Neil Kinnock was leader as he was with the Government of Mrs Thatcher. It was particularly irritating to listen to critics of the Labour Party in London who were always willing to attack the left but who chose to disregard the very good record of Ken Livingstone and his colleagues and of the way in which they had won public support for their policies.

The Conservative Government later embarked on a policy of bus deregulation and privatisation. The comprehensive system which had been introduced with the formation of London Transport was broken up. It brought back the old problems which had disfigured the transport system in London when it was operated by so many different companies and organisations. The attitude of the new leaders of London Transport to these changes was to support them. It was a sorry spectacle.

Towards the end of 1992 the magazine of London Transport, entitled *LT News*, was published with a front page headline announcing, 'It's all go for buses sell-off'. The report under this headline said that all the block grant routes would be operating on a contract basis in readiness for privatisation in 1994. The announcement made by the Minister, it was reported, had been welcomed by London Transport. It was seen as the best way forward for the London bus subsidiaries.

The same report made clear, however, that it was not known what effect privatisation would have on jobs or whether garages would be sold with the subsidiaries. I regarded it as deplorable that those responsible for the direction of London Transport should have expressed their support for these changes. I am certain that their views were not supported either by a majority of the staff or of the passengers of London Transport.

One of the fascinating aspects of my job at London Transport was that it gave me an opportunity to experience the different methods and 'culture' of the various trade unions representing the workforce of the organisation. I was involved in negotiations of one kind or another almost every day, and I soon appreciated that the kind of approach appropriate in negotiations with one union was not necessarily appropriate for another union.

Because of my experience in the engineering industry, I was reasonably familiar with the style of the engineering unions. Their officials were strongly influenced by the views of their stewards and district representatives. With the NUR and the ASLEF, great importance was attached to precedents affecting the wages structure and the line of promotion. Their officials, as mentioned earlier, entered into negotiations with carefully prepared briefs and the attitude of their respective executive committees was central to their standpoint. The railway unions demonstrated stamina in the pursuit of even relatively minor claims. The same items sometimes appeared on the agenda month after month until some progress towards a settlement was made.

The special characteristic of the TGWU was that nearly all their officials with whom I negotiated had at one time or another worked for London Transport and were thoroughly familiar with the organisation. The national officer then responsible for the passenger transport industry was Larry Smith. He was formerly an LT employee. Larry Smith conducted the main negotiations, but many of the day-to-day negotiations were conducted by other officials.

The lay representatives of the TGWU always played an important part in the determination of claims and in decisions about settlements. The Central Bus Committee of lay members had a long and vigorous history. Bill Jones of Dalston Garage, for example, who had retired by the time I worked for London Transport, was said to have been one of the most influential figures ever to have worked for the organisation. I came to know Bill and greatly respected his judgment. He served for many years on the General Executive Council of the TGWU. Because of his membership of the Communist Party he was 'purged' at the time when Arthur Deakin was General Secretary of the TGWU. He later left the CP, but remained strongly on the left and was elected once again to the General Executive Council. He was widely respected.

Another earlier prominent communist among London busmen was Bert Papworth. He was elected to the General Executive Council of the TGWU and became one of the few lay members of the General Council of the TUC. He too was 'purged' when the TGWU excluded communists from office. He remained in the CP and was then elected as Secretary of the London busmen's convalescent home. He was assiduous in his new responsibilities and was a popular figure.

Larry Smith finally became the number three in the hierarchy of TGWU national officials. He was an able spokesman for the bus employees, and I remember him particularly for his understanding of the problems faced by LT and its workers.

It was my experience at London Transport that the unions sought to settle the claims and grievances of their members by negotiations. They were rightly insistent that procedures should be observed both by management and by workers and that the procedures should require negotiations before changes were made affecting conditions of employment. If agreement could not be reached – which was rare – then either side was free to take such action as it felt to be necessary.

Another interesting part of my job at London Transport was to serve on a number of committees with other employers' representatives. I was appointed to the industrial relations committee of the Confederation of British Industry. London Transport had by then joined the CBI. I was pleased to find that most of the industrial relations specialists of the very big firms took, as I saw it, a reasonably progressive view. In general they were sceptical about the effect of increased legislative interference in industrial relations.

I also served on a committee consisting of board members of nationalised industries responsible for industrial relations. The purpose of the committee was to exchange views and experiences about common problems. My main recollection of this committee was of the conflict between the pressure of government for the observance of pay restraint and the specific and various needs of the nationalised industries to recruit and retain labour to meet their objective.

My period at London Transport coincided with the new industrial relations legislation introduced by the Heath Government. London Transport sought to act lawfully and, in agreement with the unions, made it clear, as it was legally entitled to, that it did not intend its collective agreements to be legally enforceable. Agreements were written in words which suited the purpose of the employer and the union. They were not intended to provide the basis for expensive litigation and for interpretation by lawyers and courts.

In my view, the legal changes introduced by the Heath Government contributed nothing to the improvement of industrial relations at London Transport. When they were swept away following the miners' strike and the election of a Labour Government in 1974, it was to the advantage of all concerned.

14

ACAS and Conciliation

In the early summer of 1974 I received an invitation to become the Chairman of a new organisation to be established by the recently elected Labour Government, the Conciliation and Arbitration Service. The structure and purpose of the new body generally accorded with an agreement reached in the TUC-Labour Party Liaison Committee in 1972.

I had no hesitation in accepting the invitation, because I strongly supported the intention of the Government to encourage the extension of collective bargaining and to develop an independent and voluntary conciliation service in industrial relations. The new organisation was to be under the control of a Council consisting of members appointed by the Secretary of State for Employment. Some were to be nominated by the TUC, some by the CBI, and some were to be independent. I was aware that the proposal for such an organisation owed much to the initiative and drive of Jack Jones, the General Secretary of the TGWU.

Despite my pleasure at being invited to become the Chairman of the new conciliation organisation, I left London Transport with very considerable regret. I had enjoyed my period there and valued highly the experience it had given me. It had provided an opportunity to apply ideas which I had developed about industrial relations, based upon a full and constructive dialogue with trade unions representing all employees, an acceptance of the right of workers to join in the regulation of their conditions of employment and to contribute their views and influence on all matters of mutual concern, including the conduct of the organisation.

I was fortunate to have been at London Transport at a time when it had very good leadership from its Chairman, Sir Richard Way. I was appreciative of the support that he and other board members had given me. The trade union representatives of the 60,000 workforce also played a constructive role and demonstrated that a commitment to workers' interests and support for efficiency in a public service are compatible. London Transport in my time included a large number of dedicated staff who had worked for the organisation for many years. Subsequently, with creeping privatisation, London Transport has degenerated as a public service.

The Conciliation and Arbitration Service came into existence on 2 September, 1974. The title was changed in January 1975 to the Advisory, Conciliation and Arbitration Service, to reflect the full range of its functions. In a letter sent to me on 8 August, 1974, the Secretary of State for Employment, Michael Foot, explained that at the outset the Service was to be brought into existence by administrative means, but that it was to be put on a statutory basis when the necessary legislation had been passed by Parliament.

Michael Foot explained in his letter that the terms of reference of the Service were:

'to provide conciliation and mediation as a means of avoiding and resolving disputes, to make facilities available for arbitration, to provide advisory services to industry on industrial relations and related matters and to undertake investigations as a means of promoting the improvement and extension of collective bargaining.'

The letter emphasised that the Service should be independent and so attract and retain the support of all sectors of employment. The Government would not seek to interfere. The functions of the Service would be such that parties in dispute could seek its voluntary assistance. In other situations the Service itself would want to take the initiative to explore whether it could be of assistance. In general, the Service would be expected to pay due regard to existing negotiating procedures and not normally seek to intervene unless there had been a failure to obtain a settlement within those procedures.

Michael Foot suggested that conciliation and mediation should be carried out by the full-time staff of the Service, but that arbitrators should be appointed from a panel or panels of persons experienced in industrial relations. They would not be full-time members of the staff of the Service. Arbitrators would be appointed at the joint request of the parties in a dispute and on agreed terms of reference. Michael Foot also said that he proposed to pass to the new Service the advisory services on industrial relations operated by the Department of Employment. The Service would also be able to undertake longer-term investigations into industrial relations problems.

In 1975 Parliament passed the Employment Protection Act. ACAS became a statutory body under the terms of this Act on 1 January, 1976. The Secretary of State appointed a strong Council to control the new organisation. There were three trade unionists, Jack Jones of the TGWU, Richard Briginshaw, formerly the General Secretary of the National Association of Operative Printers, Graphical and Media Personnel (NATSOPA), and George Smith, the General Secretary of the Union of Construction, Allied Trades and Technicians. The employers were Tony Peers, the Industrial Relations Director of the Engineering Employers' Federation, Alan Swinden, Deputy Director of the CBI, and Bert Farrimond of the British Railways Board. The independent members were three professors, Hugh Clegg, John Wood and Laurie Hunter.

There were occasional changes in the membership of the Council. The original members were all men. When Professor Wood resigned in January 1976 to become the Chairman of the Central Arbitration Committee, he was replaced by Dorothy Wedderburn, the Director of the Industrial Sociology Unit of Imperial College. Dorothy Wedderburn was a good member of the Council and made a critical and constructive contribution. She was not a 'token' woman. She later became the Principal of Bedford College and Royal Holloway College. Other trade unionists to serve on the Council during my time as Chairman were Len Edmonson and John Boyd of the AEU,

Harry Urwin of the TGWU, Les Wood of UCATT and John Monks of the TUC. Other employers who became members of the Council include Oscar De Ville and Cliff Rose. Professor Ben Roberts was appointed when Hugh Clegg retired.

One of the principal reasons for the formation of ACAS, independent of the normal machinery of government, was that the conciliation function in industrial disputes had to be separated from the enforcement of whatever incomes policy the government of the day might favour. It was pointless in certain disputes for employers or unions to approach conciliators under the direct control of the Department of Employment when this same Department had the responsibility to seek observance of an incomes policy.

One of the early tasks of the Council of ACAS was to consider how the conciliation service was to operate in the light of the then Government's incomes policy, set out in a White Paper entitled 'The Attack on Inflation'. The Council decided that conciliation should be available to help the parties to a dispute, and that ACAS should not act as an interpreter or as an enforcement agent for an incomes policy. It was not unusual in a dispute for ACAS to ask the parties whether they had taken account of whatever incomes policy was in existence at the time, or to advise them, if any doubts arose, to consult the CBI or the TUC or to seek an interpretation from the Department of Employment. If, however, either or both parties did not accept the incomes policy or any interpretation of it, the conciliation facilities were not withdrawn.

During my period as Chairman the successive Secretaries of State for Employment, Michael Foot, Albert Booth and James Prior, were scrupulous in respecting the independence of ACAS. On only one occasion, during the period of office of the Labour Government, was I approached by a Minister, with no connection with the Department of Employment, who sought to influence ACAS in the settlement of a dispute. I was able to remind him of the requirement of paragraph 11 of Schedule 1 of the Employment Protection Act, which stated that, apart from the presentation of accounts, ACAS:

'shall not be subject to directions of any kind from any Minister of the Crown as to the manner in which it is to exercise any of its functions under any enactment.'

I have sometimes been asked whether it was possible for me, with views strongly supportive of trade unionism, to act impartially as Chairman of ACAS, or alternatively whether my successor, Pat Lowry, with a lifetime of experience representing employers, could also be expected to be impartial. My answer is that, providing the holder of the office of Chairman subscribed genuinely to the purposes of ACAS, the task could be discharged satisfactorily.

The Purpose of ACAS

The strategic purpose of ACAS was set out in the first section of the Employment Protection Act.

'The Service shall be charged with the general duty of promoting the improvement of industrial relations, and in particular of encouraging the extension of collective bargaining and the development and, where necessary, reform of collective bargaining machinery.'

The requirement of impartiality did not mean that ACAS was without a standpoint on industrial relations. The duty 'to promote the improvement of industrial relations' was not explicitly defined in the Act, except that it included encouraging the extension of collective bargaining and the development and, where necessary, the reform of collective bargaining. It had a commitment in its favour. Significantly, this commitment to the extension of collective bargaining was later removed from the statutory duties of ACAS by the then Conservative Government.

This commitment, in my view, constituted a recognition of the democratic right of employees to join, by means of collective negotiations, in the regulation of their conditions of employment and to influence other matters affecting their welfare, prosperity and security of employment. Collective bargaining is also of advantage to employers because it provides for the orderly determination of conditions of employment, for the ventilation and settlement of grievances and for the constructive influence of employees on a range of issues of mutual concern.

Similarly, the requirement to encourage the development and, where necessary, the reform of collective bargaining machinery, implied a commitment on the part of ACAS. Good collective bargaining machinery should, in my view, provide for the effective representation of employers' and workers' interests at all levels, including particularly in the workplace. Such effective representation is unlikely to be possible without an acceptance of the advantages of collective bargaining by management representatives and adequate provision, with proper facilities, for the workplace representation of employees.

Good collective bargaining machinery also implies, in my view, that when issues arise which may give rise to conflict, an effort should be made to resolve them before changes are made or other action is taken. This imposes obligations on both employers and unions.

Another aspect of collective bargaining machinery of importance both to employers and employees is the extent to which it provides for the discussion of both collective interests and of the interests of particular groups. No hard-and-fast rules apply to all situations. There are disadvantages in a collective bargaining structure which is highly fragmented between different trades and occupations, and, similarly, there are disadvantages in a structure that fails to provide for the discussion of particular problems affecting different groups of employees. Each situation has to be examined and account taken of the needs of both employers and employees.

Another important aspect of collective bargaining machinery is its scope. It should be possible for any issue to be raised which is of mutual concern or which is causing or likely to cause friction and a sense of grievance. This also imposes obligations both on unions and employers. Employers should not argue that an issue raised by a union is outside the scope of the procedure because they regard it as a 'managerial prerogative' or because they find it inconvenient to provide a response. To refuse discussion of an issue does not ensure that it will disappear. On the contrary, an insistence on 'managerial prerogatives' encourages workers in different circumstances to become equally insistent that certain work practices are not matters for joint regulation.

The improvement of industrial relations is sometimes interpreted as meaning nothing more than the absence of strikes, even when this is achieved through repressive legislation. Some Conservative leaders give the impression that the only or main index of good industrial relations is the number of days lost through industrial disputes. It is a shallow interpretation.

A low level of industrial disputes, measured by days lost because of strikes, may indicate very little about the real state of industrial relations but a great deal about the existence of fear. This is particularly true in periods of heavy unemployment. Workers are afraid of losing their jobs, and will often put up with all kinds of discomfort and injustice because they fear that if they protest they will be marked out for dismissal or redundancy.

This fear is made worse when there is repressive legislation which imposes restrictions on trade union action but leaves employers free to change conditions unilaterally, providing that notice is given. It is even worse when notice is not given and workers feel that they have no choice but to 'take it' or be dismissed. Such legal rights of redress as may exist may mean very little if the reality is the threat of unemployment.

The state of industrial relations in an enterprise can rarely be assessed without a study of the behaviour and attitude of all concerned. A high incidence of strikes may indicate serious and unresolved problems. Conversely, the absence of formal disputes, even in conditions of prosperity, may not be an indication of good relations. It is also necessary, for example, particularly when there is a generally high level of employment, to have regard to the labour turnover figures. Employees may be so dissatisfied that a substantial number seek employment elsewhere, providing other jobs are available.

Good industrial relations exist when both the employer and the employees feel that within the employment relationship they are able, as far as possible, to achieve their respective objectives. This requires that arrangements should exist for a satisfactory dialogue between them on all matters of mutual concern. An employer's objective is usually to establish conditions in which business is prosperous, preferably with the possibility of expansion if this is desired, and a motivated workforce. The objective of workers is for decent and steadily rising living standards, reasonable security of employment, and, in many cases, opportunities for training and promotion.

In many countries the role of trade unions and employers' organisations is specifically upheld by law. The 1978 Spanish Constitution, for example, recognises the right of trade unions and employers' organisations to exist and to operate. It confirms that they 'contribute to the defence and promotion of the economic and social interests which they represent'. Article 7 of the Spanish Constitution reads:

> 'Trade unions and employers' associations contribute to the defence and promotion of the economic and social interests which they represent. Their creation and the exercise of their activities shall be unrestricted in so far as they respect the Constitution and the law. Their internal structure and operation must be democratic.'

This committed point of view on the value of collective organisation in industrial relations expresses the kind of approach which the formation of ACAS represented. Unfortunately, this central pillar of commitment to collective bargaining was undermined by successive pieces of legislation under Mrs Thatcher and Mr Major, culminating in the elimination of the duty on ACAS 'to encourage the extension of collective bargaining'.

A commitment to collective bargaining does not imply that a conciliator in an industrial dispute, except in a dispute where the right to bargain collectively is itself an issue, need lean in the direction either of a union's claim or of the employer's response. The purpose of the conciliator is to promote a settlement. It is not to act as judge or jury on the merits of the claim or the response.

Conciliation

The first requirement in conciliation is for the conciliator to listen to the point of view of the parties to a dispute. The conciliator, far from acting in judgment, should seek to understand sympathetically the circumstances and reasons which have led the parties to adopt their respective stances. This essential preliminary phase of conciliation is nearly always best conducted by separate meetings with the parties to the dispute. The conciliator must not give the impression that he is conducting an adversarial investigation. On the contrary, it is helpful towards an eventual settlement if the parties feel that the conciliator understands their respective points of view.

For conciliation to succeed, there must be a readiness by the parties to reach a settlement. Frequently in the preliminary phases of conciliation, which may last many hours before the parties are brought face to face, possible areas of compromise begin to emerge. An employer may indicate that his reluctance to move from an earlier stance in negotiations did not represent the final word, but that any movement had to be reciprocal. The union may convey a similar message to the conciliator.

The conciliator must respect the confidence of both parties and must not disclose information which might weaken their respective negotiating stances. On the other hand, the conciliator has to explore the possibility of movement, particularly if it is reciprocal, and has to try to create in the minds of the parties a readiness to consider new possibilities. At an appropriate stage the conciliator may decide that it is desirable to bring the parties together for face-to-face discussions and to concentrate not on the points of entrenched difference, but on possible points of movement. Once the discussion gets going, and providing there is a wish for a settlement, the negotiations find their own momentum and the profile of a possible agreement may begin to emerge. This whole process may take many hours and, sometimes, even days. Conciliation does not always lead to a settlement. One of the parties to the dispute may decide that in the existing circumstances there is no basis for a settlement which they would find acceptable. They may hope that attitudes will change after an interval of time. During this interval steps may be taken to exert pressure on the other party, either by strike action, resistance to a strike, a lockout or by other means.

From the standpoint of the conciliator, this kind of response may be disappointing but it is legitimate. Power is an ingredient, though not the only ingredient, of every settlement of an industrial dispute. Even governments occasionally exert their power in disputes which they regard, justifiably or unjustifiably, as damaging. The conciliator may hold the private view that the attitude of one of the parties to a dispute is unreasonable, but care has to be taken to ensure that in conciliation the parties themselves find their own solution. It is not the job of a conciliator to seek to impose a solution, even if this were possible.

Disputes involving the government of the day may pose a special problem for conciliation. ACAS must act independently and be prepared to provide conciliation, even if the government does not want a settlement or, alternatively, wants a settlement on its own terms. Conversely, the government is entitled to react in the same way as any other employer and to indicate that it does not think that conciliation is appropriate. Normally, however, in disputes directly affecting public organisations or government departments, the process of conciliation proceeds as in disputes in the private sector.

Very occasionally, a dispute in the public sector is seen by the government as so important that conciliation, for all practical purposes, is excluded. This is not a decision which should ever be taken by ACAS. It must always remain prepared to conciliate. In the mining dispute of 1984–85 it was clear that the Government of Mrs Thatcher did not want a settlement on any terms other than the defeat of the NUM.

During my time at ACAS, the Chief Conciliation Officer for most of the period was Andrew Kerr. He was admirably suited for the job. He brought to it a wide knowledge of industrial relations, sympathy for the aspirations and problems of employers and unions, a belief in the value of collective bargaining and a personal attitude helpful in his role as conciliator. He came to ACAS from the Department of Employment, where he had occupied a similar post. When he retired he was followed by Dennis Boyd, who also had a background in industrial relations in the Civil Service. He too was successful and developed and displayed the same knowledge, understanding and helpful personal characteristics as his predecessor.

Most of the conciliation function was conducted by the Chief Conciliation Officer and staff responsible to him, both in London and in the regions. I was sometimes drawn in to help with conciliation in major disputes, and always found it a fascinating experience. Each industry has its own 'culture', and this 'culture' usually has to be respected if a settlement is to be found to a dispute.

Among the disputes which I remember most clearly – not always because they had the greatest economic significance – were those concerned with the newspapers, TV journalists, the baking industry, stable lads, iron and steel, Ford, British Leyland, Chrysler, road haulage, road passenger transport and the National Health Service. Other memorable disputes were concerned with claims for trade union recognition, but more will be said of this later.

I was involved in a number of newspaper disputes when Lord Goodman was the principal spokesman for the proprietors. He was a persuasive and courteous representative. On the union side, the workers were also ably represented by the officials of the National Graphical Association and SOGAT. It became clear to me that though the employers often complained of the control then exercised by the unions, many of the arrangements had come into existence because it had suited particular proprietors to depend upon the unions for the supply of trained labour at short notice and for temporary contracts for night shifts or weekend working. The collective bargaining structure was fragmented to cater for different groups of workers. Abuses took place, and ACAS sought to promote negotiating arrangements which would better serve the long-term interests of the industry, including the application of the latest technology.

In the dispute affecting stable lads Lord Wigg, a former Labour Cabinet Minister who had risen from the ranks in the army and who was a horse-racing enthusiast, sought energetically to promote a settlement, though he had no official standing in the dispute. His sympathies were with the stable lads, and it was not easy to deal with his unofficial intervention. The problem was that though he represented no-one but himself, he appeared to have the ear of influential people and to be well informed. I tried as carefully as I could to explain that it was the practice of ACAS to deal directly with parties to a dispute. He responded by indicating that the role of unofficial informant was one that was very familiar to him from various experiences in his career, and that he had acted in that role when Harold Wilson was Prime Minister. I did not press him for details.

In one of the iron and steel disputes concerning blastfurnacemen at a South Wales plant, there was a particularly able representative from the workforce. He was a very good example of the exceptional talent which is revealed from time to time among rank-and-file workers in the trade union movement. Such experiences provide a sobering answer to the claim that our modern system provides higher education for all who could benefit from it.

In disputes affecting engineering workers there was the memorable experience of negotiating with Reg Birch or being present when he was in negotiations with employers. Reg Birch was a member of the small full-time Executive Council of the AUEW, elected from the London and Home Counties area. He was for many years a member of the Communist Party, but finally broke with them and became associated with a Maoist trend.

306

Reg Birch was often an elusive figure when a dispute was in progress. I think he took the view that pressure from the workforce was often effective in bringing a dispute to a satisfactory conclusion, and he saw no purpose in what he regarded as a premature intervention. He had a very sharp mind behind a strong London accent and a calm style. He was always very courteous during his presence at ACAS, but he was not easily shifted in negotiations.

ACAS was able to help towards a settlement in the overwhelming majority of disputes in which its assistance was invoked. The proportion of interventions culminating in a settlement was something like three out of four cases. The total number of requests for collective conciliation during my period of office at ACAS were:

1974–75 (covering 16 months' work) – 3412 requests
1976   – 3460 requests
1977   – 3299 requests
1978   – 3338 requests
1979   – 2667 requests
1980   – 2091 requests

The reduction in the number of requests for conciliation in 1979 and 1980 was due to changes in industrial relations. In 1979 formal pay policies were relaxed and there was a reduction in the number of applications under the Fair Wages Resolution and under Schedule 11 of the Employment Protection Act, which enabled claims to be considered under obligatory arbitration that a particular employer was not observing recognised conditions of employment, or, in the absence of recognised conditions, was not observing the general level of conditions for the particular kind of employment. In all such claims ACAS had a formal duty to offer conciliation. In 1980 the number of requests for conciliation was again reduced, but some of the disputes were of lengthy duration.

Most of the requests for conciliation arose from disputes concerning pay and the terms and conditions of employment.

Another significant group of requests concerned claims for trade union recognition. These requests for voluntary conciliation were separate from the claims made for trade union recognition under the statutory procedure of the Employment Protection Act. In later years the assistance of ACAS was often requested in disputes about redundancy.

ACAS continues to receive the support of the principal employers' organisations and trade unions because it is seen to do a useful job. It does not impose itself on the parties to a dispute, but seeks to assist them to find their own solution. ACAS can thus be likened to a lubricant which helps to set in motion a jammed mechanism.

ACAS does not provide a panacea for fundamental industrial relations problems arising out of the nature of the economy. It does not replace conflicts of interest, though it may help the parties to achieve an acceptable compromise or equilibrium. Such a compromise or equilibrium may be only of temporary duration, but it is usually none the less welcomed by employers and workers. Similarly it is not within the competence of ACAS to resolve problems of widespread unemployment. These problems have far-reaching effects on industrial relations.

Statutory Employment Rights

An important function of ACAS is to conciliate in individual complaints that certain statutory employment rights have not been observed. Though this attracted less press publicity than conciliation in major collective disputes between employers and unions, it consistently occupied more working time on the part of ACAS staff.

The development of individual employment rights marked a significant step forward in British industrial relations under both Labour and Conservative governments until the trend was reversed in the 1980s. Up to the 1960s there was little state intervention, with the exception of the Truck Acts, health and safety legislation and Wages Councils legislation, in the contractual relationship between an employer and an individual employee. In 1963 a new phase opened with the passing of the Contracts of Employment Act, which stipulated that employees were entitled to minimum periods of notice and that, in most circumstances, employees were entitled to receive from their employers details of certain terms of their employment.

In 1965 the Redundancy Payments Act laid down minimum levels of compensation for employees made redundant. In 1968 the Race Relations Act prohibited discrimination in employment on racial grounds. The provisions were strengthened by the Race Relations Act 1976.

The Equal Pay Act 1970 and the Sex Discrimination Act 1975 established the right of women to equal treatment with men in their contracts of employment, and made unlawful both direct and indirect discrimination on grounds of sex or marital status. The Industrial Relations Act 1971 provided for legal protection against unfair dismissal.

The law on individual employment rights was drawn together and extended in the Trade Union and Labour Relations Act 1974, the Employment Protection Act 1975 and the Employment Protection (Consolidation) Act 1978. This represented the high point in protective legislation for employment rights. ACAS had the responsibility to conciliate on individual complaints concerning alleged unfair dismissal, equal pay, sex and racial discrimination in employment, certain guaranteed payments in employment, suspension on medical grounds, maternity rights, time off for public duties and for trade union duties and activities, time off in the event of redundancy to look for work or arrange for training, an entitlement to a written statement of reasons for dismissal, itemised pay statements, certain rights concerning redundancy, the right of trade union membership, rights when the ownership of an undertaking is being transferred and unlawful deductions from pay.

Since 1980 many of these rights have been eroded by new legislation, and new opportunities have been opened for individuals to take action against trade unions. Important changes have been made in the qualifying conditions for bringing complaints about the alleged infringement of employment rights. The effect has been to reduce or to eliminate the protection given to many workers.

Every complaint made to an industrial tribunal about an alleged breach of statutory employment rights automatically involves ACAS. A copy of the complaint is passed to ACAS, and it is then the task of an ACAS conciliation officer to seek a voluntary settlement by conciliation between the individual employee and the employer. It is not the job of the conciliation officer to adjudicate on the complaint, though he is often able to assist by explaining the general requirements of the law. If the parties want a conciliated settlement, the conciliation officer is there to assist them. If they do not want a settlement or if no settlement is reached, the complaint then goes forward for hearing by an industrial tribunal, providing that the complainant does not withdraw it.

During my period at ACAS the number of cases received for individual conciliation was on average in excess of 40,000 a year. By far the majority were complaints about alleged unfair dismissal. About a third were settled by voluntary conciliation, and about a quarter were withdrawn. Thus a majority of cases were resolved without a hearing by an industrial tribunal.

Legislation on employment rights is important for the welfare of working people and helps to protect minimum standards of industrial behaviour. It is not, however, a substitute for strong and effective trade unionism. It is much more a supplement to, rather than a substitute for, collective bargaining. Nowhere is this better illustrated than in the area of women's rights, including equal pay for equal work. Women's wages are influenced by traditional notions of what constitutes women's work. This all too often has provided an escape from the application of the principle of equal pay for equal work. It is better to argue for equal pay for work of equal value.

Another problem associated with statutory employment rights is that their interpretation depends upon the courts. No-

310

one with experience before industrial tribunals and before the various appellate bodies is likely to deny that sometimes decisions are reached which, far from strengthening workers' rights, go some way towards undermining them. Moreover, the existence of a means of legal redress may discourage workers from relying on their own collective strength to secure redress against an injustice.

Despite these problems, the legislation on employment rights has had a positive effect on industrial relations. The very existence of a provision against unfair dismissal has done much to encourage civilised conduct when dismissals are being contemplated. This reform was long overdue.

Some of the resources of ACAS were devoted to advisory work on industrial relations. This advice took various forms, ranging from a response to a telephone enquiry about the law relating to unfair dismissal to an in-depth survey of an industrial relations problem in a particular undertaking. The number of enquiries answered each year exceeded 400,000, an indication itself of the need for knowledge about industrial relations problems among employers and employees.

ACAS also arranged from time to time for more formal enquiries to be undertaken, either at the request of the Secretary of State for Employment or on its own initiative, but with the support and cooperation of employers and unions. Requests for enquiries were received from the Secretary of State into the operation of certain Wages Councils. Reports were prepared, usually with recommendations for future action.

A significant advisory function was the preparation of codes of practice on industrial relations issues. These codes, which were submitted to Parliament for approval, were not enforceable at law but could be quoted as relevant evidence in proceedings before industrial tribunals. They were also designed to influence employers and union representatives in their conduct of industrial relations. Codes were prepared and approved on disciplinary practice and procedures, the disclosure of information for collective bargaining purposes and time off for trade union duties and activities.

311

15

ACAS and Trade Union Recognition

Under Section 11 of the Employment Protection Act 1975, provision was made for independent trade unions to refer claims for trade union recognition to ACAS. There was no obligation on a union seeking recognition from an employer for collective bargaining purposes to use the statutory procedures. It was clearly preferable, wherever possible, for a settlement to be reached by voluntary negotiations. Moreover, even when seeking a voluntary settlement a union could still ask for conciliation assistance from ACAS. In 1978, for example, after two years during which the statutory procedure had been in operation, ACAS reported that about two-thirds of the recognition claims which had arisen were still being dealt with under its general duty to offer voluntary conciliation. Only about one-third of the recognition cases had been referred under the statutory procedure. Nevertheless, the statutory procedure provided a possible means of resolving a recognition issue when there was no voluntary settlement.

The statutory provisions affecting trade union recognition were brought into operation on 1 February, 1976. By 'recognition' was meant recognition of a union by an employer for the purposes of collective bargaining. Collective bargaining was defined as negotiations relating to or connected with one or more of the matters listed in the Trade Union and Labour Relations Act 1974 which could be the subject of a trade dispute. These included the terms and conditions of employment, the engagement, termination or suspension of employment of workers, the duties of employment, matters of discipline, membership or non-membership of a trade union, facilities for officials of unions and the machinery of negotiations.

The Employment Protection Act required ACAS when dealing with an application for recognition to observe certain procedures.

It had to examine the issue and make such enquiries as it thought fit, including ascertaining the opinions of workers to whom the issue related.

To consult all parties who it considered would be affected by the outcome of the reference.

To have regard at all times to the desirability of encouraging the settlement of the issue by agreement and, where appropriate, to assist by conciliation.

If the issue were not settled and the application had not been withdrawn, to prepare a written report setting out the findings of the Service, any advice in connection with those findings, and any recommendation for recognition, with reasons, or the reasons for making no recommendation.

To send a copy of such a report to every trade union and employer concerned in the issue and to such other persons as the Service thought fit.

ACAS sought to follow strictly and scrupulously these procedures. Neither I nor, I think, the other members of the Council of ACAS anticipated at the outset that so many legal problems would arise from disputes about their interpretation. The general approach of ACAS was based firmly on its commitment to the importance of voluntary consent in the settlement of industrial relations issues. But when consent is missing, as in so many of the statutory recognition claims, employers may seek to use legal means to avoid a recommendation for recognition being made.

The problems of the statutory recognition procedure were not confined to those which arose because of the attitude of certain unsympathetic employers. There were also serious problems arising from competitive trade union claims. In the great majority of cases such competitive claims were avoided because of the influence of the TUC and the application of the so-called Bridlington principles and procedures for the regulation of relations between affiliated trade unions. The TUC was always helpful to ACAS. Nevertheless, there were a small number of affiliated unions and some non-affiliated unions that insisted on submitting competitive recognition claims. In a number of cases these claims resulted in legal action. ACAS had to weigh its obligation to promote good industrial relations against its obligation to encourage collective bargaining. Did, for example, the fragmentation of existing bargaining arrangements improve or damage industrial relations? At the end of 1979 no fewer than 79 recognition references were in suspense because of inter-union problems.

No Agreed Criteria

A fundamental problem for ACAS when considering claims for recognition was that there were no agreed criteria for deciding whether or not a recommendation for recognition should be made. No such criteria were set out in the Employment Protection Act, other than the general duty of promoting the improvement of industrial relations, encouraging the extension of collective bargaining and developing and, where necessary, helping to reform collective bargaining machinery. It could be argued, and was on occasions argued, that these objectives were not always compatible one with another.

The assumption of the Act was that the members of the Council of ACAS, to whom fell the responsibility of considering and determining recognition claims, would be able to develop their own agreed criteria based upon their experience of industrial relations and the general duties imposed by the Act. To some extent this proved possible, largely because of the goodwill shown by the individual members of the Council and their readiness not to push their individual views to the point of rupture. Nevertheless, the experience of difficult cases, the effect of various legal decisions, the hostility shown by a number of employers to the operation of the Act and the determination of a small number of unions to pursue claims without proper regard to the machinery of the TUC for regulating relations between unions, all contributed to a worsening situation.

There were a number of issues affecting the criteria for recognition which were never satisfactorily resolved. The first concerned the boundary of a proposed bargaining unit. Unions usually took the view that the boundary should correspond to the area where they had a reasonable membership or where, in the absence of a reasonable membership, they felt that there was sufficient support among the employees to maintain effective collective bargaining. Some unions took the view that a claim for recognition was a claim for bargaining and representational rights for all who were members, irrespective of the proportion who were members or non-members. In the federated firms of the engineering industry, for example, most of the unions were entitled to recognition for their members, even though they might constitute only a small minority in a particular workplace.

Employers often had a different view about bargaining unit boundaries. Sometimes they were prepared to accept that, irrespective of other considerations, the unit should be that claimed by the union, providing that it did not overlap an area where another union had already been recognised. On the other hand, they sometimes argued that it was not sensible to determine a bargaining unit by sole reference to the claim of a union. The claim might be for a restricted area where the union had been able to recruit members, but in the view of the employer it would be artificial to separate this particular area from other areas affected by the same wage structure or other conditions of employment. These differences had particular relevance for any proposal for an opinion survey to determine whether there was sufficient support to maintain effective collective bargaining. The drawing of a particular boundary could materially affect the outcome.

Where a claim for recognition was made on behalf of a special occupational group, the problem of defining the bargaining unit boundary could be more easily resolved, because both employers and unions usually recognised the distinctive characteristics of the unit. There were difficulties if a claim were made for an occupational group within a wider unit for which bargaining rights had already been recognised. In such a case the Council of ACAS were guided by their general duty to promote the improvement of industrial relations and the development of collective bargaining machinery. The fragmentation of existing machinery might worsen rather than improve industrial relations. In any case ACAS expected the unions concerned to seek the assistance of the TUC in resolving their differences.

When ascertaining the opinion of workers to whom a recognition claim related – as required by the Employment Protection Act – it was the practice of ACAS to enquire about the employees' wishes for collective bargaining. The views expressed were of material influence in determining the outcome. They were not, however, the only consideration. Account was also taken of the current union membership, the employees' wishes for representation by the referring union, the potential union membership in the event of recognition and the history of support for the union among the employees.

Where there was majority support among employees for collective bargaining, there was usually no disagreement among Council members about making a recommendation for recognition. It was a different matter where support for collective bargaining was confined to a minority of employees within an agreed area. It could be argued, on the one hand, that providing that there was 'sufficient' support for collective bargaining, recognition should be recommended. On the other hand, it could be argued that the wishes of the majority should prevail, and if 51 per cent did not support collective bargaining there should be no recommendation for recognition.

In the early days of the recognition procedure, the Council tended to the view that support from about 30 per cent of the workforce within a suggested bargaining area was sufficient to maintain collective bargaining. After a time, as the opposition of some of the employers affected by recognition claims became apparent, the Council tended towards a higher required minimum percentage of support for a recognition recommendation. A number of unions not affiliated to the TUC and not, therefore, party to the Bridlington arrangements for the regulation of relations between unions, sought to gain recognition in areas of employment which other unions, affiliated to the TUC, claimed were already covered by existing bargaining arrangements or, alternatively, were within the 'sphere of influence' of TUC unions. This usually meant that a TUC union had unsuccessfully been seeking recognition but had established only limited membership in face of the hostility of the employer. The non-TUC unions included the United Kingdom Association of Professional Engineers, the Shipbuilding and Allied Industries Management Association, the Steel Industry Management Association and the Association of Polytechnic Teachers.

During 1977 legal action was taken against ACAS in seven cases concerning the recognition provisions of the Employment Protection Act. In one case the issue was whether ACAS, when seeking employees' opinions, should specify the name of an employee organisation other than the union making the claim for recognition. The court upheld the ACAS view that only a union making a reference under the Act was eligible for a recognition recommendation, but rejected the contention that only the applicant union should be mentioned in the questions. Following this judgment ACAS, when taking an opinion survey, named all unions known to have members among the workers taking part.

One of the most frequent issues of controversy was the framing of questions to test the opinions of employees. Some employers alleged that the questions were biased because they did not seek endorsement for existing arrangements for individually negotiated contracts. ACAS was challenged legally on more than one occasion, but the discretion of the Service in its choice of questions and the way in which the Service exercised its discretion were upheld by the courts.

A legal case concerning a recognition claim made by the United Kingdom Association of Professional Engineers went eventually to the House of Lords, where judgment was given in favour of ACAS. This reversed earlier judgments against ACAS in the High Court and in the Court of Appeal. The main issue in the case concerned the relationship between industrial relations and the encouragement of collective bargaining. UKAPE was not part of the recognised negotiating machinery of federated engineering firms. The Law Lords found that the Employment Protection Act should not be interpreted as requiring ACAS to encourage the extension of collective bargaining if to do so would be, in the view of ACAS, to worsen rather than to improve industrial relations. This legal case extended over a lengthy period and influenced the work of ACAS.

Another case which went eventually to the House of Lords centred on a recognition claim by the Engineers' and Managers' Association, an affiliated union of the TUC. EMA had taken legal action against the TUC to challenge the validity of an award by the TUC Disputes Committee in favour of another affiliated union. The ACAS Council decided to defer action on a recognition claim by EMA until the decision of the High Court was made known on the EMA case against the TUC. This decision of the ACAS Council was challenged legally by EMA. ACAS won the case in the High Court, but the decision was reversed in the Court of Appeal. ACAS appealed to the House of Lords, which decided by a three to two majority that ACAS had discretion to suspend its investigation on a recognition claim while other relevant industrial relations activities were taking place. In the view of the Council of ACAS, the statutory recognition procedure was being used as an alternative means of pursuing a recognition claim not acceptable under the TUC's guidelines for inter-union relations.

Grunwick

The best known of the legal cases in which ACAS was involved concerned a recognition claim on behalf of process workers employed by the Grunwick Processing Laboratories Company in London. The employer was engaged in the mail-order business and received film for processing. The dispute began in the late summer of 1976, when an employee was dismissed for alleged disciplinary reasons. The evidence was that a stern disciplinary regime existed in the workplace. At the time there was no trade union organisation among the workpeople. A number of the workers walked out in sympathy with the dismissed worker. By the end of August there were 137 employees on strike, including regular employees and temporary employees recruited from among students. The company said that before the dispute began the number of weekly paid staff was 429. A large proportion were from immigrant families.

After the strike began a number of the employees joined the white-collar union, APEX, which then sought recognition by the company and the right to negotiate on behalf of its members. The company dismissed the strikers, and in the middle of October APEX referred a recognition claim to ACAS under the terms of the Employment Protection Act.

The dispute was not resolved by conciliation. Postal workers took sympathy action in support of the Grunwick strikers. Legal action was then taken against the postal workers for interrupting the mail. The company agreed, however, that if the sanction were lifted they would cooperate in the ACAS enquiries. The Union of Post Office workers acted to restore the company's access to its mail.

Following further discussions it became clear that the company was not prepared to accept or cooperate with the enquiries proposed by ACAS. They objected to the inclusion of the strikers in the opinion survey, and they objected to any reference to APEX within the proposed questionnaire. ACAS had arranged for the questionnaire to be written in both English and Gujerati. The company said they had reservations about the degree of dependence on the translation.

There seemed no likelihood of the problems being resolved by agreement. ACAS decided to proceed. Without the cooperation of the employer it was not possible to obtain the names and addresses or opinions of non-union members working for the company. ACAS offered to ascertain replies to its question-naire through Grunwick's own solicitor, but this was not accepted. The union provided the names and addresses of its members, and after excluding those who were no longer available for employment, their opinions were sought. By 93 to nil they indicated that they wanted APEX to negotiate their pay and conditions of employment. At the time the company said that the number of weekly paid staff still working was between 225 and 250.

In its report ACAS said that it would have preferred to have had the cooperation of the company, both for information to assist in determining an appropriate negotiating group and for facilities to seek the opinions of all the workers. In the absence of such cooperation, it had examined the issue in the light of the facts and opinions available to it. About a third of the workers had been asked to express their opinions, and they had expressed a wish to be represented by APEX for collective bargaining purposes. The Council of ACAS recommended that the union should be recognised.

The Grunwick case attracted considerable publicity, and the claim for trade union recognition was supported by large demonstrations of sympathisers. There was discussion at one stage of the possibility of supporting action by public service workers, other than postal workers. In a number of other countries solidarity action of this kind would have been legal, providing that the initial dispute was itself legal which, of course, in the Grunwick case it was. The indications were that many of the local public service workers were prepared to take supporting action, providing that there was official support. The problem was that the unions were concerned about the possibility of any supporting action being declared unlawful.

ACAS felt that it had discharged its statutory duty and had taken all reasonable steps to ascertain the views of all the workers. It had no power, nor sought power, to compel the cooperation of the employer. On the other hand, it was felt that the employer should not be able to defeat a claim for recognition by frustrating ACAS in carrying out its statutory duties.

The recommendation in favour of recognition was challenged in the courts, and the case went eventually to the House of Lords. The main issue was the proper construction of the Section of the Employment Protection Act, which said that ACAS 'shall ascertain the opinions of the workers to whom the issue relates'. A majority of the Law Lords decided that, before making a recommendation for recognition, 'ACAS should ascertain and take into consideration the opinion on that issue of the workforce as a whole, and where there is a reasonable possibility that there may be conflict of opinion should ascertain and take into consideration those that are held by every group of workers of any significant size that forms part of the workforce that would be affected by the recommendation'.

Thus the Law Lords, in their judgment of December 1977, found that the word 'shall' was to be construed as mandatory on ACAS, but that there was no mandatory requirement on an employer to cooperate with ACAS in carrying out its statutory function. Where ACAS was unable to ascertain the opinions of the majority of a workforce because of the non-cooperation of an employer, it was debarred from making any recommendation.

I found this interpretation of the law by the House of Lords deeply disappointing. It seemed to me also to be socially unfair and not in keeping with the stated intention of the Employment Protection Act to promote the improvement of industrial relations and collective bargaining. I accepted, of course, that under the terms of the Act trade union recognition was not automatic and that ACAS had to make every effort to ascertain the opinions of workers before making a recommendation, but it did not seem to me to be socially just that a hostile employer could successfully frustrate the whole process by non-cooperation. The Grunwick case strengthened my, by then, growing conviction that the recognition procedure under the Employment Protection Act was seriously flawed.

At the end of June 1977, more than two months after the publication of the ACAS recommendation but before the final stages of the legal action taken by Grunwick against ACAS, the Secretary of State for Employment announced the setting-up of a Court of Inquiry into the Grunwick dispute under the Chairmanship of Lord Scarman. The two other members of the court were Pat Lowry, the then Personnel Director of British Leyland, and Terry Parry, the General Secretary of the Fire Brigades Union.

Their report was published towards the end of August and found predominantly in favour of the union. It said that by dismissing all the strikers, refusing to consider the reinstate-ment of any of them, refusing to seek a negotiated settlement and rejecting ACAS offers of conciliation, the employer had acted within the letter but outside the spirit of the law. Such action, it said, was unreasonable when judged by the norms of good industrial relations practice. The Court said that whilst it was never the intention of the union, the mass picketing had on occasions led to forms of civil disorder. This, it suggested, could have been foreseen.

The Court recommended that, if at all practicable, the dismissed strikers should be taken back and that there should be the right of union representation for individuals who had a grievance. On the issue of trade union recognition for collective bargaining purposes, the Court said that ACAS was the body established by law to determine recognition in the absence of agreement. They were aware that the company had taken legal action against ACAS with a view to its recommendation for recognition being declared invalid. The Court of Inquiry did not propose to prejudge the issue. Nevertheless, they said, 'we have no doubt that union representation, if properly encour-aged and responsibly exercised, could in the future help the company as well as its employees'. The Grunwick Company rejected the main recommendations of the report.

More Problems

By the end of 1978 no less than 90 recognition references were being held in suspense by ACAS at the request of applicant unions because of inter-union problems or because of legal issues concerning trade union independence. Additionally, there was a small but growing number of employers who were very reluctant to cooperate with ACAS on recognition issues. In 35 cases ACAS was unable to ascertain the opinions of workers because employers declined to cooperate. The cumulative effect of these problems was to delay the completion of recognition references. The average time taken in each case was about 12 months.

By the end of the following year, 1979, the number of references in which ACAS was not able to carry out its statutory duty had risen to about 90 out of 339 under current review. Even in the references where cooperation was secured, there were frequently protracted discussions with employers on the proposed questionnaire to ascertain the opinions of workers. Much of my own time as Chairman of ACAS and that of senior colleagues was being spent not on conciliation but on dealing with legal problems.

In 1979 the Council of ACAS decided to write to the Secretary of State about the difficulties of the recognition procedure, including the effect of judicial decisions. It concluded that ACAS could not satisfactorily operate the existing statutory provisions. The Government subsequently secured parliamentary approval for the repeal of the statutory recognition provisions.

Among some members of the Government and among some Conservative MPs, the ending of the legal procedure for trade union recognition was, in my view, welcomed for the wrong reasons. They did not support the view that the state should encourage the extension of collective bargaining. In fairness, I do not believe that this criticism should be levelled against the then Secretary of State, James Prior. My experience was that he supported ACAS in the tasks given it by the Employment Protection Act.

The repeal of the statutory recognition procedure left a gap in British industrial relations legislation. The problem was made worse by the policy of the Conservative Government to impose numerous restrictions on the trade unions. It indicated by its attitude on many occasions that it did not want to encourage collective bargaining, and it removed the statutory obligation on ACAS to encourage collective bargaining. The Government's view was expressed clearly in a House of Commons debate on 11 March, 1993, when an Employment Minister said that it was for an employer to decide whether to recognise a union for collective bargaining. The law, he said, 'should recognise the fact that it is the employer who offers work and the employee who undertakes to do that work in accordance with the terms offered by the employer.' This could aptly be described as a 'master and servant' mentality, in which the wishes and rights of employees for collective representation can be totally disregarded.

Some trade unionists have urged that the statutory procedure for trade union recognition under the Employment Protection Act should be restored, perhaps with an amendment making it obligatory on employers to provide ACAS with access to employees when a recognition claim is being investigated. This, it has been claimed, would avoid the difficulty highlighted by the judgment in the Grunwick case. On the other hand, it would leave unresolved the problems of determining agreed criteria for recognition and the perimeters for disputed negotiating areas.

Another suggestion put forward is that there should be a scale of legal recognition dependent on the measure of support which a union enjoys among a particular group of workers. At a given minimum level a union might be granted the right of representation on individual grievances. At a higher level it might be granted consultative rights on employment conditions, and at a still higher level full collective bargaining rights.

Such a system of scaled recognition has been likened by some trade unionists to a 'greasy pole', with hostile employers constantly seeking to push the unions downwards by a combination of coercion, legal challenge and inducements to surrender collective bargaining rights. It might also lead to more disputes between employers and unions about the perimeters of negotiating areas. Unions would favour areas where their strength was concentrated, and employers would favour perimeters where union strength might be diluted by the inclusion of workers unsympathetic to collective bargaining. The system of scaled recognition has little to commend it.

Yet another suggestion is that all workers should have the right of representation on unresolved grievances. Thus any worker with an unresolved grievance could secure representation from a trade union or from anyone else, and the employer would be required to receive the representations. There would be no obligation on the employer to negotiate in good faith, any more than there would be an obligation on a worker not to pursue a trivial claim. Nevertheless, so it is claimed, an industrial custom would be promoted favourable to negotiations on workers' claims and grievances.

The problem with such a limited right of individual representation is that it might have little effect in encouraging collective bargaining. Indeed, some employers might argue that as their workers had the right of individual representation, nothing further was necessary. There is a wide gulf between the right of representation on individual grievances and bargaining rights for collective agreement.

A fundamental problem with some of the canvassed options, and certainly in any system of recognition ballots, is that they accept the possibility that recognition can be denied to a group of workers who want it. Such a group may be a minority in a given workplace, enterprise or industry, but, nevertheless, why should those who want to bargain collectively be denied it? If the principle had always been accepted that collective bargaining can be denied to those who want it simply because others do not want to exercise this right, it would have been impossible to develop trade unionism and collective bargaining over the last 180 years. Trade unionism and the request for collective bargaining always puts up 'green shoots' among a minority of workers. The Tolpuddle Martyrs were such a minority.

A Fundamental Social Right

The right of citizens to vote in local government elections is not denied because on many occasions the majority do not exercise their right to vote. The right of trade union representation and collective bargaining is a similar fundamental social right, and those who want to exercise it should not be denied the opportunity because of the indifference or hostility of others.

The principle of balloting under a statutory procedure for trade union recognition, with the possibility of recognition being refused, is an American practice which was first introduced under President Roosevelt's New Deal in the mid-1930s. It was designed to redress to some extent the imbalance of power between extremely powerful employers in mass production industries, who were violently hostile to trade unionism and were prepared to employ thugs to frustrate the unions, and a growing demand among workers in these industries for collective bargaining. In the circumstances of its time this statutory procedure was a step forward for the USA. In more recent times this procedure, though still favoured by the American unions, has not prevented the steady decline in the proportion of American workers who are trade union members and covered by collective bargaining arrangements.

In continental Europe the right of workers to collective representation in negotiations with employers is not, as in the USA, subject to balloting as to whether they want trade union recognition. In many continental countries collective representation is accepted as a basic right of employment. Balloting does take place, not on whether there should be representation, but instead on who should be the representatives.

This system of representation has much to be said for it, though it would not be without problems and it would mark a significant change in British industrial relations. If it were adopted in Britain there could be a legal requirement that in every workplace with more than, say, 10 or 25 employees there should be an obligatory ballot every two or four years to choose representatives. In my view, the trade union representatives could be expected to win the majority of these ballots. The elected representatives would then have certain negotiating and consultative rights protected by law. The TUC would have an important role in promoting voluntary good practice in inter-union relations.

The main disadvantage of such a system, it is sometimes argued, is that it might weaken the relationship between elected workplace representatives and the trade unions. Some workers might feel that it was unnecessary to join a union, providing they voted for a trade union nominee in a workplace ballot. It does not appear to have had this effect in Germany, though in both France and Spain many workers who vote for trade union nominees do not join the appropriate union. Nevertheless, in Spain in particular, the system has given the unions a legitimacy of leadership, and they have proved capable of mobilising the support of millions of workers in industrial disputes.

No system of industrial relations can be satisfactorily translated from one country to another. But if a choice has to be made, for purposes of collective bargaining rights, between the American system and the European system – with all its variations – my preference is for the European system.

The encouragement of collective bargaining should not depend solely on a statutory procedure for trade union recognition. The objective should be to promote voluntary collective agreements by a variety of public measures. In the first place, ACAS should again be required as a statutory duty to encourage the extension of collective bargaining. There should also be a system of indirect 'props' designed to make a refusal by an employer to recognise an independent representative union as unattractive as possible. Thus, for example, any employer seeking assistance from public funds, e.g. special investment allowances or regional assistance, should be required to satisfy the Minister that suitable arrangements exist for collective bargaining. In return for the privilege of limited liability, there could be an obligation to bargain collectively with an independent representative union/s of the employees.

A requirement for collective bargaining could be written into all public contracts, and a fair wages policy could help unions to extend minimum conditions of employment to other badly treated employees in the same sector of industry. New legislation for Wages Councils could be drafted to take account of suggestions made by unions, to assist them to extend recruitment among the workers covered by the Wages Councils. The right of unions to take unilateral arbitration in certain circumstances against employers offering low wages and poor conditions in comparison with other similar employers could be restored. This right used to exist in British legislation, but was repealed. Legislation on health and safety, pensions, the control of working time, and provisions for the employment of part-time and temporary workers could also insist on agreements with workers' representatives. It could also be made unlawful for employers to seek to persuade employees to surrender collective bargaining rights by offering individual contracts. Such contracts might supplement but not replace collective bargaining.

There is no legal system for trade union recognition that is without problems. The task is to support measures that are likely to bring more advantages than disadvantages. It is also essential to acknowledge that in the ultimate it is not so much the law as trade union consciousness and organisation that is the decisive factor. Trade unionism also helps the climate of opinion and can help to ensure that both the law and custom uphold the right of representation and collective bargaining.

16

Zimbabwe and Zambia

I retired from the Chairmanship of ACAS on my sixtieth birthday in January 1981. I was under no compulsion to go on that date, but I decided, on balance, that in view of the Government's industrial relations policy it would be better if I pursued my interests elsewhere. The Employment Act 1980 had already introduced changes affecting trade unions and certain employment rights, and further legislation was likely. I was not in sympathy with the thrust of the new policies.

Some time before my retirement from ACAS I was invited to talk to the Permanent Secretary at the Department of Employment about the possibility of my being suggested for a knighthood. I replied that I had no wish to be knighted. I did not think it would have helped me in my job at ACAS when talking to trade unionists. My private view was, and remains, that the honours system in Britain is inextricably bound up with privilege and the perpetuation of hereditary institutions. I wanted no part of it. The proposed discussion with the Permanent Secretary did not take place, and I heard nothing further of the suggestion.

Some time earlier, however, I accepted an invitation to join with five or six other guests to have lunch with the Queen and the Duke of Edinburgh at Buckingham Palace. I recall the circumstances of the invitation with some amusement. One day whilst in the office at ACAS I received a telephone call from someone at the Palace, inviting me to lunch with the Queen on a stated date. I remember saying to the caller that I would have to look at my diary to see if I were free. I found that I was free and responded accordingly.

Colleagues on the staff at ACAS subsequently pointed out that my instant reply was not one that would have been expected. I explained that my response was a natural one. I enjoyed the subsequent lunch and, though the conversation was limited, I thought that the Queen displayed a genuine interest in the activities of her guests. I have always held republican views, but I believe the present Queen has performed her duties with diligence and competence. I think it would be sensible if she fulfilled her reign and the monarchy were then abolished. An hereditary monarchy, with all the accompanying family and related trappings, is incompatible with democracy.

In the summer of 1981 I went to Zimbabwe and Zambia on behalf of the Commonwealth Trade Union Council and the British TUC. The visit had a dual purpose. The first was to assist the Zimbabwe Congress of Trade Unions to respond to a lengthy report to the Zimbabwe Government prepared by a Commission of Enquiry (the Riddell Commission) into Incomes, Prices and Conditions of Service. The second purpose was to visit Zambia and to make enquiries, but without ostentation or publicity, about the detention, on the orders of the Zambian Government, of four prominent Zambian trade union leaders.

Early in 1980 in Zimbabwe, Robert Mugabe led the main party of liberation from white colonial rule, ZANU (PF), to an election victory. It was estimated that ZANU (PF) gained 63 per cent of the total vote and 87 per cent of black votes. The election was held as a result of the Lancaster House Agreement for the independence of the former Rhodesia. This agreement was concluded following considerable pressure on the British Government from a number of Commonwealth leaders, and recognition by influential Conservatives that it would not be possible to sustain white rule in face of the strong demand for independence and democracy from the African majority.

The struggle for independence in Zimbabwe had a long history. From about 1890 Africans had sought, in the words of ZANU (PF), 'to remove the burden of racist oppressive rule and socio-economic disabilities that followed in the trail of European occupation and settlement'. Economic power in the hands of the white minority was given legal backing, for example in the 1930 Land Apportionment Act, so that by the 1960s the white minority, who constituted less than 5 per cent of the population, held more than 50 per cent of the land acreage of the country, including virtually all the fertile areas. Millions of Africans lived a deprived existence.

ZANU was formed as a political party in August 1963. Its distinctive characteristic was its commitment to armed struggle as the principal method for overthrowing the colonial system. Its objective was national independence, but it was more than a nationalist movement. It coupled national independence with the need for social transformation, for ending the rule of the white settler bourgeois class. One of the pamphlets issued by ZANU (PF) stated:

'From its very inception ZANU was unequivocal in its approach to the liberation struggle. It purposefully chose war as a means of achieving liberation. It must always be borne in mind that a system sustained by violence can only be overthrown by violence.'

The 1980 election manifesto of ZANU (PF) said that the Party's ideological belief was socialism.

'We believe that the achievement of political power by the people will remain hollow in terms of their material development unless it can translate itself into quantitative and qualitative benefits deriving from their economy. Such translation of political power must necessarily be by way of economic power in social form. ZANU (PF) thus believes in the development of a socialist economy.'

The election manifesto made clear nevertheless that a ZANU (PF) government would recognise the 'historical, social and other existing practical realities of Zimbabwe'. One of these existing realities, it said, was the capitalist system, 'which cannot be transformed overnight'. The Party said that 'while a socialist transformation process will be brought underway in many areas of the existing economic sectors, it is recognised that private enterprise will have to continue until circumstances are ripe for socialist change.'

Social Division

One of the central problems facing the liberation government of Zimbabwe was that of land distribution. Millions of black peasants wanted land on which to farm. Their dissatisfaction and bitterness was the result of generations of deprivation. Many of them were the descendants of families driven from land ownership to make way for white settler farmers.

The social conditions of black families on white commercial farms were described in the report of the Riddell Commission in the following words:

'Employees live on the property of their employer and are available to be called out day or night. They depend on the farmer for medical services and for the education of their children. In some cases even social recreation can come under the direction of the employer. Some employers run weekly or monthly inspections of the residential areas of their employees and families. In short, the farmer is the provider and regulator of everything, and the employees and their families are practically totally dependent on the farmer.'

The report described this state of affairs as a 'feudal type structure'. There was widespread illiteracy, and even in the available schools there was a very high proportion of unqualified teachers.

All rural hospitals, it was reported, were seriously handicapped by a financial inability to provide food for patients. The majority of children brought to the rural hospitals were already suffering from various degrees of undernourishment. On the commercial farms there were extremely low standards for the majority of black families. These low standards affected housing, water supply and sewage disposal. There was also extensive malnutrition. The Riddell Commission said that 'the social conditions on some commercial farms are below an acceptable standard of human decency'.

In the rural areas where black peasants sought to scratch a living – as distinct from the white commercial farming areas – it was estimated that the number of family units, given the poor quality of much of the land available to them and the very low level of agricultural husbandry, was two-and-a-half times its safe ecological carrying capacity. Only a very small minority of peasants owned a cart or even a wheelbarrow, and there were very few time-saving modern implements. In some areas as many as 70 per cent of the cultivators owned no draught animals to help with heavy work such as ploughing, and even the available draught animals were frequently under-nourished.

A feature of the Zimbabwe economy was the big difference between the proportion of men and women in the rural and urban areas. Among the peasants there were twice as many women as men in the over-15 age group. In the urban areas the imbalance was almost exactly the reverse. These figures were an indication of male migration to the towns in search of work. In 1977 over a third of peasant land holdings were run by women 'dependants' of migrant workers. At one period legal restrictions inhibited the movement of migrant workers' families.

The crux of the problem facing the Mugabe Government was that economic and political power were in different hands. The Government had been elected by a black majority, but economic power resided in the hands of the white settler minority. It was this minority who owned most of the land, who owned nearly all the productive sectors of commercial agriculture, who owned the mines, who operated the main banking, trade and commercial operations and who controlled most of the education, health and social services.

The division between the white minority and the black majority was plain for all to see. It was a division between affluence and poverty. In the capital city of Salisbury, as it was then called, many of the white minority lived in very comfortable circumstances, with spacious bungalows surrounded by large well-tended gardens, each with a swimming pool and barbecue area. A substantial part of the black urban population were crowded into surrounding townships, where the housing was of a very poor standard and where facilities and amenities were often at a primitive level.

I could have had arguments almost every hour of the day with individuals among the white population. Frequently they referred to the liberation movement, now the Government, as 'the terrorists'. The number of white citizens who expressed what I would have regarded as a progressive viewpoint was very limited. It was mainly confined to a few trade unionists and active members of religious communities.

The most pressing issue was the land hunger of black peasants and their families. This was not an issue capable of immediate solution, even given the maximum goodwill and determination of the Government. White farmers were in occupation of the most fertile land and they possessed the capital equipment, management skill and education without which productivity would fall. The Government proposed to concentrate, therefore, on the acquisition of land which was unused or had been abandoned in the liberation struggle, was under-utilised or was owned by absentee landlords. With the acquisition of this land it was hoped to resettle a section of the black peasant population and to encourage collective agriculture and the formation of new villages.

There was, of course, no possibility of this programme being fulfilled during my short period of weeks in Zimbabwe, but it was clear that Robert Mugabe and his colleagues had before them an enormous task. Years later I read of the progress made by the Zimbabwe Government, particularly in the development of housing, health care and education. Unfortunately, like so many developing countries in the world, Zimbabwe was handicapped by debt, by the monetarist demands of the International Monetary Fund, by severe drought and by trade problems caused by the solidarity of Zimbabwe with the liberation struggles in South Africa, Angola, Namibia and Mozambique.

The Trade Union Movement

My main concern in Zimbabwe was with the trade union movement. Its strength, such as it was, was drawn mainly from urban areas. The proportion of employed workers who were in trade unions was small, though it was impossible to provide an accurate figure, partly because of inflated claims by some unions and partly because of the very primitive registration of members. The density of membership was probably somewhere between 8 per cent and 20 per cent. Even the largest union, which at that time was the Zimbabwe Agriculture and Plantation Workers' Union, claimed no more than 16,000 members.

Despite its low density of membership, the trade union movement had a history going back to the First World War. In its early years it was almost entirely confined to white workers employed on the railways and in skilled engineering, construction and printing trades. Efforts to organise African workers were met by hostility from employers and authorities.

During the years of the liberation struggle trade union organisation took root among African workers, but the unions were divided according to the political orientation of their leaders. At one time there were no fewer than six separate national trade union centres claiming to represent organised workers. With victory in the liberation struggle, the unions were encouraged by ZANU (PF) to come together to form a united trade union movement. The principle of collective bargaining was supported by the Government.

The founding congress of the Zimbabwe Congress of Trade Unions took place in February 1981 and was attended by 200 delegates, representing 52 separate unions, with a total membership of about 200,000. The trend associated with ZANU (PF) was in the majority, and the principal officials of the new Congress were supporters of ZANU (PF). Among the main unions, apart from the Plantation Workers', representing employees on commercial farms, were a railwaymen's union, a municipal workers' union, an African engineering workers' union and a clothing workers' union. One or two of the traditional unions of white skilled workers did not participate.

335

One of the traditional white unions, the Railways Association of Locomotive Enginemen (footplate workers), played a constructive role in the new Congress and, during my period in Zimbabwe, gave considerable assistance to the creation of an effective multiracial trade union national centre. The union was led by men who had emigrated from Britain and had been active members of the Associated Society of Locomotive Engineers and Firemen. The union invited me to attend a meeting of the Executive Council, and I gained the impression that they were determined to help in the creation of a genuinely multiracial trade union movement. Opportunities were also being provided for Africans to become footplate workers on the railways.

Despite the low density of trade union organisation among African workers I quickly became aware, from meetings I attended, that there was a high level of political consciousness among the majority of Africans. This consciousness was of a very fundamental kind and embraced an awareness of exploitation and of the deprivation of political rights. Indeed, this consciousness was so deep among many of them that it expressed itself in support for revolutionary action and the armed struggle of the liberation movement. I met a number of active trade unionists who had returned to urban townships after years of armed struggle in the bush.

Immediately on my arrival in Zimbabwe I was asked to attend a meeting of some 50 trade unionists, convened by the Zimbabwe Congress of Trade Unions, to consider the Riddell Commission report and to prepare a response to it. Most of the representatives were general secretaries of affiliated unions, and all were Africans, with the exception of representatives of the Locomotive Enginemen and the National Union of Railwaymen, both of whom were British immigrants. It was an indication of the esteem in which the representative of the Locomotive Enginemen was held that he was elected to be the chairman of the gathering. The meeting lasted for four days.

The meeting decided to divide into three separate groups to study different aspects of the Riddell Commission report. Each group then reported to a plenary session and recommendations were made, which I was asked to draft into a formal response on behalf of the Zimbabwe Congress of Trade Unions.

My draft followed closely the recommendations made by the meeting, but one or two amendments of special interest were subsequently made by the assembled representatives. The most significant of these amendments was to delete any reference in my draft to 'independent trade unions'. In the discussions I had tried to explain what was meant by 'independent'; namely that, whilst recognising that the unions supported the proclaimed social objectives of the Zimbabwe Government, including the elimination of all forms of discrimination, the promotion of economic development, the raising of living standards, improving the status of women and progress towards socialism, it was important that the unions should retain their organisational independence of the Government, the machinery of state and the employers. Only in this way, I suggested, would they be free at all times to express workers' interests and grievances. Experience had shown in many countries that governments pledged to enlightened social policies could, nevertheless, act sometimes in a manner contrary to workers' interests and could make serious errors of judgment. In such circumstances, the organisational independence of the unions and their fidelity to workers' interests was the best safeguard to ensure that warnings would be sounded and the necessary remedial measures taken.

These views were not dismissed by the African trade union representatives, but they argued that the issue of trade union 'independence' should be put within the context of the liberation struggle in Africa and, in particular, in Zimbabwe. The African trade union representatives contended that the unions should never be 'independent' of this struggle. Only those who had opposed the liberation struggle had called for the unions to be 'independent'. The trade union movement among Africans, it was pointed out, was inseparable from the liberation struggle. The formation of the Mugabe Government was the culmination of this struggle. It was a revolutionary process of which the workers formed an essential part. The African trade union representatives rejected the word 'independent' to

337

describe the stance of their movement and preferred instead the words 'representative and effective'.

The second significant amendment made to my draft was to include a section warning against the provisional registration of new unions in industries where there was an already registered industrial union. The commitment of the Zimbabwe Congress of Trade Unions to industrial unionism was explained by two main considerations. The first was that industrial unionism placed emphasis on the unity of interests of all workers in an industry or service, rather than on their occupational differences. It was more likely to promote solidarity. Secondly, craft unionism, in the circumstances of Zimbabwe, was seen as a form of organisation to consolidate race discrimination. White skilled workers, it was felt, might prefer craft unionism in the knowledge that they, the white workers, constituted a substantial proportion of the skilled workforce. Thus craft unions of skilled workers were likely to be dominated by white workers.

Apart from the amendments already described in the preceding paragraphs, the draft statement I prepared on the Riddell Commission Report was adopted by the Zimbabwe Congress of Trade Unions. It followed very much the lines suggested in the conference with the trade union representatives. It emphasised at the outset that the unions wanted to play a constructive role in the social and economic development of Zimbabwe, and wished to be involved in the formulation and implementation of policies that would bring about a healthy industrial relations system and the improvement of the living standards of working people.

The statement supported the recommendation of the Riddell Commission that wage rates and wage levels should be determined through a system of collective bargaining. The Commission's recommendation that a Wages Commission should be established was, however, rejected. It was pointed out that it was the responsibility of employers and unions to determine wage rates. The Zimbabwe unions also wanted the agreed minimum rates to be legally enforceable, in order to protect workers in establishments where trade union organisation was weak or non-existent.

The Zimbabwe unions also supported the recommendation of the Riddell Commission in favour of a national minimum wage. This, it was said, should not be less than a 'poverty datum line'. Differentials should be narrowed because they often reflected not only differences in skill but differences between white and African workers.

The statement of the Zimbabwe Congress of Trade Unions expressed support for the price control of basic items entering into workers' expenditure, for the development of a system of social security, for occupational training in all industries and for the holding down of transport fares, particularly for travel to and from work.

In relation to trade unionism, the ZCTU called for the development of democratic practices in all unions and said that subscriptions should be at a rate sufficient to provide adequate funds for trade union purposes. Nearly all the representatives at the meeting convened to discuss the preparation of the ZCTU statement argued in favour of obligatory trade union membership in industries covered by collective agreements. They accepted, however, that provision should be made for workers who, on grounds of conscience, objected to joining a trade union. The objector, it was urged, should be required to contribute the equivalent of the union's basic subscription without being required to become a member of the union. It was felt strongly that non-unionists who made no contribution to the benefits of collective bargaining should not be at a financial advantage because of their conscientious objection.

The ZCTU recognised the need for an ambitious programme of training for trade union representatives. The Congress expressed the view that such training would make a major contribution to good industrial relations and to the strengthening of democracy. This, it was said, was in the national interest, and hence the cost of financing trade union education and training should not fall exclusively on the trade union movement. The necessary money should be raised by a training levy on employers, by a contribution from the Government of Zimbabwe, by grants from international agencies and by a contribution from trade union funds.

The ZCTU accepted that conciliation under the Ministry of Labour could play a vital role in industrial relations, but warned against any kind of system under which industrial relations became primarily a forum for lawyers. The unions rejected the proposal of the Riddell Commission that a new National Labour Relations Board should become 'the forum for hearing and resolving all disputes in the industrial relations field'. The resolution of disputes, it was pointed out, was primarily for direct negotiations between employers and union representatives at all levels. The emphasis should be on the development of adequate and effective negotiating machinery between employers and unions. Assistance where required should be provided through the Ministry of Labour.

On employment legislation the ZCTU urged that financial information should be made available by employers to unions to assist in effective collective bargaining, and that a scheme for redress against unfair dismissal should be introduced. The unions offered to join in consultations with the Government and employers in working out suitable proposals. The ZCTU also expressed support for a recommendation of the Riddell Commission that a national joint economic advisory committee should be established as a forum for consultation, consisting of representatives of the Government, employers and trade unions.

The Government responded sympathetically to the views on the Riddell Commission Report submitted by the ZCTU. I do not know, however, how far their subsequent actions corresponded to their declared intentions. I returned to England within a period of weeks, and I was no longer in touch with detailed developments.

I was also conscious of the immense difficulties faced by the Government. Though they exercised political power, nearly all the levers of economic power were in the hands of the white minority. In addition, the Government were still dependent to a considerable extent on a civil service machine inherited from the old regime. The African population had high expectations, and among the peasantry there was hunger for land. Economic transformation depended upon the development of a skilled and educated workforce, including a new corps of managers.

Externally, Zimbabwe faced hostility from the apartheid regime in South Africa and impediments to trade. Zimbabwe was also committed to giving support to African liberation movements in adjacent countries.

One of the senior civil servants I met who was in total sympathy with the Mugabe Government was a new Permanent Secretary at the Ministry of Labour. He was a very able young African of left-wing views who had received a university education in Britain. Unfortunately, whilst I was in Zimbabwe, he was killed in a motor-car accident. It was a loss which Zimbabwe could ill afford.

I had met this young Permanent Secretary in discussions not only about the Riddell Commission Report, but about a proposed new Industrial Relations Act to replace the old colonial legislation. A draft Bill had been prepared and submitted for consultation to all concerned. The ZCTU asked me to help in preparing a response.

The new Bill was, in my view, objectionable. It was an opinion shared by the representatives of the ZCTU. The Bill contained a preamble of worthy objectives calling for the use of state power to promote trade unionism and collective bargaining. The detailed provisions of the Bill, however, fell far short of expectations. It borrowed heavily from United States' labour legislation. There was, of course, little similarity between the circumstances of liberated Zimbabwe and the conditions of US industry in the mid-1930s, when the US National Labour Relations Act was first introduced. There was even less similarity with the political circumstances of the USA during the period of the Cold War, when new legislation was passed to weaken trade unionism.

I learned subsequently that the Bill had probably been drafted by civil servants with American legal training. It seemed as though the statement of objectives had been drafted to correspond to the intention of the Government to encourage trade unionism and collective bargaining, but that the detailed provisions had been drafted by civil servants on the basis of American experience but in a manner unrelated to the Government's objectives.

I prepared a memorandum of comment on the Industrial Relations Bill and suggested that, except for the preliminary statement of objectives, it should be withdrawn entirely. Albert Mugabe, the General Secretary of the ZCTU – and half-brother of the head of Government, Robert Mugabe – with whom I discussed the memorandum, expressed his agreement with the request that the draft should be withdrawn. This view was endorsed by the ZCTU. Albert Mugabe explained that the Government was still heavily dependent on a civil service machine which did not always reflect the thinking of the new leaders. Shortly before I left Zimbabwe, I was told by Albert Mugabe that the Government had decided that the proposed new legislation on industrial relations should be redrafted.

Strengths and Weaknesses

The Zimbabwe trade union movement had one important resource; a very strong sense of commitment on the part of many of its active members. Years of armed struggle by ZANU (PF) had developed among Africans a cadre of men and women with intense militant fervour and a readiness to accept almost any sacrifice. It was impossible not to be moved by this immensely strong political consciousness. When I visited the headquarters of ZANU (PF) or met Africans who had been active in the armed struggle and who were now expressing their enthusiasm for the new order through trade unionism, I was conscious of the very deep and strong roots of the liberation movement.

Beyond this sense of commitment among its active rank-and-file, the Zimbabwe trade union movement possessed very few resources. It had very little money, poor premises and a scarcity of equipment for typing, printing and elementary bookkeeping. There were very few people with literary and numeracy skills for writing letters and keeping accounts. There was very limited experience of collective bargaining and the preparation of claims for negotiation.

Manningham Workers Dispute Committee, December 1890 – May 1891. Note that the majority of the committee are women. (see page 14)

... Workers' Movement, shown leading a strike in Leeds, c.1920.

The author's maternal grandfather

Author, front left, on a national youth leaflet, issued by the Labour Party in 1938.

Author's mother.

the school football team c.1936, author back row, second from left.

Advisory, Conciliation and Arbitration Service. October 1974.

Cortonwood Colliery, S. Yorks, where the national mining dispute began. Author (centre) is with Joyce Gould (now Baroness) and the late Eric Heffer, MP.

Tony and Caroline Benn, with the author, outside the Marx Memorial Library.

The headquarters of the ZCTU were no more than two or three rather dilapidated rooms above a fried chicken shop. My impression was that the typing and answering of the telephone were done mainly by two African women who had been sent on a training course to Bulgaria, paid for by the Bulgarian trade unions. In some of the unions the registration of members and the financial records were very primitive.

There was, therefore, an urgent need for training in the elementary but fundamental techniques of trade union organisation. I attended a seminar of trade union educationalists addressed by an African representative of the International Confederation of Free Trade Unions. The ICFTU representative came from Malawi and was very competent.

One of my most interesting experiences in Zimbabwe was to visit a large mission in the bush, run by Jesuits of the Roman Catholic Church. It was known as Silveira House and had a staff of more than 150. When I visited it the principal officer was an Irish Jesuit. He was one of the very few white people I met who was in total sympathy with the liberation struggle and with the new Government of Robert Mugabe.

The mission had been established in the early 1960s, following discussions in the African townships surrounding Salisbury. These discussions had revealed that the majority of young people were unemployed and that those who had jobs were paid very low wages. A sense of depression, oppression and frustration was widespread. Silveira House was acquired as a centre for leadership and development, with courses for civic and national leaders, workers and youth. The mission survived for the first four years on a month-to-month basis from private donations.

It later received assistance from abroad, and its scope was broadened. An agricultural training project was launched, followed by a commercial school, two dressmaking schools and a project for the improvement of nutrition, hygiene and child care. This latter project was run by two sisters of Prime Minister Mugabe. In 1980 a department of technology was established.

Silveira House continued throughout the period of the war

343

of liberation. It survived because the liberation fighters recognised that it was helping Africans to acquire new skills. After liberation the mission was encouraged to expand its activities. When I visited Silveira House it had an industrial relations department with a staff of 10. I was invited to open a discussion on the fundamentals of trade unionism with a group of African worker-students. It was for me a memorable occasion to be seated with a group of African workers in the middle of the bush in the setting sun of the evening, discussing trade union organisation, solidarity and collective bargaining.

At that time the mission was conducting in its various departments over 100 short training courses with about 3,500 students. It was also conducting field courses for over 24,000 students. The orientation of the mission was undoubtedly towards the training of Africans in skills essential for the development of the new Zimbabwe. I am not able to say to what extent the students were encouraged to embrace the teachings of the Roman Catholic Church, but there was no doubt of the socially progressive commitment of the Jesuits with whom I spoke. I enjoyed a long discussion with two priests about the relationship between the moral teachings of the Church and the ethical case for socialism. We agreed far more than we disagreed.

My impression during my time in Zimbabwe was – though I have no figures to prove it – that Britain was not up-front in the aid it was providing. The countries with a good reputation were the Scandinavian group, Canada, the German Democratic Republic and, in some respects, China and North Korea. It was amusing to find that at that time assistance in military training was being provided both by British and North Korean contingents. China seemed to be regarded with rather more favour than the Soviet Union. Mao's views on the importance of the peasantry in a war of liberation found sympathy among some of the Zimbabwe freedom fighters.

I left Zimbabwe with real regret, even though I had been there for only a few weeks. It was an exhilarating experience. There was so much to do, and every kind of skill was valuable. How exciting it was to listen to English programmes on television, to read newspapers in the English language and to talk to Africans who had fought in the struggle for liberation; all speaking of the need for social advance and of the immense challenges and problems facing Zimbabwe.

Zambia

From Zimbabwe I went to Zambia. Lusaka, the capital, was a very different kind of city from Salisbury (Harare). It was an African city, whereas Salisbury had been the sophisticated centre of a white settler minority.

At the end of July 1981 four trade union leaders had been detained in Zambia under Presidential Order made under the Preservation of Public Security Regulations. They included the Chairman, General Secretary and Deputy General Secretary of the Zambian Congress of Trade Unions and the Deputy Chairman of the Mineworkers' Union. My mandate from the Commonwealth Trade Union Council was to find out as much as possible, but without publicity, of the circumstances surrounding their detention, and to make reasonable representations for their release.

I was able to obtain copies of written statements of the grounds of detention of two of the detainees. They related to speeches which they had made many months before. It was also alleged that both the detainees had incited illegal strikes. But what, I enquired, constituted an 'illegal strike'? Under the then current legislation strikes were forbidden if they had not been authorised by a secret ballot, if they were not in further- ance of a collective dispute to which the employee or trade union were party, or if the dispute was under conciliation or had been referred to the Industrial Relations Court for decision. I did not regard this piece of legislation as satisfac- tory.

I went to the town of Kitwe in the Copper Belt to find out more at first-hand about the attitude of trade unionists. There had been considerable unrest among the miners about the relationship between wages and the rise in prices and about

345

proposals for changes in local administration. African graduates, supervisors and artisans had also claimed equal pay with expatriate counterparts.

The defenders of the Government's decision to detain the trade union leaders offered two principal reasons for their action. The first was that at a time of very great economic difficulty for Zambia the union leaders had incited illegal strikes on the Copper Belt. The economic difficulty, it was explained, had been caused by external events. The price of oil had risen steeply, and Zambia depended on imported oil for its industrial energy. The sanctions, which Zambia supported, imposed against the regime of Ian Smith in the former Rhodesia, had a very damaging effect on the Zambian economy. The severing of trade links with South Africa and Rhodesia meant that supplies of many kinds of equipment, materials and food were cut off. This economic isolation had been made worse by the breaking of communications as a result of civil wars in Zimbabwe, Mozambique, Angola and Namibia. Moreover, Zambia had given homes and bases to thousands of exiled guerrilla fighters, who were being maintained by the Zambian economy.

All these problems coincided with a fall in the world demand for copper and a consequential fall in price. Over 90 per cent of Zambia's foreign earnings and some 50 per cent of Government revenue, it was said, came from copper. At one period copper was being produced at a loss. By the standards of Zambia the miners, it was suggested, had a relatively high standard of living.

The second reason advanced for the detention was an allegation that a coup was being prepared, organised by the American Central Intelligence Agency, to overthrow the Government of Dr Kaunda, and that a number of military men, business leaders and trade union leaders were implicated. According to reports from Government sources the Zambian Foreign Affairs Ministry had 'smashed a CIA spy ring' in June 1981. Two senior US diplomats were expelled.

During my stay in Kitwe, which is the main centre of the Copper Belt, I met the principal officials of the Zambian

346

Congress of Trade Unions and of the Mineworkers' Union. The head office of the Mineworkers' Union was a substantial building and an indication that the union had a regular and substantial income from its members. The officials vigorously defended the activities of the unions which, they said, were in pursuit of the industrial interests of their members. The unions, they pointed out, had no alternative, if they were to retain the support of their members, but to express the discontent of the workers.

The union representatives argued that they supported the stand of the Zambian Government in giving aid to the struggle for African liberation in other countries, but that the economic difficulties had been exacerbated by the Government's economic policies. In particular, they said that whilst the trade unions were not opposed to public ownership in principle, the change from private ownership in some sectors of the economy had been made too quickly. The result had been inefficiency, the growth of corruption and bureaucracy.

This criticism of public ownership by the union leaders was said by some of the supporters of the Government to indicate a deeper ideological division. President Kaunda himself said that he had been astonished at the thinking of some of the trade union leaders. He added:

'I am sure these leaders must be some of the very few trade union leaders in developing countries who think that capitalism is good for workers. Yet the history of trade unionism is one of struggle between capitalism and the workers.

'Our own experience in this country shows that capitalism cannot be the custodian of workers' interests. This is inconceivable. For we are backward because of capitalist exploitation. We were oppressed and denied political rights because of capitalist interests. Indeed, racism in South Africa is the creation of capitalism. Do these people know what they are talking about?

'Fellow countrymen, socialist policies are the only policies that will truly liberate our workers from exploitation.'

347

In Kitwe I learned that some of the union officials had been in the USA for training with American unions. One official I interviewed had the Stars and Stripes flag on his desk. The officials denied any involvement in CIA plots but pointed out that as Zambia was a one-party state, any kind of sustained criticism was regarded as subversive.

I also interviewed a Labour Commissioner on the Copper Belt, and the Acting Permanent Secretary of the Ministry of Labour. The Acting Permanent Secretary was emphatic that the union leaders had not been detained because they had expressed workers' grievances. He said that the Government was not anti-union and all employers were obliged to recognise unions and to enter into negotiations with them. Workers' committees had extensive rights to information, consultation and negotiation, and on some issues decisions could not be taken against their wishes. The Acting Permanent Secretary said that the detentions had nothing to do with trade unionism. They were a matter of state security.

I thanked the Acting Permanent Secretary for granting me an interview, and emphasised that the Commonwealth trade unions and the TUC were not making representations in any spirit of hostility towards Zambia or its Government. They recognised the part played by Zambia in supporting the liberation movement throughout the African continent, and were conscious of the immense problems the Government faced.

I pointed out that in the absence of detailed charges against the detained union leaders and the examination of evidence in open court, it was not possible to form an opinion about allegations of subversion. It was, however, disturbing when leaders were detained as the outcome of labour unrest. The illegality of the strikes that had taken place was more a commentary on the restrictions of the existing labour legislation than on the actions of trade unionists and their leaders.

I urged that in relation to the allegation that the union leaders had been involved in a CIA plot against the Government, as distinct from criticisms of Government policy, specific charges should be made and the trade union leaders should be brought to court. If not, they should be released.

On my return to Britain I reported my conclusions to the Commonwealth Trade Union Council and to the TUC. I did not discount the allegations of the Zambian Government of the hostile involvement of the CIA, and pointed out that in Zimbabwe, too, I had received complaints of attempted political interference from an American organisation with plenty of money to spend. The American organisation sought to influence political developments through trade union contacts in a direction unsympathetic to the policies of the Mugabe Government. On the other hand, this did not justify detention without formal charges and trial. Nor did it in any way justify restrictive labour legislation.

After my return to Britain I had no means of keeping up with day-to-day news of developments in Zambia. I was aware, however, of continuing problems. The conclusions which I drew from the experience in Zambia were that industrial relations problems cannot be divorced from the economic problems facing underdeveloped countries, that in the short-term there is a price to pay for solidarity between liberation movements, but that this in not a valid argument against solidarity, that underdeveloped countries dependent for their income upon a very limited range of crops, raw materials or metals are particularly vulnerable to the business fluctuations of the world economy, that trade union rights should be upheld, that foreign intervention in underdeveloped countries can take many forms, and that in a one-party state grievances accumulate without redress and finally lead to unforeseen social consequences.

I valued very much the short period I had spent in Zimbabwe and Zambia. Throughout the mission I was accompanied by my partner, Pat. With her commitment to trade unionism, to colonial liberation and her many skills on the preparation of reports, she was an invaluable collaborator in everything I was asked to do.

17

The Labour Party

In September 1981 Ron Hayward, the General Secretary of the Labour Party, informed the National Executive Committee of the Party of his intention to retire in June 1982 upon reaching the age of 65. Ron was a good chief officer. He had worked for the Party for many years and had a wealth of experience at every level. His particular attribute was his ability to identify himself with the active rank-and-file membership and to see the affairs of the Party through their eyes. He was totally without affectation, and was capable of speaking in blunt terms at the highest level of the Party when he thought it to be necessary.

I remembered Ron from many years earlier, when he had a regional responsibility. He was well liked and respected in the constituency party of which I was then a member. I recall a comment of my partner, Pat, that when Ron Hayward visited a constituency party he always succeeded in conveying the impression that he did so not as a 'policeman' to enforce discipline, but as a helpful colleague. He was deservedly held in warm regard by constituency activists in all parts of Britain. My respect for him was confirmed during the weeks I subsequently worked with him at the head office of the Labour Party in Walworth Road, London.

I was approached by a number of prominent members of the Party and unions to stand as a candidate for election as General Secretary. One such approach came from Judith Hart, who was due to take the chair at the 1982 annual conference. I had known her personally for many years. She indicated that her approach was supported by a number of other members of the NEC. I also received expressions'of support from a number of prominent trade unionists in the centre and on the left of the party.

Up to that time I had not regarded myself as a possible candidate, but I thought it preferable that the new General Secretary should have no reservations in supporting the new Leader and Deputy Leader of the Party, Michael Foot and Denis Healey, should be in broad sympathy with the NEC and should not be hostile to the constitutional changes introduced within the party for the selection of parliamentary candidates and the election of Leader and Deputy Leader. I decided to apply for the post of General Secretary.

A shortlist of candidates was drawn up by the NEC, and the candidates were interviewed at a special meeting of the NEC held in December 1981. Among those on the shortlist were Alex Ferry, the General Secretary of the Confederation of Shipbuilding and Engineering Unions, David Hughes, the National Agent of the Party, Joyce Gould, the Assistant National Agent, and Dick Clements, who for many years edited the weekly journal, *Tribune*. The final vote was between Alex Ferry and myself. I was successful by a majority of one vote. It was a secret ballot, so I do not know how individual members of the NEC cast their votes, but from subsequent conversations it seems likely that the division was mainly and, perhaps, almost entirely on political lines.

At the time I do not think I regarded any of the candidates as particularly right-wing. Alex Ferry was a very competent trade union official and was held in high regard by the affiliated unions. David Hughes was an unostentatious but deservedly very popular National Agent. I worked with him closely during my period at Walworth Road, and have nothing but good memories of his contribution. Joyce Gould was probably more inclined towards the left than to the right in her personal views, and she was always energetic in her work. Dick Clements' views were well known from his editing of *Tribune*. He was certainly not on the right.

A number of trade union leaders made it clear to me in private conversations that, in their view, my principal tasks were to help to maintain unity around the new leadership of the Party after the damaging withdrawal of so many MPs and a number of former Ministers to form the Social Democratic Party, and to make financial changes on the lines recommended in a report of a Commission of Enquiry published in 1980. This, they felt, was the most effective way in which I might contribute to the organisational recovery of the Party after the breakaway of the SDP.

I accepted both tasks without reservation. I strongly supported Michael Foot, both politically and personally. My support for Denis Healey was on rather different grounds. My personal view was that over many years he had been closely identified with the right-wing policies, both in home and foreign affairs, that had eventually contributed to electoral defeat for successive Labour governments. On the other hand, he had been elected by the Party as Deputy Leader, and his presence was symbolic of the need to maintain a united party around the policies determined by the annual conference. He was also an effective spokesman.

The Labour Party Commission of Enquiry was required by the 1979 party conference to examine the finances, organisation, membership and political education of the party. It had three co-chairmen, David Basnett, Michael Foot and Eric Heffer, drawn respectively from the unions, the Parliamentary Labour Party and the NEC. Ron Hayward and Joyce Gould provided the secretariat.

The Commission conducted a widespread examination and received no fewer than 2,460 pieces of evidence from party organisations, trade unions, other bodies and individuals. The Commission appointed three working panels to examine in detail the financial, organisational, membership and political educational aspects of the party's work. The respective chairmen were Clive Jenkins, Moss Evans and Tony Benn.

Financial Problems

The Commission reported that 'the party has effectively no reserves, a thoroughly inadequate income and is moving into serious deficit and debt'. This, it explained, was not a recent trend. It said that for the majority of the previous ten years the party had been running at a deficit on its general operations and had drawn heavily on its reserves. It concluded: 'It now has little in the way of reliable assets and the party's expenditure in 1979 grossly exceeds its income'.

The Commission made various recommendations to improve the finances of the Party, including staff changes for more effective budgetary control, the introduction of a five-year operating plan, the creation of a capital base to finance the Party's activities, and increased membership subscriptions. The Commission expressed concern at the very low membership in some constituencies, particularly in constituencies where the Labour vote indicated strong electoral support. It was suggested that the Party should set itself an initial recruitment target of 5 per cent of the Labour vote.

The report of the Commission pointed out that nearly 90 per cent of the Party's income at national level came from trade union affiliation fees. It recommended an immediate increase of 25 per cent in the rate of affiliation fees and said that at constituency level a concerted effort should be made to encourage trade union branch affiliations. For the long term it was suggested that the Party should look to public funds for the financing of political parties.

Of special significance – in view of the subsequent controversy about the links between the Party and the unions – were the recommendations of the Commission concerning trade union involvement in the Party. There was not even a hint of any loosening of the links. On the contrary, the Commission called for a much greater effort to be made to involve trade union branches in the Party at constituency level, and for closer co-ordination at regional and trades council level. It was suggested that the principle of workplace branches should be accepted.

Important recommendations were also made for the provision of more full-time agents, with trade union assistance, and for the stimulation of political education and discussion throughout the Party. It was suggested that political education

353

working groups should be formed at constituency level. Recommendations were also made concerning party political broadcasts, the monitoring of television and radio programmes, the promotion of theatre groups, closer cooperation with trade union journals and the use of opinion polling. It was also suggested that consideration should be given to the possibility of establishing a press agency and a printing and publishing house.

Inevitably, given the terms of reference of the Commission of Enquiry, there was a missing element in the final report: the political decline that had contributed to the Party's organisational and financial problems. In my view, this decline had been accentuated by the failure of the Labour Party to grapple effectively with the problems of British capitalism in the post-war world. A good start had been made in the early years of the first post-war Labour Government, but then the Government had associated itself with the USA in the Cold War and had embarked on a massive rearmament programme which made inevitable the subsequent cuts in industrial investment, cuts in the social services and the holding down of living standards. Labour lost office and remained in opposition for 13 years.

When Labour regained power in the mid-1960s there were again many good social policies implemented by the government. Unfortunately, the problems of the economy remained and Britain still spent a much higher proportion of its national product for military purposes than Germany, Japan and nearly every NATO member in Europe. The need for industrial investment could not be left to market forces, even with various measures of encouragement. The failure to tackle effectively the problems of the economy, including a much overvalued pound, finally led to crisis measures with a very stringent incomes policy, cuts in many directions and the intention to introduce industrial relations legislation which the unions opposed. Labour was defeated.

When Labour again regained office in the mid-1970s, it did so on a radical programme worked out in cooperation with the unions. The new Labour Government had a very good social record, particularly in its earlier years, but economic management was once again its weakness. It continued to spend heavily on arms, and industrial investment for renovation was never as high as it should have been. Unemployment continued to rise, though to nowhere near the figure later reached under the Conservative Government. The Labour Government was finally defeated following the Winter of Discontent, when the Government sought to hold down the wages of lowly paid public sector workers below the rise in the cost of living.

It was not surprising, following these experiences, that many Labour supporters felt a measure of disillusionment. Enthusiasm for the Labour Party declined, even among millions who still voted Labour in elections. The situation was made worse at the beginning of the 1980s by the stark disunity in the Party, by the breakaway of a number of MPs and former Cabinet Ministers to form the SDP, and by the intensity of their criticism of the Labour Party.

When I started work at Walworth Road I found that the financial situation was, if anything, worse than the description given in the report of the Commission of Enquiry. The report of the National Executive Committee to the 1982 annual conference described it as 'extremely grave'. This was a fitting observation. The general fund deficit for 1981 was £320,000. In 1980 the deficit was £165,000. The accumulated deficit was £547,000, and the Party had been in deficit for each year since 1976. Revised rates of pay for staff had been introduced following comparability studies, but at the end of 1981 the unpaid arrears of wages amounted to no less than £416,000.

The main 'asset' of the Party was unsold literature. The Party did not own its own head office in Walworth Road. The Party's bankers had authorised an overdraft up to £500,000, but the Party was heading for an overdraft of somewhere between £750,000 and £800,000. At the 1982 annual conference the auditors reported that there was very little in the general election fund of the Party.

At the 1982 annual conference the Party's treasurer, Eric Varley, said that there were several reasons for the Party's deteriorating financial position. He pointed to two in particular. The first was the commitment to pay head office and regional staff increases in pay in line with the salaries paid by the TUC. Commitments had been made for which, he said, 'absolutely no provision had been made'. Secondly, Eric Varley pointed to the extra cost of the Party's new headquarters in Walworth Road. For many years the Party had been accommodated at Transport House, Smith Square, the head office of the TGWU. The generosity of the TGWU, he said, had been replaced by higher rents and rates. Walworth Road, he pointed out, was now costing the Party more than £250,000 a year.

During my period of tenure at Walworth Road, my priority for attention was the financial situation of the Party. Without some improvement everything else was in jeopardy, including essential staffing, campaigning and, indeed, the head office itself. It would have been pointless to have claimed to work for the unity of the Party around its policies and leadership if the fabric of the Party had disintegrated because of a crippling financial situation.

By 1985 the arrears of wages of more than £400,000 were paid off. In 1982 I proposed that there should be a pay freeze, and this, to their credit, was accepted by the staff. Both in 1983 and 1984 the staff accepted pay increases less than the increase in the cost of living. At the regular meetings of the heads of departments discussions took place on reducing staffing. It was a difficult road to tread but cuts were made, overwhelmingly by natural wastage and voluntary means. This reduction in the total number of staff employed was secured, despite the creation of a small number of new posts to carry out earlier commitments.

One of the problems of reducing staffing was that the Party had no reserves to meet redundancy payments under the terms of collective agreements with unions representing the staff. There was, therefore, no alternative but to depend on 'natural wastage'. One exception to this general rule concerned a departmental head who was affected by one of the organisational recommendations of the Committee of Enquiry. Alex Kitson, who was then the Chairman of the Finance

Committee, came to the rescue and volunteered to 'pass the hat round' to a number of unions to raise the necessary sum of money. Alex did this in his own inimitable style, and to the great relief of all of us he succeeded.

The effect of these various measures was to bring about a modest improvement in the financial situation of the Party. In 1983 the Party made a surplus of £132,000, in 1984 a surplus of £42,000, and in 1985 a surplus of £39,0000. Throughout my period at Walworth Road I had full support for the necessary financial measures from the National Executive Committee, from the successive treasurers, Eric Varley, Albert Booth and Sam McCluskie, and from the successive Chairpersons of the Finance and General Purposes Committee, Alex Kitson, Alan Hadden and Audrey Wise. As Leader of the Party, Michael Foot was totally supportive and always interested in measures to improve the finances.

During the 1983 General Election a tight grip was kept on expenses. A special committee was established to administer the fund and we met regularly on more than a dozen occasions. A close scrutiny was kept on all major items of income and expenditure. The Party made a surplus of more than £200,000 on the whole election period.

The unions responded very well to the appeals for money from their political funds. The General and Municipal Workers' Union took much of the initiative within an organisation called Trade Unions for a Labour Victory, to raise money and support for the Party. Much of this was due to David Basnett of the GMWU. Larry Whitty, who was in charge of research for the GMWU and was later to become General Secretary of the Party, acted as secretary of TULV. There was some suspicion among the left in the constituencies that TULV was to become an instrument to change the policy of the Party. I found no evidence to support this view. Conversely, there were some on the right in the AUEW who were unsympathetic to TULV because it had no place in the constitution of the Party.

During the 1983 Election campaign a decision was reached in a legal case concerning Labour Party finances arising from

357

the 1979 General Election. During the 1979 Election the League Against Cruel Sports made two donations to the Party in support of its stance on animal rights. A number of members of the League took legal action, alleging that the board of the League had acted beyond its powers in making these donations. The case was heard during the 1983 campaign. The League's board was held to have acted within their powers in making one of these donations, but to have acted outside their powers in making the other donation. The Party repaid the donation, together with interest and legal costs. The total cost to the funds was more than £80,000.

The Militant Tendency

One of the early problems in which I became involved when I went to Walworth Road was the existence of a national organisation of Labour Party members known as the Militant Tendency. In 1981 a number of complaints had been received by the then principal officials of the Party that groups of Party members were associated with the Militant Tendency in a manner which contravened the constitution.

The main allegation against the Militant Tendency was that its leaders, over a long period, had joined and had been active within the Labour Party not to support its existing principles, programme and policies, as required by the constitution, but instead to build an organisation within the Labour Party with a view to gaining support and winning positions of leadership for different principles and a different programme and policies. It was alleged that the leaders of the Militant Tendency were a particular faction of Trotskyists.

The activities of the Militant Tendency were centred around the newspaper, *Militant*, which was particularly directed towards the Labour Party Young Socialists. There was no doubt that *Militant* supporters had the predominant influence in the LPYS.

Those who supported *Militant* claimed that it was a newspaper similar to other left-wing publications circulating among Labour Party members. It had gathered around itself groups of supporters who helped to sell it and gave money to sustain it. It also organised meetings to stimulate interest in socialist politics. It did not deny that it was critical of the right-wing of the Labour Party, but its supporters claimed this was no justification for any attempt to silence the paper. They pointed out that there was a long tradition within the Labour Party of publications expressing different political tendencies. *Tribune* on the left and *Socialist Commentary* on the right had sought to win support for their respective points of view, and had organised meetings and other activities for this purpose. Groups of this kind existed not only in the constituencies but also among Members of Parliament.

Many on the left who did not support the views expressed in *Militant* were, nevertheless, opposed to any kind of disciplinary action against its supporters. They argued that some who were pressing for disciplinary action had a wider objective. Their purpose, it was alleged, was to stage a right-wing counter-offensive against the changes made in recent years in the policies and constitution of the Party. By concentrating the attack on *Militant* it was hoped to discredit the whole of the left within the Party. The danger, argued some on the left, was that the purge would not be confined to the leaders of the Militant Tendency but would be extended, and that the wider campaign against the left would be taken up enthusiastically by a hostile press. The only ultimate beneficiaries, so it was claimed, would be the Conservative, Liberal and Social-Democratic parties. The Labour Party, it was said, was a 'broad church', and should remain so.

At the end of 1981 the National Executive Committee of the Party set up an inquiry into the Militant Tendency. The members of the inquiry were the then General Secretary, Ron Hayward, and the then National Agent, David Hughes. They interviewed a number of leading people around *Militant* and asked the Party's regional organisers to submit reports on the activities of the Militant Tendency. They also received considerable correspondence from individual party members and MPs. The Labour Solidarity Campaign, which drew its main support from the right of the Party, submitted what the enquiry described as 'a great deal of documentation'.

The Hayward-Hughes enquiry reached a number of main conclusions. It said that the Militant Tendency denied having individual membership, but it was, nevertheless, clear that income was received from regular weekly contributions from some readers of *Militant*, collected in the main through its full-time employees or through bankers' orders. The Militant Tendency, it was pointed out, was a well organised and centrally controlled caucus operating within the Labour Party, and that it was in control of the Labour Party Young Socialists.

The report of the Hayward-Hughes enquiry supported the view expressed by the Leader of the Party, Michael Foot, in his 1982 New Year message opposing proscription lists, witch hunts and expulsions. Nevertheless, said the report, 'The National Executive Committee has the right and duty to safeguard the Party's constitution and rules.' The Militant Tendency, it continued, was not a group formed solely to support a newspaper. It had a hard core of supporters, including full-time employees, and it had its own organisation with a separate programme, policy and propaganda outside the structure of the Labour Party. It was thus, said the report, in conflict with the Party's constitution, in particular with the clause stipulating that political organisations not affiliated to or associated under a national agreement with the Party on 1 January, 1946, and having their own programme, principles and policy for distinctive and separate propaganda, or possessing branches in the constituencies, or engaged in the promotion of parliamentary or local government candidates, or owing allegiance to any political organisation abroad, were not eligible for affiliation to the Party.

This clause of the constitution had been amended from time to time, but was intended to permit dual membership with the Cooperative Party but to exclude the Communist Party and any similar organisation, whether overt or covert. The Militant Tendency was held to be an inadmissible organisation.

The report of the Hayward-Hughes enquiry drew an important distinction between an inner leading group, who were aware of the nature and objectives of the Militant organisation, and a wider group of supporters, who were not fully aware of the objectives and believed themselves to be working for socialist objective and for the Party. The report emphasised that its authors did not wish to curtail genuine discussion and debate by pressure groups within the Party, providing that all groups were open and free to any Labour Party members to attend and participate. The Militant Tendency, they said, did not fulfil this criteria. Its centrally controlled structure prevented its supporters from participating in its decisions.

The Hayward-Hughes report suggested, as a way forward without reinstituting a list of proscribed organisations, that a register of permitted non-affiliated groups of members should be created. Groups accepted by the NEC would be permitted to operate openly within the Party. To be accepted a group would have to be open and democratic, and would not be permitted to operate its own internal discipline nor be associated with any international organisation not supported by the Labour Party or the Socialist International. The register, it was recommended, should be updated annually. The final recommendation of the report was 'that the Militant Tendency as presently constituted would not be eligible to be included on the proposed register....'

Almost immediately on my becoming General Secretary of the Party, I was required to implement the decision of the NEC to accept the recommendations of Ron Hayward and David Hughes. It was no secret that the recommendations pleased neither all on the right nor all on the left of the Party. Some on the right felt that the recommendations were too weak and that active supporters of Militant, whether in the inner core of leaders or among a wider circle, should have been expelled. Some on the left felt that the recommendations, though cautiously drafted, prepared the way for a much wider attack on the left wing of the Party.

Michael Foot supported the recommendations, and I discussed them at length with him. His primary concern was to deal with the top leadership of Militant, which he regarded as a threat to open democracy within the Party, but not to embark on a witch-hunt against individuals who might have been attracted to particular aspects of policy supported by Militant, and even less against the left in general. He was concerned to consolidate the unity of the Party, including both right and left, but felt that a secret, disciplined leadership of a group with its own distinctive ideology and organisation could not be disregarded. He was aware of vigorous complaints being voiced from some on the right of the Party.

Following the NEC decision to accept the Hayward-Hughes recommendations, and taking into account my discussions with Michael Foot, I sent a letter to all constituency parties and affiliated organisations, outlining the decisions that had been taken. I included the following paragraphs:

'It cannot be emphasised too strongly that the purpose of the NEC decision is to uphold the existing constitution of the party and to protect it from organised internal groups who, though they do not seek affiliation, nevertheless, have their own programme, principles and policy for distinctive and separate propaganda and, in effect, have organised branches or groups and discipline for this purpose. It is not in any way the intention of the NEC to inhibit open and democratic debate within the party. Moreover, the NEC recognises the valuable and legitimate role played within the democratic processes of the party by many organised groups of members.

'The NEC's decision will be implemented with understanding and respect for the rights of members and of organised groups within the Labour Party. It is our wish to answer enquiries sympathetically. No group need fear exclusion from the register without discussion and without having the opportunity to bring their arrangements into conformity with the party's constitution.'

A letter was sent to *Militant* before the 1982 annual conference, drawing their attention to the recommendations of the

Hayward-Hughes enquiry and, in particular, requesting information as to the changes they proposed to make to conform to the constitution of the Party. No reply was received within three months of this letter being sent.

As General Secretary I was asked to move at the 1982 annual conference of the Party the section of the annual report dealing with the Militant Tendency. Judith Hart, who was to preside over the conference, expressed her view to me privately that I should decline. She felt that I should not be identified with a move which would inevitably lead to a purge of dissidents and would serve the purpose of the right wing to discredit the left.

I recognised the danger to which Judith was pointing, but there were other relevant considerations. First, there was the reality of the charges against Militant. I had read all the many documents accumulated at Walworth Road dealing with the activities of Militant. There was no doubt in my mind that the Militant Tendency was organised as a secret, disciplined organisation within the Party, with its own long-term programme, principles and policy. It had its own structure at national, district and local level, and its own core of full-time organisers. It possessed a publishing house and a fund-raising organisation to maintain a shadow organisation within the Labour Party. It had its own international network of like-minded groups. The evidence for these charges came from its own published documents, from minute books and other records, and from statements made by former and present associates of the Militant Tendency.

The Militant Tendency and the organisations from which it arose were not of recent origin. The lineage could be traced back to the 1930s through sectarian and rival Trotskyist groups. For many years there had been controversy among these groups about the theory of 'entry' into socialist parties and about the manner in which transitional demands on the way to socialism could be realised.

It was not, in my view, incompatible with the requirements of Labour Party membership to hold views which owed something to the writings of Leon Trotsky, providing that the

363

obligations of membership were observed. Members of the Labour Party, even at the highest level, take their inspiration from many different sources. In my personal experience I had never been attracted by Trotskyist views, but similarly there were other viewpoints within the Party which I had never shared. The obligations of membership are not compatible, however, with support for a secret, disciplined organisation existing within the Party, with its own structure, funds, organising staff, programme and policy.

The second consideration which weighed with me in agreeing to speak for the NEC against Militant was that a refusal to do so on my part would not stop the report being presented. I shared the view of Michael Foot that the report should not be seen as a prelude to a general purge of the left, and I had the opportunity to say so to the conference. All who observed the rules, whether from the right, centre or left, had a legitimate place in the broad stream of opinion from which the Labour Party was constituted.

I spoke for the NEC on the subject of the Militant Tendency at the 1982 annual conference. The conference approved the relevant sections of the NEC report by a more than three to one majority. It also carried a resolution reaffirming that the NEC had a duty to uphold the constitution of the Party and to declare that 'organisations not in conformity with that constitution are incompatible with membership of the Labour Party.'

A notice of motion was tabled for the December 1982 meeting of the NEC, stating that in accordance with the duty placed upon it to enforce the constitution, the NEC noted that the 'Militant Tendency' exists as a group within the Labour Party, was a Trotskyist 'entrist' group with its own programme, principles and policy, and hence was ineligible for affiliation to the Party. A copy of this notice was sent to the editorial board of *Militant* and they were invited to meet the NEC to submit their views on it.

The members of the editorial board applied unsuccessfully to the High Court for an injunction to prevent the NEC from considering the motion. The members of the editorial board than met the NEC and expressed their views, denying that they constituted an organisation ineligible for Labour Party membership. The notice of motion was carried.

At the beginning of 1983 the NEC, after taking legal advice, took the disciplinary procedures a stage further. It was decided that anyone charged with involvement in 'financial support for and/or the organisation of and/or the activities of the Militant Tendency', should be given written particulars of any such alleged involvement. Further, it was agreed that anyone so charged should have the opportunity to make written and oral representations. I was instructed as General Secretary to prepare a case against the five members of the editorial board of *Militant* and to present it in their presence at a meeting of the NEC held towards the end of February 1983.

At this meeting each of the five members of the editorial board of *Militant* made a statement in their own defence. In my view they did not, nor was it possible for them, to reply effectively to the constitutional charge against them. Their defence was primarily political, on the grounds that it was legitimate for them to argue through the columns of their paper for the policies which they supported, and to organise meetings of their supporters for this purpose. They pointed out that wherever their supporters existed they campaigned energetically for Labour candidates in elections. Following discussion on the NEC, a resolution was carried expelling the five editorial board members from the Party.

In the period between the 1982 and 1983 conferences a considerable amount of time was spent at Walworth Road in the preparation of the register of non-affiliated groups of Labour Party members. The various groups were asked to apply for registration. If they did not respond, they had to be traced. They were asked to answer a number of questions, and the representatives of some of them had to be interviewed. The responses had to be examined and reports prepared for the NEC. Various enquiries about the register had to be answered. It was reported to the 1983 conference that nearly 40 organisations had been accepted on to the register.

All this took place in the months preceding the General Election. It was not a sensible allocation of resources, but it

365

was in accordance with the decisions of the NEC and the annual conference. It added weight to the argument of those who had predicted that the purge of Militant would distract the Party from more important tasks. My impression was that the register was never taken very seriously by the Party, and once the purge of Militant was under way it was regarded as having served its purpose.

Bermondsey By-election

In July 1981 Robert Mellish, the Member of Parliament for Southwark and Bermondsey, announced that he would not be seeking re-election. He complained that a group, with whom he was not in sympathy, had taken over the leadership of the local party. The Southwark and Bermondsey constituency was regarded as a safe Labour seat. It consisted of the former dockside borough of Bermondsey and part of the working-class area of north Southwark. Constituencies in this part of London had been rearranged to take account of the shift of population, but Bob Mellish's constituency was still overwhelmingly working-class in composition. The heart of the constituency was Bermondsey, with its long tradition of Labour control. Bob Mellish had been a Bermondsey MP since 1945 and had held high office.

Changes had, indeed, taken place in the Southwark and Bermondsey constituency Labour Party. The group which had hitherto been dominant in the party, supporters of Bob Mellish and of John O'Grady, the leader of the Southwark Council, had been successfully challenged by a new group who were critical of the policies of the old group. The policy differences ranged over a wide area. The new group wanted priority for housing in the Bermondsey docklands scheduled for redevelopment. It was argued that the Conservative Government wanted to give priority to commercial development and to higher-priced housing for 'yuppies'. Early in 1980 Bob Mellish had indicated his readiness to become Vice-Chairman of what was to become the London Docklands Development Corporation.

His point of view was that it was likely to be more effective to influence Docklands development from the inside than to confine criticism to the outside.

Another major difference concerned proposals being discussed on the Southwark Council for a new Southwark Town Hall, to cost many millions of pounds. The critics of the O'Grady leadership argued that there were other more urgent social priorities on which the limited resources of the local authority should be spent. Yet another area of difference concerned the attitude of some of the dominant old group to the Social Democrats. John O'Grady, it was said, was a supporter of those who were wanting to influence the party in a social-democratic direction. The Social Democratic Party was eventually formed under the leadership of David Owen, Shirley Williams, Roy Jenkins (who first entered parliament in a by-election in 1948 from one of the old Southwark constituencies) and William Rodgers.

Those who challenged the old dominant group claimed that the local party had been neglected and that an active and critical rank and file had not been encouraged. The members, it was alleged, were seen as no more than supporters to be called into activity at elections. The dominant group countered, in reply, that the support given to Labour in elections was proof that its existing representatives enjoyed substantial local support.

Those who felt that a challenge had to be made to the dominant old group in Bermondsey were by no means exclusively on the left of the Party. They were drawn from a wider cross-section, but those on the left took the initiative in organising the opposition. At the annual general meeting of the constituency party in 1980, the hold of the old dominant leadership was broken. Peter Tatchell was elected secretary, and others on the left or centre were elected to the remaining main positions.

In 1981 the Bermondsey party opposed the nomination of John O'Grady and a number of other councillors for re-election. This sharpened the controversy within the party. By far the majority of sitting councillors were, however, renominated. Towards the end of the year a parliamentary selection conference was held to choose a prospective candidate to follow Bob Mellish. Peter Tatchell was selected. In the final vote he had a majority of 37 to 30 over Arthur Latham, the former MP for Paddington, who was also a left-winger.

The selection of Peter Tatchell displeased Bob Mellish, and he criticised the decision. The press developed a campaign to discredit Tatchell and to convey the impression that the Bermondsey Labour Party had been taken over by people on the extreme left. In December 1981 a Social Democrat MP, James Wellbeloved, asked the Prime Minister, Mrs Thatcher, whether she had seen a statement by the prospective Labour candidate for Bermondsey advocating extra-parliamentary action to challenge the Government's right to rule. The question, though addressed to the Prime Minister, was also intended for the attention of the Leader of the Opposition, Michael Foot.

In the subsequent exchanges in the House of Commons Michael Foot pointed out that 'the individual concerned' was not an endorsed prospective candidate, and that as far as he (Michael Foot) was concerned, he never would be. The press seized upon this exchange, and the campaign to discredit Tatchell gathered strength.

The statement to which James Wellbeloved had referred appeared in an article written in the spring of 1981 by Peter Tatchell for *London Labour Briefing*. In the article Peter Tatchell argued that 'talking shop' committee politics implied that 'the realisation of socialism can basically be left to a handful of wise and articulate MPs and councillors debating and voting through the committee structures of Parliament and local councils'. It was, however, in Tatchell's view, not the leaders but the rank and file of the Labour Party membership and the working class at large who were crucial for the success of the struggle. Without such a mass popular base, the prospects of halting the Tory government's attack on living standards and of electing a radical Labour government looked bleak.

The sentences in Peter Tatchell's article to which particular objection was taken were:

'Reliance on the present token and ineffectual parliamentary opposition will advance us nowhere....

'Debates and parliamentary divisions are fruitless cosmetic exercises given the Tories' present Commons majority. And if we recognise this, we are forced to accept Tory edicts as a *fait accompli* or we must look to new more militant forms of extra-parliamentary opposition which involve mass popular participation and challenge the government's right to rule...'

Peter Tatchell subsequently made it clear that he did not disparage parliamentary representation but felt that it had to be supplemented by extra-parliamentary activity. Such a contention can be confirmed by any number of examples from British history. Trade unionism itself is a form of extra-parliamentary activity which has enabled working people to win many improvements. In recent times, the resistance of millions of people to the Poll Tax not only led to the withdrawal of the tax but contributed in no small measure to the downfall of Mrs Thatcher.

It is, therefore, legitimate and, indeed, sensible for commentators within the labour movement to point to the limitations of parliamentary debate against a government with a substantial majority and to urge that if progress is to be made on substantial issues, the activity of working people outside parliament is essential for success. Even where success is not achieved, agitation and activity at meetings, demonstrations and in industrial struggles help to prepare the way forward, including eventual electoral success.

This, however, does not imply that socialists should encourage the view that parliament and local councils are of little consequence. The tradition of the British labour movement from the time of the Chartists is to seek representation in parliament and in local authorities, and to use the opportunities provided by such representation to protest against injustice and, where possible, to use any instruments of power in the interests of the people. The democratic opportunities which have been won by struggle should never be belittled.

369

Though I felt that Peter Tatchell could have expressed himself differently in his article, the whole issue was being used by opponents of the labour movement to give it a significance which it did not deserve. In particular, it was exploited to sustain and give strength to the contention of the SDP that Labour was being taken over by dangerous extremists who threatened the system of parliamentary democracy.

The Labour Party decided by a very narrow majority within the National Executive Committee and in a barrage of press publicity, not to endorse Peter Tatchell as a prospective candidate. Tatchell was not given the opportunity to defend himself before the NEC. Following this decision of the NEC, Bob Mellish indicated that he intended to continue as MP for a while. Many in the Bermondsey Labour Party felt that if the NEC had endorsed Peter Tatchell a by-election might have been precipitated by the resignation of Bob Mellish.

The controversy continued. There were many protests against the decision not to endorse Peter Tatchell. In Bermondsey the Labour Party refused to accept a small number of 'old group' councillors for the approved list for the forthcoming borough council elections. On the insistence of the NEC the excluded councillors were restored to the approved list, but most of them were not selected by the wards.

In one ward a deselected councillor decided to run as an Independent Labour and Tenants' candidate, together with two other candidates. The deselected councillor was supported by Bob Mellish. The three candidates standing against Labour won by large majorities. Moves were then initiated within the Party with a view to the expulsion of Bob Mellish for supporting candidates in opposition to official Labour candidates.

In August 1982 Bob Mellish resigned from the Labour Party. In the meanwhile the NEC of the party, thanks largely to the efforts at compromise by Eric Heffer, had agreed that a new selection procedure should be held, in which Peter Tatchell could participate. Tatchell won the nomination overwhelmingly.

This time Tatchell's nomination was endorsed by the NEC

of the Labour Party. Hostile newspapers sought not only to discredit Tatchell but also the leadership of the Labour Party for its alleged inconsistency.

The subsequent by-election was one of the most disgraceful in the history of British politics. There was no limit to the depths to which some of the so-called popular press and some of Tatchell's anonymous opponents were prepared to sink in their personal attacks. He was described as a 'draft dodger' because, so it was said, he had come to Britain from Australia as an opponent of the Vietnam War. It was alleged that he was an 'extremist' who did not support the parliamentary system, and that what he stood for was alien to the tradition of 'real' Bermondsey Labour. The most despicable references, however, related to his support for the rights of homosexuals. Within the Bermondsey constituency anonymously produced posters and leaflets appeared, designed to appeal to every kind of backward prejudice among voters. Tatchell was hounded by journalists looking for any evidence to discredit him.

The task of the Labour Party was made more difficult by the decision of John O'Grady to stand in the election as a 'Real Bermondsey Labour' candidate. Sections of the press hostile to Labour used every opportunity to publicise the opposition to Peter Tatchell from O'Grady and his supporters.

Labour lost the Bermondsey by-election. The successful candidate was the Liberal, Simon Hughes, with 17,017 votes. Peter Tatchell came second with 7,698 votes, well ahead of John O'Grady with 2,243 votes. The Conservative candidate received only 1,631 votes, and none of the other candidates polled a significant vote.

The defeat of Peter Tatchell was a blow to the Labour Party. In his book, *The Battle for Bermondsey*, Peter alleges that the Labour Party leadership wanted him to lose. This was not true of Michael Foot, the Leader of the Party, with whom I was in almost daily contact, and it was not true of either David Hughes, the then National Agent of the party, or myself. Both David and I had responsibilities in the by-election on behalf of the NEC.

I can, nevertheless, understand why Peter felt that the odds were stacked against him, even within the Labour Party. There was strong opposition within the NEC to his original candidacy, and locally he had to face the hostility of those who gave support to John O'Grady. Bob Mellish, who had represented Bermondsey for many years, was one of Peter Tatchell's opponents. Peter's article in *London Labour Briefing* left him open to criticism which, given his point of view, he could have avoided. As his book on the Bermondsey by-election makes clear, he was not an anti-parliamentarian but believed that parliament does not 'monopolise or exhaust the process of representing individuals and interests groups, nor does it represent them all equally or make its own sovereign decisions'. The Labour Party, unjustifiably, has nearly always been stricter on discipline towards its members on the left than to those on the right.

During the Bermondsey by-election campaign much publicity was given in the press to the expulsion of leading Militants by the NEC. It was publicity which did not help Labour's cause. Inevitably, some among the public assumed that there was a real threat to the Labour Party from the Militant organisation, whilst others, particularly among some supporters of the Labour Party, felt that the Party should have been directing all its fire against its Conservative and Liberal opponents. Either way Labour suffered. It was made worse in the Bermondsey by-election by a local decision early in the campaign to go to a printer associated with Militant for the printing of a Labour Party leaflet in support of Peter Tatchell.

The reason advanced by those responsible for this decision was that the printer associated with Militant offered the lowest price. It was, in my view, an unwise decision which was bound to provoke hostility from those members of the NEC who were watching the campaign closely to ensure that it was conducted in accordance with national policy. The leaflets were confiscated on instruction from the Labour Party head office. I accepted ultimate responsibility for this decision, but felt that the National Party should not have been put in a position where whatever was done would have been open to criticism. The whole episode was damaging to Labour.

In subsequent years, because I moved to live in the Bermondsey constituency, I came to know much more closely most of the active members of the Labour Party. Peter Tatchell is an able person and, though generally on the left, he is not a supporter of the Militant Tendency. When he was the secretary of the constituency party and when he was the prospective candidate he did an enormous amount of work, visiting voters, taking up grievances and playing a prominent part in public campaigns on issues of concern to the electorate. In more recent years he has become less active in the Party, though, as far as I know, he is still a member. He now concentrates on other social issues, including gay rights, where he feels that his efforts are more productive of results.

Bermondsey Suspended

For a number of years I have served on the General Committee of the Southwark and Bermondsey constituency Labour Party (now known as North Southwark and Bermondsey) as a delegate, first from TASS and then, after the amalgamation with ASTMS, from MSF. In 1988 the constituency party was suspended without notice and without any opportunity for the General Committee to answer any charges. The first I heard of the suspension was when I read of it in a local newspaper. The press report made it clear that the reason for the suspension was that the party was allegedly dominated by Militant.

The decision to suspend the Southwark and Bermondsey CLP without formal charge and without an opportunity of defence was a disgrace. It flouted every principle of natural justice. I do not know to this day who initiated this injustice, but at the time it appeared to come more from within the officialdom of the London Labour Party than from the national headquarters of the Party.

My principal objection to the suspension concerned the manner in which it took place. It is elementary that when charges are levelled an opportunity should be given for a defence to be made. No action should be taken until the evidence has been considered. Nothing even remotely resembling a fair procedure was observed when the Bermondsey party was suspended.

My second objection was that I did not accept that the Bermondsey constituency party was dominated by Militant, though I would certainly have accepted that supporters of Militant had a significant presence on the General Committee. I remember more than one occasion when delegates, known to be supporters of Militant, were defeated on issues debated by the General Committee. The General Committee had a substantial majority on the left, but those who constituted the majority were by no means all Militant supporters. Some, myself included, were very clear about the extent of our substantial differences from the particular variety of Trotskyism represented by the national leadership of the Militant Tendency.

It was later discovered that a secret paper had been prepared, placing members of the General Committee into various categories in relation to Militant. It was suspected that the paper had been prepared from somewhere in the London Labour Party. I was described as a Militant 'fellow-traveller'. It was an absurd allegation and served only to demonstrate the political shallowness of the author.

The Militant supporters in Bermondsey were a mixed group of activists. Some of them were very good. They were from a younger generation and had been attracted to Militant because their inclination was to be left-wing on the main issues of the day. I anticipated that some of them at least would, as a result of experience and discussion, graduate from their support for Militant and would come to support a more traditional left point of view. A few of them were less attractive. They were always prepared to be more 'left' and 'militant' than any other left-winger.

Whilst the Bermondsey party was suspended a number of members were excluded and others suspended. The whole process seemed to me to be unsatisfactory. I have never heard at any subsequent meeting a proper report on what took place.

After an interval of more than two years, the Bermondsey party was reconstituted. I noted with interest that at the first meeting at which we elected officers the only trade union which had submitted nominations was the EETPU. Their nominees, for nearly all the main jobs, were not confined to members of the EETPU. My own union branch, together with others, had been invited to submit nominations, but as we did not know who were likely to be delegates to the General Committee or who was willing to stand for office we did not nominate.

The Bermondsey party did not recover the level of activity which it had before the suspension. This is no reflection on the newly elected officers then or since, all of whom, right and left, have done their best to keep the party going in difficult circumstances. In the ward in which I live the attendance at branch meetings has dropped from an average of about 20 to about 10. Most of the councillors elected from Bermondsey are now Liberals, and Simon Hughes has kept the parliamentary seat through four general elections since he defeated Peter Tatchell. The membership of the Bermondsey party has more recently increased. Its campaigning activity has also increased under the stimulation of its campaigns officer, Piers Corbyn, the brother of Jeremy Corbyn MP.

I did not know Bob Mellish closely, though I met him on a number of occasions. One of his sons worked for ACAS whilst I was the Chairman, and he was a very good member of the staff. He was a strong supporter of collective bargaining, well qualified and highly intelligent. Unfortunately, he died whilst still a young man. It was a tragic loss.

18

The 1983 General Election

The 1983 General Election resulted in a heavy defeat for Labour. In comparison with 1979, Labour lost 59 seats. The Conservative Party had 397 seats in the new parliament, Labour 209 and the Liberal-Social Democrat Alliance 23. In terms of votes in comparison with 1979, Labour lost more than 3,000,000, to end with 8,457,124. The Conservatives lost 685,000 votes but ended with just over 13,000,000. The Alliance were the big gainers. In comparison with the Liberal vote in 1979, the Alliance increased their vote by 3,475,000 to achieve a total of 7,780,587. Thus the vote secured by the Alliance was very largely at the expense of Labour but, to a lesser extent, at the expense of the Conservatives.

The reason for Labour's heavy defeat was primarily political disunity. Labour entered the period of the election campaign well behind the Conservatives in all the published opinion polls. The margin in the share of national voting intentions between Conservative and Labour approximately one month before the Election was somewhere between 12 per cent and 18 per cent. In the event, on Election Day the margin was about 15 per cent. The big change was for the Alliance. Their share increased during the election campaign by at least 7 percentage points, from about 19 per cent to 26 per cent. The Alliance were helped by the claims, widely reported during the campaign and welcomed in the overwhelmingly Conservative press, that they had overtaken or were about to overtake Labour.

Labour entered the election campaign burdened with a reputation for disunity. The biggest single factor contributing to this reputation was the breakaway from the Party by nearly 30 right-wing Members of Parliament, including a number of former Cabinet Ministers, and the one-time Deputy Leader of the Labour Party, Roy Jenkins, to form the Social Democratic Party. The main target of attack by the SDP was the Labour Party.

The attack on Labour and on its policies from people who had originally been elected to parliament to support Labour and had served as Labour Cabinet Ministers undoubtedly had a serious effect. This damaging blow came from the right and not from the left of the Party.

Those who argue that the responsibility for such a situation rested originally with the left, because of the policy and constitutional changes made in earlier years, are in effect saying that policy and constitutional changes are only acceptable as a basis for unity when they are endorsed by the right. It is an argument that is totally one-sided.

In any case, the control of the Party at the time of the 1983 General Election was not in the hands of the left. The Leader of the Party, Michael Foot, was from the left, but he did more than anyone, understandably in the circumstances, to ensure that the right continued to have the opportunity to share in influencing the conduct of the Party. He saw this as essential for preserving the unity of the Party after the defection of the SDP. The left was in a minority on the National Executive Committee of the Party, the Shadow Cabinet was overwhelmingly right-wing in composition, and the main national speakers at the election campaign press conferences were drawn predominantly from the right wing of the Party. One of the myths of the 1983 General Election, fostered by some on the right of the Party, was that everything at the time was under the control of the left.

The 1983 General Election manifesto placed the need to reduce unemployment at the centre of Labour's programme. As Michael Foot said in his foreword to the manifesto, '...if nothing can be done about unemployment, nothing truly enduring can be done about anything else'. The manifesto outlined the Party's proposals for an emergency programme of

377

action, including a major increase in public investment in transport, housing and energy conservation, a substantial increase in resources for the social services, increased investment in industry, especially in new technology, with public enterprise taking the lead, and a programme for training. The programme also said that the pound should be made competitive, a clear warning against the policies advocated in subsequent years both by the Tories and the leadership of the Labour Party that had the effect of locking Britain into an exchange rate with an overvalued pound.

Labour's manifesto gave a straight answer to the question: how will we pay for it? It would be wrong, it argued, to finance the initial boost to spending by increased taxation. Only if the economy had already achieved full employment would increased taxation be the right way to pay for increased investment. In conditions of widespread unemployment, idle plant and unused savings, the programme of investment should be financed by borrowing. The choice, in effect, was between borrowing for employment and expansion or borrowing to pay for the dole queues.

Labour's manifesto pointed out that spending generates new income and new savings. As the economy recovered under the impulse of public investment, less would be spent on unemployment benefit. When more people went back to work they would also pay income tax and spend more on goods which were taxed. Savings could also be made, the manifesto pointed out, by cancelling the massive expenditure programme on Trident and on PWR nuclear reactors. Savings in military expenditure, it was emphasised, should not lead to unemployment for those working in the defence industries. Labour would give material support to plans for industrial conversion so that the resources of the defence industries could be used for the production of useful goods.

It fell to Peter Shore, as Labour's principal economic spokesperson in the 1983 General Election, to expound and defend the Party's programme on employment. As far as I recall, I took the chair at every one of the national press conferences addressed by Peter Shore. In my view he did extremely well. I

378

have nothing but praise for the manner in which he described Labour's policy, analysed the causes of unemployment and pointed the way forward. He was never put on the defensive, and he never resorted to meaningless waffle to conceal discomfort under questioning.

Some on the right of the Party, after the General Election, criticised the election manifesto as a recipe for defeat. One described it as 'the longest suicide note in history'. Denis Healey, in his autobiography, blamed the 'extreme left' for two election defeats in 1979 and 1983, though Denis, in his various ministerial roles, was at the very heart of policies which contributed to the defeat in 1979. In 1983 he acknowledged, in a report which he put to the National Executive and which he quoted in his book, that the Election was not lost in the three weeks of the Election campaign but in the three years which preceded it. He claimed that if Michael Foot had gone well before the Election Labour might have won. He added: 'We had no chance whatever so long as he was Leader'.

Denis Healey mistook cause and effect. Yes, he was right in emphasising that Labour lost the 1983 election in the years preceding the election campaign. But the primary responsibility for this rested with the substantial number of right-wing MPs, including Cabinet Ministers, who broke away from the Party because of their policy differences, and then concentrated their attack on the very Party which had brought them into prominence. The special merit of Michael Foot, within the Labour Party, was that both by his personal characteristics and his political contribution he emphasised and symbolised the vital importance of keeping the Party together around the policies determined by the conference, whilst at the same time not excluding either left or right from influence. This was a role which Denis Healey, despite his many attributes, could not have played.

In assessing the years and events preceding the 1983 General Election, account needs to be taken of the roots of the right-wing breakaway that led to the formation of the SDP. They were not primarily about organisational questions such as the accountability of MPs and who should elect the Leader of the

Party – though they were of importance – but about political policies. Differences about Britain's attitude to the Cold War and the economic consequences of high military spending first came to the surface during the Attlee government. Differences about the likely consequences of the obligations of the Common Market went back at least to the early 1960s.

Significantly, in his autobiography Denis Healey acknowledges that he was mistaken on a very vital issue of policy that dominated so many of the debates within the Labour Party throughout the post-war years. He wrote: 'Like most Western observers at the time, I believed that Stalin's behaviour showed he was bent on the military conquest of Western Europe. I now think we were all mistaken.' He went on to state that Stalin concealed the full extent of Russia's wartime losses, but that these losses did much to explain his determination to create a buffer zone in Eastern Europe.

It is, I think, arguable whether the extent of the losses of the Soviet Union in the Second World War were not known to the West. Certainly my impression from my first visit to the USSR in the early 1950s was that the authorities were most anxious to convey to Western visitors the extent of the devastation and human loss resulting from the German invasion.

This apart, however, the acknowledgement by Denis Healey of his mistaken estimation of Soviet intentions carries with it far-reaching implications for Labour's policy not only in foreign affairs, but in defence policy, military spending and in the economy. To his credit, Denis Healey has demonstrated in more recent years his responsiveness to changes in the world situation, a responsiveness not based on formerly held assumptions.

A very important difference between Michael Foot and Denis Healey in the early 1980s was that Michael was not handicapped in the labour movement by a reputation as a long-time supporter of policies based upon the mistaken assumptions of the Cold War. This in no way suggests that he was soft on the injustices of Soviet power. Indeed, he was among the sternest of critics, but this had never led him into general support for US policy as expressed through NATO.

The Influence of the Right

One further illustration of the falsity of the allegation that the Labour Party was controlled by the left at the time of the 1983 General Election is provided by an examination of the list of main national speakers for the Party in the Election campaign. More were drawn from the right than from the left wing of the Party. Other than Michael Foot, the principal political figures on the left, Tony Benn, Eric Heffer, Judith Hart, Frank Allaun and Dennis Skinner, were not invited to play any role at national level. The most influential figure in London, Ken Livingstone, was also not used.

The extent to which the right and not the left in the Party – other than in the person of Michael Foot – were predominant in the presentation of policy in the 1983 General Election is shown by the choice of leading figures for the daily national press conferences and the Election broadcasts. At the national press conferences, according to my own records, the most frequent speaker was Michael Foot, with about a dozen appearances. He was followed closely by Peter Shore and Denis Healey. The next most frequent speakers were Roy Hattersley, with about five appearances, and John Golding with three. John Smith, Neil Kinnock, Ann Taylor and Gwyneth Dunwoody each appeared twice. Others who spoke included Sam McCluskie, Joel Barnett, Ann Davis, Stan Orme, Joan Lestor, Brynmor John, Gerald Kaufman and a small number drawn from outside parliament or the trade union movement. Tony Benn was not used once.

For the television party election broadcasts there was similarly a balance between the right of the Labour Party and the centre-left. Michael Foot appeared twice, but so too did Denis Healey, Roy Hattersley, Peter Shore, Neil Kinnock, John Smith and Joan Lestor. Others to participate in television election broadcasts were the MPs Denzil Davies, Sam Galbraith and Ann Taylor, and the academics Maurice Peston and Roger Opie. For the radio election broadcasts the speakers were the MPs Denis Healey, Roy Hattersley, Gwyneth Dunwoody and John Prescott, the trade unionist Roy

Grantham, and two women personalities who were not MPs, Patricia Hewitt and Glenda Jackson.

For Scottish broadcasts the party's speakers included Bruce Millan, Gavin Strang, Gordon Brown, Norman Godman, Bill Spiers, John Maxton, Robin Cook and Michael Connarky. For the broadcasts in Wales the party's speakers included Denzil Davies, Jane Hutt, Alun Griffiths, John Morris, Betty Williams and Gareth Wardell.

A significant point about the range of speakers for the Election broadcasts in 1983 was the exclusion – with the single exception of Neil Kinnock – of any from the members of the National Executive Committee elected by the constituency parties. At the 1982 conference the seven successful elected members in order of their votes were Tony Benn, Dennis Skinner, Eric Heffer, Frank Allaun, Neil Kinnock, Jo Richardson and Audrey Wise. In the following year, 1983, after the General Election, the seven successful candidates in order of the votes cast were Tony Benn, Eric Heffer, Dennis Skinner, Michael Meacher, David Blunkett, Jo Richardson and Audrey Wise. In 1983 Neil Kinnock had been elected Leader and Frank Allaun had retired. In their places were elected Michael Meacher and David Blunkett, both of whom were regarded as being on the left of the Party. Clearly it was the left among the elected leadership who were under-represented in the range of speakers for the national press conferences and election broadcasts in the 1983 General Election.

On the National Executive Committee the predominant influence was also that of the right. A key role was played by John Golding. He not only held the chair of the Home Policy Committee, but he was widely regarded as one of the principal organisers of right-wing influence at the top level of the Party. John, who had considerable ability, gave support to Michael Foot during Michael's period as Leader, but sought to ensure that the influence of others on the left was minimised.

The Chairperson of the Organisation Committee was Russell Tuck of the National Union of Railwaymen, and the Chairperson of the Press and Publicity Committee was Gwyneth Dunwoody. Neither was on the left.` Of the principal committees of the NEC, the only one with a Chairperson with views to the left of centre was the International Committee. The Chairperson was Alex Kitson of the TGWU. The Chairperson of the Finance Committee was Alan Hadden of the Boilermakers' Society, whose views were generally towards the centre.

The Campaign Committee for the General Election similarly did not have a left-wing majority. It was nominally a fairly large body and met early each morning. The committee had deliberately been made large to accommodate various interests, including not only the parliamentary leadership and representatives of the Shadow Cabinet, but also representatives of the National Executive Committee, prominent figures in the trade union movement and the departmental heads at Walworth Road. This arrangement was itself a reflection of the tensions in the Party and of the insistence of various groups that they should not be excluded. One prominent figure who was not a member of the Campaign Committee was Tony Benn.

The attendance at the daily meetings of the Campaign Committee was usually substantially less than the nominal membership, and consisted of either the Leader or Deputy Leader, if they were available from their heavy programmes of provincial meetings, the principal speakers at the daily press conferences organised nationally by the Party, and departmental heads who reported on their various responsibilities for organisation, for the arrangement of rallies, for opinion polling and for the preparation of campaign material. The nominally large Campaign Committee was an unwieldy arrangement, and during the campaign a smaller inner committee was established. The two most influential members, other than the Leader and Deputy Leader when they were available, were John Golding and Roy Hattersley.

Among the departmental heads at Walworth Road the political opinions varied from left to right, but all worked hard. David Hughes, Walter Brown and Joyce Gould were responsible for organisation and for arranging rallies and tours for main speakers. Joyce Gould took on the role of Campaigns Officer in the period leading up to the General Election. Nick Grant was responsible for publicity, and Geoff Bish and Jenny

Little for the preparation of material for the main issues of the campaign. They were also in close touch throughout with those commercially responsible for opinion polling. It would be absurd to suggest that the departmental heads constituted a network from which the left in the Party controlled or even strongly influenced the 1983 campaign.

At the 1983 Labour Party conference in the debate on campaigning strategy, John Golding said:

> 'Brother Chair, being on the Campaign Committee was the nearest I have got to life among anarchists. I am talking about the professional politicians, not the staff. It was not the staff of Walworth Road that let us down; it was we in the leadership.'

This comment was, in my view, less than generous to the Party's principal representatives at the time of the 1983 Election: Michael Foot, Denis Healey, Peter Shore, Roy Hattersley, Neil Kinnock, John Smith and John Golding himself. The immense electoral burden of disunity and of the breakaway of the SDP predated the Election campaign. The impression of disunity in the labour movement caused by the controversies of the late 1970s and early 1980s, culminating in the formation of the breakaway SDP, was reinforced during the approach to the 1983 General Election by suggestions from a small number of MPs that Michael Foot should be replaced as Leader by Denis Healey. I was aware of these suggestions, and so too were a number of journalists who were ready to give them encouragement, not only because it was regarded as good publicity to sell newspapers, but also because it was regarded as embarrassing to Labour. Denis Healey himself was not involved in the circulation of these suggestions.

At one of the national press conferences at which I was in the chair, and at a time when there was press speculation about the leadership, Michael Foot made it clear that he spoke as Leader of the Party. He said: 'I am the leader, and I am expressing the views that we will carry into operation under a Labour government.' I followed with an assertion that the

384

Campaign Committee was insistent that Michael Foot 'is the leader of the Labour Party and speaks for the Party'.

I came in for criticism for this observation from some newspapers which described it as an 'own goal' and, not surprisingly, from some in the Labour Party whose sympathies were different from my own. I think their criticism was wrong. I do not regret, that at a time when there was an effort to undermine the leadership of Michael Foot, I made it clear that this effort found no sympathy in Walworth Road.

'Own goals' are more often than not the invention of journalistic chatter. They allegedly occur in every general election, but they have very little influence on public opinion. Voters expect strong words in an election campaign, and they expect newspapers to publish sensational reports. They only have an effect when an issue of substance is involved.

In the 1983 General Election both Denis Healey and Neil Kinnock made observations which newspapers described as 'own goals'. Denis Healey referred at the end of one of his campaigning days to Mrs Thatcher's exploitation of the so-called Falklands factor. He said that she 'gloried in slaughter'. He afterwards apologised for the remark.

Neil Kinnock's alleged 'own goal' concerned comments which he made to the effect that fighting men had left their 'guts on Goose Green (in the Falklands) to prove that Mrs Thatcher had guts.' As with Denis Healey's observation, this comment was unjustified. Nevertheless, I do not believe that it caused Labour to lose votes. I do not recall anyone, other than journalists or commentators in the inner circle of politics, ever mentioning to me these alleged 'own goals'.

A more serious problem is caused in an election campaign when leading members of the Party criticise directly or indirectly the policy being placed before the electorate. In the 1983 campaign James Callaghan, the former Labour Prime Minister, made it clear that he did not agree with the Party's policy on nuclear weapons. James Callaghan's speech was widely reported, with front-page headlines. Its effect, as Michael Foot subsequently pointed out, was to strengthen the appeal of the Conservative Party on the related issues of nuclear arms and disarmament, and to divert attention from Labour's proposals for stopping the arms race, accepting a nuclear freeze and rejecting Cruise missiles. James Callaghan's speech was an expression of his deeply held views and, no doubt, he felt it right that he should express them on an issue of such importance. Perhaps he could have done it in a way less damaging to Labour?

Harold Wilson, another former Labour Prime Minister, also intervened in the 1983 General Election in a manner very unhelpful to Labour. In an exclusive interview with the *Daily Mail* he spoke at length of the errors of the Labour Party and of Michael Foot's conduct of the campaign. Michael Foot's subsequent comment on the article was that it 'contained not a single attack on the Tories. ... The whole piece might have been another brilliant advertisement designed by Saatchi and Saatchi themselves...' Michael Foot's opinion of Harold Wilson's *Daily Mail* interview was that it was 'a gratuitous display of vanity'.

An important element in Labour's failure in 1983 was that Labour governments had in some respects helped to create a public mood favourable to the thrust of Conservative policy. Thus, for example, Labour had subscribed to the idea that inflation was the most pressing of economic problems, without at the same time criticising the extent to which the economy was distorted by heavy military spending. The effect was to encourage the idea that the main problem was the strength of the unions, and that this problem could only be tackled effectively by curbing the so-called power of the unions.

Similarly, in the very final stages of the Callaghan Government the idea was given currency that the principal cause of the rise in unemployment was inflation, and that Britain could not 'spend' its way out of a recession. In reality, the very opposite was nearer the truth. To 'spend' on investment would not only have created jobs but it would have provided a basis for longer-term recovery.

None of these criticisms can be levelled at the manner in which Michael Foot led the Labour Party in the 1983 General Election. He had to face not only a cruel campaign of personal denigration but also a shameless advertising campaign by the Conservative Party which distorted Labour's policies.

Michael Foot did everything he could to win support for the Party's policy. He could not, of course, overcome the known division of views between some of the Party's prominent leaders, nor the inconsistencies in the Party's policy from one period to another relating, for example, to nuclear weapons, the Common Market, trade union rights, incomes policy, the causes of inflation and the means to deal with it. These known divisions of opinion and inconsistencies in policy served to reinforce the public impression of disunity following the break-away of the SDP.

Nor was it possible to take from Mrs Thatcher the widespread public perception of her as a determined leader with a pronounced sense of commitment. This perception had been strengthened during the Falklands war, when the Labour Party had given support to her policy. My personal view at that time was that more might have been done by using the machinery of the United Nations to resolve the issue without the use of force. It was, however, a difficult decision, and there was certainly no assurance that the use of UN machinery would have led to a satisfactory solution. I respected the view of Michael Foot that when faced by aggression from a reactionary dictator there is no acceptable alternative but to stand firm.

The argument about the Falklands conflict was, nevertheless, complicated by the surrounding circumstances. Britain, in my view, had no moral right to the Falklands as an outpost of empire thousands of miles from Britain's shores. Admittedly the views of the population, no more than about 2,000 in number, were in favour of Britain, because the settlers were nearly all of British extraction, but the existence of the settle-ment could not be divorced from the history of colonial conquest. Since the sixteenth century Britain, Spain and the USA had all been involved in the control of the Falklands. On the other hand, the Argentinean government used the issue as a means of diverting domestic attention from their appalling record on human rights and on social policy.

387

Attitude Towards the Unions

One of the issues of the 1983 General Election on which Labour was on the defensive was that of trade union rights. The argument that 'the power of the unions had to be curbed' found a response among a substantial section of the public. This was confirmed at the time by the private opinion polls conducted by the Labour Party. This hostility was hardly surprising, given the criticisms made of the unions not only by the Conservative Party and Mrs Thatcher's government but by the Labour Government during the Winter of Discontent and the persistent campaign conducted against the unions by a substantial part of the press.

My view on the appropriate way to deal with this problem was for the Labour Party to present its proposals for employment protection and workers' rights by emphasising the democratic need to redress the existing economic imbalance of power in favour of employers. In this way Labour could present its proposals within a policy framework which it believed to be right and which did not convey the impression that the Party was on the defensive about trade unionism.

In my foreword on the 1983 General Election, published in the report of the National Executive Committee to the annual conference, I stated:

'No socialist worthy of the traditions of the Labour movement should refuse, on occasions, to go against a strong current of public opinion if in so doing he believes such a course is necessary for the purpose of social progress.'

At the 1983 Labour Party conference I went further in support of the view that there should be no compromise on the defence of employment rights and trade union rights. I said:

'I do not believe we should yield one inch on this issue. We have to defend trade unionism; we have to point out that trade unionism is essential for the protection of working people. To put it in my own terms, I believe that the labour

388

movement stands for the right of working people to organise in trade unions; the right to bargain collectively; the
right to withdraw labour if necessary (that is not an advocacy of strikes but a recognition that workers have a right
to strike if they have no other way of resolving their problems); the right of solidarity action; and the right of trade
unions to conduct their own affairs without state interference. All these rights are being undermined by the Conservative Government, and the labour movement must put
itself four square behind trade unionism in the defence of
these fundamental civic rights.'

During the years since 1983 there have been a succession of
attacks on employment rights and trade union rights. By the
beginning of 1998 not one of the fundamental rights to which I
referred at the 1983 Labour Party conference was satisfactorily
upheld in British law. Indeed, one very important right, that of
solidarity in industrial action, had been made unlawful except
in the most narrowly defined circumstances.

One of the arguments used to support the limitation of trade
union rights is that in an industrial dispute there are not only
two parties involved, the employer and the employees, but
three parties, and the third party is the public. The curbing of
trade union rights is essential, it is suggested, to protect the
public interest.

There are two legitimate responses to this argument. The
first is that there should be no assumption that in an industrial
dispute the responsibility for the conflict lies with a trade
union. If a union is denied recognition for negotiating
purposes, the real responsibility for the conflict lies with the
employer. Similarly, if a trade union representative is victimised for trade union activity, it is the employer who has
precipitated the dispute. An even more frequent cause of
disputes is the unilateral act of a manager or employer in
seeking to change the terms and conditions of employment
without agreement or, in the absence of agreement, without
exhausting whatever negotiating arrangements exist or should
exist. Even in a dispute about pay it is unrealistic to suggest

that the responsibility rests exclusively with a trade union. It takes both the employer and the employees to make an acceptable contract of employment. As the law stands in Britain, the balance of power is heavily weighted on the side of the employer.

The second legitimate response to those who suggest that there should be public intervention to protect the public interest in industrial disputes is that this intervention should be designed to help the resolution of disputes. This requires not the suppression of workers' rights but their proper recognition, including the encouragement of collective bargaining, the development of collective bargaining machinery and the provision of voluntary conciliation in disputes. This was part of the purpose of the Advisory, Conciliation and Arbitration Service when it was established by the 1974 Labour Government.

Organisation

For the 1983 General Election the Campaign Committee of the Labour Party decided at an early stage to appoint an agency, Wright and Partners, to prepare ideas for the presentation of Labour's policy to the electorate. The aim was – to use the jargon of the day – to give the Party's campaign a 'professional image'. It is, of course, important always to present the Party's policies as effectively as possible, but it is also essential to recognise that presentation cannot be divorced from the political content of a campaign. Wright and Partners were regarded as competent in their field, and the two partners dealing with the General Election account were both members of the Labour Party. Wright and Partners had already done previous work for the Party.

The agency conducted enquiries about the kind of message that was likely to prove most attractive to electors. The suggestion was that the electorate wanted and would respond to positive proposals from Labour, rather than negative attacks on the record of the Conservative Government. I shared the view of colleagues that there was substance in this finding, but

I was not enthusiastic when it was decided to use as the main slogan for the election: 'Think Positive, Act Positive, Vote Labour'. It seemed to me to be almost meaningless in content.

In the discussion at the National Executive Committee on the report of the Campaign Committee, Frank Allaun expressed disappointment at the choice of the main slogan. He suggested instead: 'For jobs and peace: vote Labour'. His suggestion was not accepted by the NEC. In my view, however, it would have been preferable. It satisfied the requirement that Labour should be positive and that its main slogan should have political content.

Labour entered the 1983 General Election with a seriously depleted force of full-time constituency agents. At one time Labour had something like 300 full-time agents. By 1983 there were less than 70. This reduction took place over a number of years. It was the result of the Party's financial problems, which, in turn, reflected a decline of activity and enthusiasm among sections of the rank-and-file membership. Those who belittle the importance of maintaining the enthusiasm of the membership, based primarily on political consciousness, do not always grasp the full consequences of their standpoint. Enthusiasm is more easily maintained when Labour is seen to offer a clear, distinctive and radical alternative to the Conservative Party. Consensus politics on a range of issues are damaging to Labour Party activity.

There were, nevertheless, outstanding examples of success in maintaining the agency service and in providing a substantial financial income to the Party. Some of the East Anglian constituencies were particularly noteworthy for the success they achieved. Their success was all the more remarkable because East Anglia was not a Labour stronghold, though Labour's vote was usually higher than might otherwise have been expected. In Scotland, on the other hand, Labour's electoral strength in some constituencies was not reflected in the size of local party membership or activity.

When at the 1983 Party conference Russell Tuck of the National Union of Railwaymen replied on behalf of the NEC to the debate on Party organisation, he said:

'... we require an increase in the number of paid agents.... The National Executive Committee has accepted it; the commission of enquiry on the last occasion accepted it. A correction was made this morning. It is not 70 – the delegate was right – it is 63, I believe, at the present moment, down from 300. These are the people who keep the machine working all the time; these are the people who are the backbone of the organisation during the election. If we only have 60, one in ten for all the constituencies in the country, we are starting every election with our hands tied behind our backs...'

As in every general election campaign, so in 1983 the Party received substantial financial assistance from the unions. More than £2,250,000 was contributed to the central fund from the political funds of affiliated trade unions. Over £500,000 was provided by the TGWU, and over £300,000 by the GMB. NUPE was also a substantial contributor with £220,000. In proportion to membership, the National Union of Mineworkers was among the most generous of contributors. They donated more than £234,000.

The administration of the fund was in the hands of a special committee which met regularly both before and during the General Election campaign. John Bull of NUPE acted as the chairman of this committee, though he was not a member of the NEC of the party. He played an outstanding role in managing the affairs of the fund. The committee reported regularly to the main campaign committee, and was able to report at the end of the campaign that the Party had not only covered its expenses but had emerged with a surplus.

During the Election campaign of 1983 the majority of national newspapers displayed their usual bias against the Labour Party. Some conducted a personal campaign designed to discredit Michael Foot, and most underplayed any news which pointed to the gravity of Britain's economic problems. They also joined in fostering the impression that Labour was being overtaken by the Liberal-Social Democratic Alliance.

This they saw as a self-fulfilling prediction, designed to bring about a switch of votes from Labour to the Alliance.

On 16 May, 1983, at the beginning of the Election campaign, the *Daily Mail* carried a front-page lead story to the effect that the Japanese car manufacturer, Nissan, would abandon plans for a £500,000,000 British plant if Labour won the Election. It said that up to 35,000 jobs were at stake, many in areas of high unemployment which were Labour strongholds. The story was headed '35,000 jobs lost if Foot wins', and was supported on the same day by a *Daily Mail* editorial.

On the following day the *Daily Mail* published on its front page various comments on its earlier report of alleged job losses if Labour won the election. Readers were left with the impression that Nissan's withdrawal from Britain would probably be confirmed, but the *Daily Mail* acknowledged that a Nissan spokesman in Tokyo 'would not confirm that a general election victory for Labour would mean Nissan pulling out.'

Other newspapers gave little or no credit to the story. Nissan officials in Tokyo described as 'utterly groundless' the story that they would refuse to invest in Britain if Labour won the election. *The Observer* made special efforts to check the facts, and its Industrial Editor reported that the *Daily Mail* story 'appears to be utterly without foundation'. A particularly relevant observation was made by Lord Marsh, who was described as a 'consultant to Nissan about a UK car-making plant'. He was reported as saying: 'There could be no possible truth in the story published in the *Daily Mail*'. He 'formally, officially and totally denied' that Nissan would refuse to locate a factory in Britain if the Labour Party won the General Election.

The Labour Party decided, after consultation among a number of its leaders, that a letter of complaint should be sent to the *Daily Mail*. It was published by the *Daily Mail* though it did not, of course, receive anywhere near the same prominence as the original and follow-up stories. A complaint was also sent to the Press Council, on the grounds that the *Daily Mail* story appeared to be a fabrication designed to deter citizens from voting for the Labour Party.

At the Press Council's hearing of the complaint the Labour Party submitted a letter from Moss Evans, the General Secretary of the TGWU, recording that in 1981 on a visit to Tokyo he had discussed with the President of Nissan possible investment by the company in Britain. Further discussions with Nissan representatives had been held in Britain during the following year. No reference had been made in these discussions to any fear that Nissan might have about investment in Britain related to Labour's policy and Britain's membership of the European Economic Community.

The *Daily Mail* defended its publication of the story on the grounds that information had been supplied to its motoring correspondent, a journalist of long experience, by a personal contact high inside the Nissan organisation in Europe. The *Daily Mail* was not prepared to disclose the name of its source, but its motoring correspondent produced his shorthand notes to confirm that he had spoken to his contact. I represented the Labour Party at the Press Council enquiry and, after listening to the evidence, accepted that the motoring correspondent was an honest witness and had received information to form the basis of his story. This, however, did not justify the manner in which the story had been presented.

The adjudication of the Press Council was:

'The council concludes that the published story on 16 May, 1983, was not a fabrication. Mr Mortimer, on behalf of the Labour Party, having heard Mr Kemp's evidence, accepted that he was an honest witness and that he did have an interview and a telephone conversation with sources close to the Nissan organisation in Europe.

'Insofar as the first complaint is founded on fabrication it is rejected.

'But the council finds that the headlines and the introductory paragraph and presentation were not sufficiently qualified and were likely to mislead readers into believing that if Labour won the General Election the Nissan management had decided to abandon plans to open a British plant.

'The council considers that the story as presented apart from its first paragraph was reasonable conjecture from the information supplied to Mr Kemp. The headlines and opening paragraph, however, improperly presented conjecture as fact and omitted the vital connection between a Labour victory and withdrawal from the EEC.

'To this extent the first complaint is upheld.

'The council further finds that although no formal denial was issued by Nissan, insufficient prominence was given the following day to their refusal to confirm that a Labour general election victory would mean Nissan pulling out, and to a statement by a company spokesman that if Labour got to power that event would not substantially affect Nissan's proposals.

'Accordingly, the Labour Party's second complaint against the *Daily Mail* is upheld.

'It is fair to add that as soon as the Labour Party wrote to the *Daily Mail* to complain (which complaint was not received until 26 May, 1983) the newspaper published the letter in full.'

Perhaps the final words on the 1983 General Election should be left to two prominent speakers at the Labour Party conference. One was Sam McCluskie of the then National Union of Seamen. He was the Chairman of the 1983 national Party conference. In his opening address from the chair, he said that Labour did not lose the Election because of its policies but because of internal strife and lack of unity. The British people, he said, would not elect Labour if the Party continued to give the impression that its leaders were at each other's throats all the time. Internal arguments in the preceding years had done a disservice that would live with the British people for some time. He went on to give one example of the disunity of the Party; it was around the commitment to nuclear disarmament. He described himself as a committed unilateralist and pointed out that the Party's official policy was that Polaris would be included in the disarmament negotiations, that the Trident programme would be cancelled and that Labour would seek to prevent the deployment in Britain and in Europe of Cruise and Pershing missiles. The Party's defence policy, said Sam McCluskie, was 'never argued to its fullest extent' and could be read as 'meaning everything to anyone and everything to everybody'.

In the light of later developments, when Labour under Neil Kinnock embarked on a far-reaching review of policy, Barbara Castle's warning words to the conference were also timely. She said:

> 'We cannot launch our comeback on a reversal of all the policies on which we fought the General Election. That would be a very curious way of demonstrating conviction politics.'

She said that in relation to the EEC she was 'not prepared to say to Roy Jenkins, Shirley Williams and the rest of the Gang of Four that on the Common Market they were right and we were wrong. Because it is not true. All my experience in the European parliament for the past four years has validated everything the Labour Party said about the Treaty of Rome and the disadvantages to this country of membership on the present terms.'

Labour subsequently changed many of its policies in the direction originally advocated by the SDP's Gang of Four. Nevertheless, despite the continued decline of the British economy, high unemployment and ever-widening inequality, Labour lost the two subsequent General Elections in 1987 and 1992. The loss could not be blamed, as in 1983, primarily on disunity. Labour failed to convince the electorate that its policy offered an effective alternative.

By 1997 the Conservative Party was discredited in the eyes of many voters. There was sleaze in high places, disunity over Europe, a widening gap between rich and poor and widespread criticism of public services. There was a mood for change. In the 1997 General Election Labour was elected with about 44 per cent support on a relatively low turnout.

19

The Miners' Strike 1984–85

Of the various events that took place during my period as
General Secretary of the Labour Party, the one that aroused
my strongest feelings was the miners' strike of 1984–85. I
valued the opportunity throughout the strike to express
support for the miners on behalf of the National Executive
Committee of the Party, to witness the immense outburst of
solidarity from the rank and file of the Party and to help
organise this solidarity. I also had the opportunity to participate in many extremely well-attended meetings and rallies in
support of the miners in different parts of Britain.

The strike could, in my view, have been won if the miners
had received the support they deserved. That they did not
receive this support was due primarily to failings among
some of the leaders of the Labour and trade union
movement. Certainly their hesitations helped to foster doubts
among some workers, whose support in solidarity action was
vital for success. This criticism, however, is by no means
directed against all in the leadership of the Labour Party and
the main unions. There were many who, within the circumstances of their unions, did everything that they could to
bring success. The leaders of the two big general workers'
unions, the TGWU and the GMB, together with ASLEF, the
seamen and many of the unions affiliated to the TUC,
sought, often with success, to encourage solidarity action.
The electricians' leaders, on the other hand, who were strategically placed in the dispute, permitted their criticisms of the
leadership and policies of the NUM to weigh more heavily
than their sense of solidarity with tens of thousands of

miners who were fighting for their jobs and their communities.

In the Labour Party there was a contrast between the attitude of the National Executive Committee and the parliamentary leadership, though even within the Shadow Cabinet there were a number, notably Stan Orme, who sought energetically to bring about an acceptable settlement. Some in the Shadow Cabinet who were also on the NEC of the Party were less critical of the miners' leaders at NEC meetings than they were at Shadow Cabinet meetings. On the NEC they would have encountered counter-criticism of their attitude.

The NEC of the Party adopted resolutions of support for the miners on a number of occasions during the dispute, and encouragement was given to the holding of solidarity meetings throughout Britain. Calls were also made for collections to assist miners and their families, and Party members were asked to contribute to a weekly levy. Large sums of money were raised by the efforts of the Labour Party. The response of the Labour Party membership and of hundreds of thousands of supporters was an inspiration to all of us among the staff at Walworth Road, the Party headquarters, who felt strongly about the mining dispute. The response revealed what immense power there is in the labour movement when people are aroused by the example of workers engaged in a struggle for a just cause.

The criticism of the main parliamentary leadership was that they failed to identify themselves firmly with the movement of support for the miners. They were hesitant and reluctant in their support, and they regarded the dispute as an embarrassment to their efforts to portray themselves as a responsible Opposition, not closely identified with trade unionism and even less with the leadership of the NUM. In my view, these considerations guided their actions and they failed to grasp the historic significance of the struggle of the miners against the destructive policy of the Conservative Government.

There was no such failure on the part of Mrs Thatcher and her colleagues. They saw the true significance of the dispute. In their view, a defeat for the miners would inflict a crippling blow on the entire trade union and labour movement. It would make it much easier for the Conservative Government to carry through its economic policies and its anti-union measures.

Because of the support given by the NEC of the Party to the miners throughout the dispute, I was able, without any real problems, to identify my own attitude and, as far as it was within my power to do so, the machinery of the Party with the miners' cause. I was deeply disappointed by the parliamentary leadership, but my responsibility was primarily to the NEC.

Part of the duties of the General Secretary was to attend the regular weekly meetings of the Shadow Cabinet, and I was well aware that the misgivings of the predominant section of the parliamentary leadership about Arthur Scargill, Michael McGahey and Peter Heathfield were inhibiting the important task of mobilising maximum support for the tens of thousands of miners and their families in the titanic struggle in which they were engaged.

Even from the standpoint of the parliamentary Party, it did not seem to me that the attitude of the predominant section of the parliamentary leadership was wise. The defeat of the miners was likely to give a boost to the Government in many directions. It would dishearten the labour movement and help to persuade some workers that trade unionism could be defeated when faced with a tough employer backed by a reactionary government. It would also, I felt, give credibility to the effectiveness of anti-union laws and widespread police intervention in a dispute. More than 10,000 miners were arrested during the strike, and the police were mobilised on a national scale to prevent the free movement of miners from one area to another.

The defeat of the miners would also, as I saw it, provide a frightening example of the successful intervention of the courts to declare unlawful a strike which had been given official support. The strike in Yorkshire, for example, was declared unlawful, even though it was supported by the Yorkshire Area Council of the NUM and by almost the entire workforce of the area. It would also provide the most damaging example so far of the draconian effect of the legal sequestration of union funds in the course of a dispute.

On wider industrial and economic grounds there were also, in my view, the strongest reasons for vigorous parliamentary support for the miners. The policy of the Government, not only in mining but also in other industries, was destroying jobs and diminishing Britain's industrial base. The struggle of working people against unemployment is a vital element of political opposition. It cannot and should not be divorced from the use of Parliament as a platform for the denunciation of destructive policies. Popular struggle and effective parliamentary opposition are not opposed each to the other; nor are they alternatives. They should be seen as complementary.

I did not question that Neil Kinnock and others who shared his point of view were convinced that the Government's policies on coal were wrong and that they wanted to see those policies reversed. But history does not always present these problems on a stage of one's own choosing. In the language of the street: 'When the chips are down, you have to decide whose side you are on.' The mining dispute was of truly historic significance, and it was deliberately precipitated by the enemies of organised labour.

During the dispute the Labour Party was approached by the NUM to provide an official speaker for four main rallies to be organised in Yorkshire, Scotland, the North-East and South Wales. It would have been preferable for the Party to have been represented at these rallies by either the Leader or the Deputy Leader. The NUM would have been very pleased to have had such support. It was not to be. I recall that Neil Kinnock had other engagements. I was then invited to represent the Party and to speak at each of the rallies. I willingly accepted, and rearranged my diary accordingly. I did not regret it, either then or later.

The four national miners' rallies were not, of course, the only big meetings to be organised during the strike. Many demonstrations, marches and local meetings took place in almost every part of Britain. I attended and either spoke or otherwise participated in a number of them. Even in Tory strongholds, meetings in support of the miners attracted large audiences. Everywhere people were ready to show their sympathy for the miners and to give money for the support of miners' families. Collecting baskets were organised outside many supermarkets, and a substantial proportion of shoppers readily donated a package or tin of food to be sent to the mining areas. In thousands of workplaces regular donations and levies were organised. I have never known a cause to which the public so readily responded with gifts. At the Labour Party headquarters I had the feeling that the sleeping giant of the labour movement had come to life.

The four national miners' rallies in Yorkshire, Scotland, the North-East and South Wales were each packed to the door. Support for the NUM and its leadership was very strongly evident. At the South Wales rally, held in Port Talbot, the press made much of an indefensible incident directed against Neil Kinnock. Those responsible were no more than an extremely tiny group. They dangled a symbolic noose from roof rafters. They were wrong in what they did, and their action served only to give a hostile press the opportunity to attack the miners' struggle and to point to differences within the top level of the labour movement.

After these four national rallies a further rally was organised to take place in the Midlands, with the participation of Neil Kinnock. I gained the impression – though I was not party to the detailed arrangements – that a principal organiser of this further rally was John Golding. From the gossip at Labour Party headquarters I soon learned that special care was being taken to ensure that critical miners from Yorkshire and South Wales were, as far as possible, to be excluded. It was an all-ticket demonstration. I thought it was helpful, nevertheless, that agreement had been reached for Neil Kinnock to speak with Arthur Scargill at a miners' rally. John Golding deserved credit for his part in making it possible.

The cause of the mining dispute of 1984–85 was the determination of the Government, expressed through the policy of the National Coal Board, to run down the coal-mining industry through a programme of pit closures. This programme could not be justified on economic or social grounds. It was not a programme of closures confined to pits where coal reserves had been exhausted or where the geology was such that coal could not be mined economically. It was a programme dictated by the Government's determination to reduce the capacity of the industry to but a fraction of its potentiality, and in so doing to throw tens of thousands of miners out of their jobs and to devastate many mining communities.

The person who most clearly and emphatically warned the public of the Government's real intention was Arthur Scargill, the President of the NUM. Nothing can take this away from him.

Those who thought at the time that he was exaggerating the extent of the threat to the mining industry have been proved wrong. If anything, even Arthur Scargill's forecasts have been modest in comparison with the appalling reality of the Conservative Government's subsequent actions.

The dispute about the closure of pits did not start in March 1984, but the announcement on 1 March that the Cortonwood colliery in South Yorkshire was to be closed almost immediately was the lighted fuse that precipitated the strike. The announcement took the miners and the Yorkshire officials of the NUM by surprise. They had previously been assured that the pit had a long-term future. At least £1,000,000 had been invested on improvements only a few months earlier. Miners displaced from another colliery had recently been transferred to Cortonwood. The pit did not have a particular reputation for militancy.

The NUM officials and the miners at Cortonwood saw the impending closure as a new turn in NCB policy, probably dictated by the Government. There was no suggestion that the pit was exhausted or that the extracted coal was expensive. The purpose was to contract the industry. If the closure of Cortonwood were accepted without resistance, no pit in the Yorkshire coalfield would be safe.

Within days of the announcement of the closure, the miners at Cortonwood decided at a mass meeting to resist. They called upon the Yorkshire Area Council to support strike action, and reminded the delegates that in 1981 the Yorkshire miners had voted overwhelmingly in a coalfield ballot to support action against the closure of viable pits. Miners at other pits rapidly demonstrated their solidarity with the men from Cortonwood, and the strike in the coalfield was supported by the Area Council.

Eric Heffer, other officials from Walworth Road and I visited the village of Brampton, where the Cortonwood colliery was located. Eric was at that time the national Chairman of the Party, and was very firmly in support of the miners. I discussed the mining dispute with him frequently, and our attitudes were identical. We agreed that if we had been miners at Cortonwood we would have supported strike action. Similarly, if we had been delegates to the Yorkshire Area Council or if we had been officials of the Yorkshire Area, we would have had no hesitation in supporting solidarity action. We both felt that it would be totally inconsistent if we failed to make clear our total commitment to the miners' struggle. Eric Heffer never wavered throughout the dispute, and I valued very much his support and encouragement.

The visit to Brampton was a moving experience. We spoke to miners and their wives and went to a communal feeding centre in the village. The impending closure of the pit had devastated their lives. The chances of new employment were very limited. Most of the men with whom we spoke had young families, and they had planned their future in the expectation, confirmed to them previously by the National Coal Board, that their pit was not under threat.

NEC Policy

At the first meeting of the NEC of the Labour Party held after the beginning of the strike at Cortonwood, full support was expressed for the miners. It was not only the members of the NUM in the Yorkshire coalfield who were in dispute, but there was also a strike in Scotland against the closure of the Polmaise colliery. Under the rules of the NUM the National

403

Executive Committee of the union were empowered to endorse strike action in particular areas. This they had done in response to requests from Yorkshire and Scotland.

The resolution of the Labour Party NEC adopted in March 1984 not only supported the miners but also expressed 'deep concern at the extent of the police operation in the current mining dispute, which, from press, radio and television reports appears designed to prevent picketing at collieries'. It went on to point out that the right to picket peacefully was lawful and 'must, therefore, be upheld by the police'. The resolution deplored all forms of violence and added that the massive police presence had contributed to it. In particular, the resolution protested against the decision of police chief constables to interfere with the free movement of the British people 'by giving instructions to the police to arrest bus drivers and miners' pickets from Yorkshire, Kent and elsewhere'. By giving permission to chief constables to act as they had done, the Home Secretary had committed a serious breach of the 'traditional and normal practices of the country'. The resolution concluded by demanding that the right to picket peacefully and to move freely within the country should be upheld. It made the important point that it was not the job of the police to regard civil liability under the Employment Act as grounds to justify the prevention of peaceful picketing.

The resolution of the Labour Party NEC was, as far as I recall, adopted without anyone voting against it. It also expressed my own point of view. Together with tens of thousands of other Labour supporters in the country, I was deeply disappointed at what we felt to be the half-hearted manner in which the parliamentary leadership subsequently gave voice to the Party's official policy.

At the meeting of the NEC of the Party held in May support for the miners in their struggle against pit closures was reaffirmed. The resolution adopted by the NEC drew attention to the determined efforts of the Government to defeat the miners, including the establishment of a 'War Cabinet', the buying of extra oil for the power stations and the 'penal operation and manipulation of the social security payments system'.

404

The Government, the resolution said, were trying to starve the miners back to work. The NEC of the Party called upon all members to levy themselves to raise money for the support of the miners.

During my visits to mining areas I found that the Government's manipulation of social security payments to the detriment of miners' families caused intense feelings of bitterness. It was not only that miners themselves were denied benefit because they were involved in a dispute, but the Government reduced the benefit payable for dependants, including a wife and children, on the grounds that miners were receiving a notional payment from the union. In fact, no such payment was made and would have been beyond the resources of the NUM. On a number of occasions I heard miners and their wives comment that mining families were being treated worse under the social security system than the families of convicted murderers. This was a living example of the creation of a legacy of human bitterness.

The cooperative efforts of mining communities to sustain the minimum means of existence during the year-long dispute was a testimony to all that is good in human nature. The communal feeding centres and the soup kitchens were maintained without any motivation of private advantage or profit. Tribute needs also to be paid to the efforts of countless numbers of trade unionists and other sympathisers in every walk of life, who ensured that every week donations and food were sent to mining communities.

At its meeting in May 1984 the NEC of the Labour Party not only reaffirmed its support for the NUM but, significantly, welcomed the decision of the Shadow Cabinet to press for a full day's immediate parliamentary debate on a motion on the mining industry. This affirmation not only expressed approval of the decision to press for a parliamentary debate but also gave vent to a sense of frustration on the part of a number of members of the NEC that it had taken so long for such a decision to be reached.

The NEC also commended the efforts of Stan Orme MP, Labour's energy spokesman, to establish a basis for discussions between the NUM and the National Coal Board. Though these efforts did not succeed in bringing a settlement, this was not due to any failing on the part of Stan Orme. He worked hard to achieve his purpose, and he was strongly committed to finding a conclusion to the dispute that would protect the future of the coal mining industry and mining communities. The basic problem, as throughout the dispute, was that the Government were determined that there should be no settlement except on terms that left the way clear for a drastic curtailment of the mining industry and defeat for the miners.

At the May meeting of the NEC attention was drawn to the manner in which the social security system was being manipulated by the Government as a weapon to drive the miners back to work. Each week £15 was being deducted from the benefit payable for dependants, on the pretence that miners were receiving this 'notional' amount of strike pay. Miners' wives were being denied their entitlement to family income support on the false assumption that family income remained at the level of six months earlier, before the imposition of an overtime ban by miners in support of their dispute with the NCB. Discretionary maternity benefits were also denied to some miners' wives, and the payment of supplementary benefits was delayed. Other cases were also reported of deductions from benefits payable to miners' families, on the grounds that they were receiving gifts of food and other essentials through communal feeding centres, soup kitchens and other solidarity measures.

In May the TUC-Labour Party Liaison Committee expressed deep concern at the attempt by the NCB, abetted by the Government, to force through a programme of pit closures. In June the Liaison Committee, increasingly conscious of the role of the Government in preventing any kind of discussions that might lead to a settlement, called upon the NCB to ignore Government pressure and to resume talks immediately with the NUM. In the same month, June, the NEC of the Labour Party decided to consult urgently with the NUM, with a view to launching a joint national campaign to publicise the full strength of the miners' case against pit closures.

TUC Policy

At the 1984 congress of the TUC a statement was adopted
which, if it had been fully implemented by all unions, would
have represented a major step forward towards creating the
conditions for a settlement. It read:

'The General Council condemn the NCB's efforts abetted
by the Government to run down the coal industry and
affirm total support for the following:
'1) support for the National Union of Mineworkers' objectives of saving pits, jobs and mining communities:
'2) a concerted campaign to raise money to alleviate hardship in the coalfields and to maintain the union financially:
'3) to make the dispute more effective by:
  a) not moving coal or coke, or oil substituted for coal
     or coke across NUM official picket lines, or using
     such materials taken across NUM official picket lines;
  b) not using oil which is substituted for coal.
'The NUM acknowledges that the practical implementation
of these points will need detailed discussions with the
General Council and agreement with unions who would be
directly concerned.
'The General Council call for a fresh commitment of all to
an expanding coal industry.
'The General Council call on the NCB to resume negotiations immediately with the NUM to resolve this damaging
and costly dispute in line with the Plan For Coal.'

In moving this statement on behalf of the General Council, the
General Secretary of the TUC, Len Murray, made a good
speech and pointed the way forward towards securing a satisfactory settlement. He called for support for the NUM in its
effort to protect jobs and mining communities, and pointed out
that the fight was 'to protect the nation's coal reserves for the
twenty-first century'. He paid tribute to the stand being made
by miners, their wives and families, and then said that the
purpose of the General Council was 'to bring concentrated

power of the movement to bear on the National Coal Board and the Government, to get the Board back to the negotiating table and to ensure that it does so in a frame of mind to make an agreement.'

Len Murray was specific in explaining what was expected of unions in support of the miners. He said that they would be expected, where necessary, to take action in support of the miners. There would be problems, but the option of standing aside was 'not there'. The whole trade union movement, he said, 'must be aware of the serious consequences for all if the movement fails to give proper support that the NUM needs and is defeated in this dispute'.

Len Murray was followed by Arthur Scargill, who stated that the cause of the dispute was the announcement by Mr MacGregor, the NCB Chairman, of a closure programme in violation of a signed agreement between the Government, the NCB and the NUM. The initial programme was to close 20 pits with the loss of 20,000 jobs, but the real objective was to close 70 pits and to wipe out 70,000 jobs. How right he was, except that even he, Arthur Scargill, underestimated the extent of the eventual butchery of the industry!

Arthur Scargill went on to emphasise that the Government's intention was not only to defeat the NUM but to inflict a defeat on the entire trade union and labour movement. He expressed appreciation for the support given by a number of unions, and emphasised that the General Council of the TUC were calling for the movement of coal, oil and oil substitutes to be stopped. Arthur Scargill also referred to the thousands of miners who in the course of the dispute had been arrested. Over 90 per cent of them had no previous connection with the police and no criminal record. In addition, more than 3,000 members of the NUM had been injured in the dispute and five men had died; two whilst travelling to a picket line, one whilst working voluntarily underground to save his pit, and two on picket lines.

Supporting speeches were made on behalf of the National Union of Railwaymen, the National Union of Seamen, the two general workers' unions, ASLEF, the furniture workers, the engineering workers, Sogat and the distributive workers. Jimmy Knapp of the NUR paid tribute to the many railwaymen who had already refused to move coal in Lancashire and Nottinghamshire and had refused to move imported coal. He dealt also with the charge that the strike of the NUM had been politically motivated. It was the Government, he explained, that had planned for six years to defeat the miners. Nicholas Ridley had first presented the plan to the Conservative Party in 1978. His plan had contained the very measures that the Government had implemented.

Strong opposition to the General Council's statement was expressed by Eric Hammond on behalf of the Electrical, Electronic, Telecommunication and Plumbing Union. He alleged that the majority of the General Council had voted for the proposal to stop the movement of coal, oil and oil substitutes only in the expectation that it would be ineffective. They relied, he said, on the power workers to disagree. He went on to explain that in May, when the talks between the NUM and the NCB had broken down, he had sought to find a basis on which his union could take action in support of the miners. He had made it clear that the EETPU was opposed to violence and opposed to the use of strikes to bring down elected governments. He asked the NUM to disavow overt political objectives and to unite their union in a national ballot.

Eric Hammond's opposition to the General Council's call for solidarity action was also supported by John Lyons on behalf of the Engineers' and Managers' Association. He said bluntly that the members of his union employed in electricity supply and distribution would not take the action called for by the General Council. The reason, he said, was simple: 'the electricity supply industry is not, and never has been, available to solve industrial disputes external to it, not even for the miners'.

A rather different note, though still one of opposition to the call for solidarity action, was sounded by the spokesman for the blastfurnacemen. He alleged that if fuel supplies were stopped the steel industry in Britain would be destroyed. It was in competition with the rest of the world, and there was already over-capacity of production. He called for further consultation with the steel unions, and concluded by stressing that the blastfurnacemen supported the miners and did not want to see them lose.

In their reply to the discussion, both Arthur Scargill and Len Murray answered some of the objections made to the General Council's call for solidarity. Arthur Scargill said that the NUM had not sought the dispute. They had become involved because of the political decision of the Government. Ian MacGregor had been appointed as Chairman of the NCB to do to British Coal what he had already done to British Steel and British Leyland. The anti-trade unions laws and mass unemployment made it more difficult to fight back, and the Government expected to be able to isolate and then defeat the miners.

Len Murray, in his reply, acknowledged that there were difficulties in organising solidarity action, but the dispute 'would not go away'. It had to be settled, and the unions had to give every assistance they could to secure a speedy settlement. The statement submitted by the General Council was overwhelmingly approved by the TUC.

Neil Kinnock addressed the same congress of the TUC. In his speech he referred at some length to the mining dispute. I thought it was a disappointing speech because it did not provide a clear expression of support for the struggle of the miners, and it gave unjustified emphasis to the condemnation of violence, as though many miners had initiated violence on picket lines. This condemnation of violence, was, of course, exactly what the Tory press wanted to hear and to report. Whatever the intention of Neil Kinnock, the amount of time he devoted to the denunciation of violence served the purpose of those who, in a hostile media, wanted to discredit the strike.

The condemnation of violence should, in any case, have pointed in the first place to the violation of the rights of the mining community. Promises of continued employment had been broken, the future of whole communities was under threat, the police had been mobilised in an unprecedented manner, the free movement of miners from one area to another had been interrupted, the social security system had been

410

manipulated to impose severe hardship on miners' families, and the courts had been used to prevent the NUM from operating as an effective trade union.

There were, on the other hand, some positive features in Neil Kinnock's address. He paid tribute to the efforts of Stan Orme to promote a settlement of the mining dispute, and he expressed his conviction that coal was not just the fuel of today but was also the fuel for the future of Britain. He referred to the prospects of energy shortage, the hazards of depending on nuclear energy and the risks of depending for supplies of fuel on some of the most unstable countries in the world.

A month later, at the 1984 annual conference of the Labour Party, the delegates from the constituencies and unions had the opportunity to hear Stan Orme for themselves. His was an outstanding speech. He opened by emphasising that the miners wanted a negotiated and an acceptable settlement. The solution, he suggested, should be based on the Plan for Coal, which was a tripartite agreement drawn up by a Labour Government and endorsed by the NCB and NUM. It had also been endorsed by the Conservative Government in 1981.

Stan Orme urged that the unilateral proposals of the NCB to close 20 pits and to make 20,000 miners redundant should be withdrawn. He also urged that the five pits threatened with immediate closure should be restored to production. He rejected the claim of the NCB that they should have the right to close at any time any pits which they deemed to be uneconomic. This was not in accordance with the Plan for Coal, under which each participant had conceded some sovereignty. What was at issue was the future shape of the industry, jobs now and in the next decade, and the preservation of communities. The industry could not be written off on the basis of an accounting procedure.

Stan Orme urged strongly that the agreement embodied in the Plan for Coal should be the basis for settling the dispute. He said that he had put forward a suggestion as to how the central issue of the dispute might be resolved. After discussion Arthur Scargill, Peter Heathfield and Mick McGahey had

411

accepted that his proposal was an acceptable basis to continue negotiations and, possibly, to reach an agreement. The proposal had not, however, been accepted by the NCB. In Stan Orme's opinion, this was because of the intervention of the Government. They did not want a solution to the dispute.

In his concluding remarks, Stan Orme reminded the delegates that it was not the miners or the NUM who had closed a quarter of British industry, who had created over four million unemployed and who had put anti-union legislation on the statute book. The struggle of the miners, he said, was a fight for jobs and for the preservation of communities. He closed by expressing support for the miners. It was a speech worthy of a Labour leader.

The 1984 Labour Party conference carried a statement on 'A Future for British Coal', prepared by the National Executive Committee. It expressed full support for the miners and their families in their struggle to defend the coal-mining industry. It spoke of the targets set out in the Plan for Coal and said that the Tory plan to run down the industry must be resisted. It expressed support for the policy of the TUC and its determination to make the dispute more effective. It condemned the intransigence of the NCB and said that the proposals of the Coal Board could not be justified on social, economic or environmental grounds. The cost to the nation in redundancy payments, social security benefits, lost tax revenues and extra rent and rate rebates would run into thousands of millions of pounds, and would dwarf any accountancy 'savings' made by the Coal Board in closing pits.

The NEC statement pointed out that Britain had enough coal reserves for hundreds of years ahead. These reserves would easily outlive the reserves of oil and gas. Coal could also be used as a feedstock for the production of oil and chemicals. It was the fuel of the future. The statement concluded by stating that the Labour Party would 'continue to stand shoulder to shoulder with the miners in their struggle to save the mining industry'.

Unfortunately, the call for solidarity action made by the TUC did not receive the response it deserved. The transport unions, to their credit, reaffirmed their determination to give full support, and did what was possible to implement their pledge. The steel unions, on the other hand, said that whilst they wished to assist the miners they were not able to accede to the request that coal and coke should enter steelworks only at a level sufficient to ensure the safety, care and maintenance of the equipment, but without any steel being produced. In the production and distribution of electricity the railway unions, the GMB and the TGWU did what they could to help, but the vital support of the EETPU was missing.

The weaknesses in the solidarity of some of the unions and the coolness towards the miners' struggle of the top leadership of the parliamentary Labour Party encouraged the Government in its determination to defeat the miners. The NUM indicated their readiness to accept the assistance of the Advisory, Conciliation and Arbitration Service, but there was no shift in the attitude of the NCB in their insistence that they should have the unilateral right to close any pits which they regarded as 'uneconomic'.

The policy of the NCB caused deep concern among the members of NACODS, the colliery overmen, deputies and shotfirers' union. A ballot of NACODS members resulted in a majority of 82.5 per cent in favour of strike action in opposition to the NCB's pit closure programme and the NCB's instruction that deputies must cross NUM picket lines or lose pay. This decision of the deputies alarmed the Government because, if implemented, it would have brought the industry to a standstill. Deputies have statutory responsibilities for safety.

NACODS and the NCB then entered into discussions under the auspices of ACAS for a revised colliery review procedure affecting closures. At first these discussions did not result in a settlement, and NACODS called upon its members to strike from 25 October, 1984. Before this date, however, further discussions took place between NACODS and the NCB when the NCB sought a separate agreement with NACODS. On 24 October, the day before the intended beginning of the deputies' strike, NACODS felt that sufficient progress had been made in the discussions with the NCB to call off the strike. NACODS felt that they had achieved their claim for a revised procedure. The NUM remained critical of the revised procedure and said that it was unsatisfactory.

In the meanwhile the courts had given judgments which very seriously impeded the functioning of the NUM. An application under common law, that the rules had not been properly observed, was upheld and one of the areas of the NUM was prevented from disciplining non-strikers. The strike in Yorkshire was also declared legally unofficial, and a court issued an injunction preventing the union from describing the strike as official or from trying to dissuade members from going to work or crossing picket lines. Arthur Scargill was then served with documents alleging contempt of court for statements he made that the strike was official. His view was confirmed by the National Executive of the NUM. The NUM was fined £200,000 and Arthur Scargill £1,000. An anonymous person paid Arthur Scargill's fine without his knowledge or authority.

My view was that these court judgments were a gross injustice against trade unionism in general, and against the NUM in particular. The courts were seeking to prevent the Yorkshire area of the NUM from giving official backing to the dispute, when almost every man in the coalfield was already on strike. In public statements I expressed my point of view. A writ was then served against me to prevent my repeating the statements I had made. I reported receiving the writ to the NEC of the Labour Party, and they agreed that I should be given legal support. There was an exchange of correspondence between lawyers, but nothing further developed. It was an example of the pressure being exerted to prevent the expression of opposition to legal decisions against the NUM.

When the NUM did not pay the imposed fine of £200,000 for contempt of court, a judge ordered the total sequestration of the union's funds. Moreover, legal advice received by the TUC confirmed the fear that any financial assistance given directly to the NUM would render the donors also liable to contempt of court. The full force of the machinery of state was being used to defeat the miners. A separate hardship fund was established, with separate trustees, including prominent religious leaders, to enable the hardship of mining communities to be relieved.

Throughout November and December 1984 and January and February 1985, strenuous efforts were made by the TUC to create the conditions in which a negotiated settlement might be possible. In particular, the TUC sought, with the consent of the NUM's national officers, to secure an agreed form of words which did not include explicit references to the economics of pit closures, but recognised the NCB's right to manage the industry and the NUM's right to protect its members and their employment opportunities. In February the TUC had a meeting with the Prime Minister, in which they drew attention to an NUM document which:

a) accepted the NCB's duty to manage the industry efficiently and to secure sound developments in accordance with their responsibilities;
b) confirmed the acceptance of the modified colliery review procedure as set out in the NACODS agreement;
c) accepted the NCB's responsibility to decide on the future of a colliery;
d) committed themselves to reconciliation and a restoration of relationships.

All this represented a significant shift in the position of the NUM, and – contrary to the impression created by most of the media in Britain – demonstrated that the NUM was not intransigent. It was to no avail. Further statements from the NCB appeared to retreat even from their previously declared position. The reality was that the Government were by now confident of victory and were determined to prevent a settlement on any terms which might have been acceptable to the NUM. The mobilisation of the forces of the state, the intervention of the courts, the sequestration of the funds of the NUM, the prejudiced reporting and, indeed, the hostility of the majority of the press, the manipulation of the social security system to impose severe privation on miners' families, the failure of most of the parliamentary Labour leadership to give adequate support to the miners, the formation of a breakaway union among a section of the Nottingham miners and the uneven pattern of solidarity from unions, all combined to make it impossible for a negotiated settlement to be achieved. Among miners' families there was by now very serious deprivation, with tens of thousands short of the essentials of life and burdened with mounting debt. The result was that in some areas where the strike had previously been solid there was a slow trickle of miners back to work. In the highly productive Nottingham coalfield, the majority of miners remained at work throughout the strike.

The Aftermath

On 3 March, 1985 a delegate conference of the NUM voted to end the strike. A return to work took place within days. In many pits the men went back to their jobs behind their union banners. In one of the most memorable disputes in British history, the labour movement and the NUM had not succeeded in halting the destruction of the mining industry and of many mining communities. The strike had aroused an immense wave of sympathy among many British people but, with many exceptions, the vital support of sections of the trade union movement and the Labour Party leadership had been missing. Hundreds of miners were victimised by the NCB and lost their jobs. In subsequent months and years more than 90 per cent of the miners were to be made redundant in succeeding waves of industrial destructiveness by the Conservative Government. The devastation exceeded even the most dire warnings made by Arthur Scargill before and during the strike.

At the 1985 congress of the TUC there were two composite motions on the mining dispute debated by the delegates. The first was moved by Arthur Scargill on behalf of the NUM. It paid tribute to the 'heroic struggle of all who have been associated with the miners' strike of 1984–85'. It said that the NUM and its membership had been the subject of a 'concerted and vicious attack by the whole power of the state, including the unprecedented and combined strength of the police and the organised use of the judiciary...'. The motion called upon the TUC to campaign for the next Labour government to review all cases of miners imprisoned as a result of the dispute, to reinstate miners sacked for activities arising out of the dispute, to reimburse the NUM and other unions for money confiscated as a result of fines, sequestration and receivership, and to end pit closures other than for reasons of exhaustion.

In speaking in support of the motion Arthur Scargill said that 11,000 members of the NUM had been arrested during the dispute, 7,000 had been injured and 60 men were still in prison. Norman Willis, the General Secretary of the TUC, speaking on behalf of the General Council, called for the rejection of the motion moved by the NUM. He paid tribute to the struggle of the miners, but said that the call for the reimbursement of trade union funds confiscated as a result of fines, sequestration and receivership could not be accepted. The TUC, he suggested, should not seek to put unions 'in a special category for special treatment from a future Labour government'. Trade unions, he said, respect the law. They wanted fairer laws, but the law should not be brought into disrespect. Are we to sanction, he asked, an attitude that could well encourage a Tory government to release employers from penalties that may be needed on certain of their activities? Despite the opposition of the General Council, the composite motion moved by the NUM was carried by 4,649,000 votes to 4,585,000.

The second composite motion on the mining dispute was moved by the National Union of Railwaymen. It was supported by the TUC without a card vote. It paid tribute to the miners and their families, 'who faced starvation and privation in their struggle' against pit closures, and it protested against the erosion of civil liberties brought about by police action during the dispute. It called for continued support for mining families, including the hundreds of miners who had been victimised, and protested against decisions of the NCB

417

and British Steel to reward road hauliers for transporting coal through NUM picket lines.

In moving the composite motion, Jimmy Knapp of the NUR recalled that 75 per cent of railwaymen in Nottinghamshire and Leicestershire had refused, despite immense pressure brought to bear on them, to move coal produced during the strike. The NUR and the ASLEF still had outstanding claims for damages against them, amounting to £300,000, because of actions taken during the strike.

One month later at the 1985 Labour Party conference the arguments about the aftermath of the mining dispute were given a further hearing. The NUM tabled a motion similar to that adopted by the TUC, calling for a review of all cases of imprisoned miners, the reinstatement of sacked miners and the reimbursement to unions of funds confiscated as a result of fines, sequestration and receivership. It was again moved by Arthur Scargill. Neil Kinnock accepted the responsibility on behalf of the National Executive Committee of the Party to ask for the rejection of the motion. He made a long speech in which he said that the NEC supported the call for a review of the cases of imprisoned miners and for the reinstatement of victimised miners, but opposed the call for retrospective reimbursement.

In his speech Arthur Scargill had mentioned that in 1982 the Labour Party conference had passed by 6,800,000 votes to 66,000 a resolution 'to provide for the reimbursement of any fines levied against trade unionists as a result of Tory legal measures.' Neil Kinnock argued that this was irrelevant to the common-law procedures that inflicted the financial damage on the NUM. Was anybody seriously suggesting, he asked, that the common law should be torn up?

Neil Kinnock went on to make a number of other criticisms. He referred to the absence of a ballot among all miners, and said that as the strike wore on 'the violence built up because the single tactic chosen was that of mass picketing.' He also said that by their attitude to the court actions the NUM leadership had ensured that 'they would face crippling damages as a consequence.'

The debate, much more than the similar debate at the TUC, revealed the extent of the differing views and personal feelings between some of the principal speakers. Eric Hammond of the EETPU strongly criticised the leaders of the NUM because of the failure to hold a national ballot. He said the miners were 'lions led by donkeys'. In a speech supporting the NUM motion, Ron Todd of the TGWU said that as an animal lover he preferred donkeys to jackals. The NUM motion was carried by 3,542,000 votes to 2,912,000.

I retired from the secretaryship of the Labour Party in 1985 during my sixty-fifth year. I was glad to have had the opportunity to be at the Party's headquarters throughout the miners' strike, to express the support of the NEC of the Party for the miners, and to participate in and to help to stimulate the solidarity shown towards the miners by so many British people.

Early in 1987, after my retirement, I received a letter from Peter Heathfield, the General Secretary of the NUM, stating that the NEC of the NUM had agreed to confer on me honorary membership of the union. The letter said: 'thank you on behalf of all our members for the support you have given to this Union through some of its most difficult days'. It was and remains an honour which I greatly value.

20

Retirement – a New Opportunity

When I retired from full-time employment with the Labour Party in 1985, I looked forward to the prospect of doing whatever I wanted to do within the labour movement. I was particularly keen to complete the history of the Boilermakers' Society, which I had promised to write some years earlier. I had already completed two volumes, covering, in the first volume, the period from the formation of the union in 1834 until 1906, and, in the second volume, the period from 1906 until 1939. The two volumes had been published by George Allen and Unwin.

In the third volume, which I thought was likely to be the longest of the three when I started on it, I intended to cover the period from the outbreak of the Second World War until the amalgamation of the Boilermakers' Society with the General and Municipal Workers' Union, to form in December 1982 the General, Municipal, Boilermakers and Allied Trades Union. I was later asked by Jim McFall, the then National Secretary of the Boilermakers' section of the new union, to continue the history up to 1989, which marked the centenary of the founding union of the GMWU.

The founding union was the National Union of Gas Workers and General Labourers, which came into existence as a result of the 1889 strike of workers at the Beckton gasworks in the East End of London. This strike was led by Will Thorne, a man of extraordinary talent who, it was said, was virtually illiterate when he first went to London as an itinerant labourer in search of work. One of the people who influenced him and helped him to learn to read and write was Eleanor

Marx, the daughter of Karl Marx. Will Thorne had a long and distinguished record of service, as a leading trade unionist and Labour MP for many years after the formation of the National Union of Gasworkers and General Labourers.

The original invitation to me to write the history of the Boilermakers' Society had come from Danny McGarvey, when he was the President of the Society. In issuing the invitation he had the support of his Executive Council. I first came to know Danny McGarvey fairly closely when we were both delegates to the Metalworkers' Committee of the International Labour Organisation in Geneva. Danny had been elected to the Executive Council of the Society in 1951. The leader of the Boilermakers' Society in the 1950s was Ted Hill.

I developed a friendship with McGarvey, and we spent much time together when we were in Geneva. He was intensely interested in trade unionism and dedicated to the interests of boilermakers. He was born of a Glasgow Irish working-class family, and his ambition as a boy was to become a plater in a shipyard. Platers are responsible for the assembly of the large heavy plates which constitute the hull of a ship. There is more to it than may seem at first thought. The full range of skills associated with shipyard boilermakers include the safe handling of heavy plates, marking-out for shape and for drilling, shearing and flame-cutting, bending and rolling, riveting and welding, and caulking to make the plates watertight. Over this whole range of functions shipyard boilermaking is a highly skilled operation. The repair of ships damaged by storm, collision, rocks or accident in dock also calls for a high level of skill from boilermakers.

In modern shipyards the various skills of boilermaking are usually divided into separate trades. Uninformed critics sometimes allege that this division of labour is attributable to the insistence of the union on lines of demarcation. In reality the division of labour was originally introduced and encouraged more by the employers than by anyone else, to increase productivity. It is certainly true that in earlier years, particularly in times of depression, the members of the Boilermakers' Society did not accept that it was the unilateral right of employers to insist on the division of labour when it suited their purpose and then to impose flexibility when they saw that it was to their advantage. The members of the Boilermakers' Society were confronted with serious employment problems caused by the decline of riveting and its substitution by welding, and by the introduction of flame-cutting.

The Boilermakers' Society responded to these problems by accepting the need for change, by embracing the principle of interchangeability and by pressing for the retraining of workers whose old skills were no longer required. Sometimes there was resistance, but the Society sought persistently to explain its point of view on the acceptance of change and to win the voluntary support of members. Always a key factor was the attitude of employers to retraining and the avoidance of unemployment wherever possible. The reality was that in the course of a few years the techniques of shipbuilding were radically changed, and this could not have taken place without the cooperation of the Society and of its members.

When he left school McGarvey did not achieve his ambition of securing an apprenticeship as a shipyard plater. When he went to a shipbuilding firm for a job, he was asked which school he had attended. According to McGarvey, when he told the story to me, this was not so much a genuine enquiry as to the standard of his education but a question designed to find out whether he was a Roman Catholic or a Protestant. McGarvey was a Roman Catholic, and this was revealed by his answer. He did not get a job as a plater apprentice, but was offered an apprenticeship as a caulker, which was generally regarded as being lower in the hierarchy of trades associated with boilermaking.

McGarvey was brought up as a Catholic and as a supporter of Irish nationalism. He sometimes spoke of his mother's strong support for the cause of Irish nationalism. McGarvey remained a Catholic, and occasionally I discussed his religious beliefs with him. He accepted the responsibility of the Catholic Church to give guidance on faith and morals, but on trade unionism and social affairs he took the view that priests were no more qualified, and sometimes less qualified, than others to pronounce on what course should be followed. McGarvey took orders from no-one in determining his views on trade unionism.

One of the reasons for our friendship was that we were both on the left and we had a common interest in shipbuilding. McGarvey's convictions developed almost entirely through experience, coupled with a natural determination to stand up for himself and for those who were similarly placed. He was very class-conscious. He had a strong personality, and sometimes he could become domineering by the very force with which he expressed his opinions.

From the Executive Council of the Boilermakers' Society he was elected General Secretary and then, following the retirement of Ted Hill, he was elected as the President of the Amalgamated Society of Boilermakers, Shipwrights, Blacksmiths and Structural Workers. He served on the National Executive Committee of the Labour Party and then on the General Council of the TUC. Tragically he died, at the age of 57, in the year he was due to take the presidential office of the TUC.

I completed the first volume of the boilermakers' history whilst I was working at London Transport. It was published in 1973. The second volume was written during my period at ACAS and was published in 1982. Both volumes had been drafted entirely at weekends, on holidays and occasionally during evenings after work. I also at one stage broke off my work on the boilermakers' history to write a history of another trade union, the Institution of Professional Civil Servants. I wrote the first draft of this history at the request of the union, but the final draft was a joint effort with Valerie Ellis, who was then an official of the union. There were episodes in the history of the IPCS, associated with security procedures and the 'purge', which were better told by an input from within the union. This volume was published in 1980.

The IPCS was the third union whose history I had written. The first was the union of which I was a member, the Association of Engineering and Shipbuilding Draughtsmen. This volume was published in 1960. The AESD, the IPCS and the

Boilermakers' Society, despite their dissimilarity, had a common feature. They all had roots in shipbuilding. The draughtsmen's union was formed in John Brown's shipyard, Clydebank, during the period of industrial unrest in 1913. In its early history its membership was drawn heavily from the shipbuilding and marine engineering industries. Earlier attempts to form a draughtsmen's union, going back well into the nineteenth century, had failed because of the victimisation of the pioneers by hostile employers.

The initiative for the formation of the IPCS came largely from engineers employed within the Admiralty. There had been a professional association in the Royal Corps of Naval Constructors since the 1880s. In the immediate aftermath of the First World War, efforts were made to extend organisation to other technical and scientific staff. The IPCS began to take shape. Many of its members were reluctant to acknowledge in the early years that its main functions were those of a trade union. Experience was the teacher. In 1976 the annual conference of the IPCS, after an extensive consultation among the members, decided to seek affiliation to the TUC. Today the IPCS, under its present title of the Institution of Professionals, Managers and Specialists, is a well-established affiliate of the TUC. Its General Secretary, Bill Brett, sits on the General Council of the TUC and leads the British workers' delegation in the International Labour Organisation at Geneva.

My initial work on the third volume of the Boilermakers' Society, after my retirement from ACAS, got off to a good start when I was fortunate to be given a temporary Ward-Perkins residential Research Fellowship at Pembroke College, Oxford. It enabled me to study at length the original documents made available to me by the Boilermakers' Society and also to read other works of history, particularly concerning developments in the shipbuilding industry.

It was Bill (Lord) McCarthy of Nuffield College who suggested that I should apply to Pembroke for the award. If he had not done so, I would have been unaware of its existence. I was appreciative of his interest. I had a room in the college, and was in residence for a term. I enjoyed the experience, not

424

least because of the numerous discussions I had in the Senior Common Room on all kinds of subjects with members of the teaching staff of the college. College life can, however, become introspective, and for someone in his sixties living in temporary accommodation can be somewhat of a spartan existence.

My work on the third volume of the boilermakers' history was almost completely interrupted for a period of nearly four years when I became the General Secretary of the Labour Party. It was not even possible to work on the history at weekends. Work with the Labour Party was demanding, and the number of weekends when I was free of engagements was very few.

When I retired from the Labour Party in 1985 the boiler-makers' history became my main activity. The Boilermakers' Society made all the relevant documents available to me, and in the next four years I completed my reading of every annual report, every monthly report and every conference report for the period since 1939. I read also all the main debates in which spokesmen of the Society participated at the TUC, and at the annual conferences of the Confederation of Shipbuilding and Engineering Unions and the Labour Party.

When I had completed the draft, and after it had been read by Alan Hadden, a prominent national official of the Society and a former national Chairman of the Labour Party – who made a number of helpful suggestions – I was disappointed to find that the publisher of the first two volumes, George Allen and Unwin, had gone out of business and had been taken over by HarperCollins. The Boilermakers' section of the GMB agreed that I should approach HarperCollins, but I had little expectation that they would undertake publication. Trade union histories were not within their normal publishing scope. My fears proved justified.

All this caused a delay which I had not expected. It was then that Robin Blackburn, the editor of *New Left Review*, suggested that the publisher Verso might be interested. They were, but by then the GMB were feeling the financial effects of the industrial depression and the loss of membership. They indicated that for financial reasons they were not able at that stage to proceed with publication. Their support was, of course, essential, because trade union histories have a very limited sale and are usually offered to members at a subsidised price. I understood the reason for their decision, but I was, nevertheless, disappointed. I had spent hundreds of hours on the third volume, and the thought that it might not be published was depressing. Fortunately, Colin Robinson, the managing director of Verso, was very supportive and expressed his confidence that a way would be found to publish the third volume. His confidence proved justified, and a financial arrangement was reached which enabled the volume to be published at the end of 1993.

The completion of the three volumes gave me great satisfaction. I felt that, with whatever limitations the volumes might have, I had recorded, not only for current trade unionists who might read it but also for future readers, an important part of the history of British trade unionism. The Boilermakers' Society was born in the period of the formation of the British working class, and its history illustrates so many distinguishing characteristics of trade unionism among skilled workers.

The history of the Boilermakers' Society is bound up with the history of shipbuilding. It was fitting that before its amalgamation with the General and Municipal Workers' Union to form the GMB, the Boilermakers' Society amalgamated first with the Blacksmiths' Society and then with the Shipwrights' Society, both with a significant shipbuilding membership. The GMWU had a substantial membership in the shipbuilding industry, and the terms of amalgamation provided the boilermakers with the required measure of trade autonomy. The Boilermakers' section of the union became the core of a wider occupational grouping, now known as the Technical Craft Section.

For a period after my retirement from full-time employment I served on the editorial advisory committee of the *New Socialist*, which had been launched by the Labour Party some years earlier as a journal of serious discussion. For a time under the editorship of James Curran it was successful and achieved a steady circulation of well in excess of 20,000. Curran encour-

426

aged a wide-ranging discussion of socialist theory and practice. His personal views were left of centre within the Party, and he gave the magazine a slant which evoked interest and sales. After his departure the magazine lost to some extent its sense of direction, and it finally ceased publication.

This failure to sustain a magazine of socialist discussion, together with the discontinuation of the publication of *Labour Weekly*, is an indication of a basic weakness of the British labour movement and of the Labour Party in particular. 'Labourism', without any ideological perspective, represents a weakening of any real socialist impetus. It is not wrong for the Labour Party to concern itself with immediate issues, but it should not do so in a manner that accepts many of the assumptions favourable to the maintenance of the existing capitalist system. The socialist challenge is thereby corroded.

The Campaign Group

In the early spring of 1986 the recently formed Campaign Group of Labour MPs decided to publish a monthly broadsheet to be known as *Campaign Group News*. Its purpose was to campaign for socialist policies within the labour movement and to provide a link between the left of the Parliamentary Labour Party and the left within the rank and file of the Party.

The Campaign Group was originally formed at the end of 1982, when it was felt that Labour MPs should play a more positive campaigning role both inside and outside Parliament. The mining dispute of the mid-1980s underlined how essential it was to combine parliamentary activity in support of the miners with campaigning among the public at large. The Campaign Group played an outstanding role in this effort, and it was this, above all, that attracted me to it.

The first editorial board of *Campaign Group News* consisted of two MPs, Bob Clay and Joan Maynard, together with Alan Meale, who at that time was acting as the Secretary of the Campaign Group. Alan was later elected to parliament for the constituency of Mansfield. It was he who first invited me to join in the publication of *Campaign Group News*, and he indicated that he had discussed the invitation with a number of colleagues. He enquired whether I might be prepared to act as editor. I indicated that because of numerous other commitments, not least the completion of the Boilermakers' history, I did not feel able to act as editor but that I would be pleased to join the editorial board. This I did, and have remained a member ever since. For a number of years I have acted as the Chairperson of the board and have contributed a regular monthly column to *Campaign Group News*. Its current title is *Socialist Campaign Group News*.

I supported and continue to support the Campaign Group because it was the most vigorous in advocacy of the kind of socialist policies needed to arrest and then reverse Britain's economic decline. After the election of Neil Kinnock as leader of the Labour Party, the dominant trend was to revise the party's policies and to move increasingly towards the views advocated by the breakaway leaders who had formed the SDP.

When Neil Kinnock was elected as Leader of the Labour Party, his principal opponent was Roy Hattersley. It was widely felt at the time within the labour movement that Neil Kinnock would have more popular appeal, though it was also widely recognised that Roy Hattersley was very able and had a strong egalitarian commitment. Years later, after Tony Blair had succeeded Neil Kinnock as leader of the Labour Party, Roy Hattersley became a foremost critic of policies that departed from Labour's traditional views on the injustice of gross social inequality. The other candidates, Eric Heffer and Peter Shore, had no chance of being elected because of lack of trade union support. In Eric's case, this was to some extent misleading. In a number of unions there were minorities who would have preferred Eric's strong commitment to the left to what were perceived to be the inconsistencies of Neil Kinnock. Nevertheless, there was not a single union in which the supporters of Eric Heffer were able to win a majority. The contest was everywhere seen as one between Neil Kinnock and Roy Hattersley. Neil Kinnock won comfortably.

The election of Neil Kinnock was not seen as a triumph for

the left, but was regarded as a continuation and expression of the trend against right-wing domination which had asserted itself in the preceding years. Ever since his election to parliament, Neil Kinnock had been on most issues a principal voice of the left within the Tribune group. In articles in *Labour Monthly* – a magazine edited by the prominent communist, R. Palme Dutt – in December 1974 and August 1975, Neil Kinnock could not have been more scathing in his criticisms of British capitalism and of policies associated with Denis Healey in the then Labour Government. He called for a 'socialist solution to the capitalist crisis' and for the 'fundamental and irreversible shift in the balance of wealth and power' promised by Labour's Election manifesto. Nevertheless, in 1981 Neil Kinnock abstained in the contest between Tony Benn and Denis Healey for the Deputy Leadership of the Labour Party.

Denis Healey won the contest against Tony Benn by the very narrow margin of 50.426 per cent to 49.574 per cent. Among the constituencies there was a heavy majority for Tony Benn, but Denis Healey won a majority among the unions and among Labour MPs. The three groups separately made up the Party's electoral college. A group of MPs, including Neil Kinnock, who had voted for John Silkin in the first ballot, after which Silkin had been eliminated, then decided to abstain. Their abstention gave the edge to Denis Healey. Moreover, a number of the MPs who had voted for Denis Healey subsequently left the Labour Party to join the SDP.

Neil Kinnock's view was that, by contesting the election for Deputy Leader after Michael Foot had been elected Leader, Tony Benn contributed significantly to disunity within the party. Some of Neil Kinnock's critics felt that he was motivated more by a concern to stop Tony Benn as a possible future challenger for the leadership of the party.

Under the leadership of Neil Kinnock, the party moved strongly to the right. Despite very high unemployment, the contraction of British manufacturing industry, a huge balance of payments deficit and cuts in the social services, Labour lost the General Elections of 1987 and 1992. Neil Kinnock then resigned as Leader and was replaced by John Smith.

John Smith was from the right wing of the party, but was held in warm regard by the left. He had been consistent in his views, and though from the right, he sought to build bridges within the party. He was tolerant towards the left, and his views were strongly influenced by his religious convictions and his Scottish background. He was not seen as a leader whose main concern was with the suburban vote of southern England. John Smith's premature death in 1994 was a severe loss to the party, and was mourned by the left as well as by the right.

Other Interests

Retirement from full-time employment gave me the opportunity to be active in a number of organisations in the wider labour movement. One such organisation is Labour Action for Peace, which gives particular attention to issues of war and peace, campaigns for international disarmament and against the international arms trade. I have served on its Executive Committee for a number of years.

Labour Action for Peace has been particularly well served by its officers. The President is Frank Allaun, former MP, national Chairman of the Labour Party and member of the party's National Executive Committee. Frank's commitment to the cause of peace has been unwavering. He is also an excellent journalist and writes regularly for a number of labour movement periodicals, including trade union journals. There is no-one who can better express a political message in simple and clear terms. Many of the publications of Labour Action for Peace, including Frank's autobiographical booklet, demonstrate both his political commitment and journalistic skill.

The Secretary of Labour Action for Peace is Ron Huzzard, who has held the honorary post for many years. I first met Ron in the trade union movement more than 50 years ago, and throughout that period he has been a stalwart in the peace movement.

My interest in the weekly magazine *Tribune* has been

maintained, though some years ago I was for a period disappointed when it seemed to me to lose its radical cutting edge. More recently, under its present editor, Mark Seddon, it has regained its traditional stance. Perhaps also its new radicalism owes something to the welcome influence of Peter Hain, with his insistence on the importance of full employment as a policy objective of the labour movement.

Because of my pre-war membership of the Socialist League I have always felt an affinity to the tradition of *Tribune*. Leading supporters of the Socialist League were responsible for launching the publication of *Tribune* and I remember well buying the first issue. I have served as a staff trustee for *Tribune* for a number of years, and regularly attend the annual meetings. During the period of Neil Kinnock's leadership, membership of the *Tribune* group among Labour MPs in Parliament became more a badge of adherence to the dominant trend than a mark of left-wing radicalism. Fortunately, there are now signs that a number of Labour MPs in the *Tribune* group are sympathetic to the need for change.

Another organisation which I have actively supported since my retirement from full-time employment is the Marx Memorial Library. The library was established in the early 1930s. Its present rules specify that its 'sole and exclusive object shall be the advancement of education, learning and knowledge by the provision and maintenance of a library of books, periodicals and manuscripts relating to all aspects of Marxism and of the history of socialism and the working-class movement'. The library occupies premises in Clerkenwell Green, long associated with the labour movement. The building in which the library is housed was at one time occupied by Twentieth Century Press, the publishers of many early socialist tracts, including the journal *Justice*.

One of the rooms in the building was used as an office by Lenin when he was an exile in London in the early part of this century. It was from this room that he edited *Iskra (The Spark)*. The room is preserved in much the same style as it was used by Lenin, and is visited by people from many parts of the world.

The Marx Memorial Library houses tens of thousands of books on all aspects of the labour movement, and has a unique collection of various periodicals published in earlier years. Its constant problem is finance. It depends on subscriptions and voluntary donations for its income. It has a reading room which is open on most days, including evenings, and members of the library can borrow books to read at home. The library has an extremely small but enthusiastic and efficient staff. They are assisted by volunteers. The management of the library is in the hands of an elected committee, on which I have served for a number of years.

The maintenance of the Marx Memorial Library and of other libraries – very few in number – specialising in the labour movement is of great importance. It is not only the availability of books which is important, but also the collection of the innumerable publications of the labour and trade union movement. This is a resource of historical value. Unless special care is taken, there is always the danger that libraries associated with working-class history will be broken up, either because of financial problems or because of industrial changes affecting the demand for books. Many of the libraries associated, for example, with the South Wales miners are said to have been broken up and sold to second-hand dealers. There is no likelihood of this happening to the Marx Memorial Library, but its continued existence depends upon voluntary financial support and voluntary labour.

The Marx Memorial Library arranges both a spring and autumn programme of lectures. They are designed to provide a forum for the discussion of social, historical, cultural and scientific problems. They are not propagandist or agitational in tone, but intended to extend knowledge and stimulate informed debate. Many distinguished scholars have lectured at the library.

Ever since retiring from the head office of the Labour Party I have been pleased to receive invitations to talk to local constituency parties, trade union schools and other meetings of the labour movement. The memorable feature of these meetings is the number of dedicated people who are inspired to continue their efforts within the labour movement by their vision of a new kind of society, based not on private profit but on the satisfaction of human needs. This motivation transcends differences about immediate issues of policy. Too many of those who claim to be 'modernisers' in the Labour Party tend to disregard or to give too little weight to the importance of this motivation for the long-term health of the labour movement.

This basis motivation often finds expression in the speeches of Tony Benn. It is, in my view, one of his most distinguishing characteristics. It is the reason why he is one of the very few politicians who arouses real enthusiasm and support among a section of the population. This is not to deny that there are also some who dislike or even fear his radicalism. There are some in the labour movement, including prominent personalities, who, mistakenly in my view, have seen it as one of their principal tasks to diminish his influence.

In the late 1980s Tony Benn was the principal initiator of a new organisation called the Socialist Movement. It attracted many supporters and held successful conferences at Chesterfield and Manchester. The purpose of the new organisation was to give impetus to socialist ideas within the labour movement, but it was not confined to Labour Party members. I attended a number of the conferences of the Socialist Movement, and recognised their value in attracting many young people who for various reasons were not attracted to the Labour Party.

Nevertheless, an essential element for effective work in the labour movement is influence within the main stream of activity. The Socialist Movement should not be seen as an alternative to the mainstream, as it has been by a few of its supporters, but, in the manner of Tony Benn himself, as a supplement and stimulus to the mainstream.

January 1993 marked the centenary of the formation in Bradford of the Independent Labour Party. A committee was established some months earlier to commemorate the occasion, and I was very pleased to be invited to join it. The committee consisted of people associated with the labour movement in

Bradford and neighbouring districts of the West Riding. The initiative had the support of the Bradford Metropolitan Council.

The centenary committee organised a number of functions, including the unveiling of a plaque in the city by the then Labour leader, John Smith. A brochure was produced, describing the formation of the ILP and some of the buildings associated with its early years. A special effort was made to get the brochure into local schools so that pupils would be made aware of a very significant event in the history of their city. A function was also held in the City Hall, at which I was invited to speak. It was for me a memorable occasion.

Shortly after my retirement from full-time work, I undertook to produce every two months for what was then the British Soviet Friendship Society a bulletin of facts and figures about the Soviet Union, taken from the Soviet and British press. Some years earlier I had taken a night-school course in the Russian language and had gained GCE and Royal Society of Arts certificates in the subject. Every day when I was a trade union official, we received at the office a complimentary copy of *Trud*, the Soviet trade union newspaper. I was later able to persuade the publisher to send this copy to my home address. I received it for many years, and made a habit of reading one or two of the main stories during my journey to work.

I wrote every word of about 35 issues of the bulletin *Facts and Figures* before it ceased publication with the collapse of the Soviet Union. Each bulletin contained about 5–6,000 words, but it was not a bulletin of opinion. It did no more than report factually interesting pieces of information coming from the USSR. I think it conveyed to its readers at an early stage the impression that the Soviet Union was approaching a crisis of existence. With the collapse of the Soviet Union, my free supply of copies of *Trud* and of other Soviet publications ceased. As I no longer had the opportunity to read *Trud* I was surprised how quickly my ability to read the Russian language degenerated. I was never able to read it fluently, but I had sufficient knowledge to get the general sense of an article without too much difficulty. In more recent years, I have tried each day to read something in Spanish. I find it impossible at my age to try to study two foreign languages. I find Spanish more useful than Russian, not least because of the opportunity to visit there for holidays.

With the collapse of the Soviet Union the London South-East branch of the British Soviet Friendship Society ceased to exist, but a number of the members decided to form a monthly discussion group to be known as the London South-East International Friendship Discussion Group. It is a modest group, but its monthly meetings have an attendance of between 12 and 18. It has no particular political orientation, and it invites speakers from a variety of organisations specialising in international problems. I acted as the secretary of the organisation from about March 1993 until the beginning of 1997.

21

Rank-and-File Union Member

One of the most pleasant features of retirement from full-time employment was the opportunity it gave me to attend my trade union branch as a member without wider responsibilities, and to take an interest in the activities of the branch. Strictly I was neither a retired nor an unemployed member of the union, but a member with occasional earnings derived from writing, speaking and undertaking special consultative projects. The local branch of the union to which I belonged, TASS, met only a few minutes' walk away from my address in the Bermondsey constituency. The members of the branch were employed almost entirely in the engineering industry, and were based mainly on a Babcock and Wilcox establishment very near the Elephant and Castle junction in south London.

My partner, Pat, was also a member of TASS. Until her retirement she was employed as the editor of the *TASS Journal*. She had been active in the labour movement for nearly all her life since adolescence. She was born of working-class parents in North Battersea, and her early ambition was to be a journalist. Her father, a building trade worker with left-wing ideas but who was frequently unemployed, wrote before the Second World War to the then left-wing Labour MP, D. M. Pritt, to ask for advice as to how his daughter, who was approaching 15 years of age and was leaving a central school, might step out on the road to become a journalist. Pritt replied generously, and Pat remembers taking her school essay book to him so that he might judge the quality of her work. More than 40 years later, she was able to remind him personally and to thank him for his interest and encouragement. Pat was by then a magistrate and was in correspondence with D. N. Pritt about an article he had written in which he referred to the role of the magistracy.

Pat eventually found her way into journalism, but not without difficulty. During the war she worked in the fire service, and there was no way she could leave such essential work to pursue her ambition to become a journalist. After the war she found other employment, and went for a period to Canada. On returning to Britain she worked for *The Times* Book Club, as it then was, and eventually in about 1952 or 1953 she came to work on the publications of the Association of Engineering and Shipbuilding Draughtsmen. It was there that I met her.

Pat first joined the Labour League of Youth as a teenager, and has throughout remained a member of the Labour Party. She has occupied a number of constituency party jobs, including constituency President and delegate to the annual conference. She served as a Labour councillor in Richmond for about 13 years. She was appointed to the Employment Appeal Tribunal almost at its outset, and remained a member for about 14 years, until she reached the age limit. She is now an office-holder in the Southwark and Bermondsey constituency Labour Party, Minutes Secretary and committee member of the London South-East branch of MSF, and delegate to the Southwark Trades Council. She attended many conferences of the AESD, then DATA and then TASS. She has also been a branch delegate to the annual conference of MSF.

Pat and I were pleased to find that our local branch of TASS was well organised and had members in a number of local engineering factories, in addition to the Babcock and Wilcox works in Southwark. It was the custom at the branch meetings to receive reports on pay, conditions and negotiations at each of the factories. Regrettably, soon after my retirement from full-time employment in 1985, this changed. Increasingly the reports were dominated by threats of redundancy and even closures. These threats soon became reality. Our branch membership declined rapidly, and when the Babcock and Wilcox establishment closed the existence of the branch was in danger. Fortunately new younger members from Dolby, the sound equipment specialists, came forward and held the branch together. I was elected as Chair of the branch, and Pat became the Minutes Secretary.

Shortly afterwards it was suggested that we might amalgamate with another TASS branch in south-east London. This branch too had suffered heavily from closures and redundancies in engineering factories. It was agreed that the amalgamated branch would meet in Deptford. One of our active members employed at Dolby became the Secretary of the new branch. Unfortunately, this did not last long. The Dolby establishment was moved to the West Country, and we again had to find a Secretary. Fortunately, one of our members, who had been a design engineer but had since found employment as a university lecturer, volunteered to fill the vacancy. Both he and his predecessor from the Dolby establishment proved to be very good secretaries.

By this time TASS and ASTMS had amalgamated to form the Manufacturing, Science and Finance Union (MSF), and we were then approached to amalgamate with yet another branch that had suffered heavily from redundancies. This was an old ASTMS branch, but with numerous redundancies it had not been able to find sufficient officers to maintain its existence. We were told that at one time this former ASTMS branch had 1,000 members. We saw two of them at the meeting at which we arranged the amalgamation, but since that time not one of their members has attended a branch meeting. Closures and redundancies have reduced their former membership to no more than a very small number. By 1998 the total membership of the three amalgamated branches had fallen to under 170.

This experience was not unique in the London area. The majority of large or medium-sized engineering factories have disappeared. They have either been closed or their operations have been transferred to establishments outside London. How different it now is from the time when I was working in the engineering industry! It was then possible for a skilled worker to find employment in every district. I recall the time when a toolmaker, machine setter or jig and tool draughtsman could go along the Great West Road between Chiswick and Slough and be offered employment in almost every factory where there was any kind of engineering activity.

The Left

When the MSF amalgamation was first formed, the Broad Left in TASS attempted to extend membership to all in the new union. I was invited to take the chair at a special meeting held at one of the early conferences after the amalgamation. It was attended by hundreds of delegates, some, no doubt, to do no more than to make themselves aware of the activity of the left. At that time there were many prominent members of the union, both from TASS and ASTMS, who regarded themselves as on the left of the labour movement.

The existence of the Broad Left in TASS went back for many years. In the earliest days of the draughtsmen's union, there was a strong body of active members in Glasgow and in London who were identified with the Independent Labour Party and other even more militant organisations in the labour movement. From the formation of the union in 1913 they had substantial influence, and they sought to act cooperatively as a pressure group of like-minded members. In 1920, for example, the Executive Committee of the union was represented at a special conference of trade unions called by the Council of Action to stop the war of intervention against the newly formed Soviet Republic. The Executive Committee agreed to 'do its utmost to assist in the prevention or stoppage of war with Russia over the Polish question so far as it is possible under the rules of the Association.'

The draughtsmen's union was one of the earliest organisations to affiliate to the Labour Research Department, and remained affiliated to it when it was proscribed by the Labour Party. Similarly, the union always refused to apply the call made by the TUC in the middle 1930s to 'prevent members of disruptive bodies' (in reality this was directed against communists) from being elected to official positions within the trade

439

union movement. The union at its annual conference urged the TUC to withdraw the so-called 'black circular' in which this request had been made.

This is not to suggest that the draughtsmen's union was at all times under the dominant influence of the left. Some of the most prominent early left-wingers moved to the right in their later years. They included George Thomson, who for 30 years between 1918 and 1948 edited the union's journal and became the President of the TUC in 1947, and Archie MacKellar, a one-time stalwart of the ILP who became President of the Scottish TUC and a strong opponent of the left.

When I first joined the draughtsmen's union in 1942, I was soon introduced to the left. I worked as part of the left throughout my period of activity in the union, when it was both the Association of Engineering and Shipbuilding Draughtsmen and the Draughtsmen's and Allied Technicians' Association. During this time it consisted mainly of Labour Party members, but it always included communists and others not identified with any particular political party.

I have already commented in an earlier chapter that one member on the left who probably had more influence than any other in shaping the policy of the union on international issues was Ron Huzzard, who contested parliamentary elections as a Labour candidate and served as a Labour councillor for many years. In Scotland, an influential member was James Lamond, who became a Labour MP. In the West Midlands, where the left for many years was strong, there were not, as far as I recall, any prominent communists. Three or four of the most influential members on the left in Birmingham were also local magistrates. George Doughty, who became the General Secretary of the union and who, before becoming a full-time official was a principal lay leader on trade union industrial issues, was also from Birmingham and remained consistently on the left. He was a member of the Labour Party. John Forrester, who became the Deputy General Secretary of the union and the union's first elected member to the Labour Party NEC, was another consistent left-winger.

The idea held by some that the left leadership in TASS was

of recent origin and was identified with the Communist Party, particularly during the period when Ken Gill was General Secretary, owes something to the claim which I have heard made by a number of left-wingers that DATA, and before it the AESD, was 'captured' from right-wing domination when the union was not much more than a 'slate club'.

The reason for this false claim is that there is a tendency for each new generation of left-wingers to perceive the struggle primarily in terms of their own participation and that of their contemporaries. It is not easy for them to acquire knowledge about struggles that took place, say, 20 years ago, and even more difficult to acquire knowledge about struggles in the union 50 or even 70 years ago. It is more than 38 years ago since my volume *A History of the Association of Engineering and Shipbuilding Draughtsmen* was published, and it is now out of print. There is no other written source, apart from the original documents, conference reports, minutes and union journals, from which information about the earlier history of the draughtsmen's union can be obtained.

Even in more recent times a history of TASS, written by former full-time official Tony Foley, has not been given the publicity and circulation it deserves. It is a good book which brings out clearly the vigorous and radical activities of the union, and it tells the story in a very readable style. The current leadership of the MSF has given it very little publicity. In my view, this is because they find the radical tradition of TASS not to their liking.

In earlier years in the draughtsmen's union it was usual to have sessions on the history of the union at many district or divisional weekend schools. At one time each district or division was entitled to hold three weekend schools each year. They were well attended. This meant that many active members were made familiar with some of the high points in the history of the union.

The emphasis in trade union education has shifted heavily towards training. This, without doubt, is an important activity. Workplace representatives and active members are vital for the effective functioning of trade unionism. The introduction of new legislation on trade unionism, employment rights, health and safety and the growth of occupational pensions makes it essential that unions should provide facilities for training representatives and active members in all these areas of interest. But the training of representatives, essential though it is, is not a substitute for education about the history and purpose of trade unionism and its place within the broader labour movement.

MSF has its own residential training college. This was inherited from ASTMS and owes much to the initiative and support of an earlier generation of ASTMS leaders. It is expensive to maintain. It provides a wide range of training courses and, though it devotes some of its resources to education in a wider sense, I would prefer it do more.

In earlier years social education in the trade union movement was much assisted by the National Council of Labour Colleges and the Workers' Educational Association. The NCLC ceased to exist some years ago. Despite certain shortcomings because of financial constraints, shortage of tutors and inevitable controversies about its political orientation, it provided a valuable service.

My personal experience gave me a warm regard for the work of the NCLC. I started taking an NCLC correspondence course, through my membership of the Amalgamated Engineering Union, when I was an apprentice of 15 years of age. Altogether, through the AEU and then through the draughtsmen's union, I completed nine NCLC correspondence courses before I went to Ruskin College and then the London School of Economics. Among these courses were three on economics at different levels, one on finance, one on trade unionism, one entitled 'The Scientific Way of Thinking'(!), one on socialism and two on English grammar and written English. The very first weekend school I attended, in 1937 at Cowes on the Isle of Wight, was also held under the auspices of the NCLC. Since than I have attended numerous NCLC schools and classes. When I was living in Brixton I was friendly with the local NCLC organiser, William Warbey. He later became a Labour MP for Luton and distinguished himself by his early warnings of the war being conducted first by the French and then by the USA against the people of Vietnam.

The work of the NCLC was eventually taken over by the TUC. The argument for this takeover was that trade union educational facilities should be rationalised. Some unions supported the NCLC, some the WEA, and a number, including the draughtsmen's union, supported both. In addition, the TUC's own education and training programmes were being expanded. A large amount of money was being spent in different directions, and it was argued that a concentration of resources would bring better returns.

This argument was persuasive, but as so often with arguments for rationalisation, the case for diversity is not given sufficient weight. Education and training are not the same, and when the TUC took over the rationalised arrangements the new emphasis was on training. The distinctive feature of the NCLC was that it was consciously socialist in its approach to trade union and labour movement education. It claimed to be influenced by Marxism, but it was a Marxism of a particular interpretation. Some of the leading people in the NCLC, notably its General Secretary, J.P.M. Millar, and its one-time President, Arthur Woodburn MP, were on the right of the labour movement. In the later years of the NCLC a number of the full-time staff were sympathetic to or identified with a Trotskyist interpretation of Marxism. Nevertheless the NCLC introduced many thousands of trade unionists to an understanding of socialism and of the Marxist approach. The NCLC Publishing Society published a number of cheap outline textbooks, including *An Outline of Economics*, *An Outline of Economic Geography*, *An Outline of Imperialism* and *An Outline of Psychology* which sold tens of thousands of copies.

It is sometimes argued that it is improper for trade unionists to organise themselves within like-minded groups for the purpose of influencing the policy of the unions of which they are members. The suggestion is that any such group is likely to become disruptive and to represent a challenge to the elected leadership of the union. Union strength, it is pointed out,

443

depends on solidarity, and anything which might undermine the unity of the membership is to be deplored.

This is, in my view, a fallacious argument. Within trade unions there are different ideas as to the most effective way of advancing members' interests. If like-minded individual members are forbidden to come together to exchange views and to organise for the furtherance of their views, it is unlikely that the leadership of the union, whether right or left, will ever be effectively challenged. The leadership will almost certainly control the official means of communication in the union and will have an organisational structure to advocate its policies.

This is not an argument for anarchy in trade unions; it is an argument for democracy. A distinction needs to be drawn between the need, on the one hand, for one centre of authority in directing activity and, on the other, the need for democratic discussion in forming policy. Groups of like-minded members should not seek to usurp the authority of the constitutional committees of the union, but, conversely, the leadership of the union should not seek to stifle discussion, the exchange of opinion and the organisation of pressure for policy changes.

Trade unions are among the most democratic, and, perhaps, the most democratic of large voluntary organisations. Nevertheless, a concentration of power in a union can lead in some circumstances to an abuse of members' rights. It is for this reason, if for no other, that the existence of pressure groups of like-minded members should not be forbidden. Similarly, every union should make provision to some extent for the separation of power between policy-making, the execution of policy and the interpretation of the rights of members. The separation is not, of course, always clear-cut. In particular, the functions of policy-making and the carrying out of policy often overlap.

A situation in which a principal official is simultaneously at the centre of all these separate functions of trade union government is potentially dangerous for trade union democracy. It is not always easy to strike the right balance between democracy and unity of action. Both are necessary, and when the right balance is achieved each strengthens the other.

In MSF groups of like-minded members exist under the names of 'MSF for Labour', 'Campaign for a Democratic Union' and 'Unity Left'. 'MSF for Labour' consists of members whose distinction is that they are opposed to the other two groups, and, in the main, support the current trend in the policy of the Labour Party leadership. They see themselves as Labour loyalists.

'Campaign for a Democratic Union' is mainly London-based and was formed by active left-wing members from ASTMS. It has always been critical of the leadership of the union and is vigilant to assert and defend the rights of members and the lay structure of the union. It produces an informative and sharply critical daily bulletin at the annual conference of MSF. In the London Region it exercises considerable influence. There is some overlap of membership between the 'Campaign for a Democratic Union' and 'Unity Left', but in London they work closely together.

'Unity Left' emerged from the old Broad Left in TASS, but it has attracted numerous left-wing active members from the former ASTMS. It includes within its number supporters drawn from nearly every element of the left. Its strength lies in the national distribution of its support. It has groups of supporters in every region of the union and in every one of the main sections of the membership, including the manufacturing industry, the NHS, the voluntary sector, the financial institutions and, certainly not least, the craft sector.

MSF Conferences

My partner, Pat, and I have been delegates or visitors to a number of the annual conferences of MSF. We enjoyed the experience, and were particularly impressed and encouraged by the progressive sentiment and competence of so many of the delegates. The conference consists of more than 600 or so delegates, and progressive decisions are nearly always taken. The left take a prominent part in all the main debates, and though there is not a committed voting majority for the left, decisions are often won as a result of discussion. This is as it should be, and is a healthy situation for trade union democracy.

I particularly remember two of the main debates which still have relevance. In both, good decisions were taken. The first, in 1993, concerned the Maastricht Treaty. The leadership of the union were opposed to any critical decision being taken. The left pointed out that the so-called convergence criteria of the Maastricht Treaty were deflationary and were intended to be so by the participating governments. The criteria are incompatible with a policy for full employment.

One of the other main criticisms of the Maastricht Treaty was that its proposal for a European Central Bank, as a main instrument of monetary policy, should be insulated from any kind of democratic accountability. Article 107 of the Maastricht Treaty reads:

'...the European Central Bank, nor a national central bank, nor any member of their decision-making bodies shall seek or take instructions from Community institutions or bodies, from any government of a Member State or from any other body....'

It is impossible to reconcile these provisions of the Maastricht Treaty with Labour's policy for increased investment in manufacturing, the regions, the infrastructure, including schools, hospitals and the transport network, in housing, improvements in the environment and in training.

A policy for full employment would be impossible without a substantial increase in investment. Part of this investment could be met by increased taxation on those on incomes of, say, more than £50,000 a year, part could be met by diversification of military expenditure and resources, and part could be met by restricting the huge outflow of capital invested abroad in recent years. In the immediate future, there would have to be some increase in borrowing. Better to borrow for production than to borrow for the payment of benefit to millions in enforced unemployment.

446

At the 1993 annual conference of MSF, a resolution was carried stating that the 'principles enshrined in the Maastricht Treaty are against the interests of working people and should be opposed'. The resolution said that the principles were designed to require economic conditions for a reduction of government spending on welfare and education, limits on government borrowing which would prevent an incoming Labour government from introducing measures to end the recession, and the establishment of a European Central Bank without democratic accountability.

Another clear decision of the MSF conference was in opposition to the proposed constitutional changes by the Labour Party leadership to weaken collective trade union influence in the Party. The so-called proposal for 'one member one vote' but within different electoral arrangements for MPs, constituency members and trade union levy-payers, was seen as a means of eliminating the collective input of trade unions and introducing a weighted system of voting, to the great advantage of MPs and the disadvantage of trade union levy-payers. The MSF conference called for the rejection of 'misguided proposals which would weaken our relationship with the Labour Party and thus damage the organised labour movement.'

To make absolutely clear that it was the intention of the MSF conference that the union should oppose the proposed constitutional changes affecting the relationship between the unions and the Party, the delegates went on to endorse an emergency resolution, emphasising that the policy passed by the conference would be binding on MSF delegates to the Labour Party and other bodies. It was felt necessary to take this further decision because the leadership of the union had initiated a consultation exercise with the branches, which many of the conference delegates feared might be used to disregard the conference decision. As it happened, the consultation exercise confirmed the conference decision.

The London region of MSF had been particularly active in promoting among its members an understanding of the importance of the link between the Labour Party and the unions. It was decided to publish a booklet on the subject for circulation

447

throughout the London region. I was asked to draft the booklet, and it was published under the title *Unions and the Labour Party: Independent but Linked.* Its subtitle was: 'The case for a constructive relationship'. It argued that both industrial and political activities are essential for the realisation of trade union objectives. The unions, it said, needed the Labour Party as an instrument of political influence, and the Labour Party needed the unions to provide a firm basis of policy in the experiences of working people.

Despite the clear and emphatic decision of the 1993 MSF annual conference rejecting the proposed constitutional changes affecting the relationship between the Labour Party and the affiliated unions, the MSF delegation to the 1993 Labour Party conference abstained in the vital vote. By the abstention of MSF, the Labour leadership secured a majority of those who voted for their proposed rule change eliminating the collective vote of trade union branches in the selection of parliamentary candidates. The proposed rule change was carried by 47.5 per cent of those eligible to vote. This was interpreted as overriding two other successful resolutions on the Labour Party's links with the unions. They also were passed on a minority of those eligible to vote. One of these successful resolutions, moved by the TGWU, contradicted the rule change and reaffirmed the need for the representation of trade union branches at every stage in the selection of parliamentary candidates.

The decision of the MSF delegation to abstain in the vital vote at the Labour Party conference was taken only after strong efforts by the top leadership of the union to persuade the members of the delegation to abstain. The final vote on the delegation in favour of abstention was 19 to 17.

The argument used in favour of abstention was that the proposed rule change had two limbs: one relating to trade union participation, and the other relating to the introduction of a women's quota for the selection of parliamentary candidates. The leadership of the union said that the delegation was faced with an irreconcilable conflict between its obligation to oppose the proposed rule change on the relationship with the unions, and its obligation to support changes designed to increase the proportion of women Labour MPs.

The kindest observation to be made about this contention that there was an 'irreconcilable conflict' is that it represented a serious error of judgment. The main issue in the debate, as seen by every commentator, was the determination of the Labour leadership to eliminate the collective vote of affiliated trade union branches from the selection of parliamentary candidates. The need for more women candidates was thrown in to provide plausibility and, in any case, could have been pursued in other ways and in other debates.

The decision of the MSF delegation at the Labour Party conference to abstain in the vital vote met with widespread protest within the union. At the 1994 MSF annual conference, the members of the delegation responsible for the abstention were condemned for their action.

Within a few months of the 1993 Labour Party conference the labour movement used the new so-called 'one member one vote' system to elect a leader following the tragic and premature death of John Smith. Whatever else might be said about this system, it certainly did not provide for 'one member one vote'. On the contrary, it instituted a system under which many had multiple votes and the weighting of the votes was grossly disproportionate. The electoral college was divided into three sections, representing respectively MPs and MEPs, constituency individual members and members of affiliated organisations. The effect was to give each MP a vote equal in weight to at least 12,000 levy-paying members of an affiliated trade union. Such a weighted system in any other part of the world for an election would have been condemned as a distortion of democratic practice.

Many of us in the Labour Party also had more than one vote. I, for example, voted, legitimately according to the rules of the election, on four separate occasions. I voted once as an individual constituency member, once as a trade union levy-payer, and twice as a member of other affiliated organisations. Nominating rights for the election were restricted to MPs, representing but a tiny fraction of those eligible to vote and

449

those who contribute to the funds of the Party. Moreover, to be eligible to stand in the election an MP had to secure 34 nominations from colleagues. Ken Livingstone MP did not secure the necessary number of nominations, and was thus excluded.

I voted in the election for Margaret Beckett. John Prescott was my second choice. Tony Blair, with the support of almost every newspaper, was elected, but with a surprisingly narrow majority among the less than 20 per cent of trade union levy-payers who exercised their right to vote. Among the affiliated membership who voted, Tony Blair received 52.3 per cent of the votes.

Ted Knight

One of the prominent members of MSF in the London region is Ted Knight, one-time Leader of the Lambeth Borough Council. He serves on the London Regional Council of MSF, its Executive Committee and on the committee responsible for advising on political work. I first met Ted Knight when I was working at the head office of the Labour Party, but it was not until after my retirement from full-time employment that I came to know him more closely.

I recall that he once came to the General Committee of the Bermondsey Labour Party to speak on behalf of the Labour councillors in Lambeth who had been disqualified and surcharged in 1986, because they had unlawfully delayed setting a rate in their determination, as they saw it, to defend local jobs and services. I was favourably impressed by his appeal on behalf of the surcharged councillors. He did not concentrate on his personal problems – which must have been very great at the time – but emphasised constantly the political lessons to be drawn from the experiences in Lambeth.

The crux of Ted Knight's case was that the Lambeth councillors had sought to carry out the official policy of the Party, to defend jobs and services in accordance with local wishes expressed through the ballot box. A composite resolu-

450

tion adopted at the 1984 Labour Party annual conference called upon the NEC of the Party and the parliamentary leadership to encourage Labour councils to construct their budgets to defend services, jobs and living standards, 'even when this may mean consideration of strategies and policies which can be defined as technical illegality.' Only a few weeks earlier the NEC of the Labour Party had adopted a statement entitled 'Tory Attack on Local Democracy: Labour's Response', recommending that Labour local authorities 'should not act as agents for central government, even if the resulting budget is out of line with government policy'. In the following year, 1985, the annual conference of the Labour Party carried a resolution calling upon the Party to campaign 'for non-compliance with these unjust laws'. Ted Knight and the other surcharged councillors had a strong case that, at the time of their action, they were not infringing Party policy.

Ted Knight served for 12 years as a Lambeth councillor. For 8 years he was the leader of the Labour Group. During his leadership Labour increased its majority or reduced a Tory/Liberal majority in a succession of by-elections. In only one by-election was Labour's majority slightly reduced. In the 1986 Borough Council elections, Labour increased its majority on the Lambeth Council from the casting vote of the Chairman to 16. Ted Knight and a number of other councillors were disqualified by surcharge in 1986. They were surcharged because in resisting cuts and services, they failed to set a rate by the due date.

The financial appeal to support the surcharged and disqualified Labour councillors was officially supported by the Labour Party. A sum of £350,000 was raised in response to this appeal. When, after an interval of about four years, a further belated surcharge was imposed the labour movement, again with the official support of the Labour Party, raised another £110,000.

In 1993 Ted Knight was nominated for the Labour Party's panel of local government candidates for the 1994 elections in Lambeth. The surcharged and formerly disqualified councillors were now eligible to stand. Ted Knight's nomination was

451

supported by no less than five of the ward branches in the constituency in which he was living. He was also nominated by the Crystal Palace branch of MSF and the Lambeth General branch of NUPE. The London Regional Executive Committee of the Party decided to exclude him from the panel. Unfortunately, the Lambeth Local Government Committee of the Party, which in normal circumstances would have decided whether or not he should be placed on the panel, had been disbanded in 1989. It was accused, at that time, of breaching Party rules.

Ted Knight appealed against his exclusion from the panel, and his appeal was heard by an interviewing group of the London Regional Executive Committee of the Labour Party. He was informed shortly afterwards that his answers to questions 'did not show commitment to a necessary long-term improvement and change in performance for Lambeth Council and for the image of Labour in Lambeth.' Other surcharged and formerly disqualified councillors who had been nominated for the panel were also rejected.

Ted Knight appealed against this decision, and he was supported by the London Regional Council of MSF. He pointed out that he had not been a member of Lambeth Council since 1986, so that he could not be held responsible for more recent problems. Moreover, no current or recent investigation or report into the affairs of Lambeth Council concerned the period when he was a councillor. As for the public standing of the Labour Party during the period of his leadership, the election results provided the answer. Labour had gained increased support.

The London Regional Council of MSF asked me to represent them at Ted Knight's appeal before an interviewing committee of the NEC of the Labour Party. Ted himself submitted a written statement of appeal, outlining the background to his case. He was supported by written statements from the Brixton Neighbourhood Community Association (a significant organisation in the Brixton area of Lambeth), the Labour Group on the Lambeth Council, John Fraser (the local MP), Jeremy Corbyn MP, who recalled that for 10 years he was the voluntary agent in Hornsey, where Ted Knight had stood as parliamentary candidate in 1979, John Austin MP, the former leader of Greenwich Borough Council, and Alan Simpson, MP for Nottingham South, who pointed out that the disqualified councillors from Clay Cross had been accepted back on the local government panel once their legal ban had expired. Alan Simpson stated that he had been involved in interviewing candidates for the local government panel in his own area for many years.

In his statement of support for Ted Knight, John Austin MP recalled that Ted Knight and the other surcharged Labour councillors were, at the time, carrying out a policy which had the endorsement of the Labour Party conference. It was a policy followed, he said, by a number of prominent activists who were now Members of Parliament, including himself. He also pointed out that Labour's fortunes in Lambeth were better during the years of Ted Knight's leadership than subsequently.

A statement of support for the excluded candidates was also submitted by Joan Whalley MP, then a member of Labour's Front Bench team. She pointed out in her statement that she too had been a surcharged Lambeth councillor. The position we took, she said, 'followed Labour Party policy, and was taken at some personal risk, and only after considerable heart-searching and after the most extensive consultation with the local community'.

I also submitted a written statement on behalf of the London Regional Council of MSF and accompanied Ted Knight at his appearance before the Labour Party NEC Disputes Committee. Two members of the NEC were in attendance, Tom Burlison of the GMB and Colm O'Kane of the Confederation of Health Service Employees. David Gardner, the Secretary of the Disputes Committee, was also in attendance.

The appeal was conducted in a reasonable and friendly manner. Ted Knight was invited to state his case, and he did so without interruption. He was courteous and informative. I also was invited to speak in his support. I did so, and I too was not interrupted. There were a few questions, and they were

453

asked in a manner designed to obtain helpful information. They were not provocative.

Both Ted Knight and I felt at the end of the interview that we had been given a fair opportunity to state our case. Nevertheless, Ted Knight was informed shortly afterwards that his appeal had been rejected.

I make no complaint about the attitude of the members of the Disputes Committee. On the other hand, it seemed to me that the system itself was defective and did not satisfy the requirements of natural justice. Specific charges should have been made against Ted Knight and his colleagues, instead of the general complaint made by the London Labour Party Regional Executive Committee that 'your answers did not show commitment to a necessary long-term improvement and change in performance for Lambeth Council and for the image of Labour in Lambeth'. Those who made the complaint should have been asked to substantiate it, and Ted Knight and the others should have been given the opportunity to reply to specific points. If there were other complaints or charges, they should have been stated and an opportunity given for a reply to be made.

Ted Knight has continued to play an active part in MSF in his branch, as a member of the London Regional Council and as a delegate to the union's annual conference. He is a capable person and has, in my view, an indomitable attitude. He shows total commitment to the cause of labour. The Labour Party should be broad enough in its appeal not to exclude him from eligibility as a candidate in public elections.

22

Clause IV

The elimination of the old clause IV, part 4, from Labour's
constitution, and its replacement by new words, was a turning
point in the history of the Party. It formalised the rejection of
the notion that the extension of common ownership was an
essential ingredient of socialism. In reality it meant that
socialism, in the traditional meaning of the word, had been
rejected. Labour had become a political party committed to
the maintenance of the capitalist system, under which productive assets and the control of investment are overwhelmingly in
private hands and the dominating motive of economic activity
is the pursuit of private profit.

The old clause IV, part 4, said:

> 'To secure for the workers by hand or by brain the full
> fruits of their industry and the most equitable distribution
> thereof that may be possible upon the basis of the common
> ownership of the means of production, distribution and
> exchange, and the best obtainable system of popular admin-
> istration and control of each industry and service.'

It is, of course, true that even in its most ambitious period,
notably at the time of the 1945 General Election, Labour did
not propose as an election commitment to extend public
ownership beyond a few basic industries. Nevertheless, clause
IV, part 4, was much more than an election commitment for
the lifetime of a single parliament. It served as a signpost,
pointing the way to Labour's objective of a socialist society.

To those who argue that public ownership was electorally

unpopular, it should not be forgotten that in October 1974, in the last of the four out of five General Elections won by Labour under the leadership of Harold Wilson, the Party committed itself to an extensive programme of public ownership. It reaffirmed its support for the proposals first put forward only a few months earlier, in the manifesto for the General Election of February 1974 (also won by Labour, but with a narrow majority). These proposals included the taking into common ownership of land needed for development, the taking over of mineral rights, and the public ownership of ports, shipbuilding, ship repair, marine engineering and the aircraft industries.

The Party promised in the February 1974 manifesto not to confine the extension of the public sector to loss-making and subsidised industries, but to set up a National Enterprise Board to administer publicly-owned shareholdings and to extend public ownership into profitable manufacturing industry by acquisitions, partly or wholly, of individual firms. The manifesto also said that Labour regarded it as essential that the development of oil resources off the coast of Britain should be under public control. To this end, Labour proposed to take a majority public participation in all future oil licences and to negotiate to achieve majority participation in existing licenses. The Party also committed itself to the setting up of a British National Oil Corporation, to enable the government to exercise participation rights and to play an active role in future developments, including exploration and the refining and distribution of oil.

In addition to this programme of public ownership, the Party manifesto called for a system of planning agreements between government and key companies, to ensure that the plans of the companies were in harmony with national needs and objectives, and that government financial assistance was deployed where it would be most effectively used.

In the October 1974 manifesto, the proposal to take over profitable sections of individual firms was set out in more detail. Firms, it said, would be included from sections of pharmaceuticals, road haulage, construction and machine tools. Proposals were also being considered, as originally stated in the February 1974 manifesto, 'to ensure that banking and insurance make a better contribution to the national economy'. The October 1974 manifesto also promised that assets and licences hived off by the previous Conservative Government would be restored to public ownership.

These proposals have been set out at some length because in the debate on clause IV, part 4, there was all too frequently an assumption on the part of the advocates of change that public ownership had long ceased to play any part in Labour's economic programme. The reality was that Labour's programme for public ownership put forward in the successful General Election campaigns of 1974 was clearly motivated by traditional socialist considerations. It is impossible today to contend that the thinking behind the new clause IV is consistent with the policy commitments made for the two successful General Elections of 1974.

To move away from the advocacy of public ownership was very much part of the point of view of those former Labour leaders who formed the SDP, and whose defection played a significant part in the electoral defeat suffered by Labour in 1983. This rightward trend was then continued under Neil Kinnock's leadership.

Those who argue that the old clause IV, part 4, played no part in the pragmatic approach of successive Labour leaders should not exaggerate their case. Clement Attlee as well as Harold Wilson – the two most successful of Labour's earlier leaders – regarded the extension of common ownership as a vital part of Labour's policy for overcoming the failings of capitalism. In his book *The Labour Party in Perspective* Clement Attlee wrote:

'The Labour Party stands for such great changes in the economic and social structure that it cannot function successfully unless it obtains a majority which is prepared to put its principles into practice. Those principles are so far-reaching that they affect every department of the public services and every phase of policy. The plain fact is that a

457

socialist party cannot hope to make a success of administering the capitalist system because it does not believe in it.'

At another point in his book Attlee discussed the necessary elements of a short programme acceptable to socialists. He wrote:

'...it must contain measures which will take the country a long way on the road to the desired goal. It must contain a big instalment of nationalisation. The subjects of nationalisation must not be those about which there is little controversy, because they are not vital, but those which are really vital for the transformation of society and are called for in the national interest.'

The economic problems faced both by the Attlee government in its final years and by Harold Wilson immediately before his resignation and retirement, were not caused by public ownership. The Attlee government ran into difficulties because it accepted, at the request of the US Government, a commitment for a steep increase in the arms programme, even though the economy was already fully stretched and the balance of payments under strain. Inevitably there was an increase in inflationary pressure, with demands from the Government for the exercise of strict pay restraint at a time of rising prices and greatly increased profits. Cuts were also made in industrial investment and in the social services to accommodate the arms programme.

Harold Wilson's final period before his resignation was marked by a sterling crisis and steep inflation. No doubt, as Harold Wilson himself claimed, international difficulties had aggravated Britain's problems, but the fundamental cause of Britain's relative decline, namely its low level of investment in industry and the infrastructure, persisted. Arms expenditure remained at a higher level than the European NATO average, and at a proportionately much higher level than in Germany or Japan.

The importance of the old clause IV, part 4, was not that it provided an immediate programme for the lifetime of a Labour government, but that it provided a compass to guide the Labour Party towards its destination of a new kind of society. It embodied the recognition that the achievement of the basic values to which socialists are committed, economic justice, the abolition of poverty, full employment and greater equality will not be secured without changing the economic basis of society. The anarchy of production based upon the pursuit of private profit needs to be replaced by economic planning, based upon democratic accountability and the control of resources, and the promotion of human welfare.

When Hugh Gaitskell was the leader of the Labour Party he sought to change the old clause IV, part 4, but in doing so he observed the constitutional requirements for an attempt to change the rules. His attempt was defeated. Resistance to change came from within the trade union movement, from some of the constituency parties and from a section of Labour MPs, including some not normally associated with the left. In 1994–95 there was no such scrupulous regard for the constitutional requirements relating to proposed rule changes.

In the contest for the leadership of the Labour Party following the death of John Smith, there was no indication from Tony Blair that he wanted to ditch the existing clause IV, part 4. In an interview with David Frost on 12 June, 1994, Tony Blair said:

> 'I don't think anyone actually wants the abolition of clause IV to be the priority of the Labour Party at the moment. I don't think that anyone is saying now, looking ahead to the next two years in the run-up to an election, that is what we should focus on.'

If Tony Blair had revealed before the leadership election that it would be his intention, if he were successful, to drop the existing clause IV, part 4, it would not have helped his chances of victory. Not to have revealed his intention in the election campaign was an unworthy act.

Tony Blair raised the possibility of revising the constitution of the Party – in effect, dropping the old clause IV, part 4 – in his main speech as Leader to the 1994 Labour Party conference. It has since been widely reported that this move was planned in advance by Tony Blair and some of his closest supporters.

Two days after Blair's speech, the conference discussed and carried a motion which explicitly reaffirmed support for clause IV, part 4. The successful resolution deserves to be quoted in full. It said:

'Conference welcomes the 1993 conference decision to reaffirm Labour's commitment to clause IV, part 4 of the Party constitution.

'Conference notes with concern that the electoral strategy currently being pursued by the Shadow Cabinet places little emphasis on this constitutional aim.

'Conference moves that the Parliamentary Labour Party adopts a firmer public line on issues of social justice.

'Conference believes that to achieve a fair society, the redistribution of wealth must be a prime aim. To achieve this, the taxation system and public ownership should be used. Labour must present itself as a real and credible alternative. The Party must inspire hope and enthusiasm. If we are to win the battle of hearts and minds, we have to offer people a real sense of difference a Labour government will make to their lives.

'Conference recalls that Labour won elections when it presented itself as a united team with a radical programme for national regeneration.

'Conference strongly believes that to win, Labour must set out a positive and radical agenda which will unlock the great energies of the labour movement.

'Conference must recognise where the core Labour support resides and be prepared to reinforce its strength.

'Conference believes that Labour must be presented as a far more distinctive party and should be demonstrating this by making use of MPs and members from all shades of Party opinion. Accordingly, conference resolves to reinstate into

Labour's manifesto the commitment to bring about a fundamental and irreversible shift in the balance of wealth and power in favour of working people and instructs that the popular objective of public ownership be fully incorporated into the party's policies.

'Conference calls on the National Executive Committee to draw up a socialist economic, industrial and social strategy which will give effect to this priority; give credibility to our pledges to bring about high levels of employment and a better welfare state; enable minority groups (disabled, gays, ethnic minorities, etc.) to benefit to the same extent as all other working men and women; and make Labour a clear alternative to the other parties.'

This resolution was carried by a very narrow majority, but that it succeeded at all was indicative of the dissatisfaction felt by many active trade unionists and Party members at the trend of Party policy. The resolution expressed a view with which I was in agreement. It not only reaffirmed support for clause IV, part 4, but expressed concern that the parliamentary leadership showed little commitment to the Party's constitutional aim. In particular, it reaffirmed the Party's commitment to bring about 'a fundamental and irreversible shift in the balance of wealth and power in favour of working people', and recognised that the extension of public ownership was an essential instrument for achieving it. The thinking behind the conference resolution was very different from that expressed by Tony Blair throughout his successful campaign to get rid of clause IV, part 4.

Meetings

The meetings and debates in which I participated during the clause IV controversy – numbering about 20 meetings in all – gave me a fair idea of the approach of many active members. I do not claim that these meetings were representative of opinion in every part of Britain because most of them, though not all,

461

were in the south-east of England. Nevertheless, the experience is worth recounting.

First and foremost, Labour Party members wanted to rid Britain of its Conservative Government. They wanted a return to somewhere near full employment, a decent National Health Service, the elimination of market forces from the organisation of health care, better state retirement pensions, more resources for education and training, an end to soaring pay for the bosses of the privatised utilities, a reduction in crime, an ambitious housing programme and effective measures to reverse the continued decline of manufacturing industry. Labour was seen as the only alternative to the Conservatives, and Party members wanted to win the next general election. They recognised that Party disunity is a very serious electoral drawback. Hence, when Tony Blair launched his campaign to get rid of the existing clause IV, part 4, many were prepared to give him the benefit of their doubts about the wisdom of such an action.

Secondly, many members, including some who supported the retention of clause IV, part 4, felt that the existing clause was not an adequate statement of their socialist objectives. They agreed that within the kind of socialist society they envisaged there would be space for a wide range of private businesses, particularly in retail distribution and in the provision of services. They favoured the common ownership of the commanding heights of the economy, but did not feel that it was necessary for the Party to commit itself, certainly within the foreseeable future, to extend common ownership beyond the basic industries, the public utilities and the big financial institutions.

There was also a widely expressed view that the Party's objects should include a commitment to full employment, a free National Health Service and an educational system to provide everyone with adequate opportunities for learning and training throughout life. Another widely expressed view was that the Party's objects should include a strong affirmation of the need for equality of treatment between men and women, for equal rights for all ethnic groups and for the ending of discrimination based on sexual orientation.

I had sympathy with all these views, and I did not argue at any of the meetings at which I spoke that if I had been asked to write clause IV anew, I would have used the same words as in the existing clause. To my mind, however, this was not the main issue. The purpose of the campaign to rewrite the existing clause was primarily to eliminate the commitment to the extension of common ownership. This was consistent with the whole trend of Labour's policy and with its current programme. The Labour leadership had expressed its support for the retention of public ownership in the Post Office and the railways, but there were no proposals for the reversal of other privatisation measures introduced since 1979. This programme of privatisation had been very extensive and had included, for example, British Petroleum, British Aerospace, Amersham, a number of ports, British Telecom, Jaguar, Enterprise Oil, Britoil, Cable and Wireless, British Gas, British Airways, Rolls-Royce, British Airports Authority, British Steel, National Power, Powergen, the water authorities in England and Wales, Scottish Hydro, Scottish Power, the regional electricity authorities and the coal industry.

To accept that all these industries and enterprises should remain in private hands, even after the election of a Labour government, marked the formal acceptance by the Labour Party that its aim was not to change capitalism but to manage it better than the Conservative Party. There is, of course, nothing wrong with seeking to mitigate the evils of the capitalist system. It is, however, deceptive to suggest that periodic widespread unemployment and gross inequality can be overcome without far-reaching change to the economic system. Moreover, in the circumstances of British capitalism, the need for change to stop the decline of manufacturing industry, to increase substantially the level of investment and to eradicate the class-ridden structure which disfigures and cripples so many activities, is even more urgent than in some other advanced capitalist countries.

One of the positive features of the Labour Party and trade union meetings on clause IV that I attended was that no-one among the rank and file argued that the necessary changes

463

would be brought about by market forces operating within capitalism. Not once was it even suggested that the way forward would be through partnership with big business. The emphasis on all sides was on curtailing the power of big business. There was widespread scepticism about the possibility of doing this through the regulation of private industry.

The one argument that was used against a programme for common ownership was that when Labour came to office there were other more urgent projects on which to spend money than on compensation to private owners. Most agreed that compensation should be paid in the event of public ownership, if for no other reason than that pension funds had large sums of money invested in the public utilities. Some argued that any funds available for social reform should be directed in the first place towards the National Health Service and higher state retirement pensions.

This argument rests on the belief that the introduction of common ownership imposes an additional cost on society. This is not necessarily so. If the compensation terms offer a return to investors less than their current return, the net effect may be a saving rather than a cost. The compensation can take the form of non-redeemable bonds with a given rate of interest. The rate of interest should be less than the current rate of return under private ownership because of the elimination of risk and because, in certain industries, the current rate of return includes profits that reflect monopoly or near-monopoly conditions.

Among those who were prepared to support a rewrite of clause IV, there were many who believed that it would have been wiser not to launch the controversy. They were, however, anxious that the Labour Party should not appear to be disunited. They would have preferred a rewrite that emphasised the importance of extending the frontiers of common owner-ship but also made reference to other social objectives.

At the conference of the Greater London Labour Party held towards the end of February 1994, the supporters of the existing clause IV secured a significant victory. I attended the conference as a delegate on behalf of MSF, and was pleased to be given the job of seconding the successful motion. Attempts had been made to keep the motion off the agenda. Fortunately, due mainly to trade union efforts, they failed.

The successful motion deplored the creeping privatisation of London's economy and expressed the belief that the regeneration of industry in the London area would depend on vigorous public intervention, including the restoration of the public utilities and transport to public ownership. It supported the retention of clause IV of the Party's constitution and called for educational activities on the need for public intervention and the extension of public ownership.

The resolution was carried on a card vote by 58.771 per cent to 41.229 per cent. Significantly, the resolution failed to secure a majority among the constituency parties, but had an almost two-to-one majority among the unions.

The campaign by the leadership of the Party to eliminate the existing clause IV was totally one-sided. It flouted the constitution. The first sentence of clause VII of the constitution at the time of the campaign stated that:

'The work of the party shall be under the direction and control of the party conference which shall itself be subject to the constitution and standing orders of the party.'

The National Executive Committee did not uphold the decision of the 1994 conference in favour of clause IV. They sought deliberately to reverse it.

The NEC initiated a consultative exercise throughout the Party on the Party's objects and values. All the emphasis was on the need to change the constitution, and no reference was made to the decision of the 1994 conference in support of the existing clause IV. A consultative booklet was circulated, containing a response sheet, which made no mention of the debate and the decision of the 1994 conference. The questions in the response sheet failed to ask whether members were in favour of retaining the existing clause IV, either in its entirety or in an amended form. Indeed, the very first question in the response sheet made clear that the thrust of the argument in the consultative document was to urge that the constitution should be revised. It read:

> 'Thinking about an updated statement of Labour's aims and values, do you agree with the argument in the booklet that the current clause IV does not set out Labour's actual values in a clear and concise manner?'

The consultative document was circulated to all constituency parties on 16 December, 1994. In an accompanying letter, the General Secretary stated that the consultative document was being issued following Tony Blair's speech to the annual conference, 'where he stated his desire to update our constitution in order to set out our identity as a party in our own terms for our own age'. The letter, like the document, made no reference to the decision of the annual conference taken after Tony Blair had spoken.

In January 1995 the Labour Party issued what they described as a special edition of *Labour Party News*, circulated to all members, including the full text of the very one-sided consultative document. It also contained statements from a number of senior figures in the party. Most of them were sympathetic to changes being made. Statements for the retention of clause IV were published from Tony Benn MP and Stan Newens MEP.

The NEC also sent a video to every branch and constituency. The purpose of the video, according to a letter sent by the General Secretary to all constituency parties, was to allow 'branches to understand the views of the National Executive Committee and to fully participate in the consultation'. The decision of the annual conference was, as usual, disregarded.

The one positive feature of the consultative exercise was that it stimulated discussion among constituency party members. For the first time for many years, members were attracted to meetings to exchange views on Labour's objectives. I debated clause IV with a number of MPs. At some meetings the majority were in favour of retaining clause IV and at others the majority wanted either to add to it or to revise it completely. Of the meetings I attended there was not, in total, a decisive majority either way. The debates with MPs, including Malcolm Wickes, Bridget Prentice, Margaret Hodge and Helen Liddell, were conducted in a comradely manner. Chris Smith concluded a debate in his own constituency, in which I participated, and he was constructive. Of the MPs with whom I debated, there was only one, Paul Boateng, who introduced a note of sourness. He accused me of dishonesty in the arguments I employed. I was not conscious of having said anything which I disbelieved.

In my own constituency of Southwark and Bermondsey we debated clause IV at a meeting of the General Committee. There was a majority in favour of retaining the clause as it stood. It was then decided to call a general meeting open to all Party members in the constituency, and thus to widen the debate. This general meeting was attended by some 50 to 60 members. No vote was taken, but the balance of opinion appeared to be in favour of the existing clause IV. The General Committee of the Southwark and Bermondsey Party had, however, decided to respond to a request from the National Executive Committee that the NEC's proposal to revise the clause should be submitted to a ballot vote of all constituency members. This was done, and approval was given to the proposed revision by a large majority.

The experience of Southwark and Bermondsey was typical of a number of constituency parties. Where members participated in local discussion on Labour's objectives, there was a significant vote either to retain clause IV as it stood or to add to it. In nearly every constituency, however, the postal votes were overwhelmingly in favour of the National Executive Committee's proposal. Those who had not participated in discussion formed their opinions on the basis of the information supplied to them in the official communications of the Party and on what they saw, heard or read on television, radio and in newspapers.

The timetable for the consultation, drawn up by the National Executive Committee, ensured that a decision would be taken before the majority of trade union conferences took place in the summer of 1995. Of the big unions, only the Union of Shop, Distributive and Allied Workers held its 1995 annual conference in advance of the special Labour Party conference on 29 April.

At the special conference called to consider revising the constitution, the only proposal admitted to the agenda was the one submitted by the National Executive Committee. No amendments were allowed. The proposal of the NEC was adopted by 65.23 per cent of the total vote to 34.77 per cent. In the constituency section, which accounted for 30 per cent of the vote, support for the proposed revision was 90 per cent against 10 per cent. In the trade union and affiliated organisations section, which accounted for 70 per cent of the vote, the majority in favour of the proposed revision was much closer – 54.61 per cent against 45.38 per cent.

The major unions to vote in favour of the proposed revision were the GMB, AEEU, USDAW, MSF and the CWU. Those against included the TGWU, Unison, the printworkers, RMT, NUM, UCATT, FBU and ASLEF.

The Revised Clause IV

The terms of the revised clause were as follows:

'1. The Labour Party is a democratic socialist party. It believes that by the strength of our common endeavour, we achieve more than we achieve alone; so as to create: for each of us the means to realise our true potential and for all of us a community in which power, wealth and opportunity are in the hands of the many not the few, where the rights we enjoy reflect the duties we owe, and where we live together, freely, in a spirit of solidarity, tolerance and respect.
'2. To these ends we work for:
   – a dynamic economy, serving the public interest, in which the enterprise of the market and the rigour of competition are joined with the forces of partnership and co-operation to produce the wealth the nation

needs and the opportunity for all to work and prosper, with a thriving private sector and high quality public services, where those undertakings essential to the common good are either owned by the public or accountable to them;
  – a just society, which judges its strength by the condition of the weak as much as the strong, provides security against fear, and justice at work; which nurtures families, promotes equality of opportunity and delivers people from the tyranny of poverty, prejudice and the abuse of power;
  – an open democracy, in which Government is held to account by the people; decisions are taken as far as practicable by the communities they affect; and where fundamental human rights are guaranteed;
  – a healthy environment, which we protect, enhance and hold in trust for future generations.
'3. Labour is committed to the defence and security of the British people, and to co-operating in European institutions, the United Nations, the Commonwealth and other international bodies to secure peace, freedom, democracy, economic security and environmental protection for all.
'4. Labour will work in pursuit of these aims with trade unions, co-operative societies and other affiliated organisations, and also with voluntary organisations, consumer groups and other representative bodies.
'5. On the bases of these principles, Labour seeks the trust of the people to govern.'

Clause XVI of the party's constitution states that the constitution may be amended by resolution, carried on a card vote, at an annual Party conference. The conference held on 20 April, 1995 was a special conference, convened by the National Executive Committee, but it was not an annual conference.

The constitution distinguishes between annual conferences and special conferences convened by the NEC. Thus it was constitutional for the NEC to convene the special conference on 29 April, 1995 as part of its consultative exercise, but the special conference had no power, in my view, to amend the constitution. This power was reserved for the annual conference. This distinction was underlined in another clause of the constitution which outlines the duties and powers of the NEC. Clause IX (1) reads:

> 'To propose to the annual party conference such amendments to the constitution, rules and standing orders as may be deemed desirable and to submit to the annual party conference or to any special party conference, called in accordance with the rules, such resolutions and declarations affecting the programme, principles and policy of the party as in its view may be necessitated by political circumstances.'

This requirement, that the Party's constitution could be amended only at an annual party conference, was, however, modified by precedent. In 1980 the annual conference instructed the NEC to convene a special rules revision conference, to consider proposed amendments to the constitution regarding the election of the Party Leader. The decision of the 1980 conference, moved by the then General and Municipal Workers' Union, called upon the NEC to 'arrange a special rules revision conference in three months time'. This successful resolution also said:

> 'This procedure should allow constituency Labour parties and affiliated organisations to consider the options and submit constitutional amendments on the issue.'

The special conference held on 29 April, 1995 was not convened on the instructions of the annual conference. Nor were constituency parties or affiliated organisations permitted to submit amendments. Rule 2 of the procedural rules of the Labour Party made clear that for the agenda of the annual conference, constituency parties and affiliated organisations may propose one resolution to amend the rules. The only limitation on this power to submit a constitutional amendment was:

'When the annual party conference has made a decision on a constitutional amendment, no resolution to amend the constitution or rules of the party shall appear on the agenda for a period of three years from the time such decision is made, except such resolutions to amend the constitution and rules are in the opinion of the National Executive Committee of immediate importance.' (Procedural Rule 2 (8))

It can thus be argued – persuasively in my opinion – that the whole procedure of the special conference held on 29 April, 1995 was part of the consultative exercise initiated by the NEC, an exercise mounted despite the decision of the 1994 conference reaffirming support for clause IV. The April special conference was not empowered to change the constitution because it was not an annual Party conference, nor was it convened on the instruction of an annual Party conference. Moreover, no provision was made, as provided in the existing constitution, for the consideration of amendments submitted by constituency parties or affiliated organisations.

A point that has been argued against this interpretation of the constitution and rules of the Party is that the existing constitution and rules emphasise that a decision of the NEC, subject to any modification by the Party conference, 'as to the meaning and effect of any rule or any part of this constitution and rules, shall be final'. This does not mean, however, that the NEC can say that 'black is white'. Their power to interpret the constitution and rules, though wide, must rest on a reasonable construction of the words employed, and must take into account the precedents established by the annual conference.

For the agenda of the 1995 annual conference of the Labour Party, the National Union of Mineworkers and the Bakers' Union submitted a constitutional amendment which, in effect, challenged the decision of the special conference on clause IV. The two unions did so on the grounds that the special conference had consultative status but had no power to amend the constitution.

The Labour Party took the view that the special conference

had validly amended the constitution. The Conference Arrangements Committee recommended that the proposal of the NUM and the Bakers' Union should be deferred under the ruling that, where the annual conference has made a decision on a constitutional amendment no further amendment should appear on the agenda for three years, except where, in the opinion of the NEC, it is of 'immediate importance'.

The NUM and the Bakers' Union decided to take legal proceedings against the Labour Party, on the grounds that the Party had acted against its own rules. I submitted an affidavit in support of the interpretation put forward by the NUM and the Bakers' Union. In the final two paragraphs of my affidavit I stated:

'In summary the National Executive Committee were entitled to convene a special conference to consult on Labour's objects and values but not at that conference to amend the constitution. The special conference was not an annual conference which, by the terms of the existing constitution, alone has the power to amend the constitution; nor was it a special conference convened on the instruction of an annual conference which, by precedent, also has the power to amend the constitution. In particular, constituency parties and affiliated organisations were not given the opportunity, as required both by the constitution and precedent, to submit their own amendments affecting the constitution.

'It is now open to the National Executive Committee to submit as an amendment to the constitution the consultative decision of the conference held on 29 April, 1995. Constituency parties and affiliated organisations must not be denied their right to submit their own constitutional amendments.'

Fortunately, the issue was settled by agreement. The Labour Party agreed that the NUM and the Bakers' Union would be allowed at the 1995 conference to move and second their proposition, and that there would be a debate and vote upon it before the new rule book, including the revised version of clause IV, was put to the vote. The NUM and the Bakers' Union had successfully made their point that amendments to the constitution could be made only at an annual conference or at a special conference convened on the instruction of an annual conference.

There were some who criticised the NUM and the Bakers' Union for initiating legal proceedings against the Labour Party. It was a view which I well understood, but, on the other hand, leaders of the Labour Party should not attempt to ride roughshod over constitutional requirements affecting the rights of affiliated organisations and constituency parties.

In the outcome, the revised clause IV was endorsed by the 1995 annual conference. It was a properly made constitutional decision.

MSF and Clause IV

One of the bigger unions to vote in favour of revising clause IV was MSF, the union of which I am a member. Together with many other active members, I argued that this decision was in defiance of the policy determined by our annual conference. Under the rules of the union the annual conference is the supreme authority for determining policy, and the MSF delegations to the TUC and to the Labour Party conference are required by rule to vote in accordance with conference decisions.

In 1993, when the MSF conference last considered clause IV as part of Labour's constitution, a decision was taken to 'oppose any attempt to remove clause IV, part 4, from the Labour constitution.' Notwithstanding this clear mandate from the MSF conference, the delegation decided by a majority to vote for the changes proposed by the NEC of the Labour Party. This was the position supported by the General Secretary, Roger Lyons, but opposed by the lay National President, John MacIntyre.

The MSF branch of which I am a member, London South-East and Thameside, decided to submit an emergency motion to the 1995 annual conference of MSF – which was held after the Labour Party special conference in April 1995 – deploring the action of the majority of the MSF delegation in casting the union's vote in defiance of the 1993 MSF conference decision on trade union links with the Labour Party.

It was not easy to get this emergency motion onto the agenda for discussion. As always, there is only limited time available at the annual conference, and a choice has to be made by delegates as to which issues should be given priority. Some who supported the decision of the MSF delegation did not want the decision to be challenged.

On two occasions the standing orders committee of the conference recommended that other issues should be given priority, and that the London South-East and Thameside emergency motion should not be discussed. On both occasions the majority of delegates decided otherwise. They responded to the appeal that the delegation should be held accountable to the conference. When the emergency motion finally came up for discussion the majority of delegates decided, in a charged atmosphere, to give it support. The conference reprimanded the action of the MSF delegation to the special Labour Party conference in voting for the removal of clause IV, part 4 from Labour's constitution.

My partner, Pat, played a prominent part in the controversy at the MSF conference. She was the delegate from the London South-East and Thameside branch, and moved not only the successful conference motion but also on two occasions moved successfully the reference back of standing orders committee reports, to ensure that the conference had an opportunity to discuss the motion.

In the course of the conference debate it was alleged that opposition to the removal of clause IV, part 4, and to the action of the majority of the MSF delegation was centred on Trotskyists, communists and supporters of Militant Labour. Pat pointed out in reply that she had never been a member of any political party other than the Labour Party, and that she had first joined the then Labour League of Youth shortly after leaving school. She could have added, but she did not, that for

474

many years she had served in a succession of voluntary jobs in constituency parties, including constituency Chairperson, that she was at present an office-holder and member of the Executive Committee and General Committee of the Labour Party in Bermondsey. She could have referred also to her service for many years as a Labour councillor and as a magistrate.

The Inadequacy of the New Clause IV

The case against the new version of clause IV is that, among the objectives which it describes as Labour's aims and values, are a number which are impossible of achievement within capitalism. Other aims and values to which it subscribes embrace capitalism in words which conjure a dream world of unreality. This is why the new clause is an appalling substitute for the old clause. Whatever its limitations, the old clause had the merit of affirming the need to extend common ownership as an essential instrument for ending exploitation, securing greater equality and providing a framework for the democratic control and accountability of the economy.

The first paragraph of the new version of clause IV speaks of 'a community in which power, wealth and opportunity are in the hands of the many, not the few'. It is an admirable aim, but there is not a capitalist country in the world where it is anywhere near achievement. In Britain power, as never before, is in private hands, including the public utilities, the transnational corporations and the financial institutions. Wealth and income are as unequally divided as they ever were. Inequality is not diminishing. It is widening. The entire social structure, from the House of Lords to the educational system, is riddled with class division and privilege.

Opportunity for the many depends first and foremost on the availability of jobs. Yet in the advanced capitalist countries there are now tens of millions registered unemployed. The highest rate of unemployment is in Spain, which had the longest-serving socialist government in Western Europe until its defeat by the Partido Popular. The Spanish socialist government embraced economic policies similar in content to those supported by Labour's present parliamentary leadership.

The second paragraph of the new version of clause IV speaks of a 'dynamic economy, serving the public interest, in which the enterprise of the market and the rigour of competition are joined with the forces of partnership and cooperation to produce the wealth the nation needs'. In these sentiments word-spinning has replaced serious economic thought. The words glamorise capitalism and conceal the reality of the motives of big business.

It is a fundamental characteristic of private enterprise that it puts private profit before people. Human needs are disregarded when they are not expressed in purchasing power. Commitment to 'the enterprise of the market and the rigour of competition' inspired the introduction of the internal market in the National Health Service and created a two-tier system of education in Britain, with better resources for those who can afford to pay for them.

The 'rigour of competition' referred to in the new clause IV has little relationship to the real world of big business. Many of the main areas of the economy are controlled by a small number of giant firms, which between them effectively control the market.

One of the arguments used by the clause IV revisionists was that the old clause did not mention full employment or the ending of discrimination. It was a point worthy of debate. Defenders of the old clause IV pointed out that the words 'to promote the political, social and economic emancipation of the people' and 'to take common action for the promotion of a higher standard of social and economic life for the working population' could be interpreted as embracing both full employment and the ending of discrimination based upon gender or ethnic origin. Most supporters of the old clause IV would not, however, have objected to additional words to make explicit a commitment to full employment and to the elimination of discrimination.

Significantly, the new clause IV avoids using the words 'full employment'. This, almost certainly, was not an accident of drafting. The use of the words 'full employment' would have implied a commitment which the present leadership has shown no inclination to accept.

If the intention to revise clause IV had been to express Labour's socialist aims in contemporary terms rather than to move the party to an acceptance of reformed capitalism, it would have been possible to do so. A new clause would have affirmed the need for common ownership of the commanding heights of the economy, both industrial and financial, would have recognised the role of a more limited private sector, would have called for democratic accountability and would have referred to the objectives of full employment, rising living standards, better pensions and the democratic control of occupational pension schemes, a much more equitable distribution of wealth and income, a free National Health Service, an educational system open on equal terms to all, the elimination of discrimination based on gender, ethnic origin or sexual orientation, and a healthy environment. It could have been emphasised that these objectives could be achieved by the strengthening of the labour movement, including cooperation between the Labour Party, trade unions and cooperative organisations, and the readiness of the movement to cooperate with others who campaign for or support specific progressive objectives.

23

A New Labour Government

The election of a Labour Government in 1997 was due above all to a growing anti-Tory feeling among a substantial section of the electorate and to divisions within the Conservative Party. There was widespread dissatisfaction with the state of the NHS, with serious problems in the educational system and with the extent to which Conservative governments had created a social framework within which the 'fat cats' at the top of industry, commerce and the financial institutions had rewarded themselves far more generously than the rest of the community. There was also wide public concern at 'sleaze' in high circles.

An important contributory factor in the defeat of the Conservative Party was the very evident disunity among their leaders in their attitude to the European Union and a proposed single currency. In the Labour Party the divisions on Europe, although they existed, were not so publicly displayed. The wish to see the defeat of the Conservatives was a strong unifying force. It reflected a mood among many in the electorate that the Conservative Party had been in power too long and that it was time for a change.

It was significant that in this situation Tony Blair and those close to him emphasised that the Labour Party had now to be distinguished, not for its adherence to the traditional policies of the movement but for its acceptance of new policies closer to those of the Conservative Party. This shift was intended to make the Labour Party into a different kind of party, described as New Labour. In policy it had much in common with the former breakaway SDP.

478

This change did not affect the attitude of the majority of Labour voters in 1997. They went to the polls with their own agenda. They did not vote Labour because of the contents of the Party's official election manifesto. They wanted all or a selection of the following changes: improvements in the NHS, more resources for education, jobs, better pensions, the defence of social welfare, a commitment to a more equal society, the reversal of the privatisation of some of the major public services and utilities, an improvement in the rights of working people in employment and an end to corruption in high places.

The policies of New Labour did, however, influence the attitude of some business interests and sections of the press. Some were persuaded that it would be wiser from their point of view to back New Labour than to give their support to a discredited Conservative Party. They rightly recognised that the policies of New Labour presented no challenge to the power structure of British capitalism. Indeed, New Labour was seen as a lightning conductor through which popular discontent could be contained without destructive effect on the edifice of the capitalist system.

This recognition of the real nature of the leadership of New Labour explains why Labour had a more sympathetic press in the 1997 General Election than ever before. It was made all the clearer and attractive by the articulate manner in which New Labour was described by Tony Blair, and by the very obvious efforts of the New Labour leadership to seek the goodwill of big business and some of the press barons.

New Labour was thus able to attract a strata of voters who had not previously voted Labour but who wanted to vote for change and for better social services. Tony Blair was seen to epitomise these sentiments. The desired changes, however, require more than an articulate manner and an attractive appearance on the part of the Leader. Their achievement depends upon policies that challenge the causes of the failings of society.

The manifesto of New Labour made no commitment to reverse in any way the extensive privatisation programme introduced by successive Conservative governments since 1979.

Nor did it contemplate any significant redistribution of wealth or income, other than through the one-off windfall tax on the privatised utilities. New Labour promised that the public spending limits set by the previous Conservative government would continue to be observed, and that there would be no increase in the rates of income tax, despite the previous huge reductions made on the top rates by the Conservatives.

On industrial relations New Labour's promises were modest and designed to leave unchanged much of the anti-union legislation introduced by the Tories. As Tony Blair pointed out in an article in *The Times*, written shortly before the 1997 General Election, the law on industrial relations in Britain would remain the most restrictive in the Western world. On military spending New Labour appeared, if anything, to be more committed than the Conservatives to maintaining it at a high level and well above the European NATO average.

Labour's promise to cut class sizes for 5-, 6- and 7-year-olds was to be achieved, not by an injection of more resources but by using money from the assisted places scheme. Similarly, the promise to cut NHS waiting lists was said to depend on the reallocation of existing resources. The promise to reduce the number of under-25-year-olds on benefit and to get them into work was to be achieved by using money from the windfall levy on the privatised utilities.

All these proposed measures are welcome, but in total they are not sufficient to provide the improvements required in the NHS, education, the other social services, pensions, public transport and industrial investment. By accepting Conservative spending limits and promising not to increase income tax on higher incomes, New Labour has, in effect, committed itself to working within the main parameters of Conservative economic policy.

Labour won the 1997 General Election with a huge majority of seats. The labour movement understandably celebrated the victory as a rejection of the legacy of Thatcherism. Nevertheless, the voting figures did not demonstrate the emphatic acceptance of New Labour that some commentators suggested at the time. The total poll was some 2,000,000 less than at the previous General Election. Labour won nearly 44 per cent of all votes cast. The number who cast their vote was approximately 73 per cent of all who were entitled to vote. In other words, less than 32 per cent of the total electorate voted for New Labour. For every person who voted for New Labour, there were two others who either voted for other candidates or did not vote.

Labour's vote as a proportion of the poll in 1997 was lower than in the General Elections of 1945, 1950, 1951, 1955, 1964, and the first of the two General Elections in 1966, and only a very slightly higher proportion than in the General Elections of 1959 and 1970. In terms of seats, Labour lost the General Elections of 1951 and 1955, even though it secured a higher proportion of the total vote than in 1997. These figures demonstrate the vagaries of the present electoral system. The 1997 result was very much influenced by Conservative abstentions, the intervention of the Referendum Party and by tactical voting.

Government Policy

Government policy since the General Election has confirmed the expected direction to be taken by New Labour, though certainly no-one in the labour movement anticipated that one of the first decisions of the new government would be to hand over the control of interest rates to the Bank of England. New Labour's first Budget introduced modest help for education and the NHS, but reduced corporation tax on companies. The change in advance corporation tax is likely to take billions in future years from occupational pension funds. The Budget offered no improvement in state retirement pensions, though further enquiries are being made which may lead to changes. The rate of VAT on domestic fuel was reduced. In the late summer of 1997 the Government announced their intention to introduce tuition charges for students in higher education, and to abolish maintenance grants. This was another measure that had not been anticipated by the labour movement. If it had been introduced by the Tories, it would have been denounced by Labour.

The restoration of the right of trade union membership at GCHQ was seen by the trade union movement as the righting of an injustice. The Government took the first steps towards the introduction of a national minimum wage, and promised to abolish the requirement for periodic balloting for the authorisation of the deduction of trade union contributions through employers' payrolls. A new law is to be introduced, affecting trade union recognition. Unfortunately, it is likely to follow US practice. The real need is to recognise that collective bargaining is a fundamental social right. This is either explicit or implicit in the laws of a number of European countries where there is no balloting for trade union recognition. Balloting takes place solely on the choice of workers' representatives. Those who want representation and collective bargaining should not be denied it because either their employer or other employees do not want it.

On constitutional issues the Labour Government has set a course for reform. Its moves towards devolution in Scotland have been widely welcomed. In Wales the margin of support was much narrower but the Government has shown itself prepared for change. In Ireland the Government has sought to promote dialogue towards a settlement but when this paragraph was being written it was still too early to judge whether a solution could be found to meet the legitimate interests of all concerned. On the House of Lords the Government is pledged to abolish the place of hereditary peers, but it seems unlikely that provision will be made for an all-elected second chamber.

On changes to the system of welfare benefits the Labour Government got off to a bad start. There was every justification for improving child-care facilities for mothers who want to take employment outside the home and are able to find a job, but there was no justification for cutting the benefit of future claimants among lone parents.

There is a case for changes in the system of welfare payments but this should not be a cover for a drive for economy at the expense of legitimate claimants. Similarly, the existence of abuses should not be an excuse for cutting the level of benefit of those who are not abusing the system. The way to deal with abuse is to prevent it or eliminate it.

Since the General Election the leadership of New Labour has continued to centralise power within the Party. It has rejected local opinion in the choice of some by-election candidates – though its intervention was discredited in the Uxbridge by-election, where the preferred candidate of the national leadership did less well than the locally preferred candidate in the 1997 General Election – and it now seems ready to strengthen its influence over the choice of all parliamentary candidates in the future. The introduction of proportional representation, irrespective of whatever merits it has in other directions, will assist this process of the centralisation of power in the choice of candidates.

Disciplinary provisions within the Parliamentary Labour Party have been tightened, and very important changes are being made in the procedures for policy-making within the Party, to ensure that criticism from below is either muffled or diverted away from the annual conference. The leadership of New Labour has been anxious to court the goodwill of big business, and has correspondingly distanced itself from trade union influence. It appears that this trend will continue.

The Labour Movement

There are tens of thousands of people in Britain who constitute the active core of the labour movement. In his address to the 1997 TUC Tony Blair spoke of 'activist dominated' trade unions in terms which were, and were intended to be, critical. It was a view which revealed his own prejudices.

In recent years trade union membership has declined steeply under the impact of anti-union laws and unemployment. The reversal of this trend, more likely now with lower unemployment and limited but more favourable changes in legislation, will depend very much on the role of active members in workplaces and trade union branches.

Among Labour Party members there are similarly many activists who keep the structure of the Party in being. They serve as branch and constituency officers, members of constituency general committees, councillors and council candidates, and they do the work of the Party in parliamentary and local elections. They stand by the Party through both good and bad times. As with active trade union members, they deserve the respect of all who are prominent in the Party.

Among the active members of the labour movement, there are some who have left the Labour Party in recent years because of their sense of disappointment and disillusionment at the trend away from socialism. On the other hand, the strength of feeling against the Conservatives has provided new opportunities for recruitment. Tens of thousands joined the Party in the approach to the General Election. It is important that they should be encouraged to play an active part in the movement. Activity should not be discouraged or disparaged.

There is one vital additional ingredient for the success of the struggle for a new society: it is the circulation and spreading of socialist ideas. Labourism, as it is sometimes called, is not sufficient even in its traditional form. New Labour, in the way in which it is expounded by its leading advocates, represents not a contemporary interpretation of socialist thought, but a rejection of it. This is not to belittle the importance of efforts for the day-to-day interests of working people. But these efforts need to be guided by an understanding of the fundamental failings of capitalism and the essential requirements for socialist transformation. The inadequate spread of socialist ideas has so far been a key weakness in the British labour movement. It is essential that this deficiency be rectified.

24

Ideas and Experiences

My birth in January 1921 coincided with the development of the first major economic downturn of British capitalism following the First World War. In 1921, in comparison with the summer of the previous year industrial production fell by about a fifth, prices fell by about a quarter and unemployment jumped from less than 3 per cent of the insured population to nearly 18 per cent. The number of days lost because of industrial disputes in 1921 rose to more than 85,000,000. Except for 1926, the year of the General Strike, this was by far the highest for any of the years between the two world wars. The industrial area of Yorkshire where I was born, with its huge coalfield, its textile mills and its engineering and iron steel works, was badly affected. This experience confirmed in my parents the socialist ideas which they had already acquired.

There was some improvement in employment in the rest of the 1920s, but much of the industrial base of the economy of West and South Yorkshire remained depressed. At the beginning of the 1930s the situation worsened, with even heavier unemployment than in 1921. It was in the midst of the depression in the early 1930s that, as earlier recounted, my parents moved to the south of England; my father went first, he was then joined by mother, and finally by me.

My father's views, when as a boy I was old enough to become aware of them, reflected his experiences. He was bitter at the injustice of the whole system and radical in his viewpoint. He was not a member of any political party, but he described himself as a socialist rather than as a 'Labour man'. After the defeat of the General Strike – my father always described it as 'the betrayal of the General Strike' – and after the desertion of the top Labour leadership in 1931 to join with the Conservatives in the formation of the National Government, he spoke in contemptuous terms of the dominant ideas of the Labour Party and even of the Party itself. My parents voted Labour in the 1935 General Election, but my father, in particular, did so without much enthusiasm. By that time, however, my parents again had a regular income and my father was more concerned with maintaining, by then, his family's modest but, nevertheless, rising standard of living.

Though the effect of years of economic depression was a main influence on the ideas with which I became familiar as a boy, there were also other experiences which affected my parents and which helped to shape their views. They often spoke of the promise, made in the name of the British Government, that after the First World War Britain would be a 'land fit for heroes'. They knew that the British people had been deceived. It was not only the unemployment of 1921 and subsequent years; it was also the housing shortage. Early in their marriage my parents lived in 'rooms', as it was customary in West Yorkshire to describe the renting of a room or two rooms in a house of multiple occupation. Later they bought on mortgage an old terraced house in the Manningham area of Bradford, only about five minutes' walk from where I was born. It had a kitchen, which served as a living room, a 'front room', which was used only when guests were received, two bedrooms, a bath, which had been installed in the attic, and an outside lavatory, which was below ground level. Although it was an old terraced house with an outside lavatory, the street in which it was located was considered 'respectable'. It was better than the back-to-back houses or the streets of old terraced houses with covered passageways to provide access to the back yards.

My parents did not accept that the First World War had been fought for the protection of Belgium against German aggression. This, my father explained to me as soon as I was old enough to listen to him, was no more than a pretext. The war was the outcome of rivalry between the imperial ambitions and business interests of the main participating powers, Germany, Britain, France and Russia. He spoke of the cruel and reckless manner in which infantrymen had been thrown into battle, to slaughter each other on the Western Front. The name of Haig, the British military commander, was detested in our house. Approximately three-quarters of a million men from the United Kingdom had been killed in the First World War, and about twice as many had been disabled by wounds or poison gas. Among those who had been killed and wounded were family relatives. Our next-door neighbour in the street in which we lived had lost an arm in the fighting, and there were many other wounded men in the neighbourhood. The casualties among French and German troops were even higher than among British troops.

My parents had also been influenced by events in what was then known as 'the Empire'. In 1919 a British general had ordered troops to open fire on an unarmed crowd at Amritsar in India. It was reported that 379 people had been killed. The movement for national independence in India found new strength. My parents supported the aspirations of the independence movement. My father frequently predicted to me when I was a schoolboy that the British Empire would come to an end. Every nation, he said, had the right of self-determination.

Similarly in relation to Ireland, my parents – though neither had sympathy with Roman Catholicism – supported Irish nationalism and the objective of a united Ireland. They were conscious of the injustices inflicted on Ireland over many centuries, and were disgusted at the role in the early 1920s of the Black and Tans, an armed force recruited by the British and with a reputation for brutality. My father held the view that the people of Ireland, that is the whole of Ireland, had the right to rule themselves. The majority of the Irish people wanted home rule, and the majority of British people had voted for home rule before the First World War. Home rule for Ireland had been passed by Parliament, but its implementation had been deferred by the First World War. This decision for home rule had been frustrated by a threatened armed revolt, led by reactionary officers, in parts of northern Ireland.

This revolt had played into the hands of those opposed to Irish independence.

My father was an admirer of the Irish socialist leader, James Connolly, who had been executed by the British following the Easter Rising of 1916. Thus the views about Ireland with which I became familiar as a boy were not only sympathetic towards national independence but looked forward to an ultimate socialist solution. Irish employers were seen as having the same anti-labour interests as British employers. Religion was seen by my parents as a private matter for citizens, and the Irish people were entitled to follow the faith of their own choosing, but the majority were not entitled to impose their religion on dissenting minorities. My parents were always strongly opposed to denominational schools, which they regarded as training institutions for intolerance and separation.

Another important idea which I took from my parents was that of international workers' solidarity. Working people the world over have common basic interests for secure employment, decent housing, education and health care, protection against exploitation and the maintenance of peace. None of these objectives is likely to be achieved without struggle.

My parents sympathised with every reported struggle of working people in whatever country. They believed firmly in trade unionism, in radical socialist politics, in the struggle against colonialism and in democracy. They supported the left-wing socialists of the German labour movement who had revolted against German militarism and in the 1920s were striving for a new kind of German society, in which imperialism would have no place. They supported the Russian Revolution, though my father was always suspicious of bureaucratic control. His suspicions on this score had been aroused in the early years of the Soviet state, but it did not lead him into support for the hostile policies of the major capitalist powers.

One very strong sentiment of my parents was of opposition to all forms of hereditary power and privilege. They were republicans and had no sympathy with the monarchy. They were also strongly opposed to the existence of the House of

Lords, to the private system of education represented by the so-called public schools, and to the system of titles – dukes, lords and knights – which they recognised as an expression of an unjustified class system.

When I look back on these main views expressed by my parents, I am impressed by how right they were in their judgment. I often wonder how my father in particular reached his conclusions. His formal education was very limited, but he read the pamphlets and periodicals of the early socialist movement. My mother's views were influenced by her Nonconformist Christian beliefs.

This is not to suggest that my home influence was progressive in every direction. My father had what I now think were prejudiced and mistaken views about a number of issues, including education. It was due to his influence, and to what he felt were the economic pressures at the time, that I did not accept a place at a grammar school but instead went to a junior technical school as preparation for an apprenticeship in Portsmouth Dockyard.

My parents also had a strong sentiment in favour of self-help and personal responsibility. In some respects this was commendable, but it could also lead to Thatcherite conclusions. My parents frequently expressed hostility to poor people having large families, and I do not remember them at any time expressing sympathy for the idea of family allowances for children. Nor were they particularly sympathetic to the idea of subsidised housing. They believed in thrift, in saving through building societies or the Yorkshire Penny Bank, and in temperance. My father was always disparaging about workers who spent their income on drink or gambling and then expected support from public funds when faced with hard times.

My father also held the view, despite his socialist convictions, that Labour councils were inclined to spend too freely for the benefit of people who wasted their income on drink, smoking, gambling and entertainment. Rates, he argued, were levied not only on the well-off but on working-class people who exercised thrift in their everyday life. This never led him to vote Conservative, but he was not reluctant to voice his criticism of some of Labour's municipal policies if he thought they were extravagant.

He also had a number of other strongly held views or prejudices. He disliked Sunday trading, including Sunday cinemas, hire purchase, indebtedness, charity, pawnshops, cut-price shops, unconventional dress, 'posh' accents, bad language, crude jokes, crooners, untidiness, the national anthem, all forms of jingoism and the Union Jack! He was not in any way disrespectful to women in his conversation, but he had backward and fixed ideas about the role of men and women in the home. I never once saw him washing-up at the sink or dusting the furniture. He was not particularly sympathetic to married women taking jobs outside the home. He felt that this imposed a heavy burden on women and limited the employment opportunities of men.

The Case for Socialism

My personal experiences have confirmed rather than undermined some, though not all, of the main political ideas which were passed to me by my parents. Above all, the case for socialism is, in my view, overwhelming. By socialism I mean a society in which economic planning is predominant, based on the social ownership and democratic control and accountability of major industries and services. The basic motivation in such a society would be that of satisfying human needs. Democratic control in all walks of life would be the principal force for the prevention of corruption, the evaluation of the main social needs, housing, education, health care, social security and public transport, the avoidance of gross inequality and the promotion of good standards of social behaviour.

It would not be necessary or desirable to bring all industry and commerce under social ownership. Indeed, there are many activities which are more likely to be conducted effectively under private ownership. They include industries and services which need to respond quickly to consumer demand but which

490

are not decisive for determining the total level of investment in the economy, and hence the level of employment. Certainly, over a whole range of personal services and in retail distribution, private or cooperative enterprise is likely to satisfy consumer needs. In these areas the motivation of private profit within a competitive environment has many advantages, providing there are adequate controls to prevent labour exploitation, to protect the environment and public health, welfare and safety, and to provide safeguards against the development of private monopoly.

Despite the contribution which the capitalist system has made to economic development, and the role of private profit motivation in meeting consumer demand in many forms of economic activity, the deficiencies of the system are enormous. These deficiencies cause unnecessary human suffering and an immense waste of resources.

Perhaps the most serious deficiency of the capitalist system is that it is incapable of maintaining full employment. Periodic mass unemployment has been and is a feature of capitalism wherever it has developed.

Unemployment is not an act of God. It is the result of an inherent failing in the way in which the economy is organised. There is no shortage of human needs that remain to be satisfied. Unfulfilled demands are visible in every direction, even in the most advanced countries.

In Britain, for example, millions live in unnecessary poverty. Their housing in inadequate, their education stunted, their health care deficient, and too many find it difficult to afford an adequate and varied diet.

Why was it, then, that despite these unfulfilled wants some 1,400,000 (in 1998), according to official figures, were unable to find a job? The real unemployment figure, including those who in frustration have given up looking for work and those who have involuntarily accepted part-time employment, is much higher. The Conservative Government repeatedly altered the basis of calculation in order, for purposes of public presentation, to minimise the unemployment figure.

The reason why there is mass unemployment, despite so

many unsatisfied needs, is that under the capitalist system employment is provided by private industry only when it seems likely that a profit will be made. Profitable enterprise does not always coincide with the satisfaction of human needs.

Profitable enterprise depends upon what is euphemistically described as 'effective demand'. This represents the amount that the community spends for personal consumption, for the maintenance and expansion of productive resources, including services of various kinds, and for public expenditure. This 'effective demand' may be less than sufficient to keep the productive potential of society fully occupied. It was the British economist, Keynes, who in the 1930s demonstrated that a deficiency of demand, leading to periodic mass unemployment, was normal to the system. The assumption that the mechanism of the private market would create equilibrium at the level of full employment was wrong. The theory that income derived from production and services would always create sufficient effective demand to clear all goods and services from the market was fallacious.

In the real world, not all income is spent. Some is put aside or, in the language of everyday life, is saved. If these savings are not then mobilised and spent on replacing or expanding the means of production, or on social services or other items of public expenditure, the economy will find its 'natural' level at less than full employment. Large numbers among the workforce are then unable to find a job.

Keynes reached a conclusion about unemployment which Marx had anticipated by a different theoretical route many years earlier. To Marx, the key to an understanding of capitalism was provided by his concept of surplus value. It rests on the understanding that employed labour adds more to the value of a product than is paid in wages. After allowing for the cost of the materials and the depreciation of the machinery and equipment used in production, there remains a surplus (surplus value) which is appropriated by the capitalist employer. The motive force of capitalism is to maximise this surplus and then to invest more and to expand. This depends, of course, on each capitalist being able to sell his goods and services in the market. The level of demand for the available goods and services depends on the purchasing power of consumers and on those who want to invest and expand the production of goods and services. The level of demand periodically falls below the potential output of the existing productive forces. The result is mass unemployment.

Keynes argued that it should be possible for governments within the capitalist system to pursue a policy of full employment by stimulating effective demand so that it compensated for the deficiency of the free market. Various stimulants were suggested, including public works, low rates of interest to encourage investment in industry, and measures to increase the purchasing power of poorer sections of the community. Keynes pointed out that poorer people are likely to spend a higher proportion of their income than rich people. They have a greater propensity to consume. Hence redistributive taxation from the rich to the poor was likely to have a beneficial effect on employment. This is the very opposite of the policies on taxation pursued by Conservative governments between 1979 and 1997.

By the time of the Second World War, the theory of employment associated with the name of Keynes had won widespread acceptance. This was due not only to the persuasiveness of the theory, but also to the social circumstances of the time. The anti-fascist struggle and, in particular, the war against Nazi Germany encouraged progressive sentiments in many directions. A determination to avoid a repetition of economic depression and mass unemployment gripped the imagination of millions of citizens. By the closing period of the Second World War all the main political parties in Britain had pledged themselves to a policy of full employment.

What then went wrong with the Keynesian remedy? Why were the recommended policies not pursued when unemployment began once again to rise above what had previously been regarded as the acceptable level of about 3 per cent of the labour force? This level was said to be necessary to provide sufficient mobility between expanding and contracting areas of employment. A 3 per cent rate of unemployment, it was argued, was compatible with a situation in which overall there were more vacancies than people looking for work.

The Keynesian remedies were eventually rejected by some policy-makers on the right because, as they saw it, they failed adequately to take account of the social consequences of full employment. One central consequence of full employment was that it affected the balance of class forces within capitalism. Full employment, or anything near it, empowered the working class in its claims on the capitalist system.

The strengthening of workers' power expressed itself primarily through trade unionism. In Britain trade union membership increased to a high point of more than 13,200,000 in 1979. In more and more workplaces the unions were represented by effective lay representatives. Workers' pressure for higher wages and better conditions was expressed not only in national negotiations but also at workplace level. The upward movement of wages as a result of workplace pressure, as distinct from negotiated national minimum rates, was sometimes described as 'wages drift'. Employers complained of lack of managerial control and saw it as their task to regain control in the workplace.

So-called 'wages drift' was not a drift at all. It was due to rank-and-file pressure on wages and the effectiveness of this pressure made possible by a high level of employment. Employers then sought to protect their profits by increasing their prices. Indeed, if at all possible they increased their profit margins. They often found that this could be done because so many firms were operating in markets where they were able to increase prices without any significant fall in the volume of sales. In many sections of British industry and commerce employers are able to act in this way because a small number of firms are in a dominating position. Even when they do not operate a formal price ring, they take account of price movements by competitors.

This process results in inflation. It is the outcome of conflicting pressures within the economic system. Wage and salary earners press for improved conditions, and employers seek to maintain and increase their profits. Sometimes it is

494

possible to accommodate these conflicting interests within an expanding economy. Increased productivity leading to increased output may enable both workers and employers respectively to increase their earnings and their profits. If, on the other hand, there is a slow rate of growth within the economy despite a high level of employment, the pressures caused by the conflict of interests are likely to accelerate the rate of inflation.

A distinction is sometimes made between inflation caused by a 'push' on costs leading to higher prices, and inflation caused by a 'pull' on resources created by increased demand. This demand may arise not only from the claims of workers and employers to increase their pay and their profits, but also from decisions to increase the use of resources for capital investment, social spending or for military purposes. These concepts of 'cost push' and 'demand pull' are useful when thinking about the problem of inflation, but they are only the first stage of analysis. Too often in conventional thinking it is the workers who are blamed for inflation. Assumptions about the existing distribution of income in society, about the role of employers in putting up prices to maintain and increase profits, about the existence of informal price-fixing behaviour between big firms with a substantial market-share, and about the command on resources represented by heavy military spending, all go unchallenged.

Incomes Policy?

The answer to the problem of inflation was seen by some to lie in an incomes policy endorsed by employers' organisations and trade unions. In various forms this was the solution supported by both Conservative and Labour governments before 1979. A consensus was sought to restrain increases in incomes to a level not exceeding the rise in productivity. Labour governments were more likely than Conservative governments to obtain agreement from trade unions for such a policy, though even in the most favourable circumstances there was always a significant minority of trade unionists who did not accept incomes policies.

None of the formal incomes policies introduced by British governments since 1945 have proved workable in the long run. They have all ultimately broken down. This does not mean that they were all equally valueless or that there is no case for an incomes policy under any circumstances. A government pledged to progressive social measures on a wide front, but operating at the outset in a predominantly capitalist system is likely to find it inevitable that it would want to exert a continuing influence on the relationship between productivity, prices and incomes of all kinds.

Even then, difficulties are certain to arise because there is no way in which profits can be controlled in the same way as wages. Basic rates of pay are determined in advance, whereas profits are a residual sum left after deducting outgoings from receipts. The control of dividends is not the same as the control of profits. Dividend limitation merely regulates the amount paid out to shareholders. The remaining profits after taxation still belong to shareholders. The capital value of their holding is likely to increase accordingly and, indeed, may make their business an attractive target for a takeover bid.

It has sometimes been suggested that price control can constitute an effective control on profits. During the period of the National Board for Prices and Incomes the argument was advanced that productivity, prices and profits were closely inter-related and should not be considered in isolation from each other. There was much to be said for this contention, but experience demonstrated that price control did not prove a generally effective means of controlling profits. Specific price movements were investigated, but it was a time-consuming exercise. The usual conclusion of these exercises was that employers should be permitted to set a price that provided an 'adequate' return on capital. This took into account the need to maintain productive resources to satisfy demand, to provide for capital investment and to offer an incentive for productivity improvements. Regard was also paid to the general level of the return on capital in British industry and commerce.

A frequent issue of contention was the assessment of the capital employed in a business. Was it the historic cost, the current valuation or the replacement cost of the assets? Depending upon which of these valuations was used, widely differing conclusions could be reached about the prices and profits required to maintain a reasonable rate of return on the capital employed in the business.

An important consideration affecting any kind of prices and incomes policy is that the economy is never static. There are always sections of business and areas of employment that are expanding or contracting. Capital and labour have to be attracted to the expanding areas. This has repercussions on other businesses, and on the prices which they charge and the wages and salaries they pay to their employees.

In relation to wages and salaries, the relevant considerations for a 'fair' policy are also complex. There is not only the difficulty – or, indeed, the impossibility – of establishing a 'fair' relationship between profits and pay, but there are also extremely difficult problems in attempting to control wage and salary structures between one occupation and another. The starting point for any comparison may not be acceptable to those directly involved. There are then the many different considerations put forward in wage and salary claims. They include references to the cost of living; to rising profits to which workers have contributed; to the need to maintain or to widen differentials to encourage recruitment or the acquisition of skill or to undertake training; to the reward of past productivity or to changes in working practices likely to promote increased productivity in the future, or to the establishment of a basic standard below which no-one should fall. There is also the problem that the opportunities for improved productivity vary widely between different occupations, and that in some occupations no realistic measure of productivity can be determined. Productivity depends partly also on other factors of production.

These difficulties are not an argument against any kind of productivity, prices and incomes policy within an economic and social framework of a progressive government. The contribution which such a policy can make even under the most favourable circumstances is, however, limited and temporary. Within capitalism there is no way in which it is possible permanently to assess 'fairness' between income derived from profits and income derived from labour. Inflation is influenced by the struggle between different social groups for a greater share of the total product of society.

The Conservative rejection after 1979 of full employment as an economic objective was a measure of their recognition that the empowerment of the working class, resulting from a high level of employment, threatens the employers' managerial control of the system and even of the continued existence of capitalism. Hence the switch from the objective of full employment to the objective of a low level of inflation. It is not that the majority of big employers want unemployment, but they are prepared to support policies which sacrifice full employment if, in so doing, they can achieve a low level of inflation, together with what they describe as labour 'flexibility' and legislation to weaken trade unionism. This is the contemporary reality of class politics. It explains why Keynesian remedial measures to stimulate employment went out of fashion among those close to the Conservative Party and even among some in the Labour Party.

The essential requirement for a policy for full employment is that the government should have sufficient control of the economy to stimulate both supply and demand to bring back into production and into service the available unused resources. Thus it is not sufficient to concentrate on either the supply side or the demand side of the economy. Action has to be taken on both fronts.

The requirement that there should be adequate public control for a policy of full employment will not be achieved so long as the commanding heights of the economy remain under private ownership. The experience of previous Labour governments indicates that no amount of so-called indicative planning of private industry, whether within a notional plan drawn up by a Ministry of Economic Affairs or through the consultative machinery of a National Economic Development Council, will override the motivation of private firms.

For a number of years I served as the Chairperson of the National Economic Development Committee for Engineering Construction. It was one of the committees more usually known as 'little Neddies' and operated under the auspices of the National Economic Development Council. It was sometimes said that it was part of the national planning mechanism. It was an unjustified description. The whole of the 'Neddy' machinery served a useful consultative purpose between government, employers and unions but to suggest that it had a planning function was to attribute to it powers that it did not possess.

Investment will not be made if boards of directors decide that it is not in the interest of their private shareholders to do so. Nor will the big investment institutions guide their investments towards British industry if they judge that a better return is to be obtained elsewhere, either in Britain or abroad.

The trend towards a more unified world economy and the growth of the importance of the transnational private corporations, has accentuated rather than diminished the problem of investment in British industry. The 1994 World Labour Report of the ILO stated:

'Globalisation enables capital to roam the world in search of cheap and productive labour – transferring jobs from one country to another.'

The British government's response at the time to this trend was to make Britain a low-wage economy, with few regulations for labour protection and with severe restrictions on trade unionism.

Inequality

One of the main criticisms of the capitalist system is that it produces gross inequality unrelated to the kind of differentials required to encourage and reward training and skill. This gross inequality applies both to the distribution of wealth and to the

499

distribution of income. There is no justification for the existence in Britain of a very rich class, within which there are individuals or small groups with assets exceeding many millions of pounds. This kind of wealth is not derived from effort personally made; it is the result either of inheritance, or of speculation or of the accumulation of profits derived by employing the labour of others.

The majority of people in Britain have little wealth. Even among those who do not form part of the severely deprived underclass, their main asset is usually a house, frequently held on mortgage. Some also in Britain have the asset of an occupational pension or an entitlement to such a pension when they retire, to supplement their state retirement benefit. This is sometimes compared to a terminal capital asset because it provides an annual benefit to the date of death or to the death of the spouse, though it is more accurate to regard it as deferred pay. Occupational pensions have become more important in recent years, though on the other side of the balance has to be weighed the decline in state retirement benefits as a proportion of average earnings.

Apart from their house and pension, most households in Britain have very low savings. A report published by the Institute for Fiscal Studies in September 1994 estimated that more than half the households in Britain had savings of less than £450. This was the equivalent of less than two weeks' average earnings for a male full-time manual worker. It means that there is no safety net to cope with unemployment, sickness, disability or other unforeseen loss of income or exceptional expenditure. The Institute of Fiscal Studies concluded from their survey that the wealth gap between rich and poor in Britain remained as wide as ever.

Very wide existing differences in income, as distinct from capital, are similarly a feature of British society. In recent years the difference between the top and the bottom has widened. According to a report prepared by the Institute of Fiscal Studies and published in 1997, there had been an unprecedented increase in income inequality during the preceding 20 years. Among the findings were that the richest 10 per cent of the population have as much income as the poorer half of all households. The report concluded that on virtually any measure poverty in Britain had increased dramatically.

Another way of looking at the figures of income distribution is to compare from one period to another the proportion of households with an income below half the average. This is regarded by some authorities as a measure of poverty. It takes account of changes in the general standard of living. People's conception and experience of poverty is influenced by the standards of others. In Britain the number of people falling within the band of poverty so defined increased from 5,000,000 in 1979 to 13,900,000 in 1992, and included almost one-third of all children in the United Kingdom.

In the USA, the richest of the world's capitalist countries, the inequalities are equally glaring. A report published by the Carnegie Corporation in 1994, compiled by a panel of eminent doctors, educators and business executives, said that 3,000,000 children, almost one in four, were living in poverty and social deprivation with a deteriorating quality of life. These broad findings of widespread child poverty were confirmed in an official report from a US agency, the General Accounting Office, which found that the number of poor children under three years of age rose during the 1980s from 1,800,000 to 2,300,000.

In recent years in Britain, the growth in inequality in society has been accelerating. This has partly been the effect of changes in taxation. In the ten-year period 1985 to 1995, the rich became richer as a result of tax changes, and the poor became poorer. An analyses of the Budgets since 1985 made by the Institute of Fiscal Studies showed the cumulative effect of tax changes on different bands of Britain's 20,000,000 households. The poorest four bands were all worse off on average. Those who benefited most were the top band. Even within this top 10 per cent the gains were heavily weighted in favour of the top 1 per cent. The biggest losers as a result of tax changes were unemployed couples with children and one-parent families.

This comparison of the effect of tax changes between

501

different income groups underestimates the real widening of the inequality in British society. It is not only that tax changes have benefited the rich and penalised the poor, but the recipients of big incomes have boosted their incomes to even higher levels.

The increase in top salaries, not least in the privatised companies formerly under public ownership, has been the subject of wide and unfavourable comment even among those normally sympathetic to private business. In March 1994 the former Chancellor of the Exchequer, Kenneth Clarke, said in an interview:

'I disapprove of some of the high executive salaries paid by British companies, and I wish more of our business leaders showed a decent level of restraint.'

There are now a substantial number of companies in Britain where one or more directors are earning more than £500,000 a year. Some are earning more than £1,000,000 a year, and there are a handful whose annual earnings are in the multi-million bracket. They have been listed from time to time in the magazine, *Labour Research*, published by the trade union supported research organisation, the LRD. In the issue dated September 1997 it was reported that an LRD survey found 123 company directors getting over £1,000,000 a year. During the previous year directors' earnings in publicly quoted companies rose by an average 16 per cent.

Those who have sought to defend these unjustifiable payments have sometimes argued that the earnings levels have been fixed by committees of non-executive directors or that they reflect performance-related pay formulae. The determination of top executive pay by non-executive directors can be likened to a game of musical chairs. It is a closed circle of people, many of them with multiple directorships. They fix each other's salaries as they move from one board to another. As for the performance-related pay, the standards which apply in many board rooms do not apply to workers.

The double standards are well illustrated in the payoffs made to numerous top company executives whose services are no longer required. The magazine *Labour Research* has summarised the available information on the so-called 'golden handshakes' to departing directors. The issue of September 1994 named 40 directors who in the previous year had received golden handshakes of £100,000 or more. Seven of this number each received £500,000 or more. The top recipient received more than £3,000,000 from British Aerospace. *Labour Research* pointed out that the number of directors receiving massive payouts was much larger than those listed because companies are not legally required to give details of individual settlements. A particularly interesting personal case was that of Mr Bob Horton, who was reported to have received a £1,500,000 'golden handshake' from one company and then became the part-time chairman of Railtrack on a salary exceeding £120,000 a year.

There are numerous reported cases of 'golden handshakes' as a reward for failure. Some departures of top executives, for example, followed the declaration of substantial company losses. Others followed boardroom disagreements in which a departing director had lost the confidence of other board members. Tim Melville Ross of the Institute of Directors was reported as saying: 'What I do find abhorrent is people who are paid for failure.' A fund manager, Paul Manduca of Threadneedle Asset Management, observed: 'People are failing at the job who have been paid the market rate and are finding themselves rewarded for failure at the end of it.'

Top executives have not only benefited from very big pay increases, and some of them from 'golden handshakes', but some have also been able to buy shares on specially favourable terms under stock option clauses in their contracts. The dividing line in such cases between pay and capital gains has become blurred. Nor should it be overlooked that taxation changes in recent years have made it possible for high income receivers to invest substantial annual sums in schemes which provide tax-free returns.

Gross inequality is inseparable from capitalism. The private ownership of the industries and financial institutions that dominate the economy breeds gross inequality every minute of every working day. Every attempt to diminish this inequality, even to a modest extent, meets with the obstacle that the basic motive of capitalism is to maximise the return on capital.

When Neil Kinnock was the Leader of the Labour Party, he and Roy Hattersley produced a Statement of Democratic Socialist Aims and Values. It spoke of the need for a more equal distribution of wealth and power, and recognised that a society based on 'ruthless social and economic competition entrenches the privileges of a minority whilst restricting the rights of the rest of society'. It called for a collective approach to common economic problems and 'the creation of an economy which uses and develops resources in the widest national interest.'

Unfortunately, when it came to translating these broad and worthy objectives into proposals for changes in economic power, the statement became less radical. It argued for an extension of social ownership – in terms which might well not now be acceptable to the Labour leadership – but suggested that except in 'some areas which are wholly inappropriate for the application of market forces', the 'operation of the market, where properly regulated, is a generally satisfactory means of determining provision and consumption, and where competition is appropriate, socialists must ensure that it is fair and that consumers, workers and investors are protected from commercial and financial exploitation.'

The idea that a capitalist market motivated by private profit can ever be 'properly regulated' and 'consumers, workers and investors protected from commercial and financial exploitation', is unrealistic. This is not to argue against any attempt to introduce regulations and protective measures, but there should be no implication or false belief that such protective measures are ever likely to abolish periodic mass unemployment and gross inequality so long as capitalism prevails.

A belief in a more equal society has always been in Britain an important tributary of socialist thought. Roy Hattersley has articulated this belief as strongly as anyone. In an article in *The Guardian* on 26 July, 1997 he wrote:

'Finally – no doubt under the impulse of earlier influences – I found a morally and intellectually compelling theory of socialism: the good society is the equal society. Once upon a time, the Labour Party believed that too. It is the abandonment of that belief which has made me – for the first time in nearly 50 years' membership – a reluctant dissenter.'

One of the most glaring inequalities is that between the so-called developed and the underdeveloped world. Despite all its failings, the capitalist system has provided, by the long-term development of production, the basis for higher living standards. Such benefits as have been secured by working people have not been distributed as acts of beneficence, but have been won as the outcome of trade union and political pressure. Moreover, even with long-term rising living standards, millions in the economically advanced countries have suffered from exploitation, period mass unemployment, wars caused by commercial rivalry, and acute but avoidable poverty.

The inequality between the developed and the underdeveloped countries has been accentuated by capitalism. Despite the existence of aid, the underdeveloped countries have been exploited in the interests of the economically dominant powers. In some cases the economies of developing countries have been distorted, to concentrate on the production of a single crop or a limited range of raw materials for supply to the developed countries. Local reactionary rulers, resistant to fundamental social change and land redistribution, have often been kept in power by the support of developed countries. In more recent times the policies of the International Monetary Fund and the World Bank, acting in the interests of the bankers of the dominant powers, have added to the problems of the underdeveloped world.

In order to secure debt repayment the underdeveloped countries have been pressed to reduce social spending, thus harming the poorest among their population, to deregulate their labour markets, which is a euphemism for eroding employment rights and reducing pay, and to introduce stringent monetarism with high interest rates, the effect of which is to increase unemployment and retard the economy. The net result has been that in some years the flow of income has been from the poorer to the richer countries and not, as it should be, from the rich to the poor.

The World Labour Report 1994 of the International Labour Organisation stated that, with the exception of countries in East and South-East Asia, the developing countries had seen a decline in wages. Some of the most serious falls were in Africa. Since 1975, for example, according to the World Labour Report, wages in Kenya had fallen by 50 per cent and in Tanzania by 80 per cent. Over the same period minimum wages in some of the countries of Sub-Saharan Africa had fallen by 50 per cent to 70 per cent. An ILO survey of civil service pay in 14 African countries showed that between 1975 and 1985 starting salaries at the lowest levels had halved, whilst those at the highest levels had plunged by nearly two-thirds. In Latin America, one of the other continents affected by Third World debt and the pressures of the IMF and the World Bank, minimum wages went down in most countries during the 1980s. This decline now seems to have been halted, though between 1991 and 1992 real minimum wages continued to fall in Brazil (by 6 per cent) and in Argentina (by 14 per cent).

Most of the workforce in the underdeveloped countries is employed in agriculture. The ILO report confirmed that in Africa the living standards of farmers have been falling, though not as steeply as those of urban workers.

Misdirection of Resources

Another fundamental criticism of the capitalist system is that it misdirects resources. Resources are directed towards projects which yield a profit. There are many human needs, however, which will never by satisfied by the motivation of private profit. In a lecture given at the University of Wales the eminent US economist, Professor J. K. Galbraith, referred to some of the social needs for which there has to be a public responsibility. He pointed out that: 'In no country does the market system provide good, low-cost housing.' Few things, he said, were more visibly at odds with the good society than badly housed or homeless people. Similarly, health care for the needful was a public responsibility. No-one, he urged, should be assigned to illness or death because of poverty. There were also other essential functions of the state, including parks and recreational facilities, the police, libraries and the arts.

Galbraith referred also to a range of activities 'beyond the time horizons of the market economy'. Capitalism invests for relatively short-run returns, but much scientific discovery does not offer either early or certain returns. Galbraith pointed out that some of the 'truly important industrial achievements of recent generations – the great improvement in agricultural productivity, modern air transport, advanced electronics – have depended heavily on public investment'.

Another important area of activity where market forces give very misleading signals for the use of resources is in transport. The benefits of a transport system cannot be measured solely by the receipts of a transport undertaking. Similarly, the costs of optional forms of transport, or the absence of adequate transport, cannot be calculated by reference only to the outgoings of a transport organisation. With almost any form of transport, there are social costs and benefits which are relevant for any kind of calculation about the allocation of resources.

The need to take account of social costs and benefits, so obvious in the case of transport, applies, however, to all forms of industrial activity. Society should not disregard the environmental consequences of its economic activities. One example will suffice to illustrate the point. According to the World Health Organisation, up to 5,000,000 people are poisoned each year by pesticides, 40,000 of them fatally. It has been estimated that industrialised countries use 80 per cent of the world's agrochemicals, but probably suffer less than 1 per cent of deaths due to pesticide poisoning, while developing countries use 20 per cent of the chemicals but suffer 99 per cent of the deaths.

Yet another criticism of capitalism is that it has contributed in no small measure to innumerable wars and, in particular, to the most destructive wars of the twentieth century, in which tens of millions of people have lost their lives. Imperial powers sought to extend their domination over vast areas of the world. They did it not just because they wanted to fly their national flag in foreign parts, but because there were private profits to be made from the advantageous exploitation of protected markets and from overseas investment. The First World War was the outcome of rivalry between competing imperial powers. The Second World War was the outcome of the attempt of German big business, in its fascist form, to extend its power in Europe and the attempt of Japanese imperialism to extend its power throughout Asia. These ambitions were, for a period, appeased by British capitalism in the belief that fascism could be directed against the Soviet Union and that fascism was preferable to communism.

Colonialism was brought to an end by the struggle of the colonial people, assisted on occasions by progressive movements in the imperialist countries. In many cases, however, liberation was not secured without military struggle. In some areas the capitalist powers intervened militarily when, as they saw it, the cause of liberation might lead towards fundamental social change. The Vietnam War was the most costly of these acts of intervention.

The private manufacture and sale of arms has helped to stimulate the diversion of resources from the solution of the problems of world poverty. British firms have been to the fore as suppliers of arms on a world scale, including, on occasion, the supply of arms to countries with dictatorial regimes.

It would be wrong to give the impression that capitalist rivalry is the only source of war. There are other kinds of rivalries which have led and continue to lead to armed conflict, but even when there appear to be other causes the influence of capitalist interests sometimes plays a part.

These then are some of the arguments in favour of replacing capitalism by socialism. There are no blueprints for socialism, and certainly enormous injustices have been committed in the name of socialism in the twentieth century. Socialism, nevertheless, does have meaning for the future. It will be a social system within which the satisfaction of human need and not the pursuit of private profit will be the dominating motive of the economy. The levers of power will need to be in the hands of the people. Hence the commanding heights of industry· and finance will be under social ownership. The only guarantee that the resources of production will be used for the benefit of all, and that power will not be abused, is through the strengthening of democracy in all directions.

The Means of Change

It is one thing to state the case for socialism: it is another to indicate how it might be brought about. It is certain that the existing capitalist system will not be changed unless a substantial section of the adult population want it and, equally important, are prepared to do something to make their wishes effective.

Traditionally the cause of socialism has been associated with the development of a working-class movement. Even in countries where the industrial working class has been or is heavily outnumbered by a peasantry, the socialist movement has sought to base itself on ideas likely to appeal primarily to industrial workers and then to develop a programme of land reform designed to win the support of landless agricultural workers or poor peasants. Land reform is not necessarily a socialist measure, but in modern conditions, as experience has underlined in many countries, it often needs a socialist leadership to challenge the vested interests of major landowners.

In Britain the development of the socialist movement was the outcome of a number of converging but different traditions, but there was no doubt of the central role of the industrial working class as the main vehicle for social change. The traditions of radicalism, of democratic protest, of religious Nonconformity, of High Church Christian socialism, of Owenite social reform, of the Fabian Society and of Marxism all played a part

509

in the evolution of the ideas that helped to form the British socialist movement, but it was only when these ideas found fertile ground within the organised labour movement that they became of real political significance.

The emergence of a socialist movement in Britain with these different tributaries of thought depended partly upon the injection of ideas from outside, but was prompted also by the experiences of numerous working-class activists within trade unionism. This helps to explain the special role of Keir Hardie and other men and women from the industrial working class who helped to form the Independent Labour Party in 1893. The ILP had genuine working-class roots. This traditional relationship between trade union activity and socialist ideas has been carried forward in Britain by many participants.

It has become a familiar argument of recent years that the industrial working class has so declined in numbers that the movement for social change must broaden its appeal to embrace citizens who are not industrial workers, and who do not think of themselves as part of the working class. It is certainly true that in Britain the number of workers employed in manufacturing, in the extractive industries, notably coal mining, and in dock employment has declined substantially.

This does not mean, nevertheless, that the proportion of those in employment who depend for their livelihood on selling their ability to work to an employer has declined or become less significant. The composition of the workforce has changed and will continue to change. A higher proportion of workers are now employed, for example, in large retail stores, in various forms of transport other than railways, in public services and utilities, in financial institutions of various kinds and in a multiplicity of other services. The proportion of women in the workforce has risen steeply, and more and more are employed part-time and on temporary contracts. The changes in the composition of the workforce do not imply that employed workers are becoming less important in the social composition of the nation.

The decline in the number of the industrial working class,

even though this class is still large, has led to some weakening of class consciousness and the traditional base of strong trade unionism, but the expansion of employment in other directions has helped to develop and will continue to develop consciousness about pay, working conditions and security among other sections of the population. In 1997, despite unemployment, anti-union legislation and the decline in manufacturing, coal-mining and dock employment, the affiliated membership of the TUC was roughly twice what it was when Britain was beginning to emerge from the slump of the early 1930s.

In the world in general the working class continues to grow, whether the definition is confined to industrial workers or, more accurately, to all who are dependent for their livelihood on the sale of their labour power to an employer and who do not own the means of production. Millions have joined the working class as a consequence of the growth of industry in many parts of the world. This is the foundation for the strengthening of the world labour movement and for the struggle for socialism.

From its earliest days in Britain the workers' movement sought to gain the right of representation as a means of improving working and living conditions. At the centre of the demand for representation was the claim for the widening of the suffrage. Thus from the very beginning the struggle for better working and living conditions was inseparably connected with the struggle for democratic rights.

This relationship between the fight for the extension of democratic rights and for social progress is not something unique to the history of the British labour movement. It is also true of other countries. Indeed, towards the end of the last century the extension of the franchise appeared to place the German labour movement in the most favourable position for social advance of any country. In his writings in the 1890s Frederick Engels, the lifelong collaborator of Karl Marx, greeted the electoral successes of the German socialists and advocated the use of every democratic opportunity to advance the workers' cause. Unlike some of his contemporaries, however, Engels warned against any false belief that capitalism

511

would tamely accept defeat solely by the electoral process. State power had to be transformed. Drawing on the experience of the Paris Commune of 1871, he spoke of two 'infallible means' of transformation, namely the filling of all posts by election on the basis of universal suffrage and the payment of all officials at the level of workers' wages. No doubt there are problems with both of these 'infallible' instruments of popular control, but they illustrate the importance which Engels attached to democratic power in the process of social transformation.

Engels' warnings about the use of state power to frustrate the labour movement were confirmed in the most brutal manner in Germany in the 1930s. The Nazis, with support from German big business, instituted a dictatorship of capital and sought in every way to destroy the labour movement.

A related issue to that of the development of electoral and other democratic opportunities for the labour movement is that of the effect of rising living standards on the political consciousness of working people. In the economically advanced countries capitalism, despite periodic mass unemployment and gross inequality, has provided the basis for higher living standards, taking one decade with another. This is in no way to deny the existence of inexcusable deprivation among millions of people or the suffering caused by war and by the exploitation of the Third World. Nor is it to deny the depravity of standards of behaviour associated with advanced capitalism, ranging from widespread drug abuse to increased criminal activity in many directions. Nevertheless, it would be an exercise in self-deception not to accept that for the great majority within advanced capitalist countries their living standards, as measured by their own perception, are higher than they were for their parents, and higher still than they were for their grandparents. These improvements have been gained partly as a result of trade union and political pressure, but have also been made possible by advances in productivity and by benefits gained from the exploitation of the Third World.

512

The International Labour Movement

This has had a profound effect on the labour movement in the advanced capitalist countries. It provides the sustenance for policies that accept the continued existence of capitalism. This trend found expression in the controversies about 'revisionism' in the German labour movement at the end of the last century. The idea was advanced that organised labour, through its industrial and political strength, and by taking advantage of electoral opportunities, could win continuous improvements in living standards. The aim of socialism was not rejected, but emphasis was placed on activity for immediate aims.

The theories of 'revisionism' were formally rejected by the majority of the German labour movement, but for practical purposes the 'revisionist' ideas became predominant. The effect, however, both in Germany and Britain was that substantial sections of the labour movement identified many of their interests with that of their own ruling class. Thus when the First World War broke out the majority of union leaders in both countries supported their respective governments. This despite the warnings of an impending imperialist war, expressed in resolutions carried at pre-war international socialist conferences.

It was this disastrous experience that led Lenin to believe, following the Bolshevik revolution in Russia in October 1917, that it was necessary to form a new international of political parties, identified with Marxism and rejecting any suggestion of the policies of 'class collaboration' associated with the social-democratic parties in Western Europe. The Third (Communist) International came into existence but never succeeded in gaining majority support among the working class of the advanced capitalist countries.

The organisational principles of the Communist International reflected very much the experiences of illegal work of the Bolsheviks. Russia was a country without a tradition of democratic institutions. The so-called principles of 'democratic centralism', which communist parties were required to observe, gave immense powers of control to the leadership. It was not only that minorities had to accept the decisions of the majority, but discussion could be prevented except when authorised by the leadership. In later years any kind of dissent was likely to be condemned as 'factionalism'. Party members who differed from a decision of a leadership committee to which they belonged were not permitted to carry their difference downwards and to test their opinions by discussion with the rank and file.

The ultimate effect of these organisational principles was that whilst, on occasions, it gave communist parties very considerable power of mobilisation and effective action, it stifled internal democracy and accountability. Control passed into fewer and fewer hands and, in some cases, whoever was general secretary exercised very great personal power. In countries where communist parties constituted the government, this could and did lead to terrible injustices. Moreover, since no-one is infallible and all political parties make mistakes, the dangerous consequences of wrong policies were greatly magnified. There was no effective means of early democratic correction.

The affiliated parties of the Communist International also found that the main thrust of their policies was determined in Moscow. Sometimes this expressed commendable international solidarity as, for example, in the struggle against fascism following the Seventh World Congress of the Communist International in 1935, but sometimes it required parties to pursue policies which made no sense in the countries in which they were operating. Communist parties gained a reputation for sharp turns in policy or even for 'somersaults' from one position to another.

The split in the international labour movement following the First World War did not provide from either camp a satisfactory way forward towards socialism. In Western Europe the social-democratic trend accommodated itself increasingly to an acceptance of capitalism, and even its record in the struggle against fascism was mixed. In Austria and Czechoslovakia it resisted fascism energetically, in France and Spain it joined with others in popular resistance to fascism, but in Germany and Britain it rejected the call for a popular front. In Britain the role of the Labour Party in its initial support for 'non-intervention' against fascist aggression in Spain was particularly damaging. In the period immediately following the Second World War, social-democratic labour parties helped to initiate important social reforms within a number of countries, but then, with the development of the Cold War, most of them took the side of the USA and embraced policies of rearmament. Their support for American policies also helped to give currency to 'free market' ideas associated with the US economy.

In more recent years the record of social-democracy has been uneven. In Britain the Labour Party has moved increasingly to the right during a period when, more than ever, radical policies have been needed to overcome the deep-seated problems of the British economy. It is no longer possible to describe the Labour Party as a socialist party, except that socialist consciousness still motivates many of its active rank-and-file members and there are numerous socialists among its Members of Parliament. The official policy of the Party as put forward by the leadership offers no challenge to the continuation of capitalist control.

In France the Socialist Party has overtaken the Communist Party as the strongest force on the left, and it has registered some important electoral successes. In Spain a serving socialist government introduced a number of valuable social reforms but failed to tackle the highest rate of unemployment in the European Union. In Italy the socialists were submerged by corruption, and in Germany the policy of the social democrats was not dissimilar from that of the Christian Democrats. There is not a single country where social democrats in government have transformed society from capitalism to socialism. The best record is in Sweden, where changes made over a period of more than 50 years seem likely to have affected permanently the attitude of the public to social welfare, the environment, labour protection and the rights of minorities.

The record of the communist trend within the world labour movement has been more spectacular, both in achievements

515

and failings, than that of the social-democratic trend. The Russian Revolution, despite the ultimate collapse of Soviet power, is likely to be seen in the future as one of the turning points of world history. For the first time an attempt was made to construct a new kind of society based upon the social ownership of industry and cooperative farming. It had many achievements to its credit. Until the final years of stagnation it had a high rate of economic growth, even though, for many years, it had to face economic hostility from most of the capitalist world. Despite the initial backwardness of its economy, it introduced and developed many measures of social welfare. In the Second World War it played the major role in the defeat of fascism. The sharp contrast between Russia's defeat in the First World War, when Germany had millions of troops engaged on the Western Front as well as on the Eastern Front, and the Soviet Union's defeat of the Nazi armies in the Second World War, when Germany commanded virtually the whole of continental Europe and did not have to face an active second front in Western Europe until 1944, was there for all to see.

The very existence of the Soviet Union and the prestige it enjoyed as a result of the outcome of the Second World War had a strong and progressive influence throughout the world, not least in Western Europe, in the immediate post-war period. The influence of the Soviet Union was also felt in the world-wide struggle against colonialism.

The eventual collapse of the Soviet Union was not due to any one single factor. There were numerous failings, but there was one of supreme importance. The absence of effective democratic control and accountability led to bureaucracy, the corruption of power and to stagnation. When things went wrong, there were no available means of popular pressure to put them right. People were intimidated by political tyranny, under which many lost their lives. Immense resources were devoted to the arms race in pursuit of the military doctrine that the Soviet Union had to be as strong as any likely combination of hostile powers. This pursuit of military strength – for which there were strong arguments in the light of the history of capitalist hostility and military attack – nevertheless led to economic weakness. In the control of the economy, the importance of market forces was very much underestimated. The planners sought to plan every minor detail, and prices were fixed by administrators rather than by reference to costs and to demand. This led to distortion and waste.

In other parts of the world the communist trend in the labour movement played a significant part in many countries in the movement for national independence and colonial liberation. The most recent example is that of South Africa.

The most significant of all developments, however, in the period following the Second World War was the coming to power of the communists in China. A high rate of growth has been achieved with policies which appear to combine important elements of central planning with the incentives of capitalism.

There were also vast injustices and economically chaotic measures during the so-called 'cultural revolution'. Democracy will be needed in China no less than in any other country embarking on the road to socialism. It is still too early to predict the eventual course of the Chinese revolution.

Vietnam, also under communist leadership, appears to be taking much the same course as China, even though the relationship between the two countries is cool rather than warm. Living standards in Vietnam are rising, and the rate of economic growth is high. Private enterprise and foreign investment are being encouraged. Political control remains firmly in the hands of the Communist Party, and it appears that the Party leadership has taken the view that at this stage of economic development the motivation of private profit, particularly in small business, offers the most favourable impetus for growth. It remains to be seen whether at some stage in the future the balance between political control and economic power will be changed.

In Cuba, a much more rigorous form of communist economic control has had to be modified, mainly as a result of the effective but totally unjustified economic boycott conducted by the USA. This boycott is exercised not only through a US trade embargo but also by prohibitive measures against shipping operated by other countries. Ships trading with Cuba are not permitted to use US ports. The economic boycott has been condemned by the United Nations General Assembly. Despite the very severe handicap of the economic boycott, the Castro government of Cuba has many achievements to its credit and continues to be supported by a substantial section of the population.

In a number of other Third World countries political parties claiming to be Marxist-Leninist exercised political control or had substantial political influence until the collapse of the Soviet Union. In most of these countries the parties claiming to be Marxist-Leninist have now been displaced or their influence has been much reduced. It is doubtful whether there was ever any real basis in their backward economies for socialist transformation. The influence of political parties claiming to be Marxist-Leninist was due to the nature of the anti-colonial struggle in parts of the Third World and to the economic and military support of the Soviet Union or China.

It is clear from the experiences of the world labour movement in the twentieth century that there is no one pattern for socialist advance applicable to all countries. In every country account has to be taken of the specific economic and political circumstances which exist, and of the traditions which have helped to shape the form and outlook of the labour movement. The traditions of the social-democratic, communist and anti-colonial movements cannot be disregarded, and will all have a part to play in the future. The traditions of social democracy and of the communist trend, in their many varieties, have both positive and negative features. The future success of the labour movement will depend on the nurturing of the positive traditions and the elimination of the negative traditions.

Britain

In Britain the starting point for any assessment for the future is the existence of the labour movement, not as we might wish it to be, but as it is and as it has evolved. The trade union movement provides the basis for the day-to-day effort of working people to protect and advance their interests. It will remain so in the future. Its importance for the labour movement cannot be exaggerated. It reflects the strength and the limitations of outlook of working people. Any idea that the people of Britain can be won for socialist change without persuading the trade union movement to support the struggle for socialism is to engage in delusions.

The influence of trade unionism on the political leanings of the Labour Party has been demonstrated ever since the Party came into existence. The domination exercised by the right in the Party for many years, and again more recently, could not have been maintained without the support or acquiescence of a substantial section of the trade union movement. Conversely, the move to the left in the Party in the 1970s was attributable primarily to a leftward trend within trade unionism, symbolised by the ascendancy of such figures as Frank Cousins, Jack Jones, Harry Urwin, Hugh Scanlon, Alan Fisher, Dick Briginshaw, Ray Buckton, Terry Parry, Les Buck, Danny McGarvey, Alan Sapper, Ken Gill, Clive Jenkins, Jim Slater, Doug Grieve and a number of miners' leaders, including Daly, Scargill, Heathfield and McGahey. They were varied in their points of view on some issues, but none of them was on the right of the movement. This influential progressive trend reflected a deeper change in the mood of many rank-and-file trade unionists.

It was this experience of a leftward trend in trade unionism which led some Labour leaders in the 1980s to respond to the press clamour for changes to diminish trade union influence within the Party. The growth of unemployment and the anti-union legislation of the 1980s served to weaken the confidence of working people in their own strength. The right-wing trend in the labour movement was able to reassert its ascendancy, but the margin of their majority has not always been as large as they would have liked. The left is a significant force, and new opportunities for it to develop its strength are likely to come again.

The movement for social change in Britain will continue to

express itself in a combination of pressures both inside and outside Parliament. The effort for a Labour majority in Parliament, which finally succeeded in 1997, was an essential part of this process. To emphasise simultaneously the importance of the struggle outside Parliament is not to attack Parliament but, on the contrary, it is to recognise that democracy requires the fullest participation of the people. Parliament, as an institution for democratic progress, cannot be separated from the activity of the common people, expressed through trade unionism, a wide variety of single-cause organisations, meetings, demonstrations, representations and the freedom of speech and the press.

GENERAL INDEX

521

525

INDEX OF PERSONS